Sociological Theory

Contemporary Debates

John Scott

Professor of Sociology
University of Essex

Edward Elgar
Cheltenham, UK • Lyme, US

Published by
Edward Elgar Publishing Limited
8 Lansdown Place
Cheltenham
Glos GL50 2HU
UK

Edward Elgar Publishing, Inc.
1 Pinnacle Hill Road
Lyme
NH 03768
US

Paperback edition reprinted 1997, 2004

British Library Cataloguing in Publication Data
Scott, John
    Sociological Theory:Contemporary Debates
    I. Title
    301.01

Library of Congress Cataloguing in Publication Data
Scott, John, 1949–
    Sociological theory : contemporary debates / John Scott.
        p.   cm.
    Includes bibliographical references and index.
    1. Sociology—Philosophy.   I. Title.
HM24.S3775   1995
301'.01—dc20   94–40622
                                                            CIP

ISBN 1 85278 418 0 (cased)
       1 85278 427 X (paperback)

Printed and bound in Great Britain by
Biddles Ltd, King's Lynn

Contents

Figures

Acknowledgements

The ideas in this book have been worked out over a number of years, and numerous people have played a part – directly or indirectly, wittingly or unwittingly – in its production. Many will, perhaps, have forgotten the role that they played. My interest in the works of Parsons and Habermas was developed in discussions at the London School of Economics in 1971 and 1972. David Martin introduced me to the ideas of von Hayek and tolerated my interest in Habermas. A paper that I presented to a seminar run by him and Eileen Barker became the basis of my first published paper on Habermas. Sessions with Steve Ackroyd in the Robinson Room and elsewhere covered virtually all aspects of sociological theory, and I remember them and our continuing correspondence as the most stimulating intellectual occasions of my career. Ron Fletcher's love of theory – indeed, his love of sociology – was a great source of inspiration to me. Although we met on only a couple of occasions, he was extremely generous with his time in our long correspondence. He encouraged my early work on Parsons, and it is sad that he did not live to see its much belated publication in this book. Students at the Universities of Strathclyde and Leicester have intermittently been exposed to the developing theoretical ideas, most recently in the Sociological Analysis course at Leicester. They have played a great part in helping to clarify my presentation of ideas. In developing an earlier course on Theoretical Sociology at Leicester I had long discussions with Christopher Dandecker that resulted in a joint paper as well as a joint course. That paper became the basis of a book that Christopher wrote with Terry Johnson and Clive Ashworth (*The Structure of Social Theory*, Macmillan, 1984). Pressure of other work prevented me from participating in the writing of that volume, but the ideas that it embodies have their echoes at various points in this book. Derek Layder's commitment to theoretical work has shown that rigorous and original theory can be combined with clarity of expression and a commitment to empirical work. Many of the ideas in this book have been discussed with Derek, who has read the whole manuscript. David Lockwood's published and unpublished papers on theory are among the major achievements of theoretical sociology, and they have been very influential in my own work. In particular, his emphasis on the need to distinguish 'social integration' from 'system integration', and to give proper attention to each, is the cornerstone of much that I have written. My thanks to all of these people, none of whom should be held responsible for any of the views that I put forward.

This book appears just as I begin a new phase of my career, at the University of Essex. The manuscript was, however, completed at the University of Leicester and I would like to dedicate the book to my Leicester colleagues. While I was Head of Department they allowed me to carve out just enough time to get this book completed.

Preface

Theory is fundamental to the whole sociological enterprise: it defines its central concepts and it shapes empirical research. Yet discussions of theory are often presented in the most complex and obscure language, and in ways that seem to emphasize the irrelevance of theory to empirical and applied sociology. The name Talcott Parsons, for example, has become a byword for obscurity and irrelevance, his numerous and weighty books being regarded as virtually 'off limits' to those who just want to get on with 'real' sociology. What is not recognized by many who reject or ignore Parsons is the extent to which his ideas have become part and parcel of the whole framework of mainstream sociology. In view of this, it is sad that so few people bother to read him, and sadder still that so many practitioners do not perceive how much is owed to him and how much can still be learned from him.

These problems are confounded by the fact that so many of those who have engaged with Parsons and have developed powerful critiques of his work have presented their own ideas in equally obscure terms. The difficulties of the language employed by these theorists is, perhaps, obvious from the strange and obscure names given to their theoretical positions: phenomenology, ethnomethodology, structuralism and so on. As a result, the works of such important and powerful figures as Garfinkel and Althusser are discussed, if at all, within narrowly defined intellectual circles and have not had the impact that they deserve on the mainstream of sociological research.

In recent years, those interested in contemporary theory have seemed to turn away from sociological research and have looked to intellectual developments in philosophy and the more obscure theoretical products of literary and cultural studies. Distinctively social issues, as a result, have sometimes been lost sight of, and the purpose of sociological theory forgotten. The works of Lyotard and Derrida, for example, can provide us with much insight into certain aspects of social life, but they are no substitute for sociological theory.

A number of important theorists have recently begun the task of integrating philosophical ideas with the various strands of contemporary sociological theory, and they have sought to do this on the basis of a critical reconsideration of the works of Parsons and, indeed, the earlier 'classics' of Marx, Weber and Durkheim. The most important of these theorists are Giddens and

Habermas, whose works have had a major impact both within and beyond sociology. It is important for all sociologists to read and discuss their ideas. Engagement with their ideas is essential for all who wish to further the development of sociology as a discipline. Unfortunately, their own works are difficult and obscure, though not, perhaps, as obscure as their critics sometimes claim.

All sciences use concepts that are unfamiliar or that differ from everyday ideas designated by the same word, and the analysis of such concepts requires a degree of abstraction from concrete matters. Where many theorists have gone wrong is in making their ideas inaccessible by, deliberately or inadvertently, using unnecessarily complex vocabulary or dense grammar. It is my belief that theorists should actively encourage people to read – and hence to criticize – their work, and that the need to communicate should be uppermost in their minds. The aim of this book is to further this communication by presenting the leading ideas of contemporary sociological theorists as clearly as possible. To this end, I have tried to convey the nature of their arguments without getting unduly bogged down in abstract and obscure language. A certain amount of difficulty and complexity must, nevertheless, be expected in theoretical work. I hope that my summaries are clear enough to excite and encourage readers to struggle with the originals for themselves.

The book begins with a Chapter on the founding statements of sociological theory, as these formed the basis from which contemporary debates began. Those who are familiar with the history of sociology may prefer to skip rapidly through this Chapter, while others may find it useful to read it more closely. In either case, readers should not feel that it is necessary to understand everything that is touched on in the Chapter. Its purpose is not to present a potted history of sociology, nor is it to give definitive summaries of leading sociologists. Its aim, rather, is to sketch the assumptions about sociological theory that provided the starting point for the greatest of all contemporary theorists. Talcott Parsons, beginning in the 1930s, completely reshaped the discipline and moved it in new directions. Parsons undertook his work on the basis of a very specific view of the works of his predecessors, and this view was, until recently, very widely accepted as an accurate view of the sociological tradition. Chapter 1 is, therefore, an essential backdrop to my consideration of Parsons himself in Chapter 2.

The Chapter on Parsons is the longest in the book, as it is in Parsons that many of the themes in contemporary debates were introduced or were given their present form. A thorough grasp of Parsons's work is the essential foundation for understanding all that has followed. The subsequent Chapters focus on the various theoretical positions that have developed in the wake of his work. I have tried to allow the many criticisms of Parsons to develop naturally through the book, rather than listing them extensively in the Parsons Chapter itself. Critics of Parsons's view of 'action', for example, are explored through the counter-arguments of the rational choice, phenomenological, symbolic interactionist and conflict theorists, and the limitations of his view of 'system' are explored through structuralist and post-structuralist writings. This strategy is important for emphasizing the continuity and accumulation that lie behind the diversity of the various positions. The works of Giddens and Habermas, in different ways, indicate this continuity. In each of them can be found an attempt – sometimes explicit and sometimes implicit – to build on Parsons's achievements and to incorporate the arguments of his critics.

I have concentrated on the general theoretical statements of the various writers considered, but I have also tried to show how these ideas have been used to understand the modern world. Sociology arose as an attempt to understand the great transformation through which distinctively 'modern' forms of social relations were replacing the 'pre-modern' structures of the 'traditional' world. In the Chapters that discuss Parsons, Giddens and Habermas (Chapters 2, 9 and 10) I have tried to show how the insights of the founders of the discipline have been enlarged to comprehend the 'late modernity' of the second half of the 20th century. These accounts are important, I believe, in showing how the abstract theoretical ideas of the writers can be, and have been, translated into empirical research programmes.

1. Foundations for sociology

Sociology is a product of modernity, born of the great intellectual and social upheavals that destroyed the medieval European world. Inspired by the great scientific discoveries made by Copernicus and Newton, whose methods had been introduced to social thought by Bacon, Descartes and Hobbes, the intellectual culture of early modern Europe stressed the ideals of rationality and humanism that were at the heart of 'Enlightenment' thought. Rejecting religious doctrine and divine revelation as guarantees of truth, along with the traditionalism and hierarchies of the medieval world that they legitimated, Enlightenment thinkers emphasized the pivotal role of reason and experience in all matters and formulated a scientific approach to social questions. In the works of these writers, the modern world was seen as having progressed beyond the level of civilization that had been achieved in the ancient world. 'Modernity' and 'progress' were synonymous.

Today, the recognition that people's actions and characters are shaped by the societies in which they live is commonplace. It is readily accepted that there are differences in the attitudes and outlooks of the inhabitants of the various countries of the world, and we understand that this is a consequence of the varying social institutions and histories of their societies. It is equally readily recognized that vast differences in character and social structure divide inhabitants of, say, contemporary Europe from their medieval or their prehistoric predecessors. However, this awareness of society and the social constitution of the individual has not always appeared so obvious. Systematic reflection on these matters is a recent phenomenon, and it took many years and much intellectual discussion before such ideas were established as part of the contemporary cultural worldview.

Enlightenment thought had introduced a new discourse of the 'individual' that was first translated into social thought by Luther and Machiavelli (MacIntyre, 1966). According to Machiavelli, in whose work this new individualism was cast in a specifically secular form, individuals were motivated by the attainment of power, glory and reputation, and they adopted a rational and purely technical attitude towards the choice of the appropriate means to attaining these ends. The most influential early statement of this new rational individualism was constructed by Hobbes (1651), who set out a model of political order as the product of the rational, self-interested actions of individuals.

In the work of Hobbes, his contemporaries and their immediate successors, social thought was merely part of a broader framework of ideas that encompassed what would now be regarded as the separate disciplines of law, economics, politics, history, psychology, philosophy, theology and ethics, as well as the natural sciences of physics and biology. The dominant element in this encyclopaedic view of social matters was the political question of the origin and justification of government. In their approach to this question, Enlightenment writers sought to establish the grounds of political legitimacy in modern society in terms of the 'rights' of individuals and the consequent need for government through the consent expressed in a 'social contract'.

Social thought in the 18th century continued this modern outlook and elaborated the contention that social arrangements were to be seen as the direct and transparent creations of individual action. In the works of some theorists, however, can be glimpsed the emergence of a new idea. Montesquieu, Rousseau, Condorcet and the great writers of Scottish political economy were all liberals, committed to individual rights, but they recognized that individuals were the creatures, as much as the creators, of their social circumstances. Recognizing that individual wants and interests are shaped by their social circumstances, they laid the basis for a conception of 'society' as something other than a mere aggregate of individuals.

It was in the great 19th century works of Hegel, Comte, Spencer and Marx that recognition of 'society' as a distinct object received its first and most systematic statements. Their work was shaped by a clash between liberal ideals and the conservative reaction to them. Indeed, it was the impact of conservatism on intellectual culture that allowed a proper awareness of 'society' to emerge for the first time. Comte gave the systematic study of society its name of 'sociology', and this new science was established as an academic discipline around the turn of the century in the founding works of Durkheim, Weber and their contemporaries. Where the works of the 19th century pioneers had been shaped by the clash of liberalism and conservatism, that of the founding generation of university sociologists built on the pioneer statements in a climate of thought that was marked by their attempts to come to terms with the challenge posed by Marxism, which had become institutionalized in the socialist parties of Europe rather than in its universities. The development of sociology up to the 1930s continued to show the effects of this interplay of academic sociology and Marxism.

DISCOVERING 'SOCIETY'

Enlightenment thought postulated individuals with 'natural' characteristics and properties derived from a supposed 'state of nature' that existed prior to the establishment of society through a social contract. For the most part, the idea of the state of nature was recognized as a historical fiction, but it served the essential role of grounding the supposed 'rights' and powers of individuals in their inherent, natural, non-social characteristics. Social arrangements were themselves seen by social contract theorists as the results of the actions of individuals endowed with natural rights and powers.

One of the first theorists to break with this view and to formulate the idea that individuals were the creatures of their social circumstances was Jean-Jacques Rousseau (1755, 1762). When individuals entered into the social contract and abandoned the state of nature, Rousseau argued, a fundamental break was made with their attributes and qualities as 'natural' individuals. The natural attributes and qualities of individuals were distorted by the establishment of 'society', in which they were accorded distinct social characteristics that were irreducible to their natural, individual characteristics. Individuals in society are different from individuals in nature. Rousseau added the further important point that morality was a consequence of society. Only in society was the exercise of moral judgement possible. Individuals in society were moral beings, capable of reflecting on the inequalities and constraints under which they lived and judging them in terms that transcended individual self-interest. People in society, Rousseau held, could formulate a 'general will' through which social transformation could be morally justified. This insight into the cultural formation of individuals was of great significance, but Rousseau showed little concern for exactly *how* social institutions were able to shape individual characteristics. More than this, he assumed a fundamental uniformity in social conditions following the initial social contract, and so saw little reason to study social variations from one place to another.

The somewhat earlier work of the Baron de Montesquieu was of particular importance in its clear recognition of the variability of social conditions. It was also in Montesquieu's work that the first attempt was made to construct an idea of a separate 'social' sphere that was distinct from that of political action. In his work the idea of 'society' in its contemporary sense begins to acquire a substance (Montesquieu, 1748). For Montesquieu, social phenomena comprised interrelated systems of elements that were self-sustaining and expressed a specific cultural spirit (Hawthorn, 1976: 18). The social milieu in which the political sphere of law and government exists comprises a systematic structure of occupations, institutions, customs and practices that are shaped by the geographical factors of soil and climate.

Rousseau, then, showed that individuals were the products of their society, and Montesquieu showed that societies varied across time and space. Neither writer, however, showed any attempt to construct a historical model of changing social circumstances. Towards the end of the century, however, another Frenchman, Condorcet, outlined an account of how intellectual progress

involved change from one form of society to another. Asserting the intellectual progress of modern society over the classical world, Condorcet constructed a scheme of historical stages that led from tribal barbarism to the
French Republic. The key to this historical progress was provided by change
in the intellectual sphere: cultural change drove social change (Condorcet,
1794). In Condorcet, then, is found the historical dimension that was missing
from Montesquieu's account of society.[1]

It was in the work of the great Scottish Enlightenment writers, however,
that Montesquieu's discovery was first carried forward in a historical framework. Adam Smith (1759, 1766), Adam Ferguson (1767) and John Millar
(1779), drawing on the earlier work of David Hume, rejected social contract
theories of political authority and embraced Montesquieu's conception of
societies as structured wholes. Their work showed a strong historical emphasis, and they saw human history as a process of development from one stage
of society to another.[2] Despite this awareness of the existence of social
wholes, they retained a focus on the individual as the prime mover, seeing
societies as the unintended consequences of individual actions. Societies,
they believed, did not exist separately from, or independently of, individuals
and their actions. Individuals produced social institutions as the unintended
consequences of their actions, and the social arrangements that they produced
were able to shape their future actions. History was an ongoing process in
which societies and their institutions were constantly reshaped by individual
actions.

The Scottish writers postulated an economic basis to social development.
At the heart of any society were its economic activities. The forms of property and class relations through which economic activity was undertaken
were seen as the basis of political organization and of social life more
generally. Their particular concern was to understand their own society, and
they saw this as arising from the very specific commercial transformation
that European societies had undergone since the 16th century. Economic
activity had taken an increasingly commercial and 'industrial' form in modern Europe, resulting in the emergence of a distinct sphere of 'civil society', a
sphere of market exchange and contractual relations separate from the political sphere of the state. Civil society – the core of modern 'civilization' – was
seen in the context of the long-term historical progression of society from a
condition of 'savagery' and 'barbarism' to the present stage of civilization
that more perfectly expressed individual human nature than did any prior
form of society.

The English classical economists were the principal inheritors of the insights
of the Scottish writers, though they concentrated on the 'economic' aspects
of civil society. This work became the basis of the economic principles that
were subsequently developed into marginalist economics (Ricardo, 1817;

Malthus, 1820; Mill, 1821, 1848). The idea of 'society' as a structure of political, economic and other institutions was not to be further developed in Britain until later in the 19th century when Herbert Spencer set out his scheme of sociological analysis.

Social thought in 18th century England remained resolutely tied to normative political concerns and involved little in the way of an analytical or scientific study of society. The framework for political discourse was provided by the American and French revolutions, which were seen by radical writers and activists as epitomizing the democratic and egalitarian ideals of the Enlightenment. Liberals such as Wilkes and Paine drew on the same individualism that had inspired the Scottish social theorists, but they developed this into a doctrine of fundamental human rights. Tom Paine's (1792) *The Rights of Man* was the most famous product of this approach, but it had been preceded by a similar statement from Mary Wollstonecraft (1790), which was subsequently taken as the basis for her *A Vindication of the Rights of Woman* (Wollstonecraft, 1792).

Wollstonecraft's significance for social theory goes beyond her concern for individual rights. She sought to show the gendered character of the liberal emphasis on the rights of 'man', and she aimed to round this out with a discussion of the conditions for the emancipation of both men and women. Placing gender divisions at the forefront of her social theory, she argued that the socialization of women was rooted in false assumptions about the 'natural' characters of men and women and that this was the basis of their subjection to men. Their socialization confines women to a state of childlike 'innocence' and weakness and prevents them from developing their rational faculties of understanding. Instead, they are seen as specifically fitted to be 'alluring mistresses' rather than 'affectionate wives and rational mothers' (Wollstonecraft, 1792: 79). Like Rousseau she showed that individuals were shaped by their social circumstances, but she added that gender divisions were an important condition for, and product of, the social constitution of individuals. Wollstonecraft's work did not, unfortunately, have the influence on her contemporaries that it deserved, and the mainstream of social and political thought remained resolutely gendered until well into the 20th century. In the narrower political sphere it was not until John Stuart Mill (1869) took up Wollstonecraft's ideas in the middle of the 19th century that her views began to have any significant influence on political debates.

The Enlightenment and the French and American revolutions produced a conservative reaction not only to their excesses but to their very principles. The central conservative figures of the 18th and early 19th centuries were Edmund Burke (1790), Joseph de Maistre and Louis de Bonald (1796). These writers rejected the idea that society was the creation of individuals. Their fundamental assumption was that society is divinely ordained and is, therefore, prior to its individual members. It is through the social phenomena of language, knowledge and moral values that human beings are constituted as individuals. Oriented by a romantic vision of the disappearing values and institutions of medieval society, conservatives sought to defend the importance of family, religion, community and status. In so doing, they highlighted these social institutions as objects for analysis, contrasting them with the counterpart institutions of modernity. Liberalism, with its endorsement of modernity and civil society, largely disregarded the institutions of the old society and analysed only the economic and political institutions of capitalism and democracy. Where classical liberalism alone was unable to generate a full-blown sociology, the clash of liberalism and conservatism allowed 'society' as an object of sociological investigation to be properly theorized for the first time (Nisbet, 1966, 1978; Mannheim, 1925). It was in the contrasting works of Hegel, Comte, Spencer and Marx that this clash of ideas was to have its most productive consequences.

PIONEER SOCIAL THEORISTS

Social thought in the 19th century reflected the interplay of liberal 'classicism' and conservative 'romanticism' (Gouldner, 1973; Therborn, 1976: 163ff). The classicist outlook centred on an endorsement of the emergent social order of capitalist society. Romanticism, an essentially conservative reaction to this order, rested on an idealized image of the medieval past that served as its yardstick for a moral and political critique of capitalism. The political economy of Ricardo and Mill was perhaps the clearest expression of the classicist outlook, but romanticism was not so directly associated with systematic social theory.

The influence of romanticism was at its strongest in Germany. Despite Kant's construction of an individualistic and rationalistic account of knowledge and social life, the predominant approach to these issues in Germany focused on the historical development of cultures and saw societies as integrated wholes characterized by a specific cultural spirit. The clearest expression of this is found in Herder, who outlined the idea of the national community characterized by a shared language and by the particular 'spirit' that animates its culture. The *Volksgeist* – the spirit of the people – was the basis on which the cultures of nations were to be understood. Culture developed in the sphere of spirit. The particular spirit that infused each society was seen as a partial realization of a deeper, underlying spirit of 'humanity' *per se*. Herder recognized the diversity of cultures and the moral values that they embodied, but he held that they were partial, but progressive, manifestations of the underlying spirit of humanity (Herder, 1784–91). It was in Georg Hegel that this argument received its clearest expression.

Hegel's social theory revolves around the concept of 'spirit' (*Geist*), the element of meaning and purpose that he saw as the central characteristic of human life (Hegel, 1807, 1821). Individuals construct subjective definitions and conceptions around which they orient their actions. In acting purposively and thereby creating social institutions, a people express their underlying spirit in those external forms that Hegel calls 'actual spirit'. Social institutions are 'objective' forms of actual spirit, as distinct from the 'subjective' forms that it takes in individual minds. When people objectify their purposes in social institutions and practices they create spiritual phenomena that exist separately from, and externally to, themselves. Each historical period – each 'society' – can be understood as a distinct 'totality' of forms of objective spirit. Societies are cultural totalities, cultural wholes, in which the spirit of the people is expressed in its specific social institutions and practices.

Hegel took over the romantic concept of the *Volksgeist* – folk culture[3] – and turned it to his own purposes. In his hands it became the basis for showing how people are shaped by their 'national culture'. Individuals who share a culture show similarities of character that distinguish them from those who live in other cultures. Hegel held that the culture of a nation develops in and through the individual members of the nation but that it has an existence over and above these individuals. The spirit of a nation is a moral reality that cannot be reduced to individual spirits or minds (Cohen, 1978).

The immediate and 'natural' form of objective spirit, and hence the earliest historical forms that this takes, are the social institutions of the family and kinship. These are the primitive, primordial groups in which all individuality is subordinated to the community and individual consciousness is shaped completely by the collective life. It is the basis for the development of language and a common culture. The next historical breakthrough occurs with the establishment of 'civil society'. This term, taken from the liberal political economists, designates the 'economic' sphere of social relations in the division of labour and the market through which individuals seek to satisfy their wants and needs. With the growing complexity of the social organization of labour, the unity and cohesion associated with kinship are broken up, and individuals come to compete with one another and to enter into relations of conflict. Where Hegel saw the family and kinship as virtually equivalent to the 'state of nature' that had been described by the social contract theorists, he saw civil society as the equivalent of the post-contractual society in which self-interest and interdependence through exchange had become the basic principles of social organization (Marcuse, 1941). It is in civil society that social strata – 'estates' – arise from the organization of property and labour. Each estate has its own specific economic circumstances and, therefore, its own aims and interests, and these interests are expressed in distinct patterns of education, styles of life and social honour. Civil society, then, is the economic sphere of socially organized labour through which the division of society into distinct estates or classes occurs. [4]

The highest social form that is achieved by objective spirit is the politically organized nation state. The state, as representative of the spirit of the whole nation, transcends the particular interests and divisions that arise in civil society and it forges people together through their common interests (Avineri, 1972). Cultural development results in progressively higher levels of national self-awareness and in a growth in rational control over natural and social processes.

Human history, Hegel claimed, exhibits progress. National cultures are not simply different: they are superior or inferior to one another and there is a historical trend from inferior to superior cultures. Superiority and inferiority are judged in relation to the underlying spirit of humanity that they express. Hegel saw this spirit – the world spirit – as embodying the human capacity of 'reason', and world history is to be understood as the progressive *rationalization* of social life. The driving force in this rationalization is the world spirit itself: the direction of social change is not intended by individuals; history is a result of the 'cunning of reason' itself. The active role of spirit, as against intentional individual action, is perhaps the most obscure part of Hegel's work. Spirit as an active, moving force in history can only be understood if a mechanism is provided for translating the spirit into action. Hegel's solution was to invoke a religious mechanism. Behind reason, as a transcendental activating force, he places 'God': the cunning of reason constitutes divine providence.

The overall progress of human history – from its earliest stages to its culmination in the 19th century Prussian state – can be seen as a development of the 'world spirit', but this historical progress is not a simple, unilinear movement. History develops unevenly from one nation to another. World history is the development of the world spirit through the progressive rise and fall of nations. Cultures decline when they fail to promote the further self-awareness of their members, and in these circumstances the culture loses its authority. Its spirit ceases to inspire the social forms of the nation; these social forms ossify and the nation declines. Expanding nations, on the other hand, embody the advance of the world spirit. The rising, expanding nation that is most advanced in any period constitutes the 'world historical nation', the crucial historical subject that has the power to make and shape history through its collective actions. The rise and fall of nations as collective agencies is integral to the progressive rationalization of social life.

Hegel's own philosophy was seen as a part of this process. Intellectual activity occurs in the sphere of 'absolute spirit', where people attempt to develop an awareness of their own subjectivity and the forms of objective spirit through which they live. Each stage of historical development is associated with a particular form of intellectual self-understanding, and Hegel traces a three-fold move from art through religion to philosophy. Only in this final stage of philosophy does intellectual activity fully grasp the movement of the world spirit. Rational philosophy grasps the cunning of reason; philosophers ally themselves with the rising nation state; reason is united with itself. When reason is fully institutionalized in the nation state, history is at an end and true human freedom begins.

Hegel's work was encyclopaedic in character, and his social thought was but one element within a much larger conspectus of ideas. Despite this, or perhaps because of it, he had few direct heirs, and only Lorenz von Stein (1831) can be regarded as having attempted to construct a truly Hegelian social theory. More significant in the longer term was the 'left Hegelianism' of a group of critical writers that became the foundation of Marxism, and the 'right Hegelianism' that remained closer to Hegel's own concerns and became the basis of the work of Dilthey and the hermeneutic tradition.

It was Comte who gave social thought the name by which it is now known: sociology. His work is the summation of earlier ideas of cultural and social progress, drawing especially on Condorcet and Ferguson but cast in a distinctive form. His *Cours de Philosophie Positive* set out his sociological ideas within a systematic social philosophy, while his later *System of Positive Polity* broadened this into a political programme (Comte, 1830–42, 1851–54). Comte's approach to social thought embodied the 'positive', scientific assumptions of the Enlightenment. 'Positivism' was not an invention of his, but was merely a systematization of widely shared assumptions about the law-governed nature of phenomena and the appropriateness of deterministic causal explanations.

Comte saw the societies of history as forming a series of 'organic' periods of social stability that are separated from one another by transitional periods of upheaval and transformation. The organic phases of human existence are stages of social 'equilibrium' where there is a mutual balance or interdependence among the various parts of the society, which reinforce one another in a harmonious way. The principal elements in any society are its division of labour, its language and its religion. Through the division of labour people come to depend upon one another for their basic needs, through language they are able to learn to pass on knowledge from the past, and through religion they can achieve a sense of common purpose that transcends the conflict of individual interests. The most important of these elements for Comte is religion, fundamental beliefs and values. Each stage of history involves the predominance of particular patterns of religion, and the transition from one organic stage to the next occurs as a result of cultural change.

In the earliest stage of human history societies are organized around a religious culture of 'theological' knowledge and so are marked by the dominance of the priests who are the producers and guardians of this knowledge. Such societies are subject to the political rule of warriors. The second organic stage of human history – medieval society – is characterized by societies that are organized around 'metaphysical' religion and the dominance of churchmen and lawyers.

Comte saw himself as living through a period of crisis, a period of transition leading to a new, third, organic stage of history. Medieval society, dominated by its religious and militaristic culture and political outlook, was decaying under the impact of the unprecedented cultural change initiated by the Enlightenment. The metaphysical culture of the medieval world had broken up in the face of the growth of scientific knowledge. Comte saw this as laying the basis for a new social order that would be organized around 'positive', scientific knowledge and the industrial technologies in which science is embodied. These societies would be subject to the leadership of scientists and industrialists. The 'industrialists' were the capitalist employers, directors and bankers, the 'entrepreneurs' who were the active force in the growth of the technology of production. Following Saint-Simon, Comte saw these entrepreneurs as the leading element in a much larger 'industrial class' that was growing to form the vast majority in the new 'industrial society' that involved the rational, scientific organization of labour, aimed at maximum output and growth. The increasing concentration of production, in both technical and financial terms, would be the basis of the enhanced collective power of the 'managers' who run the system. The scientific knowledge of society itself, Comte believed, would become the basis of a new religion, a religion of humanity. 'Positivism' would provide a secular equivalent of the solidarity and authority that the Catholic Church had provided in the medieval period. Sociologists – the producers of this positive knowledge of society – would be the 'priests' of the new religion, controlling its education and determining its policies. Social transformation, Comte believed, was inevitable: history was not simply a process of change, it constituted 'progress'. The task of sociology was to understand this process in order to promote the development of the new form of society.

Spencer set out his philosophical ideas and the basis of his evolutionary scheme from the 1850s, publishing *The Study of Sociology* in 1873 and the *Principles of Sociology* over the following 20 years (Peel, 1971). According to Spencer the social realm comprised clusters of individuals in interaction. 'Society', however, could not simply be reduced to the actions of these individuals. Interactions are culturally organized and show persistent patterns in the arrangement of individuals. These patterns are, for Spencer, 'superorganic'. They are phenomena that have properties in their own right, distinct from the biological and psychological properties of the organic level of individual human existence. By virtue of their 'organization', societies can be regarded as 'organisms' and can, therefore, be analysed, like all other organisms, in terms of their structures and their functions.

Spencer employed a general evolutionary model in which social evolution was seen as a process of *structural differentiation* leading to *functional adaptation*.[5] Social evolution was seen by Spencer as occurring along two dimensions. The first, and most important, is a process of growing structural complexity, a progressive shift from 'simple' undifferentiated societies to more complex 'compound' societies. Through a process of structural differentiation societies achieved levels of complexity that made them better adapted to their environments. The simplest of societies are those that are organized around the family and kinship and that meet their needs through hunting and gathering, while more complex societies have a more extensive division of labour and political organization. Initially, social evolution involves the differentiation of government, then of economic activity (agriculture and industry) and then of communication processes. Subsequently, each of these differentiated structures is itself subject to differentiation into more specialized institutions. Government, for example, is differentiated into distinct political and military structures. The second dimension of evolution concerns the internal regulation of societies, which Spencer saw as varying between the 'militant' and the 'industrial'. Militant societies are those that are organized through centralized mechanisms of coercion and control that establish a high level of compulsion in social relations. Such societies are rigidly stratified into closed social hierarchies.

Spencer's concept of the industrial society has often been misunderstood. He uses the word 'industrial' to refer to involvement in constructive and productive activity within a framework of peaceful rather than coerced or violent interaction. 'Industrial' corresponds closely, then, to the idea of 'civil society' in the Scottish theorists and liberal political economists, though Spencer recognized that simpler as well as more complex societies can be 'industrial' in their internal organization. Industrial societies have weak and diffuse systems of internal regulation, actions are undertaken on a voluntary basis rather than through compulsion, and their systems of stratification are open systems of classes.

Comte had seen history as a simple unilinear sequence, but Spencer, like Hegel, recognized that social development can follow a zigzag course. The overall course of history showed a pattern of progress, but the development of any specific society could show stagnation or retrogression rather than progress. Instead of seeing societies as forming elements in a single sequence of stages, Spencer saw them showing quite divergent paths within the overall progressive development of the human species. In England, for example, he saw signs of advance towards a complex 'industrial' society, but he felt that the country had achieved such equilibrium by 1850 that further differentiation ceased and it became more rigid, centralized and 'militant'. The relative openness and freedom of English 'civil society' had been subverted by a growing collectivism and state interventionism that Spencer, as a liberal, abhorred.

Where Hegel and Comte had seen societies as totalities with distinct properties of their own, Spencer was concerned to emphasize that they were to be seen as the result of individual actions. While 'social organisms' do have a unity and coherence in their social institutions, these properties must be regarded as the consequences of the interplay of the actions of the individual members of society. This is not to say that societies are a direct result of choice and planning. Matters rarely work out as individuals intend, and social institutions must be seen as the *unintended consequences* of individual action. Societies result from the complex accumulation of consequences, which helps to ensure that individuals are unable to foresee what the results of their actions might produce. In 'industrial' societies, for example, the voluntary and contractual exchange relations of individuals produce the collective benefits described by Adam Smith and they generate a high degree of social integration and social solidarity without the need for moral or political intervention. The sociological understanding of this, Spencer felt, could form the basis of a critique of the growing levels of state intervention that characterized the late 19th century: social stability was possible without state intervention, it occurred solely as an unintended consequence of un-coerced individual action.

Spencer was one of the most influential of the Victorian social theorists. The principal inheritor of the Spencerian mantle in Britain was Hobhouse, who used the evolutionary model for a very different political purpose. Where Spencer had been a committed advocate of *laissez-faire*, Hobhouse sought to provide an intellectual rationale for collective action and state intervention allied to the Fabian political programme of social reform. From his base at the London School of Economics, where he held the first British Chair in sociology, he forged a synthesis of Spencer and Hegel, drawing on the Hegelianism of T. H. Green. Hobhouse saw consciousness and purpose playing a central role in social development, culminating in the need for ever higher degrees of co-operation and collective organization in social life.[6] Hobhouse was a contemporary of Weber and Durkheim, but he did not advance social theory beyond the first generation theorists as those writers were to do. He remained, in almost all respects, a 19th century theorist.

In the United States a 'Social Darwinist' interpretation of Spencer became the basis of early American sociology and social reform. The leading figure, Sumner, stressed the idea of the 'survival of the fittest' that Spencer had set out in an early essay.[7] For Sumner (1883), history was a continual struggle of individuals and groups that were motivated solely by the seeking of pleasure and the avoidance of pain. Through this struggle emerged those practices that maximized the adaptation of societies to their environments. These practices, the unintended consequences of human action, were the habitualized, customary ways of doing things that Sumner called the *folkways* (Sumner, 1906: 19).

Unlike Comte and Spencer, Marx's work on social theory was not defined as an exercise in 'sociology'. Whenever Marx did give a label to his own work it was 'political economy' – more accurately, he described himself as engaged in a 'critique of political economy'. Despite this concern for the economic aspects of social life, Marx's work was no mere 'economic' theory. Drawing on the Hegelian social philosophy in which he had been trained, Marx saw economic processes as embedded in a larger social context and as subject to historical transformation. His specific contribution – as this was manifested in those of his works that were published during the 19th century – was to combine Hegelian social philosophy with the analysis of 'civil society'\produced by the English and Scottish social theorists and to put the resulting synthesis to practical use in his support for the socialist and communist parties of Europe. Hegel, Smith and their followers were, Marx held, representatives of 'bourgeois' social theory, and their works had to be subjected to radical critique if they were to be of service to the 'proletariat', the working class.

The link between Hegel and the political economists was provided by their discussion of the role of labour in civil society. Hegel's discussion of labour, Marx held, was cast in idealist terms – in terms of the development of 'spirit' – rather than in the materialist terms adopted by the Scottish theorists. Marx's earliest works included a detailed critical examination of Hegel's work that attempted to 'stand Hegel on his head' and convert his historical idealism into a *historical materialism*. Much of the work through which Marx developed these ideas – including his important writings on 'alienation' – remained unpublished and unknown until well into the 20th century (Marx, 1844; Marx and Engels, 1846), but the general conclusions that he drew concerning the appropriate method for social analysis were clearly set out in his published work.

Marx's starting point was not the 'individual' of classical economics, but real people as they actually exist in specific historical periods with their particular *social* relations. From this point of view, he held, it must be recognized that the fundamental priority for real people is to secure their means of subsistence through productive labour. The fundamental social relations in any period, then, are the relations of production. These relations control the application of labour power to the means of production, and they lie at the heart of Marx's historical materialism. The social relations of production are the fundamental premise for all social theory.

For Marx, legal relations and forms of the state are not aspects of the general development of the human 'spirit', but are rooted in the social relations of material production. These social relations of production correspond to the specific level of development achieved by the material productive forces and they comprise the 'economic structure' of society. On the basis of this economic structure arises a legal and political 'superstructure', as do the various forms of social consciousness that Hegel had termed 'absolute spirit' (Marx, 1859). It is the mode of production of material life that conditions the overall social, political and spiritual life of the society; it is the 'social being' of people that determines their consciousness.

The relations of production are relations of effective control over the means of production and are legally expressed as property relations. These relations cast people into distinct *class* relations that divide those who control from those who labour. All societies are divided between the controllers of the means of production – who form the 'ruling class' – and those who are excluded from this control. The subordinate class of non-controllers depends only on its own labour power and can secure its means of subsistence only by entering into social relations with the controllers of the means of production. These class relations are antagonistic, involving a mutual conflict of interests that grows with the development of the forces of production. Class relations that initially correspond with the development of the forces of production eventually become a hindrance to the further development of those forces of production by which they were shaped. At the heart of each society, then, is an antagonistic opposition of interests between the members of the two basic classes, and these class antagonisms are seen as the driving force in history. The struggle of classes – ultimately in the form of a social revolution – leads to a transformation of the relations of production that allows the further development of the productive forces. The political and legal superstructures of societies are of secondary importance in this process of social change. While political and cultural factors may help to shape the form that is taken by class struggle, economic factors are primary and the superstructure is eventually transformed as a result of the economic transformation.

Marx uses this historical method to interpret the development of European society. There had been, he held, a transition from the medieval 'feudal' mode of production to the modern 'capitalist' mode of production. Feudal relations of production had been transformed earliest, and most clearly, in England, where the class relation of lord to serf began to give way to that of capitalist to wage labourer during the 15th century. It was in England that a true 'proletariat' of wage labourers had been formed by the early 16th century. It was in England that 'civil society' emerged in its earliest and clearest form. The political and cultural forms of modernity were superstructural changes that reflected this prior and more fundamental economic transformation. The rise of the nation state and the emergence of the ideas of the Enlightenment thinkers corresponded to the rise to power of the bourgeoisie, and Marx saw himself as living in a society that was characterized by the increasingly antagonistic class relations of bourgeoisie to proletariat. These antagonistic class relations had allowed the productive forces to develop to the unprecedented levels that were characteristic of the *industrial* production that took place in the large-scale factories that were being set up across Europe. Modern society was, then, a *capitalist* society in which industrial technology had achieved an extremely high level of development.

To understand modern capitalist society it was important to understand the nature of capitalist relations of production, and the great bulk of Marx's work was concerned with this task. In the various volumes of *Capital* he set out the economic theory that comprised the core of his analysis of modern society, seeing the production process as organized around the exploitation of labour by capital (Marx, 1867). In this process of exploitation, 'surplus value' was transferred from workers to capitalists, impoverishing the former and enriching the latter. Exploitation was the basis of the progressive 'polarization' of class relations that would precede the development of a proper 'class consciousness' among workers and would impel them towards revolution. The class relations of capitalist society had become a fetter on the further development of industrial technology and would culminate in a revolutionary transformation in which capitalism would give way to a classless 'communist' society.

The arguments of Hegel, Comte, Spencer and Marx differed considerably from one another, though there is a degree of agreement about the broad pattern of 'modernization'. For all the writers, social development had moved away from an early stage of society that was organized around kinship and religion and was marked by a degree of equality and a lack of social differentiation. There was also a common recognition that the central institutions of modernity were those of 'civil society': the market, the division of labour, property and class divisions. They diverge sharply, however, in their views on the further development of modernity. Hegel saw civil society being tamed by the power of the state, and Comte shared something of this view, seeing the state as an instrument of positivist science. Marx saw the state as a mere reflection of class division that would eventually be overthrown with the establishment of a communist society. Spencer shared Marx's abhorrence of the state, but anticipated – or, at least, hoped – that the state would be limited and the liberties of civil society would be re-established.

THE FOUNDERS OF ACADEMIC SOCIOLOGY

Hegel, Comte, Spencer and Marx can be regarded as the true pioneers in the development of a framework of sociological thought, though only Comte and Spencer defined their work in these terms. In the period between 1880 and the 1920s a major re-orientation in social thought took place. The development of academic sociology was tightly constrained by national boundaries: there was little academic contact between France and Germany, and very little between either of these and Britain. Only in the United States was there any significant drawing on work carried out in other countries. For this reason, a number of distinct 'national' approaches to sociology arose and became the bases of the institutionalization of the subject in the universities. In France and Germany, in particular, an attempt was made to establish sociology as a university discipline with its own place in the academic division of labour. Emile Durkheim was the dominant figure in France, while Ferdinand Tönnies, Georg Simmel and Max Weber prevailed in Germany. In their differing ways, they entered into a critical dialogue with the works of the pioneers and began the construction of more disciplined and more focused theoretical frameworks that could serve as the bases of empirical investigations of the kinds that had already been established in history and the natural sciences. Marxist thought had moved in a different direction to become institutionalized in socialist political practice, though a number of important economic works were produced and it began to have an influence on social science in the universities. It is from this heady mixture of influences that the founding statements of sociology emerged.

It was only from the late 1870s that Marx's economic theory became more widely known. It had a particular influence in Germany, where it was taken up by the new Social Democratic Party (SPD). Marx died in 1883, and it was largely through the activities of Engels that 'Marxism' as a doctrine became the basis of a political strategy in the SPD and the other socialist parties that were allied with it in the Second International. Kautsky, supported by Engels, was the leading figure in the SPD, and orthodox Marxism emerged under his guidance and that of Plekhanov of the Russian Social Democratic and Labour Party. This orthodox Marxism stressed the 'scientific' character of Marx's thought and, in the hands of Engels, was given a distinctively 'positivistic' interpretation. Because of its identification with organized socialism, Marx's thought did not enter the mainstream of academic debate, and its influence in the universities developed only slowly.

It became apparent to many Marxists, as it had to Marx himself, that the expectation that capitalism would involve a deepening economic crisis and social polarization was not being fulfilled. As a result, belief in the revolutionary transformation of capitalism weakened. Bernstein's (1899) *Evolu-*

tionary Socialism set out these doubts and concerns, arguing that a 'revision' of Marx's theory was necessary to correct its failings and to bring it up to date with developments in capitalism since the time of his death. Bernstein's ideas generated a storm of controversy between the 'revisionist' and 'orthodox' wings of Marxism that marked socialist debates for many years. The most fruitful theoretical outcomes of these debates were the novel arguments of Luxemburg in Germany and of Adler, Renner and Hilferding in Austria (see Bottomore, 1975).

Rosa Luxemburg (1913) revised Marx's theory to take account of the imperial expansion of the capitalist powers during the 19th century, but she sought to defend the core idea of the inevitability of economic collapse and, therefore, of the need to be prepared for revolution. The Austrian Marxists, on the other hand, saw imperial expansion as merely one aspect of the growth of a more 'organized' form of capitalism that they termed 'finance' capitalism and that would, they believed, be both more stable and more difficult to overthrow than its competitive predecessor (Renner, 1904; Hilferding, 1910).

Though he was not the only French social theorist to call himself a sociologist, Durkheim was the single most important figure in the establishment of sociology in the French university system. He undertook his principal studies from the 1890s while teaching sociology in a Faculty of Education, and he was appointed to the first Chair of sociology in France in 1913. Durkheim's work can be seen as developing a critical response to both classical liberalism and its associated individualistic framework (as epitomized in Spencer) and to the orthodox Marxism that had become an important feature of European political debates. Such writers as de Tocqueville and Le Play who, in their different ways, explored the social cohesion and authority generated in the family and the community, were important points of reference for Durkheim, but his principal source of inspiration was, of course, the 'positivism' that had been established by Saint-Simon and Comte. From these writers came the emphasis on the role of ideas in social life that was central to his critique of classical liberalism, but his critical response to liberalism also developed some of the same themes as the right Hegelians and historicists in Germany. For Durkheim the distinctive characteristics of social life, as against biological life, are to be found in the realm of ideas and values. 'Society' is not simply an aggregate of individuals, it is a collective body of ideas, values and sentiments. While societies do possess important 'morphological' characteristics that are shaped by material factors, the bonds that hold societies together are not material but ideal. The essential features of social life are the values, religious beliefs, legal norms and rules of language that bind its members together. Society is a *moral* reality, and it was for this reason that Durkheim saw his aim as being to establish a science of 'moral life'.

The aim of sociology as the science of society is to observe, describe, classify and explain the nature of and changes in these moral phenomena, which Durkheim (1895) regarded as 'social facts'. Durkheim held that a positive science must treat its objects of analysis as 'things' that exist independently of the preconceptions of individual scientists. Whether facts of nature or social facts, these things must be studied empirically and objectively. The central attribute of a social fact is its 'externality' relative to the individual members of society. Social facts are distinct from the biological and psychological facts concerning individuals and are seen as having a reality in their own right. They are general throughout a society, they endure over time and, like the facts of the natural world, they constrain people's behaviour. Although stressing that social facts are external to individuals, Durkheim later came to emphasize that moral phenomena also have a subjective reality in so far as they are internalized by individuals and become elements in their consciousness (Durkheim, 1912).

An example will clarify Durkheim's argument. Language is a social institution and, as such, a social fact. It is organized by a structure of grammatical rules that pre-date any particular individual and that will persist after his or her death. They are part of the world into which the individual is born and to which he or she must adapt. But the rules of a language have this significance only because they are learned by individuals. A native speaker of English, for example, can regard the rules of Russian or Swahili as purely 'external' factors, but the learned rules of English grammar are internalized facts about him or her as an individual. The constraining power of the moral phenomena of society, then, is not a direct effect but depends upon internalized attitudes and values, and on the reactions of others who have also internalized those same attitudes and values.

All social phenomena have these characteristics, from the morphological features of interaction patterns through social 'currents' and 'forces', to the core of the moral reality of society. Durkheim saw morality as a collective phenomenon, not a matter of individual choice. The moral reality of society comprised what he termed the *conscience collective* or the *collective representations*, the common culture or symbolic system that defined a structure of shared ways of perceiving, thinking, feeling and acting that had a specifically moral impact on the individual members of the society. Individuals are born into a pre-existing society and acquire its values and ideas through their upbringing and education. It is in this way that individuals are constituted by society. The moral reality of society *constrains* individual actions and is irreducible to those actions. Durkheim's assumption that social facts were irreducible to individual facts went far beyond the organicism of Spencer. Durkheim held that social facts were things-in-themselves that could enter into causal relations with one another without the need for any individual intention. Social facts and their causal relations are merely refracted through the individuals who are their carriers.

Durkheim's historical sociology is concerned with the transition from traditional, pre-industrial societies to modern, industrial societies, and he developed his account of this transition through a critical examination of the arguments of Comte, Spencer and Tönnies (Durkheim, 1893). Durkheim traces a process of social differentiation through which changes in the social division of labour lead to a change in the basis of social cohesion. Western society is passing, he argues, from a situation of 'mechanical solidarity' to one of 'organic solidarity'.

Mechanical solidarity is characteristic of traditional society, and Durkheim's analysis of this has much in common with those of Spencer and of Tönnies (1889).These undifferentiated or less complex societies are divided into cellular segments such as families, clans and tribes. These segments are localized in bands or in village communities, and individuals are attached to and enclosed by their domestic and communal locales. The separate segments of a society are unified through the common beliefs and sentiments of their members. There is a high level of consensus and strong, repressive systems of social control, rooted in a *conscience collective* that allows little scope for individual autonomy. Deviance is seen as a direct threat to the social order and is met with a strong, intense reaction that is geared to reinforcing social solidarity. The significance of punishment in such societies is that it directly expresses the moral consensus of the community.

Industrial societies are based around an extensive division of labour, an increased specialization of tasks that leads to much higher levels of interdependence of one individual on another. These features are associated with the weakening of the corporate character of the *conscience collective* and a consequent growth of individualism. The common culture becomes more generalized in content and more concerned with balancing the autonomy of each individual against all others. The growth of the division of labour is the basis of an 'organic' solidarity that is rooted in the interdependence of individuals.[8] This was not, however, a simple consequence of unfettered exchange relations of the kind stressed by Spencer. Durkheim argues that social solidarity cannot be derived simply from the individual pursuit of pleasure and self-interest through rational exchange in the market. Exchange relations among freely contracting individuals are based on a framework of norms and implicit understandings. In order to enter into such relations, individuals must have a prior commitment to the institution of contract and to observing its moral force over them. Such commitments are part of the *conscience collective*, and Durkheim concludes that there is a 'non-contractual' basis to all contractual relations. Spencer's account of the market, like that of Adam Smith before him, was unable to explain the existence of the very 'non-contractual' elements that it depended upon. For Durkheim, the non-contractual basis of exchange relations was to be found in a normative order, a social fact.

The Europe of his day was, Durkheim held, at a point of transition in which the old forms of mechanical solidarity that characterized the medieval world had broken down, while the institutions of organic solidarity were only unevenly developed. The crisis resulted from the rapidity with which industrialization had taken place, and he held that the crisis would disappear as organic solidarity became more firmly established. This conclusion led him to reject the Marxist view that the crisis of modern society was economic in character. For Durkheim, this crisis was a moral one and could not be resolved simply through the abolition of private property, redistribution of wealth or greater economic planning. The moral crisis of 19th century Europe was manifest in such conditions as 'anomie' and 'egoism', whose consequences were class conflict, high levels of suicide, and other forms of social discontent (Durkheim, 1897). Indeed, Marxism and other socialist ideas were seen by Durkheim as symptoms of this failure of social solidarity. The task of sociology was to identify these 'pathological' features of modern society and so to help to establish organic solidarity through the promotion of normative frameworks of regulation that combined social cohesion with a recognition of individual autonomy.[9]

From the standpoint of the sociological debates of the 1990s, Weber appears as the most important figure in German sociology. He was, however, only one of a number of writers in Germany who sought to establish sociology as an academic discipline, though he was neither employed as a 'sociologist' nor did he consistently seek to apply this label to himself. His work was, however, linked to that of a number of scholars who took up the name 'sociology' to distinguish their intellectual concerns from those of their predecessors who operated within the romantic framework of folk psychology, with its studies of custom, language and mythology. Of these 'sociologists', Tönnies and Simmel were regarded by their contemporaries as the leading figures, and Weber was an active, though not uncritical, supporter of their efforts.

Tönnies produced the first great work of German sociology in 1889 and went on to produce a central synthetic text that summarized the achievements of German sociology (Tönnies, 1889, 1931). His study *Community and Association*, preceding Durkheim's *Division of Labour* by four years, explored the transition from the 'communal' organization of medieval society to the 'associational' organization of modern society. He reiterated the interpretation of European modernity that had developed over the preceding century, but he cast it within a framework that sought to give proper attention to the creative and constructive role of individual action in producing its central cultural values. Simmel, coming to sociology from philosophy, wrote a classic study of the social consequences of money (1900) and also went on to produce two widely studied texts (Simmel, 1908, 1917). In Simmel's work individual action was again made a central concern, and he developed a powerful account of the formation of groups through interaction. Drawing on both Tönnies and Simmel, Weber (1904–5) applied sociological ideas to the specific issue of the development of capitalism in Europe and went on to undertake a series of comparative investigations in historical sociology (Weber, 1915, 1916, 1917) and an encyclopaedic statement of a framework for the study of economy and society (Weber, 1914, 1920). The latter was, in fact, written as the introductory volume for a series of studies that would contain works by the leading German sociologists and economists of the day.

Building on the works of Tönnies, Simmel and Weber, the mainstream of German sociology through the 1920s and 1930s centred on questions of 'formal' or 'pure' sociology in which the analysis of actions and social relations formed the central part. Such writers as Vierkandt (1923), von Wiese (1924–29) and Geiger were the leading contributors to this enterprise, and their work was complemented by Oppenheimer's conflict theory (Oppenheimer, 1914, 1922) and the cultural sociology of Alfred Weber (1920–21), Max Scheler (1923–24) and Karl Mannheim (1929). This flowering of intellectual effort in sociology, unmatched in any other country, collapsed with the Nazi seizure of power, which led to the suppression of most social theory and to the direct exclusion of Jews from the universities. Virtually the only active sociological theorist during the 1930s, a collaborator with the Nazi regime, was Freyer (1930), who set out a neo-Hegelian view of German society.[10]

The central theoretical assumption of the mainstream of German sociology was that the social process comprised individual actions and interactions, from which are formed the more or less enduring interpersonal relations that constitute the subject matter of sociology. These relations are not, however, 'external' to, or independent of, individuals, as Durkheim had argued. Associations, groups, states, Churches and so on were all seen as constructions in the minds of individuals and towards which they orient their actions. Such relations consist solely in the likelihood that a particular pattern of actions will occur. They constrain individual actions only because individuals *define* them as 'things' separate from their own wishes and interests. The activities of individuals interweave in such a way as to produce what Simmel termed the 'external network' of interactions that comprise society, though this network has an independent reality only when it is taken account of by individuals in their actions (Simmel, 1908: 30). If 'social structures' have any reality, it is as 'configurations' of interaction patterns that are produced by actors who orient their actions around such ideas.

Weber showed that such theoretical ideas could be used in historical investigations. 'Capitalism', he held, can be seen as a configuration of social
relations and, when formulated as a scientific concept, it can be studied in
terms of the individual actions that constitute it and that are responsible for
its emergence from traditional, pre-capitalist patterns of action. The causal
explanations that sociologists and historians produce – for example, those
concerning the rise of capitalism – must be rooted in the interpretative understanding of the subjective meanings by which individuals orient their actions.

In his analysis of the rise of capitalism, Weber took Marxist analyses as
one of his targets. In their work, he held, 'capitalism' was reified as a
deterministic system, rather than being seen as the outcome of individual
actions. Weber wished to show that the economic actions of capitalists and
workers were not to be seen as mere consequences of their economically
structured positions. They were, he argued, also shaped by cultural values
and meanings. This argument was most clearly outlined in his analysis of the
Protestant ethic and the spirit of capitalism, where he demonstrated the
importance of specific religious beliefs in the development of European
capitalism in the 17th century (Weber 1904–5). Weber's sociology placed the
cultural value choices that are made by individuals at the centre of attention,
and he showed that these choices were rooted in the historical relativity of
values. Weber, like Durkheim, highlighted the central significance of ideal or
moral factors in social life, placing these alongside material factors in the
structuring of the social actions of individuals, but he rejected any assumption that they were 'social facts' to be studied through the deterministic
methods of the positivistic sciences. Weber proposed that they be studied
through the construction of historically grounded concepts – 'ideal types' –
that illuminate the distinctive features of particular situations of action.

Weber held that the social development of Europe had followed a course of
rationalization, though he saw this in very different terms to Hegel. For
Weber, rationalization is a consequence of changing patterns of value orientation in individual actions. In particular, the 'traditional' value patterns of
medieval Europe and the forms of action with which they were associated
had given way to actions that were oriented in purely rational terms. The
modern world was 'disenchanted' as a result of the demise of the traditional
religious and magical meanings by which people had guided their actions in
the past. The rational scientific meaning systems that have replaced them are
unable to provide people with values to guide their actions. In the modern
world, individuals must make and maintain their value choices without any
guidance from tradition or religion. Thus, 'traditional authority' had increasingly given way to the rational forms of authority that are found in systems of
bureaucratic administration that operate under abstract and impersonal legal
norms. The bureaucratization of the state and of the capitalist enterprise was

the central feature of modern society for Weber, and he was very pessimistic about the possibility that individuals might escape from the 'iron cage' of bureaucratic surveillance and control. Socialism, in particular, he saw as an ideology whose implementation would increase the level of bureaucratization by furthering state control.

France and Germany were the countries in which the two principal models for academic sociology emerged. Durkheim and his contemporaries established a 'positivist' science of society that took as its objects integrated structures of social relations and cultural representations. The task of such a sociology was the formulation of causal generalizations and, wherever possible, the 'laws' governing social phenomena. This model for sociological analysis produced an image of modernity that was closely linked to the idea of an industrial society. Weber and his contemporaries, on the other hand, established an 'interpretative' science concerned with social actions and social relations and that emphasized the need to 'understand' social phenomena in terms of their subjective meanings. Their image of modernity was a combination of industrialism with capitalism, and in stressing this combination of features in modernity the German sociologists drew heavily on their critical response to the Marxist theory of capitalism.

THEORETICAL SUB-CURRENTS

The French and German, 'positivist' and 'interpretative' models were not the only forms of sociology to be institutionalized after 1880, though they were undoubtedly the most successful. In Austria and Italy ideas that centred on issues of conflict and power were developed. These ideas were also important in the early development of sociology in the United States, where they were a major element in the powerful synthesis of 'Chicago' sociology.

The leading Austrian conflict theorist was Ludwig Gumplowicz, whose work was closely associated with that of Ratzenhofer.[11] Gumplowicz (1875, 1883, 1885, 1905) rejected the fashionable historicism of his German contemporaries and their emphasis on individual action, and he also rejected the arguments of Durkheim and the classical liberals. He turned, instead, to Darwin for inspiration, seeing the conflict of groups as the driving force in history (see also Ratzenhofer, 1893, 1898, 1907; Aho, 1975). Group cohesion and discipline were the basis of power, and so the struggle of groups was necessarily a power struggle. Because of the centrality of power in social development, societies tend to be divided between a 'ruling minority' and a 'subject majority' (Gumplowicz, 1905: 203). The ruling minority, the group that commands, has control of the major levers of power, though it may be served by an 'intermediate class' that is also able to live off the subject group.

Gumplowicz rejected the Marxist view that group conflicts are rooted in economic differences, despite his use of the word 'class'. Instead he claimed that there are always 'ethnic differences between the ruling class and the ruled' (Gumplowicz, 1905: 201).The fundamental struggles of social life are based in ethnic group competition for control over scarce resources. These ethnic group conflicts are the basis of state formation and, thereby, of the division between rulers and ruled. Each nation state has its origin, Gumplowicz argued, in the rise to dominance of a particular ethnic group that seeks to expand its interests and power. Because states arise from the subjection of one population by another, ethnic heterogeneity is built into the structure of states, and it is from the fusion of ethnic groups and from their internal differentiation that economic class divisions emerge. Class positions are defined by the ability 'to appropriate the surplus economic production ... to seize a specific amount of the national wealth' (Aho, 1975: 68).

Gumplowicz was a central influence on the work of the Italian writer Gaetano Mosca, who developed the idea of the division between rulers and ruled into the doctrine of the 'elite'. Mosca was less committed to the idea of the ethnic basis of group conflict, and he constructed a model that stressed the role of will, purpose and conflict in social life, ideas taken from Machiavelli and from Nietzsche. Politics is concerned with power, and societies are dominated by a 'ruling class' or 'elite' that dominates and manipulates the masses.[12] The elite 'performs all political functions, monopolizes power and enjoys the advantages that power brings' (Mosca, 1896: 50). In 'primitive' forms of society, military force is the basis of elite recruitment, while in modern societies it is wealth that is critical. History involves the constant rise and fall of elites as the power bases of the prevailing social forces alter.

Mosca took from Nietzsche the idea that all knowledge is illusion. Nietzsche had argued that people live through the illusions of religion and politics, including the very idea of 'reason' itself.[13] The world is, therefore, inherently senseless, meaningless. There are no such things as truth and objectivity, no 'correct' knowledge or 'rational' belief. The task of philosophy and of social theory is to *unmask* the fictions by which people live in order to disclose the drives and goals that are the real springs of action. These drives are blind instincts, pure 'will' aimed at enhancing people's power. Human beings are driven by a *will to power*, an urge to enhance their capacities and resources at the expense of those of others.

Vilfredo Pareto developed similar views to Mosca on the inevitability of elite rule and the constant 'circulation' of elites. Pareto, however, gives greater attention to the bases of the underlying drive or will to power. These drives he called the *residues*, and he concentrates his attention on the residue of 'innovation' and the residue of 'consolidation'. Following Machiavelli, Pareto sees these as the bases of the character types of, respectively, the 'foxes' and the 'lions'. It is the balance of these two residues in the social forces of a society that determines the predominant character of its elite. Further echoing Nietzsche, Pareto argued that political rule by an elite depends on their use of a set of ideas that legitimizes and masks the reality of power. Pareto termed this legitimizing ideology the 'derivation', while Mosca termed it the 'political formula'.

In the United States the ideas of Gumplowicz found their expression in the work of Lester Ward, although his initial ideas on group conflict had been developed independently (see Ward, 1883). Ward saw the social process as the outcome of the struggle of organized social forces, and it was Gumplowicz's emphasis on the ethnic dimensions of this struggle that particularly influenced his work (Ward, 1897, 1903). Where Gumplowicz and Ratzenhofer had seen social development as the outcome of the 'blind' struggle of groups, Ward argued that this process could be brought under planned, purposive control. Along with Albion Small, the leading figure in the establishment of American professional sociology at the University of Chicago, Ward held that sociology itself could be a guide to action that would promote planned control. The two set out the basis of a 'pluralist' conception of modern politics (Small, 1905).

It was under the influence of Small that the so-called 'Chicago School' emerged as a fusion of the social psychology of William James, John Dewey and George Mead with Small's version of group conflict theory. The clearest expression of this Chicago viewpoint is to be found in the work of Robert Park and the writers that he inspired in studies of the struggle of ethnic and other social groups for scarce resources in Chicago and in the southern states (Park, 1921; Park and Burgess, 1925; see also Smith, 1988).

Other models for social theory, largely outside the framework of academic sociology, were provided by developments within Marxism. The First World War fractured the international socialist movement along national lines, and the Russian revolution of 1917 created further divisions. Lenin's formulation of Marx's ideas rejected the orthodox Marxism of the Mensheviks and became the basis of a new orthodoxy within the Russian and other 'communist' parties of the Third International. These ideas owed much to Hilferding's account of finance capital and imperialism, but Lenin added a much stronger emphasis on revolutionary action and on the possibility of a political revolution occurring outside the advanced capitalist countries. In 'backward' countries such as Russia, Lenin held, revolution could be brought about by an effectively organized political party that would guide the working class and mobilize the peasantry to establish a political framework for economic transformation.

Outside this new orthodoxy, a number of important critical works were produced by Gramsci, Korsch (1923) and Lukács (1923), who drew on the

f Dilthey and Hegel and recreated a form of 'left Hegelianism'.
on theme to their works was an emphasis on the incorporation of
and cultural analysis into the predominantly economic framework of
thought: it was felt that the 'superstructure' had to be theorized in its
ight.

ramsci, the leader of the Italian Communist Party from 1924 until his
arrest in 1926, developed the idea of 'hegemony' to describe the ideological
and political dominance of a ruling class and stressed the need for the working class to construct a counter-hegemonic organization if they were to successfully challenge the existing structure of power. Gramsci's work had little
influence outside Italy until its rediscovery in the 1970s, and even in Italy his
imprisonment by the Fascists meant that he played little part in the intellectual debates of the 1930s.

Lukács, a Hungarian literary theorist, carried out his main academic work
in Berlin (under Simmel) and in Heidelberg. It was at Heidelberg that he
came into contact with the historicist ideas that had been important in shaping Weber's thought. Through these works he explored many of the same
ideas that the young Marx had pursued, and so arrived at a position that
contrasted sharply with the orthodoxy that had been built from Marx's later
writings. His best-known work (Lukács, 1923) was very influential, but his
subsequent involvement in communist politics led him to repudiate it as a
juvenile work of 'idealism'.[14]

Despite his repudiation, the book was extremely influential. In it Lukács
rejected the claims of both orthodox Marxism and idealism. He developed an
account of 'fetishism' and 'reification' as the specific forms of consciousness
that arise under the conditions of capitalist production, independently redis-
covering Marx's still unknown ideas on 'alienation'. Revolutionary action,
he argued, involves the development of a form of class consciousness that
can effectively challenge the capitalist system. Critical theory – his term for
Marxism – embodies this alternative consciousness, and it enters the historical process when the proletariat recognizes it as a solution to the 'reification'
that is produced by bourgeois forms of thought. Theory enters into practice;
social structures are transformed; history is made. The key element in this
making of history is the revolutionary vanguard party – as it was for Lenin –
as it is in the party that critical theory is carried forward. Both Lukács and
Korsch saw the critical theory of Marxism as the theoretical foundation of
proletarian class consciousness. Critical theorists had the task of developing
this theory and taking it to the working class, who were prevented from
developing an autonomous class consciousness because of the hegemony of
the reifying forms of bourgeois consciousness.

The works of Korsch and Lukács were influential in the formation of the
Institute of Social Research at Frankfurt, where Horkheimer and Adorno and

their colleagues undertook a reconstruction of Marxism. Their work coincided with the appearance in 1932 of two early manuscripts by Marx himself. The *Economic and Philosophical Manuscripts* and *The German Ideology*, both dating from the middle of the 1840s, had been unpublished and had been virtually unknown since Marx had completed them. In these works, Marx set out a more 'philosophical' approach than in his economic theory and showed a far more favourable attitude towards Hegelian ideas, though he recast the Hegelian view of consciousness and politics in a rigorously materialist framework. The work of the Frankfurt Institute combined these influences into a powerful 'Hegelian' Marxism. The Institute's work in Germany ended in 1933 when its members were forced to flee to the United States, where the subsequent development of critical theory was to take place.

This, then, was the intellectual context from which contemporary debates in sociological theory have emerged. Our image of many of these writers is, today, different and, in many cases, more complex, but this is a reflection of the fact that we now approach the pioneer and founding works in sociological theory from the standpoint of our current concerns. These concerns have emerged over the last 60 or 70 years in the works of the writers who will be discussed in the rest of this book. The basis for these works was laid during the 1920s and 1930s by Talcott Parsons, who attempted to take stock of the achievements of the founding generation and set the course for subsequent theoretical work. It is with Parsons's interpretation – and misinterpretation – of the history of sociology that a consideration of contemporary debates must begin.

NOTES

1. It was not until the work of Comte that these strands were pulled together into a single theory of both 'social statics' and 'social dynamics'.
2. The Italian writer Vico had earlier presented an interpretation of history as a process of development in *The New Science*, but his work had little influence on his contemporaries (Vico, 1725).
3. The concept of the *Volksgeist* is difficult to translate, and 'folk culture' is perhaps the nearest equivalent term. It carries many of the connotations of 'popular culture', though this term has lately come to be applied principally to the products of the 20th century mass media.
4. Hegel's analysis of the formation of *Stände* within civil society reflects the arguments of the classical economists on the formation of 'classes' and was influential for the work of both Marx and Weber on social stratification.
5. Spencer's evolutionary ideas preceded those of Darwin, though they differed from the form in which Darwin was later to express them.
6. See also the later work of T. H. Marshall (1949) on citizenship.
7. An early essay on competition encouraged Galton, Pearson and others in England to link Spencer's work with a Malthusian view of population pressure and to construct a policy of 'eugenics', or selective breeding.

8. Durkheim's categories of 'mechanical' and 'organic' solidarity are, perhaps, unfortunate, as his use of the words involves a reversal of their conventional usage. This puts Durkheim's terminology at variance with most contemporary and subsequent writers, for whom modern societies are seen as 'mechanical' and as differing from the 'organic' unity of medieval societies. Durkheim's distinction might have been better formulated as a contrast between the repressive 'communal' solidarity of pre-modern societies and the 'organized' solidarity of modern societies.

9. Durkheim failed to give an adequate explanation of the link between interdependence and social solidarity in *The Division of Labour in Society* (Durkheim, 1893). It is only in his later work on political sociology that he resolved this problem by arguing that solidarity arises from the differentiated normative structures that are established around each specialized occupation and task through a 'guild' system.

10. General reviews of German sociology can be found in Abel (1929), Becker (1938), Aron (1936) and Freund (1978).

11. Gumplowicz was a Pole who lived and worked in Austria. Ratzenhofer was a native Austrian. Both writers developed arguments that were similar to those of Oppenheimer in Germany (see Therborn, 1976: 186ff).

12. This discussion draws on my forthcoming book on social stratification. It was, in fact, Pareto who introduced the word 'elite' to refer to the concept of the ruling minority (Pareto, 1901, 1902 , 1916).

13. Although a reaction to Hegel, Nietzsche's work is more directly a radicalization of that of Schopenhauer.

14. Lukács worked in Moscow during the 1930s and returned to his native Hungary when the communist regime was established there.

2. Talcott Parsons: where it all began

Talcott Parsons held a virtually unchallenged position as the world's leading sociological theorist from the 1940s to the 1960s. Over a period of 30 years Parsons produced a series of works of theoretical synthesis that were often of great complexity but were always of major importance. He inspired a whole generation of sociologists, many of whom continued to expand and to build upon his work. The style in which Parsons wrote was dense, ponderous and turgid, and this tended to obscure the rigour and the significance of his arguments.[1] Nevertheless, his work remained the fundamental point of reference for theoretical debates throughout the period. Aspects of his work were challenged by sympathetic critics such as Merton (1949) and less favourable critics such as Wrong (1961), while a more fundamental challenge was posed by conflict theorists such as Rex and Dahrendorf,[2] but no other social theorist commanded the attention that Parsons received. It was only towards the end of the 1960s that his theoretical work began to be eclipsed by more radical theorists.

Parsons was born in 1902 and he died in 1979, having spent most of his career at Harvard University. His first confrontation with the social sciences occurred during a period of postgraduate study that he spent at the London School of Economics and at Heidelberg in the 1920s. He developed an interest in economics and the sociology of economic life, and his doctoral thesis was an examination of conceptions of 'capitalism' in German social theory.

Concluding that economic processes could be understood only as elements in larger social structures, Parsons extended his work into an examination of a number of other writers who had concerned themselves with this issue. Beginning with investigations into the works of Alfred Marshall and Vilfredo Pareto, he went on to reconsider the work of Max Weber, whom he had initially studied while at Heidelberg. He then undertook a study of Durkheim.

Parsons's discovery of Durkheim had particular significance for the rest of his life's work. He was the only one of Parsons's chosen theorists who had not undertaken a major study into the sociology of economic life. He had, however, explored the embededness of economic activity in the larger social context. It was Durkheim's concern for the cultural and symbolic processes that make up this context, and his consequent focus on values, symbols and ideas, that rapidly became the central theme of Parsons's own work.

THE PROBLEM OF ORDER

Parsons identified Durkheim's (1893) book *The Division of Labour in Society* as a key text in the integration of economic and social theory, and he claimed to have detected a strong connection with the themes raised in Weber's (1904–5) *The Protestant Ethic and the Spirit of Capitalism*. Durkheim's book had highlighted religious and other cultural values as underpinning contractual economic relations, while Weber's work had studied the implications of religious beliefs for economic action. The outcome of Parsons's investigations into these issues was presented in *The Structure of Social Action* (Parsons, 1937).

The principal argument of *The Structure of Social Action* was that Marshall, Pareto, Weber and Durkheim had, independently of each other, converged upon a similar theoretical approach to social life. Each writer was concerned, he claimed, with finding a solution to 'the problem of order' that he identified in the work of Hobbes.[3] Hobbes had claimed that people in their natural state were motivated solely by their individual interests and their passions, which they pursued in purely rational ways. The rational pursuit of self-interest leads to competition and conflict, and it provides no stable basis for co-operation. There is always the possibility that an agreement to limit competition will be broken or undermined if it is in the interest of a person to do so. A 'war of all against all' is the inevitable result of rational, self-interested action. Hobbes observed, however, that co-operation and social order are, in fact, a normal feature of social life. The war of all against all is, somehow, avoided in normal social interaction. The fundamental issue in social analysis, then, is the question: 'how is social order possible?'.

Hobbes remained within an individualistic frame of reference and argued that social order could exist only if people see it as in their own individual interest to co-operate with one another. If people recognize endemic conflict – the war of all against all – as being, in the long term, contrary to their self-interest, they might be willing, in the short term, to limit the disruptive effects of their actions. No individual will do this unless he or she is certain that all others will do the same. But there are no rational grounds for believing that others will forego short-term advantages. Those individuals who restrict the pursuit of their self-interest will lose out, to the benefit of those who pursue their interests wholeheartedly. In a system of rational individual action, no one has any incentive to limit the pursuit of their interests. It is impossible to explain *how* co-operation and social order occur.

Hobbes's solution to his theoretical problem, Parsons argued, had been to invoke the state as an external force that had the power to limit individual action and to enforce a stable social order. Stability in social life, and particularly in the *economic* sphere of 'civil society', is a *political* fact. It is the outcome of coercion, or of the threat of coercion, which alters the rational calculations that individuals make. Parsons held that this is an inadequate solution to the problem of order, as it ignores the *normative* features of social life. Hobbes, he says, saw society as a system of economic and political power relations in which there was no place for norms, for altruism, obligation and duty that, Parsons argued, are important elements in actual societies. Such norms are not mere fictions or deceptions that mask power struggles. Social order, argued Parsons, depends upon a 'normative order' as well as on power and coercion. Hobbes had failed to explain how normative order was possible.

Parsons concluded that there was something fundamentally wrong with Hobbes's social theory. If it is unable to provide an explanation of a critical feature of social life, there must be something wrong with its basic assumptions. The Hobbesian problem could be resolved only by breaking with those assumptions, but those who followed in Hobbes's tradition had failed to do this and had resorted to various *ad hoc* solutions. Some followed Locke and invoked the arbitrary and unjustified idea that social order resulted from a 'natural identity' of interests, while others stressed the biological factors of heredity and environment.

Only with the work of Alfred Marshall, Parsons argued, did this 'utilitarian' tradition move towards a solution to the problem of order. Marshall's main contribution to economics had been a theory of utility in which economic activity is an expression of certain qualities of *character*. According to this, economic action is not simply egotistical, based on self-interest, it is also shaped by shared value standards (Parsons, 1937: 163, 435). But Marshall had not broken with the utilitarian tradition, and he failed to develop a proper theory of cultural values. For this it was necessary to look beyond the English utilitarian tradition.

It was in the Italian theorist, Pareto, that Parsons found a more adequate solution. Pareto aimed to overcome the limitations of the utilitarian focus on rational, 'logical' action and to build a complementary account of 'non-logical' cultural values. Two types of action – logical and non-logical – were rooted, respectively, in interests and values. Pareto introduced the concepts of 'residues' and 'derivations' to analyse these. The derivations were the values that served as political 'myths' or ideologies to legitimize and rationalize self-interested actions.

For Parsons, the analysis of elites, power and conflict were subsidiary elements in Pareto's scheme, secondary to the concepts of logical and non-logical action. The latter he saw as the core of an important theoretical advance in solving the problem of order. It was in the work of Durkheim and Weber, however, that Parsons found what he believed to be the most forceful solutions to this problem. Starting from different theoretical traditions – from 'positivism' and 'idealism', respectively – Durkheim and Weber converged towards a similar view of action.

Durkheim's advocacy of the idea that 'society' is a moral entity whose essential characteristic is a body of common values and beliefs was central to his critique of utilitarianism. Parsons saw Durkheim as having formulated a concept of social structure as 'formed mainly by a common system of norma- tive rules which ... rest upon a system of ultimate common value attitudes' (Parsons, 1937: 464). His solution to the problem of order, then, centred on a recognition of the importance of the 'non-contractual element in contract'. It involved an awareness of the system of normative rules that constrain indi- vidual exchange relations. The social structure defines an institutional pat- tern, a clustering of normative expectations that regulate actions and whose stability and change must be the focus of attention for sociological analysis.

Idealist theorists such as Dilthey saw social life as the expression of ultimate cultural values. From this standpoint, there is an ineradicable gulf between the natural sciences and the 'cultural' or historical disciplines, with the study of social action involving the 'understanding' or 'interpretation' of these ultimate values. Parsons's image of Weber is that of one who rejected the metaphysical implications of this view and sought to show that individu- als do, indeed, make value choices, but that their choices are shaped by their material circumstances. But Weber refused to subscribe to the Marxist posi- tion on the economic determination of values, which he saw as denying the autonomy of culture. Weber thus set out a theory in which religious and cultural values were accorded an independent causal significance in the struc- turing of social action.[4]

According to Parsons's interpretation of the founders of academic sociology, Durkheim and Weber had moved, from their radically different starting points, towards a similar explanatory framework in which both values and interests were given their due attention. Parsons termed this emerging framework the 'voluntaristic' theory of action. Although this new framework had not been fully developed in the work of any of the founding sociologists, there had nevertheless been a distinct convergence in their intellectual concerns. Weber and Durkheim were the most prominent exponents of this new voluntaristic theory, both having attempted to reconcile the analysis of rationality and self- interest with that of norms and values. Individuals were seen as exercising a considerable degree of *choice* in the ways in which they pursue their interests, but their choices are *constrained* by a framework of norms and values that they share with other members of their society. Their actions cannot be reduced to their material circumstances and their individual self-interest, but neither can they be seen as totally irrational expressions of 'free will'. Social actions are neither determined nor free: they are 'voluntary'. A voluntaristic theory of action revolves around the interplay of choice and constraint.

The theoretical task that Parsons set for himself in *The Structure of Social Action* was to elucidate this voluntaristic theory of action. Through a critical discussion of the works of Marshall, Pareto, Durkheim and Weber, he held, it was possible to arrive at a solid basis for the further development of social theory. The major gap in the works of the founding sociologists Parsons found in the area of methodology. The voluntaristic theory could be developed only if an appropriate methodology was also constructed. This, Durkheim and Weber had failed to do, and the task that Parsons set for himself was to outline a methodological basis for social theory.

ANALYTICAL REALISM

The methodology that Parsons set out in *The Structure of Social Action* was the foundation for all that he was subsequently to write in his long career. This framework of ideas on the nature and role of theoretical concepts in the social sciences, was modified only slightly during the early 1940s and in one or two papers during his later career. Through all the shifts in substantive focus that characterized his later work – for example, that from 'structural functionalism' to 'systems theory' – the methodological framework remained as the constant and unifying thread.

The basis of his methodology came not from the founding sociologists but from two of Parsons's senior colleagues at Harvard. Alfred Whitehead, the philosopher, and Laurence Henderson, the biologist, provided the inspiration and key ideas for Parsons's attempt to understand the scientific method. Whitehead, a collaborator with Bertrand Russell in a major work on the philosophy of mathematics and logic (Whitehead and Russell, 1910) had set out a clear and systematic view of the relationship between 'theory' and 'fact'.[5] The principal element in the views of Henderson, however, was the methodology of Pareto, which he sought to disseminate among his Harvard colleagues (Henderson, 1935; Homans and Curtis, 1934). Indeed, it had been through the influence of Henderson that Parsons had discovered Pareto's substantive sociology.

The central contention in Parsons's methodology was rooted equally in Whitehead and Henderson. This was his assumption that a science, whether a natural science or a social science, consists of knowledge that is organized into a *theoretical system*. Scientists formulate propositions about 'empirical' phenomena – the phenomena of observation and experience – and these propositions are systematically interrelated with one another in a logically ordered system. For this reason, scientific theory is always systematic and general in form.

The roots of this methodology, as it was developed by Parsons, are to be found in the work of Kant, who explored the relationship between the external world and the concepts and theories that people use to construct their knowledge of it. He had argued that things 'in themselves', as they actually exist in the world, are never directly available for everyday experience or scientific study. People can only ever be aware of 'things' as they are represented to them in their conscious experience. Such representations are not direct apprehensions of the real world, as they already involve the organizational and interpretative abilities of the human intellect. Human knowledge can only ever concern the *phenomena* of conscious experience – the *nuomena*, the things-in-themselves as they exist beyond human consciousness – remain completely unknowable. From this point of view, scientific and everyday concepts are not simple descriptions or 'names' for 'things' that actually exist in the world. Knowledge is not a picture or reflection of external reality, it is a *selective organizing* of aspects of that reality.

These ideas were taken up by the neo-Kantian writers who had influenced Weber, and it was partly through a reflection on Weber's methodology that Parsons turned to Kant. Weber and Parsons, however, drew very different conclusions. Where Weber had drawn radical, relativistic conclusions from the Kantian position, Parsons saw Kant as providing the basis for an objective and general social theory. Parsons rejected all the idealist and relativist implications of the Kantian tradition and held firmly to the 'realist' assumption that there is, indeed, a real world and that human knowledge of this world is not simply an arbitrary creation of the human mind. Human *experience* of the world is constituted through concepts, but the world itself is not. Knowledge, then, is neither a direct reflection of reality nor is it an arbitrary mental construction. In order to distance his views from both crude materialism and idealism, he termed his own methodological standpoint that of 'analytical realism' (Parsons, 1937: 730). The impossibility of knowing the things-in-themselves in their full complexity meant that it was necessary to abstract certain *aspects* of them and to organize them conceptually. Parsons held that theories are able to grasp aspects of the external world, with varying degrees of adequacy. Scientists construct theoretical systems that have an empirical reference and can be empirically tested.

Parsons' methodology also recognized the role that *general* theoretical concepts played in social analysis. The abstraction and organization that take place in a science depend upon the particular *conceptual scheme* that is used. A conceptual scheme comprises a set of interrelated and systematically organized concepts that provide a basis for selecting and organizing the phenomena of experience. Conceptual schemes are central to all human perception and experience, and not only to scientific knowledge. Indeed, scientists may often draw upon everyday conceptual schemes, but they should do so in an explicit and rational way with the aim of transforming the initially vague conceptual scheme into a fully fledged *theoretical system.*

Each science rests upon a different conceptual scheme, and so each will abstract from and organize the external world in a different way. It is not possible, therefore, to see the knowledge that is produced by any particular conceptual scheme as being 'superior' to that produced by any other. Each scheme grasps a different aspect of reality, and no one scheme can be accorded an absolute validity over all others (Parsons, 1937: 41, 181–3; see also Bershady, 1973).

Parsons held that it is 'the conceptual scheme of action' that enables theorists to talk about human action rather than about physical events or biological behaviour. This was, he believed, the great scientific achievement of the founding sociologists. The major works of Pareto, Weber and Durkheim can be read as attempts to formulate this distinctive conceptual scheme. They sought, Parsons believed, to lay the basis for the emerging science of sociology and to distinguish its intellectual concerns from those of biology, chemistry and physics, as well as from everyday and common sense ideas about action. The founding sociologists were not simply constructing specific theories, they were constructing a whole new science.

At the heart of any conceptual scheme is its 'descriptive frame of reference'. This frame of reference in Parsons corresponds in Kant's thought to the *a priori* concepts and categories that make up the necessary framework of all thought. The conceptual scheme of action involves the *action frame of reference*, 'the indispensable logical framework in which we describe and think about the phenomena of action' (Parsons, 1937: 733).[6] The spatio-temporal framework of classical mechanics, according to Kant, is built around the concepts of space, time, quality, modality and relation, together with the ideas of mass, velocity and distance. The action frame of reference involves concepts and categories that were only inadequately recognized by Kant and had to await the intellectual discoveries made by Pareto, Weber and Durkheim.

Fundamental to the action frame of reference are the concepts of time and purpose (Parsons, 1937: 733), the fundamental dimensions in terms of which action can be understood. Action is defined by the fact that it is organized over time and involves the purposive use of means to achieve goals. It is in this sense that Parsons claims that action comprises means–ends relations that are organized over time: 'An act is always a process in time' (Parsons, 1937: 45). It involves a state of affairs – an end or goal – that the person wishes to bring into being or to maintain in existence, and so it can be considered as future-oriented, as concerned with the attainment, realization and achievement of these goals.

The key ideas of the action frame of reference are summed up in its basic concept, the 'unit act'. The concept of the unit act is the sociological equivalent of that of the particle in classical mechanics. It is the fundamental concept of all social analysis, the most elementary way of conceptualizing human action and the building block for larger systems of action. The unit act comprises five elements: it involves an *actor* with a goal or *end*, who manipulates the *means* which are perceived to be available, under the limiting *conditions* of his or her situation, and who acts in accordance with certain *norms* in order to achieve this end. All descriptive statements in classical mechanics must refer to one or more particles of given mass capable of location in space, and of changing their location in time through motion. Similarly, all descriptive statements in the theory of action must refer to one or more unit acts in which actors in specific situations are oriented to certain norms and exert a certain amount of effort in the manipulation of means over time so as to attain their goals.

Inherent in this view of action is the requirement that the scientist adopt the 'subjective point of view'. This is not to say that he or she takes a personal and biased stance towards the study of action. Nothing could be further from Parsons's mind. By the subjective point of view, Parsons means that the social scientist is concerned with things and events as they appear from the standpoint of the actor, and not as they might appear to anyone else or to any supposed impartial observer. The situation in which an actor is placed is relevant to social science only in so far as the actor is aware of it, gives it a definition and takes its features into account in deciding upon a course of action. A corollary of this view is that the social scientist must recognize the centrality of 'choice' in human action. The means and ends of action are never simply 'given' or environmentally determined, they are always chosen by the actor in relation to cultural norms and values (Parsons, 1937: 44ff.). It is for this reason that Parsons describes his theory of action as 'voluntaristic'.

The first step in a scientific investigation of structured patterns of action, then, is to identify the unit acts from which they are built and to describe their features in terms of the action frame of reference. This is a process of scientific abstraction in which aspects of reality are reconstructed as idealized and logically consistent models. These models of actors and patterns of action are the ideal types that Weber referred to as 'historical individuals' or historical particulars (Parsons, 1937: 30). The concept of modern capitalism, for example, can be understood as a historical individual that is a specific combination of other ideal typical units: free markets, impersonal law, bureaucratic administration and so on.

This initial descriptive task, taken on its own, tends to lead to a static, 'mosaic' model of society: a particular society is seen simply as a tessellating combination of different ideal typical parts. The Weberian ideal type method, then, is an essential first step, but it is too limited to serve as a comprehensive sociological method. The ideal type method minimizes the dynamic features of social life. It fails to conceptualize the ways in which one form of society develops into another as a result of certain processes that may not be apparent in the individual parts.

It is when social scientists move beyond 'factual' description to theoretical explanation that they must use *general* concepts from which ideal types are constructed. In order to achieve a scientific explanation, Parsons argues, it is necessary to analyse the concrete ideal types into their constituent elements and then to organize these elements into a theoretical system. Factual descriptions of action must be broken down into what Parsons terms 'analytical elements'. These analytical elements are the variables in terms of which human actions can be analysed. They are the most general attributes or qualities of phenomena, such as the degrees of 'rationality' and of 'disinterestedness' that an action involves (Parsons, 1937: 30ff.).

'Economic rationality', for example, is an analytical element that occurs, to a greater or lesser extent, in a number of different concrete forms of action. Conversely, any particular ideal type of action combines a number of different analytical elements. 'Traditionalism', as understood by Weber, is a concrete ideal type of unit act that involves, as one of its analytical elements, a degree of economic rationality. But this element alone is not sufficient to characterize traditionalism, as it is a quality that it possesses in common with other types of action. Traditionalism is a form of action that is economically rational relative to a traditionally fixed standard of living. It is the combination of two analytical elements – economic rationality and traditional fixity – that defines 'traditionalism' as a concrete type of action (Parsons, 1937: 616–17, 35–6 n.1).[7]

Scientific explanation involves the formulation and use of 'analytical laws'. An analytical law 'states a uniform mode of relationship between the values of two or more analytical elements' (Parsons, 1937: 622). Analytical laws specify the relationships between ends, means, norms and conditions as they are taken into account by the actor in planning a course of action. They involve reference to subjective meanings: they are constructed from the subjective point of view, which is inherent in the action frame of reference, and they refer to those aspects of reality that enter into the mind of the actor. On the other hand, they specify determinate relations between analytical elements and so enable sociologists to produce *causal* accounts of action. Scientific explanations in sociology, then, combine causal adequacy with adequacy at the level of meaning.

Analytical laws are very difficult to construct and are the end results of long processes of scientific investigation. Parsons felt that sociology had not in 1937 advanced to the level at which many such laws could be formulated with any precision. Economics, on the other hand, was an area where more advances had been made in the formulation of analytical laws. Parsons (1937: 36) gave the example of the economic law of the maximization of utility: 'to the extent that an action is rational, it will tend to maximize utility'. The whole body of laws of supply and demand which figure so prominently in micro-economic theory comprise a complex system of analytical laws concerning the relations among such elements as value, utility, choice and so on. This systematic analytical framework of theory contrasts sharply with a purely descriptive focus on the concrete organization of business enterprises and of the division of labour in particular societies.

Turning to sociology itself, Parsons claimed that it is possible to identify 'the law of increasing rationality'. This law states that change within a concrete action system will tend to increase the degree of 'rationality' that it manifests (Parsons, 1937: 751).[8] The meaning and validity of this particular law is not something that need detain us at this stage, as it plays only a minor role in Parsons's early work. The important thing to note is simply that concrete factual descriptions must be broken down into analytical elements that can be formulated into analytical laws. Conversely, laws about the relations among analytical elements can be used in a synthetic way to redescribe and to predict factual occurrences.

Analytical laws do not exist in isolation from one another, but are formed into theoretical systems. The aim of social science, argued Parsons, is to develop a systematic body of generalized analytical theory, a general theory of action. The theoretical propositions that are produced by the various specialist social sciences (such as economics) must be logically related to one another into more comprehensive intellectual systems within which it is possible to derive simpler laws from more fundamental ones. Theoretical systems are hierarchical structures of analytical laws from which, ultimately, concrete descriptions can be derived with logical precision through a process of deduction (Parsons, 1937: 24, 618–19). A fully developed theoretical system will be 'logically closed', in the sense that it will have a perfectly coherent logical structure. A principal way of advancing any science, therefore, is the logical criticism of its theoretical systems with the aim of uncovering any gaps that exist in its deductive structure. By uncovering hidden assumptions and filling in the missing elements in theories, a scientist can advance the frontiers of knowledge and can facilitate the derivation of ever larger bodies of law. This is the role of the theorist, as opposed to the empirical researcher, in the advancement of science.

But logical criticism alone is insufficient for scientific advance. The real driving force in scientific development is empirical research that is aimed at the verification of analytical laws. Scientific propositions refer, ultimately, to concrete empirical phenomena and so it is necessary to gauge their empirical validity through testing the predictive adequacy of the theory (Parsons, 1938).

Scientists must examine the theory in order to derive hypotheses about actual events, and these hypotheses must be tested in empirical research. Here is seen the central tenet of Parsons's analytical realism: scientific concepts are not arbitrary constructions because the real world constrains the ability of scientists to construct empirically adequate logical systems. While it is not possible to know the world as it actually is, it is possible to produce empirically adequate, non-relative knowledge about the world.

THE ACTION FRAME OF REFERENCE

The core of Parsons's action frame of reference is the 'unit act', the most elementary form of human action. The aim of social theory, according to Parsons, is to show how complex social structures are built up from these elementary unit acts. The separate acts of any one individual are interconnected, and they intertwine with those of others to form complex interweaving chains of unit acts. These interweaving chains of action are what Parsons calls 'action systems', and much of his work has been concerned with examining the properties of action systems, rather than simply of unit acts.

A system of action is a number of unit acts that are linked together through chains of elementary interpersonal relations – 'interactions' such as co-operation and conflict – and that are associated with various *emergent structures*. These emergent structures are irreducible elements of human life that 'emerge' from the linked unit acts, but disappear from view if a system of action is broken down into its constituent unit acts. They are results of the *organization* of unit acts into systems, and hence Parsons describes them as 'organic' properties of the systems themselves. At the level of the individual actor are the emergent structures that constitute the individual personality, and that Parsons later identifies with the Freudian and Meadian ideas of the ego, the super ego, and the self. These personality elements are irreducible to the individual acts of the actor. At the social level, Parsons identifies such emergent structures as 'common values', that he subsequently defines to include such things as norms, roles and institutions.

The type of unit act to which Parsons gave greatest attention was that of 'rational action', which he derived from Weber's concept of purposive rational action (*zweckrationalität*) and Pareto's concept of logical action. Central to rational action is a normative principle that relates means to ends 'according to a logico-experimental standard' (Parsons, 1937: 210). The rational actions of an individual, for example, involve the technical choice of means on the basis of their instrumental appropriateness for the achievement of desired ends, or the economic choice of those means that will lead to the optimal allocation of resources to alternative goals. Economic theory has focused its attention on the issue of allocation, extending it to the interaction of individuals through contractual and market relations. As Hobbes showed, the economic level of action – civil society – is inherently conflictual, as each individual strives to secure the means necessary for the achievement of his or her own goals. It was this that led Hobbes to recognize the necessity for a third element, a political element of coercive power in systems of rational action. Systems of rational action, then, involve actors who seek the maximization of technical efficiency, economic wealth and political power. Wealth and power are seen by Parsons as being the fundamental, intrinsic interests of rational action, as they constitute 'generalized means' to actors' goals (Parsons, 1937: 263).[9]

The degree to which the pursuit of wealth and power will result in the greatest benefits for all members of a society, as held by the classical utilitarian writers, depends upon the level of integration that exists among their ultimate values. The liberal assumption that the individual pursuit of self-interest will maximize the interests of all, achieving the greatest happiness of the greatest number, can only be upheld if there is a system of common values that limits social conflict. If there is a common value system, actors will come to develop shared normative rules that, in turn, become the basis of social order. Where no such common value system exists, argues Parsons, there will be no normative order and social life will be in a state of 'anomie'. In anomic situations the only social order that can exist is that which results from the interlocking interests of actors. Such alignments of interests are unstable bases of order, as those rules that might be proposed by any one of the parties will have no legitimacy or moral authority (Parsons, 1937: 401–2). Common values, then, are central to *stable* social order.

Parsons's main concern in *The Structure of Social Action* was with the analysis of rational action and of the part that was played by common values in systems of rational action. He did, however, give a briefer discussion of two other types of unit act: these are ritual action and the forms of action that he described as 'modes of expression'. Where the ends pursued by an actor are 'non-empirical' or 'transcendental', action cannot be rational. A person's search for a high-paying job, for example, can be pursued in a rational way, while a search for 'salvation' cannot. In the latter case, there is no way that the person can know whether their goal has actually been achieved. This kind of action is ritual, not rational, action because the relationship of means to ends depends on a standard of 'symbolic appropriateness', rather than one of technical appropriateness or economic allocation (Parsons, 1937: 258). The principal example of ritual action that Parsons gives is the religious, where symbols of a 'sacred' character decide the appropriateness of the means that are chosen. A religious believer, for example, may pray for salvation simply because his or her belief system enjoins prayer as an appropriate way of acting for those who seek salvation.

Modes of expression, on the other hand, are forms of action in which there is no motivational structure of means to ends: the action simply 'expresses' ultimate values without regard for its rational utility or its ritual appropriateness. The artist, for example, might produce a painting in order to express a particular complex of meaning, and not as a means to any other end. Similarly, marital relationships, Parsons argued, are often expressive of the ultimate value of love (Parsons, 1937: 691).

It is not surprising, perhaps, that the concept of modes of expression plays a relatively minor role in *The Structure of Social Action*. It is, in fact, incompatible with the basic tenets of the action frame of reference, despite its importance in Parsons's general view of the social world. According to the action frame of reference, all unit acts are directed towards goals. If a mode of expression is, as Parsons claims, an end-in-itself, then it cannot also be viewed as oriented towards some external end. Modes of expression simply *are* expressive, they are not structured in terms of a means–end relationship. For this reason, we must see Parsons as outlining two distinct categories of action: rational and ritual action, on the one hand, and modes of expression on the other. Only the first of these categories is compatible with the action frame of reference and its fundamental concept of the unit act (Menzies, 1976: 45). Parsons's elaboration of 'expressive' forms of action in his later work resolved this problem by abandoning the idea of the unit act and, thereby, enlarging the action frame of reference. In his later work, as will be seen, the building blocks of action systems are no longer unit acts, they are roles.

As with rational action, Parsons sees ritual and expressive actions as intertwining to form action systems with emergent structures. Indeed, concrete systems of action are generally built from all three types of action. Because of their particular properties, each type of action has a different significance in action systems. Rational action, for example, is seen as relating principally to the problem of goal attainment in social action. Ritual actions, on the other hand, have their significance in 'revivifying and strengthening the common value elements, which are ordinarily more or less latent' (Parsons, 1937: 713), making them the basis of social solidarity. In reinforcing the common values of the society, ritual actions are fundamental to action systems as they strengthen the ultimate ends of rational actions and the norms that regulate them. Ritual actions are central to the 'non-contractual' element in contract and to the avoidance of anomie.

A FIRST STRUCTURAL FUNCTIONAL SOLUTION

Parsons's methodology emphasized that the construction of analytical laws that could explain the development of action systems rested upon a prior identification of their 'analytical elements'. The formulation of these general analytical laws, he argued, is the principal task of the social sciences. After completing *The Structure of Social Action*, he came to realize that sociology had not reached the stage at which this task could easily be achieved: the variables that sociologists employed were generally not measurable in the way that most economic variables were, and they could not be manipulated in a precise mathematical way (Parsons, 1945: 216ff). For this reason, he held, it was necessary to introduce some simplifications to the methodology. The simplification that he proposed involved a temporary abandoning of the search for analytical elements in order to uncover the 'structural parts' that make up the action system.[10]

Parsons had already argued, in *The Structure of Social Action*, that action systems could be seen as comprising certain distinct 'parts', of which the unit act itself was an example. A part is a specific and fixed combination of analytical elements whose concrete existence 'makes sense' apart from its relation to the other parts of the system. Examples of these structural parts of action systems would be those described in the various ideal types that Weber had constructed: markets, political parties, classes, states, churches and so on. The problem with such concepts, Parsons felt, was that they lost sight of the 'organic' nature of social systems and so implied a rather static, 'mosaic' image of society. The properties of a system are not simply the result of an aggregation of the properties of its constituent parts; they are 'emergent' properties. Parsons argued, nevertheless, that the construction of ideal typical concepts of structural parts could serve a very useful purpose at the stage of development that sociology had achieved in the 1940s.[11]

Parsons termed this approach to social theory 'structural functionalism', a phrase that has since become widely known but little understood. The core element in structural functionalism is the identification of the most important structural parts of a system. Structural parts are fixed combinations of analytical elements, and by formulating concepts that describe the fundamental structural parts of action systems, sociologists can begin to analyse their dynamics. The fundamental structural parts of a system are those that have a 'functional significance' for it. Parsons saw functional significance as involving both the internal relations of the system and its relations to its environment (Parsons, 1945: 217). Sociologists must identify the structural parts of action systems that play a crucial role in integrating the system or in adapting it to its environment, and must make these the fundamental points of reference for the analysis of all other processes. Sociologists must describe the structure of an action system and can then go on to analyse the dynamic processes that are involved in the maintenance or development of the structure. All processes, viewed from the standpoint of structural functionalism, must either contribute to the maintenance or patterned development of an action system, or they are 'dysfunctional'.

Action systems form themselves into personality systems, social systems and cultural systems and, at this stage in his work, Parsons concentrated his attention on social systems, the specific objects of study for sociologists.[12] The basic unit or part of all social systems, he claimed, was the 'role', which links the actor as a 'psychological' entity to the wider social structure (Parsons, 1945: 230). Roles comprise the normative expectations that define the behaviour that is associated with the holding of a particular social position. Those expectations that are sufficiently well established to be regarded as having a legitimacy, in Weber's sense, are termed social 'institutions'.[13] The role of the doctor, for example, is defined by specific expectations concerning the appropriate behaviour of doctors in relation to their patients, their colleagues and other medical staff. This role can be said to be structured through such social institutions as the norms of professional responsibility.

Roles and social institutions, as the fundamental structural parts of social systems, can further be analysed in terms of the 'functions' that they fulfil within a social system. Parsons's clearest statement on this, in line with the position that he adopted in *The Structure of Social Action*, claimed that there are two 'functional needs' that must be met if any social system is to continue to exist. He termed these the 'situational' and the 'integrative' needs, which concern, respectively, the relation of the system to its environment and the maintenance of a degree of internal cohesion or solidarity (Parsons, 1947).[14] Those institutions and roles that are concerned with situational needs are the economic and political structures that are constituted through rational actions. The institutions and roles concerned with integrative needs, on the other hand, comprise those that are concerned with the avoidance of conflict and the promotion of co-operation, and that are built from ritual actions.

The functional needs of systems, then, are used to organize the structural parts from which social systems are built. But a full structural functional analysis must go beyond this exercise in social *statics* to an appreciation of the *dynamics* of social systems. The dynamic variables that Parsons highlighted derived directly from his action frame of reference. He held that a social system can be maintained as an objective entity only because of the subjective patterns of motivation that underlie it. Roles are reproduced, for example, only in so far as individuals are motivated to meet the normative expectations that define them. Sociological analysis must explore the processes of socialization through which motivational structures are acquired by individuals, and it must show how these motives are involved in the reproduction of roles and social institutions. The functional needs themselves, then, have no independent causal role in social life. They are relevant for the explanation of action only in so far as they are taken into account in the subjective orientations of individual actors. True to the action frame of reference, Parsons eschews 'functional explanation': it is the interplay of institutions and motives that is fundamental to social systems.

Structural functionalism, argued Parsons, is a half-way house on the road to a fully scientific social theory. Only in economics had there been a move to fully analytical theory, with the construction of, for example, the laws of supply and demand in neo-classical economics. Sociology in the 1940s and 1950s was not ready to move in this same direction. The advance towards analytical laws in sociology would be possible only when sociology had achieved a complete structural functional analysis of the social system. This goal was to be achieved, he suggested, by clarifying and extending the structural parts that had been outlined in the works of Weber and Durkheim. But it is important to appreciate the distinctiveness of the theoretical strategy adopted by Parsons. Weber had employed his ideal typical structural concepts in order to produce historical and comparative investigations such as those associated with the Protestant ethic thesis (Weber, 1904–5). The ideal types were used as building blocks for explanations of specific, and unique, historical processes. Durkheim's work, on the other hand, involved the use of structural concepts to elucidate specific social phenomena, such as rates of suicide or elementary forms of religious life. These concepts were then employed in structural analyses at a more general level: Durkheim was concerned to understand some of the most general conditions of social solidarity. Parsons's theoretical strategy departed sharply from that of Weber and pushed that of Durkheim to its extreme. For Parsons, the aim of social analysis was to construct *general theory* – frameworks of theory that would be *universal* in their scope.

Parsons's theoretical aspirations, then, were based on the natural science model, where general theory is the accepted aim of scientific analysis. Structural functionalism, for Parsons, was the first step towards a general theory of systems of action. This structural functional model was developed by Parsons throughout the 1940s in a series of essays on such topics as kinship and population, politics (including studies of fascism, democracy and propaganda), the professions and the occupational structure, and the nature of social stratification (See Parsons, 1954). In 1951, however, he published *The Social System*, a full length, systematic account of the structural and functional organization of systems of social action that built upon and elaborated the themes of his early studies.[15]

THE MATURE STRUCTURAL FUNCTIONAL SOLUTION

The central element in Parsons's critique of utilitarianism was the claim that the goals of individual action are formed socially, and that they therefore reflect the values that prevail in the society. Ends, then, are not distributed at random, but are socially structured. As his work developed, Parsons came to emphasize more strongly the importance of *common values*, of consensus, in structuring action. The question that Parsons left unaddressed, however, was that of *how* these ends are socially formed: what are the mechanisms involved? In the essays that he wrote in the years following *The Structure of Social Action*, he began to develop a solution that reached its final form in *The Social System*. His solution centred on the mechanisms of *socialization*, the process through which people learn those means and ends of action that are enjoined by the common values of their society. Through socialization, values are 'internalized' by individuals, and their motivations become integrated with norms and values. When individuals internalize social values, these values form the basis of their sentiments or 'commitments'. The concept of socialization into common values came to form the lynch pin of Parsons's work; it became the mechanism around which he constructed his model of the dynamic processes that sustain societies.

It is through their socialization as children in families and in formal education that individuals learn the basic expectations that others have of them. These expectations define specific roles, and socialization consists of the learning of the various social roles that will be played or encountered in a person's life. 'Role' emerges in *The Social System* as the fundamental concept of this revised version of the action frame of reference.

A role is a complex of normative expectations concerning the behaviour of an actor, and all roles involve reciprocal relations: roles cannot be defined in isolation, but only in relation to specific other roles. The role of 'husband', for example, implies and is defined in relation to the role of 'wife', and the role of 'parent' can be understood only in terms of that of the 'child'. Action is shaped by an individual's conception of the behaviour that is expected of an occupant of their role and by their understanding of the likely reactions of role partners to their actions. It is through the anticipated reactions of others that role expectations are sanctioned and behaviour is subjected to social control.

Roles are the building blocks of sociological analysis, and Parsons looks at two ways in which roles can be formed into larger structures. From the standpoint of the analysis of *social integration*, attention is focused on the formation of 'collectivities', understood as clusters of concretely interacting roles that are characterized by varying degrees of social solidarity and cohesion. Families, small groups, trades unions, business enterprises and political parties are collectivities in this sense. The analysis of social integration involves a consideration of the action of individuals in roles, the formation of collective actors, and the relations of co-operation and conflict in which actors are involved (Parsons and Shils, 1951: 190ff.). From the standpoint of *system integration*, on the other hand, roles are seen as formed into 'institutions', understood as clusters of analytically interdependent roles that may perform certain 'functions' but are not units of action. Social institutions are the fundamental 'parts' of the social system, and its overall stability depends upon the degree of integration or malintegration among its institutions.[16] Despite his recognition of these two levels of sociological analysis, Parsons's principal concern in *The Social System* was the analysis of system integration.

Roles are 'institutionalized' when their underlying values are shared by the great majority of the participants, and when these values are internalized. Thus institutionalization reflects both value consensus and the internalization of values through which roles and sanctions are defined. Parsons recognized that institutionalization is a variable feature of social life. In some situations there may be a complete value consensus and perfect socialization, resulting in the complete institutionalization of role relations and, in consequence, in social stability. This is, however, merely one possible situation among many. To illustrate this point Parsons considers the opposite extreme, which he sees as corresponding to that which Durkheim described as 'anomie'. In a situation of anomie there is value dissensus and an absence of internalization: actions are unregulated by any established normative patterns.

There is, then, a contrast between two extreme forms of social structure – the fully institutionalized and the anomic – with all real social situations falling somewhere between these two extremes. In order to achieve a scientific understanding of social life, Parsons argued, sociologists should concentrate their attention on the fully institutionalized type of social structure. This type of social structure is more comprehensible than all the others, and its analysis can serve as a yardstick for understanding the departures from this 'ideal type' that occur in actual situations. The bulk of *The Social System* consists of Parsons's elaboration of the fully institutionalized model of the social system.

Parsons began his detailed account of social systems, then, with a discussion of social institutions. The institutionalized role relations of a society comprise its 'relational complex'.[17] This system of role relations is 'the structural core of the social system' (Parsons, 1951: 52), and its constituent roles are regulated through social institutions. A social institution is a complex of institutionalized roles that are 'of strategic structural significance'. By this Parsons (1951: 39) seems to mean that an institution has a critical significance for the 'functional needs' of the social system. While whole roles may be included in specific institutions, it is more usually the case that a particular institution involves only certain aspects of social roles. More specifically, institutions include those aspects of roles that are relevant to particular functions. Each role, then, is typically structured by one or more institutions. Thus the role of husband-as-breadwinner, for example, might be seen as structured by such distinct and functionally specific institutions as 'marriage', 'property', 'employment' and so on.[18]

Parsons divided institutions into two categories according to their function. These categories he terms the 'regulative' and the 'cultural'. 'Regulative institutions' are those that are concerned with limiting the pursuit of sectional interests and so with achieving a degree of social or collective integration. They define the appropriate and inappropriate goals and means that may be employed in actions. Economic action, for example, is normatively regulated, as Durkheim showed in his critique of Spencer. The economic activities of a capitalist business economy are not purely rational and self-interested, but are structured by definite social norms that specify restrictions on what may and what may not be produced for profit and on the conditions under which goods and services can be produced. Prostitution and the use of heroin, for example, are subject to very tight legal and moral restrictions, the sale of alcohol and tobacco is subject to somewhat looser restrictions, and the sale of most other consumer goods is regulated by norms relating to health and safety, fire protection and consumer rights over the quality of goods. Similarly, employment relations are structured by normative restrictions on hours of work, rates of pay, rights of dismissal and so on.

'Cultural institutions', on the other hand, do not directly enter into the regulation of social action. They are *latent* in role relations and in regulative institutions, but are fundamental to their regulatory powers. Cultural institutions ensure the 'acceptance' of particular values that may not be directly relevant to an actor's own role relations. Those who are not scientists, for example, may nevertheless accept the 'truth' of scientific knowledge, and this acceptance will underpin the authority and legitimacy of scientists. Similarly, Christian morality may be widely accepted in a society and may be drawn upon in legitimating more specific normative expectations.

The relational complex of a social system is seen as involving a number of distinct types of action, of which Parsons saw two – the instrumental and the expressive – as being fundamental. His contrast between these two types of action reiterates the distinction that he drew in *The Structure of Social Action* between rational and ritual action, and it assimilates the latter with the concept of 'modes of expression'. This new typology of action is the basis of the differentiation of societies into distinct relational complexes, each with their own regulative institutions.

An *instrumental relational complex* is one in which actors are oriented towards one another in a purely instrumental or means–ends way. This was, I have shown, the basis of the 'unit act' in Parsons's early work, but in his mature position it is simply one form of action. In instrumental action, actors are concerned with attaining particular goals and they adopt a purely cognitive and formal standpoint towards the conditions that are necessary for attaining them. These goal-oriented interactions stood at the centre of the utilitarian tradition of economic theory, which analysed the instrumental relational complex in terms of production, exchange and co-operation relations that were linked through the division of labour to form 'civil society' or the 'economy'. Parsons had much in common with this view. He held that the means and conditions of instrumental action are the 'facilities' that actors have available to them, and it is facilities that are basic to all instrumental processes. Instrumental actions are structured by regulative institutions, and it is the institution of property that is central to regulating the distribution and control of facilities. An instrumental relational complex must not, however, be seen as a purely 'economic' phenomenon. In addition to the economic problem of the allocation of resources, argued Parsons, it concerns the 'political' issues of power relations. In this argument from *The Social System* is repeated the concern for power and wealth as fundamental features of rational action that Parsons had outlined in *The Structure of Social Action*.

An *expressive relational complex*, on the other hand, involves actions in which immediate gratification is sought, and objects are evaluated solely in these terms and not as means to other ends. Expressive emotional actions had not been analysed by previous writers to any great extent, and there was no equivalent of the classical economists' account of instrumental actions. Parsons felt, therefore, that he had to do more work in constructing the concepts necessary for analysing this type of action. I have already highlighted the difficulties that Parsons faced with his early concept of 'modes of expression'. In *The Social System*, Parsons resolved these problems by abandoning the restrictive idea of the unit act and seeing 'instrumentalism' and 'expressivity' as analytical elements of all concrete acts, but which can be analysed independently of one another as differentiated 'parts' of social systems.

People oriented towards one another in expressive ways seek to achieve a degree of solidarity and of shared meaning among themselves. Parsons saw the relation of 'love' as epitomizing such expressive orientations: 'between two lovers a system of shared erotic symbolism will be developed which is an inherent aspect of the relationship and a condition of its integration' (1951: 77). In addition to personal love of this kind, Parsons cites patriotism (love of one's country) as an example of an expressive relation, which may become associated with a variety of ethnic symbols in the creation of national solidarity. Where objects appear as 'facilities' in instrumental relations, they appear as 'rewards' in expressive relations, and Parsons argues that the distribution of rewards in a social system is regulated by the institution of social stratification.[19]

The facilities that are involved in instrumental actions, argues Parsons, can be seen as bases of *power*. By this, Parsons meant both the 'purchasing power' that is studied in economics, symbolically expressed in money, and the kind of political 'influence' that can be achieved through the mobilization of social relations and that is symbolically expressed in authority (Parsons, 1951: 124, 126–7). The rewards that are involved in expressive actions, on the other hand, can most appropriately be regarded as bases of *recognition*.[20] The two forms of recognition that Parsons identifies are 'approval' and 'esteem'. Approval has no direct symbolic expression of its own, and money is often used as a surrogate for approval, but esteem can achieve a degree of generalization as hierarchies of *prestige* (Parsons, 1951: 130–31). Money, authority and prestige, then, are generalized symbolic expressions of the use of objects in instrumental and expressive relational complexes.[21]

Parsons identified a third type of action alongside the instrumental and the expressive. Where instrumental and expressive actions are associated with regulative institutions, 'moral' actions relate to cultural institutions. Moral action underpins instrumental and expressive action, helping to constitute them both as forms of distinctively *social* action. In the moral type, actions are oriented to evaluative concerns *per se*, and the uppermost issue is that of the appropriateness of actions themselves, rather than that of their relation to particular goals or gratifications. Moral action, then, is involved in the internal integration of instrumental and expressive relational complexes and in integrating these complexes into a cohesive overall system. Such actions are particularly expressed in what Parsons has termed 'cultural institutions', including such phenomena as ideology and religion.

A system of social relations, a society, is a particular complex of normatively patterned roles and institutions that can be regarded as 'boundary-maintaining' in relation to its environment. Relative to the environment, it is able to maintain certain constancies in the structure of its roles and institutions. Parsons did not see this as a necessary feature of actual societies. It is a consequence only of fully institutionalized social relations, though he argues that, 'it is simply a fact that ... these constancies are often found to exist' (Parsons, 1951: 483).

Although Parsons's aim was to formulate a *general* theory of social systems and their structural elements, he sees this as a basis on which sociologists can understand more concrete processes. The analysis of roles and social institutions was cast at the most general level and, having set out this framework, Parsons begins to show how typologies of social structures can be built. He argued that, in the fully institutionalized case, social structures reflect a value consensus, and from this it follows that a classification of structures can be made by classifying the underlying value patterns that they express. There are, of course, a very large number of possible values, and Parsons did not try to classify actual values. Instead, he presented a classification of the principal axes along which value patterns may vary. These axes he termed the 'pattern variables'.

Parsons held that there is a very limited number of ways in which values can define role relations and action orientations. To construct his typology he starts out from the contrast that he has already drawn between instrumental and expressive types of action. These types are particular combinations of analytical elements, and Parsons's attempt to formulate the pattern variables was his first attempt to build analytical elements into his social theory. He sees each type of action as combining 'choices' on each of five variables (see Figure 2.1). These five 'dilemmas of action', he argued, are exhaustive: all action involves a choice, conscious or otherwise, on each of the five variables, and no more than these five pattern variables are involved in the structuring of social action. Having moved from concrete types of action (instrumental and expressive) to the underlying elements (the five pattern variables), Parsons held that the pattern variables can then be used for more general classificatory tasks in sociology. Roles, institutions and whole societies can be classified in terms of the same five pattern variables.

Instrumental	Expressive
Affective neutrality	Affectivity
Self-orientation	Collectivity orientation
Universalism	Particularism
Achievement	Ascription
Specificity	Diffuseness

Source: Parsons, 1951: 67.

Figure 2.1   The pattern variables

The first pattern variable defines the dilemma of affectivity *versus* affective neutrality in action. This concerns the degree of emotional involvement that the actor has in his or her roles and relations. Affectively neutral action is that which is considered disciplined and calculative, the actor taking a purely impersonal stance, while affectively oriented action is impulsive and emotionally engaged, seeking immediate gratification. Where a relation is highly charged with feelings, then, it can be characterized as 'affective' rather than 'neutral'. The second pattern variable involves the dilemma of self-orientation *versus* collectivity orientation, and relates to whether the interests that are pursued in actions are sectional or communal. Certain roles, for example, may involve the legitimate pursuit of private interests, as with many commercial roles, while other roles may require that actors subordinate their personal interests to the common interests of the group or wider society.

Universalism *versus* particularism defines the third pattern variable. This dilemma of action concerns the extent to which others are judged from a partial, 'biased' point of view. Where actors take a universalistic orientation to one another, their relationship is structured by purely 'cognitive' standards in terms of which account is taken only of the features that the other person shares with all others of the same type. Particularistic orientations, on the other hand, are subjectively biased in terms of the particular, unique significance that the other has for the actor. A businessperson's orientation to someone merely as a 'customer', for example, is universalistic, while an orientation to him or her as a kinsperson who must be given a discount would be particularistic. The fourth pattern variable involves the dilemma of ascription *versus* achievement, or quality *versus* performance as it is sometimes described. This dilemma concerns the way in which the other person is categorized: is he or she seen in terms of ascribed personal qualities or simply in terms of their effectiveness or success in achieving certain goals? Orientation to an African American doctor as a technically competent specialist involves a concern for his or her achievements, while an orientation towards him as a 'black' or as a 'man' would involve a focus on assumed intrinsic qualities. The final pattern variable involves the dilemma of specificity *versus* diffuseness and concerns the functional scope of an actor's interest. A specific orientation involves restricting expectations and interests to narrow and limited aspects of the other, while a diffuse orientation is not restricted in this way and concerns the totality of the person or object.

Although the pattern variables involve a 'dilemma' of choice, Parsons did not claim that actors simply choose one or the other pole of each dilemma. Although actions, roles and institutions do, indeed, involve an emphasis on one pole, they will also require some attention to the opposite orientation. Choice in actions and in the structuring of relations involves giving *priority* to one or the other pole of each dilemma. To illustrate this point, Parsons examined the nature of the role of the doctor in contemporary America.

This role involves according priority to a combination of rational, 'instrumental' values that are common to all professional and business roles, but these have to be counterbalanced by some elements of the expressive type (Parsons, 1951: Chapter 10). The doctor is a scientifically trained expert who is expected to be technically competent, and these expectations accord priority to a majority of the 'instrumental' choices on the pattern variables. But the doctor's commitment to a 'professional' stance, rather than a purely universal one, means that the role cannot merely involve the self-interested pursuit of personal profit, but must also involve a commitment to the performance of a public service in conformity with the widely shared value of 'health'. 'Collectivity orientation', from the expressive side of action, must be given priority along with the other more instrumental elements.

The instrumental complex of value patterns in the doctor role involves a combination of universality, neutrality, specificity and performance. It is universalistic in that there is a requirement for the generalized impartiality that is characteristic of the 'scientific' attitude. The doctor must choose the most efficient means to a given end and must be an 'objective' practitioner. The methods of treatment should be chosen without any reference to the particular, personal circumstances of the patient: the patient is a 'case' rather than a 'person'. The neutrality pattern of the doctor role requires the elimination of any sentimental concern about the patient. Doctors must not become sexually aroused by their patients, they should not make moral judgements about them, and they should not become emotionally concerned about their sufferings.

Specificity is a feature of the doctor role that arises from its functional specialization within the division of labour: the doctor has a specific concern for the 'health' problems of the patient and should be unconcerned about his or her financial or other personal circumstances. These aspects of the patient's life are each matters for other specialists, such as lawyers, accountants, garage mechanics and shopkeepers. Finally, an achievement orientation is necessary if doctors are to attain the high technical competence that is required of them. Doctors achieve this competence through a long period of specialist training that leads to their accreditation as a practitioner.

The doctor role, then, can be characterized by a distinctive combination of choices on the five dilemmas: it involves the priority of collectivity orientation, universalism, neutrality, specificity and achievement. These are the primary orientations that are built into the role expectations of the doctor. Predominantly an 'instrumental' role, the doctor role also involves the expressive element of collectivity orientation. Other expressive elements are also involved, however, as secondary, supporting aspects of the role expectations. The doctor, for example, must show a degree of diffuse concern for the well-being of the patient, must have some concern for their suffering, and so on. The important thing for Parsons is that these elements are subordinate to the primary instrumental elements. The doctor would be seen as deviating from role expectations if his or her actions were too expressive and insufficiently instrumental.

It is on this basis, Parsons suggested, that it is possible to construct a typology of social roles and, thereby, of whole relational complexes. Looking at the 'primacy' or priority of value choices on each of the pattern variables,

Parsons suggested that it was possible to construct a typology of all the various combinations of choices that can be made. The 'instrumental' and 'expressive' types are merely two of the 64 possible combinations of choices on the five pattern variables, though Parsons suggested that the number of combinations to be considered is actually less than this. There are, he said, 32 'meaningful' combinations of the pattern variables and, therefore, 32 'types of possible role expectation pattern' (Parsons, 1951: 66).[22] The roles and institutions of a society can be described in terms of these 32 combinations of pattern variables.

Parsons also made the point that whole societies, as combinations of roles and institutions, can be classified in the same way. The number of possible combinations is mind-boggling: even if societies are to be characterized by their *dominant* characteristics, Parsons's analysis would suggest that there are 32 types of society. Parsons argued that the scheme can be simplified – and so made more useful – by limiting it to those few combinations of pattern variables that actually occur in the known range of human societies. There are, he suggests, just four main pattern variable combinations that encompass the great majority of all societies. The four patterns are, in fact, constituted from a cross-classification of just two of the pattern variables (See Figure 2.2). These four societal types are the universalistic–achievement pattern found in the United States and most 'industrial' societies, the universalistic–ascription pattern found in Nazi Germany and Soviet Russia, the particularistic–achievement pattern found in traditional China, and the particularistic–ascription pattern found in the Latin American societies (Parsons, 1951: 180ff).

	Universalism	Particularism
Achievement	United States	Traditional China
Ascription	Nazi Germany	Latin America

Figure 2.2   A societal typology

Parsons's usage of the typology was purely illustrative, though it is not difficult to see an implicit model of social development from particularism to universalism and from ascription to achievement. Modern industrial societies, of which the United States is the leading example, have developed from earlier forms of social life that were dominated by particularistic and ascriptive relations.[23] The direction of social development on a world scale is from 'expressive' (particularism and ascription) to 'instrumental' (universalism and achievement) forms of social life. Parsons (1951: 487, 501) saw this as indicating that modernization can be understood as involving a move in the direction of the rationalization of social life.[24] Indeed, he claims that the fundamental contrasts set out in the pattern variables can be derived from Tönnies's discussion of the move from traditional *Gemeinschaft* societies to modern and rational *Gessellschaft* societies (Tönnies, 1889).

The transition from 'traditional' society to modern industrial society is not smooth and crisis-free. In a discussion of Germany and Japan, Parsons showed that the rapid expansion of instrumental action patterns during the 19th century, through an untrammelled market economy and a powerful capitalist business class, had dislocated traditional loyalties and expectations. This had generated structural 'strains' among those groups that were most closely tied to the traditional order. As one commentator has put it:

> With their established system of values threatened, members of the traditional sectors vent their aggression by attacking symbolized versions of the rationalizing and modernizing interests. Correspondingly, they profess an exaggerated loyalty to the traditional values that are allegedly being eroded (Buxton, 1985: 108).

Where external groups are seen as the agencies of rationalization, this reaction is likely to be expressed in a strongly nationalistic form, as in romantic Conservatism, and Parsons saw the German fascism of the 1930s as an expression of this kind of discontent. The fascists rejected rational-legal and 'liberal' institutions in favour of an emphasis on the traditional national goals that had been subverted by modernity. Similarly, Japanese militarism gave voice to this kind of reaction.

Even in the United States and Britain, problems had resulted from the decay of traditionalism and the consequent freeing of instrumental value patterns that were unlimited by expressive normative restraints. Parsons followed Durkheim in diagnosing this as a problem of social solidarity that could be resolved only through the establishment of a particular combination of instrumental and expressive value patterns. The 'professional' form of occupational regulation, as found in the role of the doctor, provided a model for this new form of organic solidarity. The occupational division of labour in an advanced industrial society would be organized around the application of scientific and technical knowledge to economic purposes, but within a framework of collective commitments that would prevent the emergence of the unrestrained self-interest of the Hobbesian war of all against all.

TOWARDS ANALYTICAL THEORY

When Parsons introduced the concept of the pattern variables he made his first step towards the 'analytical elements' that had been his scientific goal since the 1930s. His use of these concepts, however, followed the logic of the structural functional method, as he concentrated his attention only on certain fixed combinations of these elements. In the work that he began after 1951 he relaxed this limitation and began to construct analytical theories of social systems. The initial breakthrough occurred in work that he undertook with Bales and Shils shortly after the completion of *The Social System*. This work was published in two books (Parsons *et al.*, 1953; Parsons and Bales, 1956) that converted the pattern variables into a more systematic and comprehensive 'functional' scheme. This scheme was elaborated in a further book (Parsons and Smelser, 1956) and a long collection of essays (Parsons, 1969).

The work culminating in *The Social System* had produced a complex *structural* account of social life, with the concept of 'function' being used as a loose organizing principle for classifying the relations between the structural parts of societies. Virtually all of Parsons's structural analysis was carried forward, unaltered, into his later work, although he gave increasingly more attention to the 'deeper' *functional* relations that he saw as making up the corpus of analytical theory in sociology. The outlines of his structural sociology were set out – if rather complex and far from clearly stated – and were subsequently to be refined and elaborated. They were not, however, fundamentally altered. According to this view, 'societies' were concrete collectivities, actual clusters of roles and institutions that were relatively self-sufficient, had a particular boundary and persisted over time. American society and British society were examples, as were smaller collectivities such as wandering hunting and gathering bands and larger collectivities such as Roman society. Societies were organized through such institutions as kinship, work, education and stratification, some of which might become 'differentiated' from other parts of the society. Economic institutions, for example, formed a differentiated cluster of activities in modern society – the 'civil society' of the classical economists – and political institutions, too, showed a high level of differentiation. Societies, then, exhibited structural differentiation and, therefore, a degree of internal complexity.

All of this is familiar from Parsons's work between 1937 and 1951, and it became the cornerstone of orthodox, mainstream sociology in the 1950s and 1960s (see Chapter 6). What is less familiar – and more specific to Parsons himself – is the framework of functional theory that he constructed to explain the emergence and differentiation of structures. In the framework of functional analysis, the concept of 'society' is replaced by that of the 'social system'. A social system is an analytical device that can be used to understand and to explain actual societies and that combines together certain analytical elements that are real, underlying features of social life. A social system refers to those aspects of human action that involve the integration, solidarity and cohesion of individuals in their interactions with one another.

Parsons constructed his new concept of the social system from his understanding of advances in general systems theory. He had first became interested in the idea of a 'system' in his studies of Pareto during the 1930s, and the idea had subsequently been much elaborated by biologists, mathematicians and, latterly, computer scientists. In general systems theory, the idea of the organism as a system of functionally related elements was made into a general principle for the analysis of all 'organized' processes. Social life, and human actions more generally, are organized phenomena, and Parsons saw them as prime candidates for systems theory. Through his work with Bales and with Shils, he constructed a distinctive statement of a theory of social systems and systems of action.

The 'function' of any element within a system is the contribution that it makes towards the survival or continuation of the system. All elements that make such a contribution have a specific function in maintaining the basic shape of the system. Parsons held that the very concept of a system implies that *all* its elements make some kind of contribution and that, therefore, all elements in a system have a function. If a particular process or activity made no contribution to the continuation of the system it would not, in the strict sense, form an element of the system: it would be a completely autonomous and free-standing system in its own right.

More specifically, the function of a system element is seen as the contribution that it makes to meeting the 'needs' or 'requirements' of the system. If a system is to persist over time in its current form, Parsons argued, then certain processes and activities must take place. If these processes do not take place, the system will 'die', break down or be transformed. The human body, for example, 'requires' food if it is to survive, and unless this food is obtained it will die. The digestion of food, then, is a 'requirement' of the system as a whole: digestion has a specific 'function' in the maintenance of the body. Parsons concluded that all systems that do, as a matter of fact, persist over time must – by definition – exhibit a functional interdependence among their elements. The correct method for analysing systems, then, is to identify their requirements and to show how the constituent processes and activities contribute to the meeting of these requirements.

Parsons recognized physical systems, biological systems and action systems as possible objects of analysis. While many of his ideas were drawn from general systems theory, and so were believed to be applicable to all kinds of systems, the particular functional processes that he identified in action systems involve elements that are specific to action and that differentiate action from biological and physical processes. He elaborated his ideas on these particular processes on the basis of his earlier discussion of 'functional significance' in social systems. Parsons had argued that roles and institutions could, within the framework of structural functionalism, be analysed in terms of their contribution to the internal integrity of a system or their contribution to the relationship of the system to its environment. In his systems theory these became the basic organizing principles: the functional requirements of a system concern its 'internal' connectivity and its 'external' adaptation to its environment. Functional processes, then, may have an internal or an external orientation. Alongside this distinction, Parsons introduced another that is familiar from his earlier work. He argued that the functional processes of a system may be 'instrumental' – concerned with the *means* or resources that a system requires – or they may be 'consummatory' – concerned with the *ends* or goals towards which the system is moving. Functional processes in any system, then, can be classified into the four categories that result from a cross-classification of these dimensions (see Figure 2.3). This cross-classification of functional processes creates four categories – labelled A, G, I and L – that may form themselves into distinct, specialized 'sub-systems' of the original system.[25]

	Instrumental	Consummatory
External	A	G
Internal	L	I

Figure 2.3   Functional processes within a system

In the general sphere of action Parsons identified the four functions in the following way. The 'A' function is *adaptation*, the processes through which the limits and opportunities that are set by the environment are responded to and, where possible, controlled in order to ensure that the system obtains the resources that it needs. The 'G' function is *goal attainment*, the distinguishing feature of action systems. Processes meet the G function when they formulate goals or purposes and mobilize resources that can be directed to their achievement. These processes use existing resources in order to maintain or alter the equilibrium of the system. The 'I' function is *integration* and is concerned with processes that ensure the co-ordination of the various elements that make up the system. Activities serve an integrative function when they produce an organization of the system that can withstand the disruptions that it may face. The 'L' function is *pattern maintenance*, its abbreviation coming from the original term 'latency' that Parsons used to describe it. Processes serve the L function when they build up and maintain the 'motivation' that energizes action.

Any system of action that persists over time will be meeting these – and only these – functions. Action is purposive: it is a motivated process (L) in which goals are formulated (G) and the accumulation of appropriate means (A) is co-ordinated (I) in a way that is likely to prove successful.[26]

The social system, as a system of action, exhibits these four functional processes. The I sub-system contains the 'integrative' processes through which co-ordination, cohesion and solidarity are secured. This is the core of the social system, as it creates a sense of 'community' among the members. The structures that meet the integrative function tend to form what Parsons has called a 'societal community'. In primitive societies the societal community is coterminous with the whole society, defining its communal identity as a specific 'tribe' or 'people'. In more advanced societies it becomes focused around the idea of the 'nation', from which other structural elements become differentiated. A societal community is 'the patterned normative order through which the life of a population is collectively organised' (Parsons, 1966b: 10), and in terms of which 'membership' is defined. It embodies and maintains the integrity of a common value system that unites the whole society and legitimizes its normative order. A societal community is 'a complex network of interpenetrating collectivities and collective loyalties' (Parsons, 1971: 13). As such, it is internally diverse – divided, perhaps, into numerous kinship-based household units and localities. Vertically, the units of a societal community are often formed into a system of social stratification.

The A sub-system of the social system contains its 'adaptive' processes, the processes that secure the required resources from the system's environment through processes of production and distribution. Parsons saw these processes as having an 'economic' significance. The concrete roles and institutions that are concerned with these processes – the occupations, technologies, markets and so on, that make up the 'economy' as a structurally differentiated part of modern societies – are specialized around the adaptive function. Parsons did, though, make it perfectly clear that they will also tend to have other functional implications for the system. All concrete roles and institutions tend to be multi-functional, though they may be specialized around one of their functions. Thus in many societies there is no structural differentiation of specifically economic activities. They can be described as having 'economies' only in an analytical sense, as their adaptive processes are embedded in a larger social structure.

The G sub-system of the social system is understood in a similarly analytical sense. This sub-system contains the 'goal attainment' processes through which people are mobilized to pursue collective objectives. These processes, for Parsons, have a 'political' significance. Where institutions of chiefdom, government or statehood are differentiated around this function, it is possible to identify specifically political institutions, which may comprise a distinct 'polity'. Political processes, like economic processes, are often embedded in larger structures, and it may not be possible to identify a structurally distinct polity. In relatively undifferentiated societies, economic and political processes remain embedded in the structures of the diffuse societal community.

Finally, the L sub-system of the social system contains the latent processes that ensure the maintenance of its fundamental value patterns. These processes are essential to the maintenance of social order, but they are generally latent, underlying processes rather than being explicit and structurally differentiated. Those processes of socialization that Parsons saw as being especially concerned with pattern maintenance are focused in the institutions of the family and education, but these tend to be deeply embedded in the structures of the societal community.[27]

A social system, then, was regarded by Parsons as a system of interrelated functional sub-systems. The concrete roles and institutions of a society may be analysed in terms of their functional significance, and aspects of these roles and institutions may be seen as analytical elements in the appropriate sub-systems. It is relatively unusual, Parsons felt, for a particular role or institution to have a single, exclusive function. These parts of societies are generally multi-functional combinations of two or more analytical elements. The structural parts of a society do, however, frequently have a primary significance for one function or another. In these circumstances, the lines of structural differentiation may correspond closely to the underlying functional differentiation of the social system. Societies with a high degree of structural differentiation will have an economy, a polity and a societal community – and, perhaps, some institutions that are concerned specifically with

Functional processes in the social system		Structurally differentiated parts of a society	
A Economic	G Political	A Economy	G Polity
L Socialization	I Solidarity	L	I Societal Community

Figure 2.4   Functional and structural differentiation in the social system

socialization (See Figure 2.4). It is rarely, if ever, the case that differentiated structures will contain all the relevant functional processes. Even where an economy has become differentiated from other social structures, many adaptive processes will remain outside these economic institutions embedded in the societal community.[28]

Parsons's account of structural differentiation in his last works shows a fundamental continuity with that given in *The Social System*. Figure 2.5 presents a composite reconstruction of his argument to bring out these continuities. The instrumental actions that he saw as involved in economic and political institutions are concerned with A and G functions and are the basis of the differentiated economies and polities within which money and authority are generated. Expressive actions, on the other hand, are concerned with I and L functions, and are the basis of the societal community and its stratification through the production and distribution of prestige. For all its novel terminology, then, the Parsonian system theory continues the argument of the earlier Parsonian structural functionalism and, behind that, the initial position set out in *The Structure of Social Action*.

Action and interaction		Function	Differentiated structures	Objects and media		Institutions
	Instrumental	A	Economy		Money	Property, contract
				Facilities, Power		
Moral		G	Polity		Authority	Leadership
		I				
	Expressive		Societal community	Rewards, Recognition	Prestige	Stratifiaction
		L				

Figure 2.5   Social differentiation in Parsons: a reconstruction

The social system has so far been described as an action system, but it is important to recognize the very specific sense in which Parsons meant this. An action system comprises four sub-systems, and Parsons saw the social system as being one of these sub-systems. The social system is the I sub-system of action. Those processes of action that co-ordinate and integrate the actions of numerous different individuals through the establishment of solidarity and cohesion are the truly 'social' elements of action. Following the logic of his approach, Parsons identified another three sub-systems of action (see Figure 2.6). The behavioural organism – the body – is the means through which action is adapted to its physical environment; it is the point of contact

A	G
Behavioural organism	Personality
L	I
Cultural system	Social system

Figure 2.6   Parsons's action system

between the meaningful aspects of action and the 'material' aspects of its environment. The personality serves the function of goal attainment, as it is the means through which purposes are formulated and plans of action are constructed. The cultural system serves the pattern maintenance function by providing the values and ideas that motivate and guide action.

The details of Parsons's analysis of this general level of action need not be pursued, but it is important to understand the logic of his argument. Functional analysis, he has argued, is a universal method for the analysis of living systems, and the system of action is his fundamental point of reference for identifying the four functional sub-systems of the 'AGIL' scheme: action has its biological, psychological, social and cultural aspects. Each of these sub-systems can be analysed in terms of the very same four-function scheme. The behavioural organism, for example, has its adaptive, goal attainment, integrative and pattern maintenance sub-systems, as does each of the three other systems. This idea has already been illustrated for the case of the social system, and its sub-systems can be seen as sub-sub-systems of the action system. This same procedure can be repeated for each of these systems: the 'economic' system, for example, has its A, G, I and L sub-systems. Parsons's overall image of the action system, then, is that of a Russian doll. There is a whole hierarchy of systems within systems, each involving the same four-function differentiation. This is illustrated in Figure 2.7.

The four-function scheme is also the basis on which Parsons identified an academic division of labour. At the level of the system of action, for example, human biology studies the body, psychology studies the personality, and anthropology studies the cultural system. The social system is the object of social scientific investigation, with each of its sub-systems forming the subject matter of a specific science: economics studies the A sub-system, political science studies the G sub-system, and sociology studies the I sub-system.[29] The specific object of sociological investigation, then, is the societal community and the integrative processes with which it is involved. In the

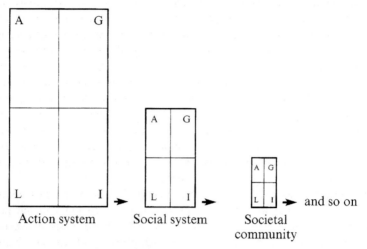

Figure 2.7   Systems within systems

case of undifferentiated societies, sociology will study whole societies. As structural differentiation advances, its focus narrows to the societal community as economic and political processes become the objects of other social sciences. In his own work, however, Parsons did not consistently maintain this distinction, and he spent much time analysing economic and political processes. Indeed, much of his late work went beyond the social system to a general consideration of systems of action in their entirety.

Parsons analysed the relations between sub-systems in terms of a model of 'interchanges' among them. The details of this model are immensely complex and, in their details, far from compelling, but the basic principles are clear. Sub-systems are not self-sufficient – if they were, they would be free-standing systems rather than *sub*-systems – and so they must be involved in relations of functional interdependence. Parsons argued that the sub-systems maintain their connections with one another through processes of interchange in which the resources that are required (the 'inputs') and the products that are produced (the 'outputs') of each system are exchanged. The four sub-systems, then, are connected through 'double interchanges' (exchange of inputs and exchange of outputs), and the functional interdependencies can be mapped as a pattern of input–output relations.

This need for functional interchanges is an essential feature of all societies, and there is a constant flow of resources among the sub-systems of the social system. In societies with a low degree of structural differentiation, these interchanges are managed with relative ease, as there is little or no separation between the various functional tasks. In societies where economic and political structures have been differentiated from the societal community, however, there is a need for more explicit regulation of the interchanges. This regulation occurs, Parsons argued, through the use of 'media' of exchange. The paradigm case of such a medium is money: the existence of money as a generalized, symbolic means of exchange with little or no intrinsic value allows the possessors of goods and services to enter into extensive and more enduring exchange relations than are possible on the basis of pure barter. Money encourages an extension of the division of labour, it allows a proper market mechanism to develop, and it permits an effective and efficient allocation of goods and services to occur. Money is generated within the economy as its own specific means of exchange, and it can be used in exchange relations between the economy and other parts of the society.

Using money as his model, Parsons argued that power can be seen as an analogous symbolic medium of exchange that is generated in the polity (Parsons, 1963b). Power can be used to regulate interchanges between the polity and other sectors of the society. Thus interchanges between differentiated economic and political structures involve transactions that are mediated by the use of both money and power. The societal community, in turn, generates 'influence' as a circulating medium, and its interchanges with the economy and the polity are mediated by influence and by money or power (Parsons, 1963a). The logic of his position requires that a differentiated L sub-system would generate an equivalent medium of exchange for use in its interchanges, and Parsons did, in fact, refer to 'value commitments' in this context (Parsons, 1968). His analysis is, however, even in his own terms, rather problematic, and the L sub-system does not generally involve the degree of structural differentiation that is characteristic of the economy and the polity.[30]

Parsons's analysis of the media of interchange – in so far as the economy, the polity and the societal community are concerned – can be seen as a reformulation of the view of 'power' that he presented in *The Social System*. There he saw money, authority and prestige as the three forms of *power* in society. In his later work, money, power and influence appear as the three principal *media* of interchange. Although the terminology varies, his basic position remained constant. Each of the principal structural parts of the society generates a particular capacity or resource that acquires a generalized significance for its internal transactions and for its interchanges with other parts of the society. In the mature Parsonian scheme, these mediated interchanges are seen as central aspects of the functional interdependence of the parts.[31]

The final piece in the jig-saw puzzle of Parsonian theory is his attempt to sort out the causal relations that exist between the various systems and subsystems. In *The Structure of Social Action* Parsons had rejected Marxist and

other 'materialist' approaches for their tendency towards deterministic explanations, but he had also rejected the alternative 'idealist' approaches that
explained social action as the mere 'expression' of values. Action, he stressed,
resulted from the interplay of material and ideal factors. At the same time, he
wished to recognize that values and norms played a specific and crucial role
in the production of social order. In his final works, he formulated this view
in terms of what he called the 'cybernetic hierarchy'.

Drawing on work in general systems theory, Parsons argued that those
processes that were high in 'information' were especially important in guiding or controlling the overall development of a system. Those processes, on
the other hand, that were high in 'energy' were able to limit or condition this
development. The overall development of a system, then, is the outcome of
both controlling and conditioning factors. Within the action system, Parsons
argued, the cultural sub-system – which produces values – is high in information and stands at the top of the hierarchy of control. The behavioural organism, on the other hand, is high in energy. It relates to the material environment of action – the physico-chemical (A) and organic (G) sub-systems – and
is the most important conditioning factor (see Figure 2.8).

Ultimate reality	Sub-system	Output	Information	Energy
	Cultural	Values	High	Low
	Social	Norms	↓	↑
	Personality	Goals	↓	↑
	Behavioural	Facilities	Low	High
Physical-organic environment				

Figure 2.8   The cybernetic hierarchy

The cultural system produces the values that actually enter into the structuring of action by virtue of their internalization during socialization. The
biological organism articulates the limits on action that are inherent in the
external conditions of the physical environment. While the conditioning factors are grounded in physical circumstances, the controlling factors are said

to be rooted in references to an 'ultimate reality'. This ultimate reality is, Parsons said, the 'environment above action', and he later termed it the 'telic system' (Parsons, 1966b: 8; see also Parsons, 1978). Values are created by individuals in order to resolve the fundamental problem of meaning with which all humans must cope. These values have a 'religious' character as their acceptance involves an act of faith in their absolute validity and they are, for this reason, frequently grounded in symbolic representations of gods and spirits that are supposed to inhabit the ultimate reality. Though Parsons did not go so far as to say that values originate in God – though it is likely that he did, in fact, believe this – he did hold that they originated in a religious quest that was, somehow, essential to the human condition. It is the *search* for a god that is the source of values.

THE EVOLUTION OF MODERNITY

Change is an ever present possibility in systems. The constituent sub-systems are engaged in a constant interchange with each other and there is always the possibility that there will be imbalances or disruptions in the flow of re- sources. Under normal circumstances the internal, integrative processes of a system will ensure that these sources of instability are contained. Systems are 'boundary-maintaining'; they maintain a state of 'dynamic equilibrium' in which the system's behaviour is contained within definite limits and the integrity of the system is not threatened. A system can, in the same way, cope with minor changes in its environment without having to alter its basic form. The normal processes of the system ensure that these environmental factors are handled with the minimum of disruption. A human body, for example, retains its basic shape and form over time, despite changes in its food supply and in the weather (Parsons, 1961).

Because this equilibrium is 'dynamic' there is always the possibility that environmental changes may be so great that the system will have to modify its structure if it is to survive. Major changes in the global climate and pressure on natural resources, for example, may force substantial changes in human social activity. Parsons also recognized that internal instabilities may pose problems that the system can handle only through structural change. A certain degree of strain and tension between the structural parts of a system will always result from imbalances and disruptions in its functional interchanges. Where these strains accumulate or are particularly great, there will be pressure for structural change. Many such internal ('endogenous') strains result from external ('exogenous') environmental sources. Growing population pressure, for exam- ple, will tend to make itself felt through its consequences for the internal distribution of resources such as food, jobs and housing.

The most important type of structural change that Parsons considers in social systems is *social evolution* through structural differentiation. Changing environmental conditions pose the need for adaptation, and more differentiated societies have a greater capacity to adapt to such changes in the future. The direction of social evolution is further shaped by cultural changes, the guiding or 'controlling' element in social life. Cultural values decide the kinds of structural differentiation that will take place and the responses that will be made to this differentiation. Through constantly adapting to a changing environment, societies undergo structural transformations that enhance their general capacity to adapt (Parsons, 1966b: 21).

Evolution occurs when each new structure has an enhanced capacity for performing its primary function, compared with the performance of that function in a less differentiated society. This implies that social evolution is merely one form of structural differentiation, as it is also possible to imagine regressive differentiation. Parsons concentrated his attention, however, on differentiation that enhances adaptive capacity. The differentiation of structures creates new problems of integration. If a differentiated structure is to persist over time as a successful adaptation, the operations of the various parts must be co-ordinated with one another and this may require new integrative structures. The achievement of this integration, Parsons argued, will normally involve a move towards the 'inclusion' of the differentiated parts into the normative structure of the society. Parsons's account of evolution is highly reminiscent of Spencer's. Parsons (1937: 1) had begun his first book by asking, 'Who now reads Spencer?', and by the 1960s it was clear that Parsons had been one of Spencer's most avid readers. In both writers is found a model of social evolution in which structural differentiation is driven by functional adaptation.

Figure 2.9 shows the evolutionary account of world history that Parsons produced. The earliest stages of human history – more strictly of pre-history – are 'primitive' societies that are relatively undifferentiated and are based around religion and kinship. Hunting and gathering societies such as those of the aboriginal tribes of Australia are almost totally organized around kinship relations, in complex articulation with a totemic cult religion.[32] They are only loosely bound to particular territories and are undifferentiated; the whole society comprises a single collectivity as the societal community forms an intricate kinship network that encompasses the whole society. As these societies become more established in bounded territories and their structures of kinship and property become more differentiated, a system of stratification emerges and there may be the establishment of monarchical power. These more differentiated societies are what Parsons termed the 'advanced primitive' type. The African kingdoms, he said, can be seen as marking a distinct advance over the primitive Australian societies.[33]

Societal type	Sub-type
Primitive	Primitive
	Advanced primitive
Intermediate	Archaic
	Advanced Intermediate
Modern	

Figure 2.9   Parsons's schema of social evolution

The crucial watershed between 'primitive' and 'intermediate' societies occurs with the emergence of a written language and the spread of literacy. This specific development within a cultural system allows the generalization and expansion of culture through the supplementing of the oral culture with a culture of documents and archives. Written documents serve as repositories of data and decisions, and they allow the creation of a historical record. Writing, then, is crucial for the breakthrough from primitive to intermediate societies.

Intermediate societies are of two types, the 'archaic' and the 'advanced intermediate'. Archaic societies have a more advanced agricultural base than primitive societies and they are characterized by the craft literacy of the priesthood which controls a cosmological religion. In these societies – and Parsons instanced Egypt and Mesopotamia – there emerges a sharper social stratification within the societal community and a clearer structuring of central political functions into separate governmental institutions. Advanced intermediate societies are those that are marked by a historic religion and 'imperial' organization. Examples are the societies of traditional China, India, Islam and Rome that were studied by Weber (See Weber, 1915, 1916). In these societies there is full upper class literacy and, echoing Comte, Parsons saw their religions as having developed a 'philosophical' systematization in which there is a conception of a 'supernatural' order that is sharply distinguished from the 'natural' world.

Modernity emerged from within medieval Europe, where the cultural system of Christianity and the institutions of the Roman Empire had laid the foundations for many of the characteristics of modernity. The slow development of modernity after the breakdown of the Empire was a result of the co-existence of factors antithetical to it – most notably the institutions of 'feudalism' that carried forward primitive and archaic elements of tribal loyalty. Medieval Europe evolved into a 'European system', an inter-societal system in which lines of structural differentiation followed geographical and regional lines of demarcation. East and west were divided by the split between the Eastern and Western Churches; Latin and German influences divided the south from the north; and in many areas there were boundary conflicts with neighbouring empires and cultures – Moorish pressure on Spain, the Saracens in the eastern Mediterranean, Turkish pressure in the south east, and so on.

Within this world social system the various regions came to be specialized around particular functions. Italy was central to the pattern maintenance processes of Europe. It was the most latinized and Christianized of the European societies and comprised a fertile seed bed for the nurturing of classical culture. The Reformation, originating in this cultural seed bed, helped to differentiate religion from other social structures, creating a distinct sphere of secular culture and creating a tendency towards the religious pluralism that came to replace the hegemony held by the Catholic Church in the old society. Eastern Europe, on the other hand, developed centralized political bodies that protected the European system from external threats from the east. In the north west, and in France and England in particular, there occurred innovative transformations that led to the territorial state and to the differentiation of economic and political structures from a societal community in which integrative processes were concentrated.[34] The territorial 'national' states that were formed in England, France and Holland were rooted in ethnic homogeneity and in solidaristic societal communities. These nation states became the spearhead of modernity, and by the end of the 17th century England had become the most advanced of the three.

In England the differentiation of religion from government and the growth of religious pluralism and secularism meant that all religious denominations were included in the secular framework of the national society. England also avoided the extremes of absolutism, and the aristocracy became the dominant element in a parliamentary system in which the monarchy was the tool of the aristocracy rather than the sole source of executive power. In this kind of framework, Parsons argued, the urban bourgeoisie could be accorded representation in parliament and was not sharply divided from the aristocracy. England was also the most advanced European society in economic terms. It had a highly commercialized pattern of agriculture, and the market orientation of landowners and farmers created a common interest with the bourgeoisie that precluded a sharp separation of town and country.

In this first phase of modernization, England and France were the 'lead' societies, England becoming the heart of the 'industrial revolution' and France of the 'democratic revolution' in the late 18th and early 19th centuries. The industrial and democratic revolutions were forces that weakened the remaining barriers to the full development of modernity in the European world. The watershed that divided intermediate from 'modern' societies was the emergence of rational, legal procedures within the integrative sub-system of the society. This was the basis for the framework of constitutional politics and the establishment of citizenship as the criterion of membership in a 'nation' that characterizes modernity. The democratic revolution established, through its attacks on hereditary ascriptive status in the name of 'liberty', 'equality' and 'fraternity', the idea of a nation of 'citizens' rather than 'subjects'. All adults were seen as equal in their membership of society as full citizens.[35] Citizenship developed through the establishment of civil, political and social rights, and it allowed the integration of societies which might have become increasingly differentiated by religion, ethnicity and territoriality. A major dynamic force in many modern societies was the tension between the solidarity of common citizenship and the cleavages of religion, region and ethnicity (Parsons, 1966a, 1970, 1971).

Thus modern societies were organized around legally grounded nation states. In these nation states evolved the central social institutions of modernity. Through the industrial revolution was established an extended division of labour that resulted in an 'occupationalization' of work and in the class opposition of property-owning capitalists and their employed workers. The cultural elements of this process were expressed in a specifically 'capitalist ideology'. 'Economic' institutions concerned with adaptive functions were sharply differentiated from other parts of society. Markets and money, rooted in property and contract, came to characterize all forms of production from physical commodities and factors of production to financial services. In the sphere of goal attainment functions, 'political' roles and institutions of a 'bureaucratic' type became all-important in government and industry, as well as in churches, universities and other organizations.

By the end of the 19th century modernity had ceased to be a purely European phenomenon and Parsons held that the lead in modernity had passed to the United States, which had successfully fused the advances that had been made in England and France. It was there that a third modern revolution occurred in the 20th century. This was the 'educational revolution' that synthesized the cultural principles of the industrial and democratic revolutions and overcame the opposition of capitalist and socialist ideologies. This helped to establish the basis for the expansion of a third cluster of modern institutions that Parsons called 'associational organization'. By this he meant the emergence of strong voluntary associations with democratic decision-making apparatuses. Associations such as political parties, interest groups, business corporations and professional bodies emerged to play a central role in the overall integration of modern societies.

It is on this basis that Parsons saw the central dynamic of modernity in essentially Durkheimian terms. The American educational revolution established an 'achievement society' that was organized around equality of opportunity and equality of citizenship, new forms of social stratification, and a strengthening of the functional significance of 'professional' and 'associational' forms of organization. Professional and associational organization was the basis of organic solidarity, as Parsons had argued in his earlier work. These are the structural features that many other American commentators had come to describe as 'post-capitalism', the 'knowledge society' or the 'society of professionals'.[36] Parsons shared much of this viewpoint, though with some qualifications. The strains that resulted from the class oppositions of early modernity and the strains of ethnic and religious conflict that resulted from the persistence of 'pre-modern' elements in modern society would, Parsons felt, be transcended as the new forms of solidarity appropriate to an industrial society were crystallized.

The patterns of organic solidarity that were pioneered in the 'associational' societal community of the United States would spread across the world. They were not mere features of 'Americanization' but were fundamental elements in full modernity. These forces would also, Parsons held, affect the Soviet Union. In that society, claimed Parsons, the break with pre-modern traditionalism had been made and many 'democratic' elements had been established, but these were combined with the tight party control and command economy of the totalitarian system. This combination involved many strains and tensions that would lead to the transformation of the society:

> We suggest, then, that the processes of the democratic revolution have not yet reached an equilibrium in the Soviet Union and that further developments may well run broadly in the direction of Western types of democratic government, with responsibility to an electorate rather than to a self-appointed party (Parsons, 1971: 127).

Parsons would have seen the collapse of the Soviet Union in 1991–2 as a vindication of his position that modernity, as epitomized in the United States, would spread world-wide.[37] Parsons (1971: 143) saw the spread of modernity as a long-term process that would take much of the next century to complete itself. Any 'post-modern' form of society was, he said, a very long way off.

Parsons's work has been subject to much criticism, and the following Chapters will make these criticisms clear. The criticisms that I consider are not purely negative, but involve the attempt to enlarge or replace Parsons's ideas with alternative ideas. Many of these alternatives have themselves been subject to criticism, as will be apparent from my discussions. Chapters 3 and 4 discuss the two main alternative accounts of individual action, while Chapter 5 looks at theories of collective action and conflict that seek to supplement individualistic theories. Chapter 6 considers mainstream extensions of Parsons's work on systems and structures, while Chapters 7 and 8 discuss more critical views on structure. In Chapters 9 and 10 I look at the recent work of Giddens and Habermas, putting these in the context of the ethnomethodological and other views on which they have sought to build.

NOTES

1. There are sociologists today who reject Parsons's theoretical position but have read barely a word that he has written.
2. The arguments of the conflict theorists are reviewed in Chapter 5. See also the early compilation of criticisms in Black (1961) and the important works of Lockwood (1956).
3. The account of Hobbes's argument which follows is that which was given by Parsons. An alternative view can be found in Macpherson (1962).
4. Parsons sees Marx as producing a historicized version of the utilitarianism that had been established by Hobbes. For this reason, he sees Weber as working on the same problem of order as Marshall, Pareto and Durkheim.
5. Parsons refers to Whitehead (1926), though the 'process philosophy' that underlies his analytical realism can be found in Whitehead (1927, 1929).
6. The conceptual scheme of action is also called, more loosely, the 'theory of action' and the 'general action schemata'. The action frame of reference, however, is always referred to as such.
7. The pattern variables in Parsons's later work mark his first attempt to construct analytical elements for sociology. Indeed, the pattern variables derive from Parsons's examination of the distinction between rational and traditional forms of action in the works of the founding sociologists.
8. This 'law' is Parsons's formulation of the Weberian idea of rationalization, which was itself Hegelian in origin.
9. This point is developed in Parsons's later work on 'generalized media' in social systems.
10. Parsons generally uses the word 'units' rather than 'parts', but the latter is closer to subsequent usage.
11. Scott (1963) has argued that there is a fundamental discontinuity between the early and later work of Parsons. The contrary argument, for continuity, is clearly set out and documented in Wearne (1989).
12. Personality systems, he said, were the subject matter of psychology, while cultural systems were the province of anthropology.
13. There is an equivocation in Parsons's work as to whether 'role' refers simply to institutionalized normative expectations – as implied in the Durkheimian origins of the concept – or refers also to actual regularities of action. Parsons often writes as if the normative *regulation* of action is necessarily expressed in its factual *regularity*.
14. These functions relate to what were earlier described as the 'goal attainment' role of rational action and the latent 'revivifying' role of ritual actions.
15. See also Parsons and Shils (1951) for a complementary discussion of the wider context of personality and culture. There are, however, a number of contradictions between this source and *The Social System*.
16. The terminology of social integration and system integration is not used by Parsons, though the distinction is clearly made. The point is developed in Lockwood (1964). Lockwood's distinction has been seriously misunderstood by such writers as Habermas and Giddens (noted below). In their application to Parsons, the two forms of integration might be clarified as referring to *collective integration* and *institutional integration*. To these might be added *societal integration*, the extent to which a social system is formed into a 'society'.
17. This is my phrase, although Parsons (1951: 70) does use it in this way. Parsons generally talks of 'relational institutions', but this is not compatible with his general definition of 'institutions', discussed below. It seems preferable to refer to this relational structure of roles as the relational complex.
18. The use of this illustration should not be taken to mean that Parsons sees all families as structured around such a 'head of household' role. He does, however, see family relations as structured by specific gendered norms and values that accord men a dominant position wherever these expectations are fully institutionalized.
19. This involves a slight departure from his earlier essay on stratification (Parsons, 1940),

but also a much larger divergence from common usage which relates stratification to class, status and political domination. Parsons's concept of stratification is concerned almost exclusively with the 'status' aspects. See also note 21 below.

20.   'Recognition' is my term, rather than Parsons's, but it is in line with his later terminology.

21.   Parsons's distinction between money, authority and prestige can be seen as a reformulation of Weber's discussion of class, domination and status.

22.   Parsons derives the figure of 32 from a combination of the pattern variables at two levels. Affectivity/neutrality, specificity/diffuseness, and universalism/particularism can be combined into eight types, and self/collectivity and achievement/ascription are used at a higher level to cross-cut these categories and produce a system of 32 combinations.

23.   Parsons is not saying that contemporary Latin American societies are precursors of modern industrial societies. His point is, I think, that the Latin American societies exhibit certain important features that also characterized the 'traditional' societies from which the industrial societies of Europe and America have developed.

24.   This conclusion is a restatement of his earlier analytical law of increasing rationality.

25.   Parsons saw a very close relationship between the pattern variables and the functional sub-systems. Self-orientation *versus* collectivity orientation was collapsed into the external/internal distinction, while combinations of the remaining four pattern variables were seen to define the specific value patterns associated with each function. Indeed, the societal typology in *The Social System* (See Figure 2.2) can be mapped onto the functional scheme. See Parsons *et al.* (1953) and Parsons (1960).

26.   Compare the essentially similar definition of action that Parsons gave in *The Structure of Social Action.*

27.   I follow the usage of Rocher (1974: 60) in writing about 'socialization' processes. Parsons's later work contained the idea of the 'fiduciary' as a description of the L sub-system, though he did not suggest that it became the object of structural differentiation in quite the same way as the economy and the polity.

28.   Alexander (1982–3) has correctly pointed out that Parsons often makes the mistake of conflating the issues of functional and structural differentiation, or, at least, of assuming that there is a direct one-to-one correspondence between them and that the word 'economy', for example, can be used to refer to *both* a concrete cluster of specialized institutions and a functionally defined sub-system.

29.   Parsons is less clear about the science that studies the L sub-system, although he tends to suggest that anthropology, once more, has a special role here.

30.   Here is again apparent his untheorized assumption that there is a one-to-one relationship between functional and structural differentiation.

31.   The underemphasis that is given to 'value commitments' in my discussion, and of the 'fiduciary' as a differentiated structure within the society, does some damage to Parsons's own presentation. It is, however, more in line with the logic of his position. The attempt to develop a concept of value commitments is necessary only because Parsons mistakenly equates functional and structural differentiation at crucial points in his work.

32.   Parsons refers to Durkheim (1912) and Lévi-Strauss (1949).

33.   Parsons's principal source here is Fortes and Evans-Pritchard (1940).

34.   Such arguments are reminiscent of Hegel's discussion of the emergence of civil society.

35.   Parsons refers to Marshall (1949) on this point.

36.   The clearest statement of this view is in Kerr *et al.* (1960). See also Bell (1973).

37.   This section was written in the week that the first properly democratic elections were held in Russia. Paradoxically, the elections enhanced presidential power and established a new fascist party as the largest block in the parliament. Parsons might well have interpreted this in the same way that he had interpreted German fascism: as a response to the strains of modernization.

3. Rational choice and social exchange

Mainstream social theory and research during the 1950s and 1960s owed a great deal to Parsons. While many of the intricacies of his position were rejected or ignored – not least his 'analytical realism' – the basic structural functionalist model of the social system was widely accepted. This contrasted sharply with the situation in economics, where 'utilitarian' theories of rational action remained central to theoretical debates. It was the apparent success of economics in constructing explanations of economic processes and in translating them into the arena of public policy debate that encouraged some sociologists to ask whether sociology might not make similar advances if its theories, too, were constructed around models of rational action. Parsons had himself, of course, recognized rational or instrumental action as one of two principal forms of action – the other was 'expressive' action – but his critics began to make far more radical claims. The conspicuous lack of success that sociologists had achieved in explanations of social action was seen as a consequence of the inadequacies of the Parsonian view of action and of his overemphasis on value consensus and socialization. A reworked theory of rational action that was constructed along exclusively individualistic lines, it was felt, would provide a simple and powerful basis for generating social explanations.

The most influential statement of this view came from Parsons's Harvard colleague George Homans. In an influential article, Homans (1964) had argued that Parsons, despite his espousal of a theory of action, had underemphasized voluntary individual action and had consistently overemphasized the structural features of whole social systems. Parsons, like Durkheim, had rejected 'psychological' explanations and had resorted to a holistic emphasis on deterministic 'social facts'. It was necessary, argued Homans, to 'bring back' a concern for individuals and their actions.[1] Homans's solution was to return to themes that he had first outlined in the 1930s, when he had produced an influential study of Pareto that stressed a theoretical commitment to the study of rational ('logical') forms of action and the need to see this form of action as the result of specific psychological processes (Homans and Curtis, 1934). His first substantive works had been concerned with social history and with small group studies (Homans, 1941, 1950), but a short book that he wrote with David Schneider in the mid-1950s (Homans and Schneider, 1955) had led him to return to Pareto's concerns. The book was aimed at criticizing the work that Lévi-Strauss had undertaken on kinship, and Homans argued that an adequate explanation of social institutions and practices had to begin from a consideration of individual, self-interested actions. This general thesis was elaborated at length in *Social Behaviour* (Homans, 1961), and it was this book that was the basis of Homans's criticisms of Parsons.

Homans's conception of rational action bears a striking resemblance to Parsons's concepts of rational or instrumental action. This should not, perhaps, be a cause of surprise if it is recalled that Pareto had been a major influence on both writers. Whereas Parsons held that rational action must be seen as structured by social norms that exist prior to any particular course of action – the non-contractual element in contract – Homans returned to a pre-Parsonian, classical view of individual rational action that re-established the very Hobbesian problematic that Parsons had sought to transcend. For Homans, social interaction and all social structures are completely reducible to individual behaviour, and the latter must be understood in terms of the principles of behavioural psychology. Such an approach to action, he held, had been comprehensively developed in economics, and the very success of economic theory was a virtual guarantee that sociology could make similar advances if it constructed its theories on the same basis. Micro-economics provided a model for sociology. Homans saw social interaction, then, as a process of social 'exchange'. Economic action involves the exchange of goods and services, and in other actions people exchange help, approval and other valued activities with one another. People enter into their exchange relationships as rational, self-interested actors.

Economic theorists have tended to adopt an instrumental model of action, seeing actors as pursuing conscious and deliberate strategies in the rational pursuit of their goals. Such a view involves an emphasis on the *cognitive* aspects of action: actors draw on their knowledge and information in order to construct plans of action that they calculate will allow them to achieve their goals. The so-called 'marginalist revolution' of Jevons, Walras and Menger had, in the final decades of the 19th century, laid the basis for these developments. The marginalists shared the classical assumptions of individual rationality and self-interest, but they moved economic theory from the analysis of supply to the analysis of demand, and they replaced labour theories of value with subjectivist theories of 'utility'.[2] A precedent for the use of marginalist ideas in sociology can be found in Weber's analysis of economic action, where ideal types of rational action were used.[3] Pareto's work, too, was firmly rooted in marginalist assumptions.

Homans drew on these ideas for his analysis of social exchange. His empiricist methodology led him to eschew any concern with internal and subjective mental states, arguing that human behaviour must be explained in terms of its purely external and objective characteristics. All that is necessary, he believed, was to assume that people have specific wants or needs that drive them to act in particular ways. 'Rationality' is a learned response, not a conscious strategy. From this point of view, he held, there is no fundamental difference between human and animal behaviour. A pet dog that runs towards the sound of a biscuit tin being opened is behaving 'rationally', as the owner is likely to give it a biscuit once the tin is open. There is no need to assume that the dog consciously formulates a rational strategy aimed at securing biscuits. It simply needs to be assumed that the dog has learned from past experience to associate this particular sound with the offer of food. Similar principles apply to human behaviour. People often praise those who help others, and so an approval-seeking individual might be seen as behaving rationally in offering to help colleagues at work. There is no need to assume that the individual consciously calculates the prospects of approval: being helpful becomes 'natural' or 'instinctive' for them because they have learned to associate the giving of help with the receipt of approval.

Homans's behavioural model of rational action was, for many years, the most influential form of exchange theory in sociology.[4] During the 1960s and 1970s, however, the exchange theories of Blau (1964) and Cook (1977) returned to cognitive models of action, converging with the attempts of writers such as Coleman (1973) to develop formal models of rational action.[5] Their work became increasingly mathematical in orientation, and they converged ever more closely with the theories of micro-economics. This trend towards formal, mathematical models of rational action was also apparent in political science (Downs, 1957; Buchanan and Tullock, 1962; Riker, 1962) and was paralleled by the attempts of some economists to apply their models of action to non-economic processes (Becker, 1976, 1981). Most recently, a number of theorists have attempted to reconstruct Marxism on the basis of models of rational action. This 'analytical Marxism' marks a striking convergence between Marxism and marginalist economics (Elster, 1983, 1986a; Roemer, 1988).

The exchange model of interaction has sometimes been compared with an earlier analysis of exchange that had been developed by Marcel Mauss, Durkheim's nephew. Mauss (1925) presented an account of the exchange of gifts in tribal societies, but he showed that these exchanges involved a norm of 'reciprocity' that was quite distinct from the economic logic of the market. Although many exchange theorists have attempted to build norms of obligation and reciprocity into their work, this has always been a problematic exercise. Economic theorists, the mainstream of exchange theory, and recent 'rational choice' theories have all been more at home with those forms of action that can be assumed to follow a purely rational 'economic' or 'market' orientation.

Such claims appear to make much sense for certain types of action in societies where 'economic' activities have been differentiated into a separate sphere of activity and where such motivations play a major part in the whole of society. It is difficult to argue, however, that the approach has a universal application of the kind posited by Homans and many of his successors.

THE BASIC MODEL OF RATIONAL ACTION

Contemporary theories of rational action adopt the standpoint of methodological individualism, the assumption that all complex social phenomena are to be explained in terms of the elementary individual actions from which they are composed:

> The elementary unit of social life is the individual human action. To explain social institutions and social change is to show how they arise as the result of the action and interaction of individuals (Elster, 1989b: 13).

These elementary actions are driven by the wants, goals or values that individuals seek to achieve and are understood as the products of the rational choices that these individuals make from among a range of alternative courses of action. It is rarely possible for individuals to achieve all of the various things that they want, as the social world is a world of scarcity. Choice is, for this reason, a necessity, and rational choice theories hold that choices are the result of a calculation of the likely outcomes of possible actions. Actors anticipate the outcomes of alternative courses of action so as to calculate the optimum course for them to take. Rational individuals choose the alternative that is likely to yield the greatest satisfaction of their various wants, goals and values (Heath, 1976: 3; Carling, 1992: 27; Coleman, 1973).

Rational action is, then, assumed to be self-interested action. This is not to say that it necessarily involves a narrow 'egotistical' motivation, as it can also encompass actions that are oriented, for example, by the pleasure that is derived from giving pleasure to another. The assumption of self-interest does mean, however, that the theory is difficult to apply to 'altruistic' actions in which an actor does something for a person or a principle, despite the pain or cost incurred. Rational choice explanations see phenomena as the consequences or outcomes of the actions of purposive actors with specific 'preferences', these actions taking place within specific, given constraints and on the basis of information that individuals have concerning these constraints and their likely effects. Actions are explained through the interdependence of *opportunities* (what people *can* do) and *preferences* (what people *want* to do – their desires).

At its simplest, the relationship between preferences and opportunities can be seen in purely *technical*, means–ends terms. Actors pursue desires on the basis of the opportunities that are available through action governed by purely technical considerations of the efficiency of the connection between the means and the end. In a broader sense, however, the relationship of preferences to opportunities involves 'economic' considerations of effectiveness in the allocation of resources among various possible uses.

Rational choice theories in economics itself have been concerned with the production, distribution and consumption of goods and services, especially in so far as these processes are mediated by money and the market mechanism. Modern rational choice theorists have, however, shown that the same general principles as are used in explaining monetary transactions can be used to understand interactions in which other resources are employed. Such resources as time, information, approval, prestige and so on have all figured as elements in theories of rational choice and social exchange.

Economic considerations arise whenever an actor ponders the allocation of money, time or other scarce resources. The choice between the purchase of tea or coffee, for example, involves the allocation of money, while the choice between voting or staying at home on election day involves the allocation of time. These technical and economic considerations are modelled through the concepts of *cost* and *reward*. The various courses of action that are open to a person – her or his opportunities – vary in their cost to the person, but they also result in varying rewards. Each of the products that is available in a supermarket, for example, has a price attached to it, these prices representing the money that a person must spend in order to obtain them. The consumption of these products provides rewards, in the form of satisfaction, to the consumer. Rational choice involves an attempt to calculate and to balance the rewards and costs of the various actions that a person undertakes.

The whole range of actions available to a person in everyday life can be seen as involving varying rewards and costs. The rewards that are involved in purchasing goods from a supermarket, for example, include the intrinsic satisfactions that can be gained from their consumption and the less tangible satisfactions that might be involved in their status display for conspicuous consumption. Stealing a car that is left unlocked in a street and with the keys in the ignition, on the other hand, is rewarding because of the pleasures derived from joy riding or the satisfaction of arriving speedily at one's destination. These same activities, however, involve costs. Items can be purchased from a supermarket only by giving up some of the money that a person possesses, and car theft involves penalties, such as imprisonment, that will be incurred if the thief is apprehended and convicted.

Rewards and costs must not be considered simply as intrinsic properties of objects and actions. Something is rewarding or costly only in relation to specific preferences. If I have no desire to drive fast in emulation of race course and rally drivers, 'joy riding' will not be rewarding to me; and if I do not like cheese and tomatoes – which I do not – then frozen pizzas will be an unrewarding purchase in a supermarket.

Homans formulated these ideas into the concept of 'profit'. The cost of a course of action, he argued, is the punishment that is incurred or the reward that is foregone. The *profit* that a person gains in interaction is measured by the rewards received minus the costs incurred, and Homans held that 'no exchange continues unless both parties are making a profit' (Homans, 1961: 61). Unless each participant finds it profitable, the interaction will not continue. The person who experiences a 'loss' finds the interaction more costly than rewarding and so will have no incentive to continue to participate. This is clearest in simple economic terms. The purchase of a jar of coffee in a shop involves the exchange of coffee for money. The coffee is regarded as a reward by the customer and as a cost to the shopkeeper; the money paid, on the other hand, is a cost to the customer and a reward for the shopkeeper. The transaction will not take place unless both the shopkeeper and the customer regard the money as being equal to the value of the coffee.

Under competitive market conditions, in fact, economic theory has shown that there seems to be an exchange of equivalents, with no profit being earned by either party. Each participant regards the rewards gained as being exactly equal to the costs incurred. If the customer regards the coffee as being less rewarding than holding on to the money (the coffee is too expensive), then she or he will not buy it. If the shopkeeper regards the money as less valuable than the coffee (the coffee is too cheap), then he or she will not sell it. A transaction will take place only when the price is at a level at which each party breaks even. In these circumstances, with no profit being earned, it is difficult to see how any shopkeeper could remain in business.

In fact, the reality is more complex than the appearance. If the shopkeeper's price for the coffee is higher than that paid to the wholesale supplier – the normal situation in business – a monetary profit is earned in the transaction and the shopkeeper will wish to stay in business in order to engage in similar transactions with other customers and suppliers. Similarly, the customer also makes a profit. The true cost of the coffee is what the customer might otherwise have spent the money on: tea, drinking chocolate or beer. The customer, in choosing coffee, makes a profit equal to the difference between the value of the coffee and the value of the alternatives that he or she might have bought.[6]

Homans's discussion of this simple type of economic transaction draws out a number of further implications, but the general outline of his argument should be clear from the simple case. Participants in social interaction engage in a calculus of rewards and costs and the interaction will continue in a stable form only if all participants are making a profit. Those who experience a loss will withdraw and will engage in alternative interactions where they are more likely to earn a profit.

Rewards, costs, profits and losses are not, of course, seen as purely monetary matters. They may involve any rewarding activity, and the overall 'profit' that a person receives is the net balance of all these rewards and costs. Thus monetary losses may be tolerated if there are compensating rewards of social approval. This might be the case, for example, when a person gives money to a charity. An actor's assessment of the overall balance of rewards and costs is extremely difficult for the social scientist to model, as there is no common yardstick. In the narrow economic sphere itself, money is the generalized medium of exchange in terms of which all marketable goods and services can be compared. Such rewards as 'social approval' have no direct monetary price, and it is difficult to see how actors are able to compare them. Nevertheless, Homans and rational choice theorists see this as a technical problem to be solved, not as an insuperable logical problem.[7] The fact is, they argue, individuals *do* make such comparisons in their everyday actions. The most successful attempts to model these comparisons have occurred in theories of preference orderings.

A preference orderings is the set of comparisons that people make among pairs of possible actions. A person who needs to make a journey, for example, may compare walking with taking the bus, walking with car theft, car theft with taking the bus and so on, and will decide which of each pair of alternatives is preferable to the other. Taking the bus may be preferred to both walking and car theft, but car theft may be preferred to walking. The preference ordering, then, would run from taking the bus (highest preference), through car theft, to walking (lowest preference). A rational actor is one who chooses the course of action that has the highest position in his or her preference ordering. If it is possible to assign numerical values to the rewards and costs that are involved in the various preferences, as economists are able to do for pure monetary transactions, then the preference orderings can be expressed as a so-called 'utility function'. It can be argued that a rational actor will act in such a way as to maximize his or her 'utility'.

Although the assignment of precise numerical values to actors' preferences may not always be possible, the laws of supply and demand that have been constructed in economic theory provide a paradigm for social exchange.[8] Homans's work on social exchange made it clear, however, that social theory cannot simply follow economic theory in a slavish way. Economists are able to predict the equilibrium point at which exchange transactions will stabilize only because they assume the existence of perfect competition, and Homans held that these conditions are relatively unusual in social exchange. Whereas economic theory can use these conditions to ground the assumption that people will act so as to equalize the 'marginal utilities' of their various activities – so maximizing their total utility – Homans will make no such assumption for social exchange in general. Indeed, as will be seen later, Homans introduced the idea of 'distributive justice' as a normative factor that limited the individual maximization of utility in social exchange.

The discussion so far has been concerned with the exercise of rational choice under conditions of certainty or of calculable risk. Under conditions of certainty, each alternative course of action has a known outcome and so choices can be made with complete certainty. Shopping exemplifies rational choice under conditions of certainty: all prices are known and precise comparisons of different goods can be made. Theories of utility maximization and 'indifference' have been the most important elaborations of this basic model, showing that certainty allows people to evaluate all possible outcomes and so to select the most preferred one as the goal of their action. In a theory of indifference, individuals are assumed to be able to construct a schedule of possible outcomes and to be able to decide whether or not they are 'indifferent' to the various outcomes. Only minor modifications to these theories are necessary in situations of calculable risk, where people must compare probabilities rather than certainties. Card games such as poker, for example, rest upon the assignment of known probabilities to alternative outcomes, and so such games can be played in a rational way. The chance of drawing a particular card and, therefore, a particular sequence of cards, can be calculated from a knowledge of the numbers of cards of each suit and value in the pack. In situations of certainty or calculable risk, then, exchange relationships will take place wherever they allow each participant to become better off than they would in any alternative interaction (or non-action). Blau's (1964) work elaborated on this idea as it applies to non-economic exchange, though Heath (1968) has shown that Blau's work involves some technical mistakes.

Situations of certainty and calculable risk involve the exercise of power. When actors are considering an exchange there will generally be a range of possible transactions that each would consider profitable. It is rarely the case that this range is so narrow that there is only one point of balance. More typically, the exact point at which an exchange will take place will depend upon the relative power of the participants. The bargaining power of actors varies with their 'dependence' on the exchange relationship, and actors are dependent on one another to the extent that there are no alternative sources of supply available to them (Emerson, 1962; Heath, 1976: 24). If a person is able to obtain something only from a single supplier, then he or she is highly dependent on that relationship and so will have little power to influence the 'price' that has to be paid. The monopoly supplier is able to use market power to command a high price from his or her customers. Power must, therefore, be seen as central to the operation of markets and, by extension, to all systems of social exchange. The operation of markets through power and dependence relations is, under conditions of certainty or calculable risk, the basis of the theory of supply and demand. This does not involve assuming the existence of 'perfect competition'. 'Oligopoly' and 'monopoly', involving progressively greater differentials of power in the market, are important forms of relationship in economics and in other forms of social exchange. Most recently, Emerson's colleagues have analysed the generation of power in extensive networks of exchange relationships (Cook *et al.*, 1983).

Market relations and card games – the paradigms for rationality under, respectively, certainty and calculable risk – do not exhaust the full range of social relations. Where actions have multiple and indeterminate consequences that ramify in unpredictable ways – the case in the great majority of social acts – actors face conditions of *uncertainty*, rather than of certainty or of calculable risk. Choices about higher education, for example, involve a great many unknown or uncertain variables: the likelihood of gaining particular classes of degree in different subjects, the likelihood of gaining employment, the returns attached to different kinds of job and so on. In these circumstances it is not even possible to assign definite probabilities to the various outcomes. If it is possible to take account of expected or anticipated outcomes and to give them a numerical value, then indifference theories can – and have – been extended to these situations. In many social situations, however, this is not possible, and no calculation of risk can be made. In these situations of uncertainty, then, theories of 'strategic' choice have to be applied.

In conditions of strategic interaction, the rewards and costs that are received by an actor depend not simply on his or her own actions, but also on the actions of others. The rational actor must try to anticipate the likely actions of others. Consider the case of two students, Alan and Barbara, who are suspected of having cheated in their assessed coursework by writing essays for one another. If they are questioned separately by their tutor, then each has the opportunity to deny or to confess to the cheating. Because they are questioned separately, neither student knows what the other will do. The possible outcomes of their interrogation can be presented in the form shown in Figure 3.1. In this diagram, the two choices facing each student have been cross-classified to produce four possible outcomes. It would be most rational for both students to deny cheating, as this would allow them to escape punishment (outcome 4). This is a safe strategy, however, only if each can be certain that the other will also deny cheating. Alan cannot be sure what Barbara will do when faced with threats and inducements from her tutor. She may, for all he knows, confess. He may, therefore, decide to confess himself: this confession may mean that the tutor will be sympathetic to his extenuat-

		Barbara	
		Confess	Deny
Alan	Confess	1	2
	Deny	3	4

Figure 3.1   Strategies under uncertainty

ing reasons for cheating and so may regard Barbara as the ringleader. Alan's punishment may, therefore, be mitigated if he confesses to cheating and Barbara denies it (outcome 2). As Barbara faces exactly the same uncertainty about Alan's actions, she may also choose to confess (outcome 1). The worst possible outcome for either student would be to deny cheating while the other confesses (outcomes 2 and 3). The one who denies cheating would, in these circumstances, be seen as doubly culpable: a cheat and a liar. Denial, therefore, involves the risk of a very severe penalty.

The best outcome of the interrogation, from the students' point of view, is for them both to deny cheating, allowing them to get away with it (outcome 4), but the most likely outcome is that both will confess (outcome 1). The adoption of a rational strategy by each student results in an 'irrational' outcome. Even if both students are aware of this paradox, there are no rational grounds for either of them to do anything other than to confess. Denial is sensible only if each student can be certain that the other will also continue to deny cheating.[9]

Strategic action under conditions of uncertainty can be analysed as an individually rational form of action: it follows a purely instrumental pattern, but it does not result in the 'optimizing' or 'maximizing' outcomes that are predicted for rational actions under conditions of certainty or calculable risk. It is, however, the most important form of rational action outside the economic sphere of the market. Indeed, market transactions where uncertainty prevails will also take a 'strategic' form. For this reason, the 'theory of games' – the mathematical analysis of strategic bargaining – has been seen to offer more to sociology than do narrower and more restricted theories of 'indifference'.

A PSYCHOLOGICAL BASIS?

The conception of 'rational action' has generally been taken to imply the idea of a conscious social actor engaging in deliberate rational strategies. For

Homans, however, rationality was an aspect of *behaviour* rather than action. Whatever 'meaning' people may attach to their behaviour, Homans argued, it is shaped by rewards and punishments, and people are motivated to seek rewards and avoid punishments. 'Rationality' is a description of such reward-seeking behaviour, it is not a description of conscious motives.

While some other writers have regarded the 'reinforcement' of behaviour as a subsidiary element in rational action (Elster, 1989b: Chapter 9), Homans saw it as playing the central role. Rational actions are reinforced, and so similar actions are more likely to result whenever the actor is faced with similar circumstances. This process of reinforcement occurs also in certain forms of animal behaviour, and this means that it is possible to turn to behaviourist psychology for insights into human behaviour.

Homans starts out from the concept of *voluntary* (or 'operant') behaviour. This was then contrasted with purely instinctive forms of animal behaviour that have no counterpart in the sphere of human action, and with reflex actions such as a knee jerk or a blink. Those forms of behaviour in which there is no voluntaristic element were seen as relatively unimportant features of human life. Voluntary behaviour, Homans argued, is learned behaviour that is shaped through its 'reinforcement' in interaction. Reinforcement, or 'conditioning', operates through the rewards and punishments that activities receive and, following Skinner, Homans termed this a process of *'operant conditioning'*. Because of his assumption that there were parallels between animal and human behaviour, Homans spent some time drawing out the general conclusions of Skinner's work on the conditioning of pigeons (see Skinner, 1953, 1957).

Skinner had showed that animal behaviour could be shaped by the giving or withholding of food. The food is a reward that reinforces the tendency of the animal to repeat the behaviour that led to its reward. In the laboratory the psychologist provides the rewards and punishments, while in natural settings it is environmental factors or the behaviour of other animals that provides rewards and punishments. Whatever the setting, behaviour is oriented by its reward and punishment. Homans concluded that it was also necessary to 'envisage human behaviour as a function of its pay-off: in amount and kind it depends on the amount and kind of reward and punishment it fetches' (Homans, 1961: 13).

Homans did not deny that people were 'conscious' in ways that other animals were not, but he did not see this as marking any fundamental difference in the ways that their behaviour was to be explained. An understanding of the conditioned behaviour of animals is the basis for explaining the equally conditioned, but symbolically mediated, behaviour of humans. People think, wish and conceptualize in symbolic terms, and this introduces a whole array of complex ideas that are not present in the behaviour of animals. What is able to serve as a 'reward', for example, depends not simply on biological states such as hunger or thirst, but also on the normative expectations and conscious interests of individuals. Homans believed, nevertheless, that the general principles of animal psychology could be applied, with little difficulty, to human behaviour. Indeed, he held that the very success of economic theory demonstrated this to be true. The principles of classical economics, he claimed, can be grounded in the general principles of behavioural psychology. Taken together, then, the two disciplines provide a firm foundation for constructing models of social interaction.[10]

Social behaviour, according to Homans, is that particular category of voluntary behaviour in which the activity of one animal rewards or punishes that of another. Social behaviour is a matter of mutual reinforcement, it is a process of 'exchange' that is oriented by self-interest in the avoidance of punishment and the seeking of rewards. Central to his concerns, then, were those activities that reward or punish other people. While any activity can, in principle, reinforce the behaviour of others, Homans identified *approval* as being of primary importance in social interaction. Most activities are very specific in their ability to reinforce another's activity, but approval is a 'generalized reinforcer' that has the capacity to reinforce a wide variety of activities. Because of this generalized capacity, Homans argued, social approval plays a similar role to money in the narrower sphere of economic exchange, and both approval and money can be seen as general means of exchange in social interaction.

The strength of a reward or punishment – its ability to reinforce behaviour – is measured by its 'quantity' and its 'value'. Quantity is easiest to measure in the case of money and those physical objects and commodities that can be added up and divided in a simple and relatively straightforward way: £1 000 is a larger quantity of money than £100. Homans held, however, that sociologists should also try to measure the quantity of other reinforcers. A measure of the amount of money that a person is able to receive in various transactions can be complemented by a measure of, for example, the amount of approval that a person is accorded for various courses of action. Time, for example, is a valuable resource that can serve as a measure of approval. Expressing approval takes time, and the length of time and the number of occasions on which approval is expressed might be used as an indirect measure of the degree of approval: the more that I approve of someone's behaviour, the more time that I am willing to spend on expressing that approval. For these reasons, Homans gave great attention to the length of time and the 'frequency' with which an action occurs.

The value of a reward is the 'utility' that it has for a person, and this subjective matter can vary greatly from one person to another. As Homans said: 'Some men find some of the damnedest things valuable' (Homans, 1961: 45).

For some inexplicable reason, for example, some people enjoy watching football, and for these people the opportunity to attend a football match would be highly valued. Other people, more understandably, enjoy listening to jazz and would regard attendance at a jazz concert as highly valuable. Those objects of utility that individuals regard as valuable are reflections of the cultural values to which they are attached, and this provided Homans with a solution to the problem of generalizing about subjective value. Despite the great diversity that exists in valued activities, Homans believed that particular cultures were often marked by the dominance of certain values. American culture, for example, involved the sharing of certain values that distinguished Americans from Chinese. Generalizations can, therefore, be made about the value of particular rewards and punishments within specific cultural contexts.

On the basis of these concepts, Homans turned to the task of constructing a deductive framework for organizing fundamental 'propositions' concerning human behaviour. There are, he held, only a small number of such fundamental propositions. The basic propositions are:

(1)   If in the past the occurrence of a particular stimulus-situation has been the occasion on which a man's activity has been rewarded, then the more similar the present stimulus-situation is to the particular one, the more likely he is to emit the activity, or some similar activity, now.

(2)   The more often within a given period of time a man's activity rewards the activity of another, the more often the other will emit the activity.

(3)   The more valuable to a man a unit of the activity another gives him, the more often he will emit activity rewarded by the activity of the other.

(4)   The more often a man has in the recent past received a rewarding activity from another, the less valuable any further unit of that activity becomes to him (Homans, 1961: 53, 54, 55; emphasis removed).[11]

These propositions can be illustrated by considering situations where approval is received in return for offers of help, as when, for example, one work colleague helps another to complete a difficult task. Someone who helps another and, in consequence, receives their approval, is likely to proffer help in other circumstances where he or she expects this to meet with approval. Conversely, the more often that approval has been given to those who help, the more often will similar help be given; and the more oriented a person is to approval-seeking, the more likely he or she is to offer help. Finally, the more often that a helper has been approved by others, the less likely is he or she to consider their approval to be so highly rewarding in the future. Homans argued that there can be an exchange of punishments as well as an exchange of rewards. Putting the four basic propositions into the negative illustrates this point. Thus, for example, a person who has been punished for an activity in the past is likely to avoid doing it wherever he or she believes that they may be punished again.

A final important point that Homans made is that the *threat* of punishment or the *promise* of a reward may motivate people as much as the punishment or reward itself. The threat of punishment, for example, may call forth appropriate behaviour from those who wish to avoid the punishment. This assumption allowed Homans to recognize the motivating role of threats and inducements in the conditioning of human behaviour.

Homans's purpose in outlining his psychological model was to provide a rigorous explanation, rooted in the principles of methodological individualism, of the findings of micro-economics and the analysis of social exchange. The descriptions of exchange processes in terms of formal models, he argued, was simply the first step, and a comprehensive social theory must go beyond these and construct realistic models of individual motivation. Such models were available, he felt, in the works of behavioural psychologists, and it was necessary only to spell out the links between their findings and those on social exchange. Such was the task that he believed he had completed in *Social Behaviour*.

COLLECTIVE ACTION AND SOCIAL NORMS

Two inter-linked problems have bedevilled attempts to depict theories of rational action as general theories of social action. These are the problems of collective action and of social norms. Critics have argued that a proper solution to these problems shows the need to go beyond, or even to abandon, the theory.

Rational choice and exchange theorists see no problem, in principle, in incorporating collective action into their theories. All that is necessary, following the principles of methodological individualism, is that the actions of groups and organizations be reducible to statements about the actions of individuals. Trades unions, political parties, business enterprises and other organizations may figure as units of analysis in rational choice theories. Such organizations have 'virtual intentions' that 'stand in some relation to the real intentions of the human individuals who are said to comprise the collective agent' (Carling, 1992: 27). Thus, Cook *et al.* (1990) have claimed that writers such as Williamson (1975), in their approach to the transaction costs of enterprises, can be seen as setting out an exchange theory with collective actors. Whenever it is possible to demonstrate the existence of a decision-making apparatus through which individual intentions are aggregated and an agreed policy formulated, it is legitimate to speak of collective actors (Hindess, 1988).

Theories of rational action do, however, face a crucial problem of showing *how* such organizations come to be formed. This has been formulated as the problem of the ability of individual motivation to explain support for, and attainment of, 'public goods', as opposed to private, sectional rewards. Put succinctly, the question is that of why individuals should join or support organizations that provide benefits that they will gain even if they do not join the organization? Why, for example, should a person join a trades union (at the cost of their time and money), if they will receive any negotiated wage increases in any case? In the same vein, why should someone not avoid or evade the payment of taxes if they are still able to benefit from public health and education policies, from national defence and so on? Assuming a strict model of rational action, rational individuals in large social groupings – such as social classes – have no incentive to support these kinds of collective action. They will calculate that their individual participation can have no significant effect on the organization's bargaining power and so there is nothing to be gained from membership. An individual's contribution to a trades union, for example, will have little or no relevance for its ability to bargain with employers and to negotiate conditions of work and pay rises. The sheer size of its membership provides it with the necessary bargaining power, quite independently of the individual's membership. This conclusion leads to a paradox once it is generalized. If each potential member makes this same calculation – and there is no reason to expect rational actors to do otherwise – then *no one* will join the union and it will not have the power to negotiate. No one, neither members nor non-members, will receive pay rises or improved conditions of work. In a variant of the 'prisoners' dilemma' model of strategic choice, individually rational decisions result in a lower profit for all.[12]

The fact that people *do* join trades unions and *do* pay taxes must mean that there is something missing from the simple rational action model. Olson (1965) has attempted to resolve this problem by suggesting that collective action in support of public goods is sustained through what he called 'selective incentives'. What he means is that there may be the use of additional rewards and punishments over and above the public goods themselves. Coercive penalties for tax evaders and the restriction of benefits to union members, he argued, can operate in this way. These selective incentives alter the rewards and costs attached to various courses of action in such a way as to make support for collective action appear profitable. Union membership is a rational choice for individuals if a 'closed shop' can be enforced, if pay rises are restricted to union members or if unions can offer advantageous insurance or legal advice to their members. Hechter (1987), for example, has argued that groups are formed if it is possible for them to monopolize a resource and to exclude non-members (See also Oliver *et al.*, 1985; Oliver and Marwell, 1988; Marwell *et al.*,1989). In the absence of these conditions, however, the problem of collective action remains.

Offe and Wiesenthal (1980) have extended Olson's argument by exploring the differential advantages that are available to different groups in society. The collective organization of workers, they hold, is problematic because of the ways that labour is structured within a system of capitalist production. The collective organization of capital, on the other hand, involves no such problems. The development of capitalist production combines capital and labour into ever larger units as capitalist business enterprises follow, of necessity, a rational strategy within a competitive market. Capital becomes enlarged through merger, amalgamation and the formation of inter-corporate cartels and, in consequence, it is rational for large enterprises to combine into employers' associations and other federal bodies. Each enterprise is large enough to make a difference to the outcome of collective action, and the consequences of collective action are easy to appraise in terms of the purely monetary interests to which enterprises are oriented.

The same business logic, Offe and Wiesenthal argue, impels an expansion of the division of labour that brings workers together into larger and more extensive units of production. This concentration of labour, however, occurs within a framework of its subordination to capital: labour is concentrated, or socialized, as an integral part of those business enterprises that are rationally oriented to the accumulation of capital. The concentration of capital, then, is facilitated by the normal, rational operations of business enterprises, and labour becomes socialized as a supportive element in business strategies. While the concentration of capital is a facilitating condition for the organiza- tion of capital into interest groups, the concentration and socialization of labour creates the very *problem* of collective action that Olson described. If workers are to combine in opposition to their employers, they must organize in ways that cross-cut the division of labour and that bring different catego- ries of worker together into cohesive and solidaristic unions that exist sepa- rately from, and outside of, any employing organization. A new collective identity has to be forged and individual workers have to be motivated to combine with one another.[13]

Offe and Wiesenthal have, perhaps, overstated their case. While they suc- cessfully demonstrate that Olson's problem is inscribed within the ways in which labour is organized in a capitalist system of production, they overstate the ease with which capitalists can be organized. They focus their attention on 'capital' considered as a factor of production and give no real attention to 'capitalists' considered as members of a class. The shareholders, executives and directors who participate in the control of capital and benefit from its use do not figure in the work of Offe and Wiesenthal. The organization of capital that they describe is the organization of capitalist business enterprises into federations and business pressure groups; they do not look at the conditions under which individual capitalists may combine, or not combine, into collective organizations to pursue their shared interests. There are, indeed, few examples of such organizations, and so it is likely that any attempt to form such an organization would face similar problems to those that Olson has described for labour organizations.[14]

While Olson, Offe and Wiesenthal have tried to remain within the framework of rational choice to explain collective action, others have argued that no satisfactory explanation can be made unless theorists go beyond rational choice itself and recognize the part that is played by social obligations. Individuals pay taxes or join trades unions because they feel that they are under an obligation to do so or because they have some kind of moral or ideological commitment to the organization. Although some advocates of rational choice have rejected any concern for considerations other than those of instrumental rationality, normative questions do find a place within theories of rational action. Rational individuals may compare themselves with others, judging their own rewards in relation to those received by those others that comprise their 'reference group'. Similarly, people may be understood to act rationally relative to those moral values to which they have a non-rational commitment. Homans, for example, developed these kinds of views in relation to feelings of 'relative deprivation'.

Individuals who are engaged in social exchange, Homans argued, may experience relative deprivation if the rewards that they receive are less than those that are received by others for similar behaviour. These feelings arise because people draw on ideas of 'justice' in the distribution of rewards and costs: they feel that certain others do not 'deserve' their rewards. There is, he held, a general assumption in all societies that rewards received should be proportional to costs incurred and, in particular, to the cost of the 'investments' that people have made. This led Homans to set out a fifth basic proposition:

(5) The more to a man's disadvantage the rule of distributive justice fails of realization, the more likely he is to display the emotional behaviour we call anger (Homans, 1961: 75).

Conversely, a person who feels relatively advantaged is likely to feel guilt rather than anger.

Normative considerations, then, may be taken account of in theories of rational action. Rational choice theories can, for example, take account of the varying comparisons that people make and of the reference groups on which they draw in making these comparisons, and they can handle rational choices relative to given moral commitments. There are, however, much greater problems in explaining the *origin* of these norms. Parsons (1937) argued that Durkheim had been one of the first to recognize that all rational actions occur within an institutional framework of norms that cannot be explained from the standpoint of rational action itself.

This problem is particularly clear in Homans's discussion of the norm of distributive justice. This normative framework of distributive justice (the basis of proposition 5, above) was invoked by Homans on the basis of little argument and no evidence. The norm of distributive justice was related to the assumption that individuals make comparisons with one another and that these comparisons involve specific reference groups. But no explanation is given for *why* individuals make comparisons, and there is no consideration of what determines the extent of these comparisons. Because Homans was unable to explain the formation of cultural norms, he could invoke distributive justice only as a universal feature of social life.

Ekeh has claimed that Homans's discussion of social norms marked a fundamental contradiction in his work:

> We can say that *Social Behaviour: Its Elementary Forms* is two books. The first book ends at page 61 and deals with *profitable exchange*. The second book begins at page 72, with an introduction on pages 61 to 72, and deals with *fair exchange* (Ekeh, 1974: 130; see also Deutsch, 1964).

The idea of fairness – a normative conception – points beyond the framework of rational choice theory itself. Homans did not show why considerations of social justice should arise or why they should prevail over considerations of profitable behaviour. The norm of fair exchange, the principle of distributive justice, cannot be explained by the logic of immediate contractual exchange. Coleman had tried to do this by looking at the emergence of 'trust' as a rational response to attempts to build coalitions, but the recent work of Cook and Emerson (1978: 762) has demonstrated that the norms of trust and justice that individuals routinely draw upon in their actions carry a moral force that runs counter to purely rational considerations, and that this sets definite limits on the use of bargaining power.

This same problem arises in Blau's (1964) account of the norm of reciprocity. This norm, he argued, arises because the provision of a service tends to create an obligation to return that service at some later date. It is, however, difficult to see why this would be the case unless there is some imbalance in the exchange relationship. If each participant makes a profit, there is no 'instrumental' reason for any such obligation to arise. If participants recognize an exchange as being non-profitable (or as being less profitable than the alternatives) but enter into it nevertheless, this could be for one of only two reasons. Either it is a result of coercion – in which case no question of obligation arises – or it is the result of a *pre-existing* sense of obligation. In the latter case, there remains the problem of explaining the origin of the obligation.

This was, of course, the core of the Parsonian critique of the Hobbesian account of social order. Parsons held that self-interested rational actors cannot generate a stable social order on an 'economic' or 'political' basis – neither 'civil society' nor the coercive Leviathan are sufficient. For Parsons, social order could be explained only through the recognition of a normative, non-contractual element in an individual contract.[15]

Blau's position had been that many exchange relations are, as a matter of fact, unbalanced as they form elements in long chains of deferred actions. Individuals are willing to incur a cost in their exchanges whenever they anticipate that this will create a sense of obligation that can be traded in at some time in the future. Although this does, indeed, give a possible explanation for the sense of obligation, it does so only by assuming that interaction is rooted in a framework of *trust*. Deferred rewards and chains of obligation are sustainable only if actors trust one another to behave appropriately in the future. The framework of norms and commitments that sustain such trust relations cannot themselves be explained through rational action processes.

A related conclusion has been drawn by Carling in his discussion of gender divisions, which emphasizes the impact of socialization. Carling shows that the exercise of rational choice is limited by the 'differential pre-commitments' that participants bring to their exchange relationships. Socialization into norms and values is structured by gender and so results in a systematic differentiation of preferences between men and women. These variations in preferences are amplified by the mechanisms of rational choice that produce systematic patterns of advantage and disadvantage along the lines of gender (Carling, 1992).

Among the recent rational choice theorists, Elster has explicitly confirmed this conclusion. Norms, he argues, are not 'outcome-oriented' (Elster, 1989a: 98; Elster, 1989b: 119), but are internalized and so acquire a compulsive character that cannot be explained in purely rational terms. Norms operate, he holds, through shame and guilt, rather than through rewards and punishment.[16] As far as the explanation of norms is concerned, Elster offers nothing:

> Norms, in my view, result from psychological propensities about which we know little. Although I could tell a story or two about how norms might have emerged, I have nothing to say about how they actually did emerge (Elster, 1989b: 123).

Norms do, nevertheless, play a central part in social action, and Elster's work is significant for the fact that he has recognized this and has attempted to build an analysis of social norms into a rational choice model. Rational choice and normative commitment, he argues, are complementary processes in the formation of social action.

Elster adopts an orthodox definition of social norms, seeing them as im-
perative rules of behaviour that are shared within a particular social group
and that are sustained, in part, by the approval and disapproval of others.
Rational choice theories are able to take account of such norms by seeing
actors as taking a purely pragmatic or calculative orientation towards them
and as seeking to maximize the approval that they receive from others. Elster
holds, however, that this point of view does not exhaust the matter. Actors
develop emotional commitments to social norms when they have been internalized. As a result of these commitments, the norms become unconditional
injunctions, and actors are oriented to the norms as ends-in-themselves. As a
result of this compelling character, infringement of a social norm results in
shame, embarrassment, guilt and other feelings of personal inadequacy. A
norm, then, is apparent in 'the propensity to feel shame and to anticipate
sanctions by others at the thought of behaving in certain, forbidden ways'
(Elster, 1989b: 105; emphasis removed).

Norms are clustered into systems of shared beliefs and common emotional
reactions and are generally unconscious or only partially conscious. Norms
need not be fully conscious and articulated to have their effect on action.[17]

Further pursuit of the question of social norms would be out of place in a
consideration of rational choice theories, and Elster does not, in fact, take his
analysis much further. His principal concern is to show the limitations of
rational choice theories by illustrating the importance of norms for a solution
to the problem of collective action. Collective action occurs, in part, because
purely rational considerations are complemented by social norms of co-
operation:

> When one is confronted with successful collective action, the task is to identify
> the precise *mix of motivations* – selfish *and* normative, rational *and* irrational –
> that produced it. Motives that taken separately would not get collective action off
> the ground may interact, snowball and build upon each other so that the whole
> exceeds the sum of its parts (Elster, 1989b: 186–7).

A shared norm of fairness, for example, can help to produce co-operation by
motivating those whose narrow self-interest might otherwise lead them to be
free-riders. It is not simply the case that the social norm's unconditional
character leads to autocratic conformity. While norms may have an unconditional character, conformity is situational and individuals – even those with a
strong sense of moral commitment – may choose to ignore or deviate from a
norm. The likelihood of conformity in a particular situation is strengthened
whenever it is apparent that most others are co-operating. If a person sees
that most others are paying their taxes, then he or she will feel a strong sense
of obligation to pay taxes as well: 'it's only fair'. If, however, only a small
minority are co-operating, then the person may feel that it would be foolish to

incur the costs of co-operation, even if he or she feels a personal commitment: the majority are 'getting away with it', so why shouldn't everybody
(Elster, 1989b: 189)?[18]

The assumption of instrumental rationality, then, cannot give a complete
explanation of social order. A full account must incorporate an awareness of
the part that is played by social norms and emotional commitments alongside
the exercise of rational choice. Heath's review of rational action theory
recognizes this explicitly. While rational considerations may explain why
particular individuals introduce and enforce social norms, they cannot explain how these norms may sometimes come to be internalized:

> The rational choice approach can only explain what people *do*. It can explain why
> people might institute a norm and might then enforce it, but it cannot explain why
> they should change their values – for this is what internalisation amounts to.
> Values ... must always remain a 'given' in the rational choice approach and to
> explain how they change we should have to introduce additional psychological
> mechanisms that have nothing to do with rationality (Heath, 1976: 64).

RATIONAL ACTION AND SOCIAL STRUCTURE

The starting point for virtually all rational choice theorists has been an
explicit statement of the assumptions of methodological individualism. This
is the position that holds that all statements about social phenomena are
reducible to statements about individual action, and that explanation of these
phenomena in terms of other social phenomena is, at best, a shorthand expression of the more detailed individual-level processes that produce them.
Durkheim's injunction to explain 'social facts' in terms of other social facts
is, therefore, rejected in favour of a Weberian emphasis on individual action.

Homans, for example, said that he was concerned with the 'elementary
social behaviour' of face-to-face interaction that he saw as comprising the
'subinstitutional' level of social analysis on which all social institutions
depended. While the social processes at work at the institutional level are
more complex than those of the subinstitutional level, this does not reflect a
difference of subject matter. The greater complexity is simply a consequence
of the more indirect nature of many exchange relations and of the greater use
of 'generalized reinforcers' such as money and social approval, and from the
more indirect nature of many exchanges. An employee of a business enterprise, for example, exchanges his or her work time for a monetary wage that
is received from a clerk in the salary department and not from a direct
supervisor or from the owner of the firm. Instead of a direct exchange between worker and the person for whom the work is undertaken, there is an
'indirect' exchange that is mediated by one or more intermediaries. Large

organizations do, however, continue to rely on the direct rewards that arise in face-to-face encounters: the approval of the supervisor or of work colleagues is an important reward that supplements the wage. For these reasons, Homans held that there are no independent and autonomous social structures:

> If you look long enough for the secret of society you will find it in plain sight: the secret of society is that it was made by men [*sic.*], and there is nothing in society but what men put there (Homans, 1961: 385).

Those features of social life that are conventionally called 'social structures' are simply chains of individual actions, and it is because many of these chains become quite extensive that social life can appear to have a life of its own. Cook and her colleagues (1990) have recently drawn on arguments from social network analysis to suggest that social structures can be understood as chains of interconnection that form exchange networks through which resources flow.[19]

Other writers in the exchange and rational choice tradition have taken a less extreme view and have followed Parsons in recognizing the 'emergent' properties of social phenomena. Blau (1964), for example, showed how complex structural phenomena can emerge from individual rational action. Most recently, Elster has presented a similar view, arguing that relations among social institutions are emergent features of social action. More strikingly, and controversially, Elster has argued that rational choice theories of action provide the best possible basis for Marxist social theory: Marxism, he holds, is a combination of rational choice and structural ideas within a framework of methodological individualism (Elster, 1985: Chapter 1; Elster, 1986a: Chapter 2).

Central to Elster's account of emergent properties is the idea of the *unintended consequences* of social action. Purposive, intentional actions have consequences, and many of these consequences are unintended. It is the compounding of unintended consequences that results in social phenomena of which actors may be only partially aware and that they experience as constraints rather than as the products of their action. Elster shows, for example, that the accumulation of unintended consequences can result in cyclical economic dislocations or – as in Adam Smith – in collective benefits. It is, perhaps, paradoxical to find such a degree of agreement between a contemporary Marxist writer and the founder of classical economics.[20]

The importance of the unintended consequences of rational action had first been recognized in the works of the classical economists and was most systematically developed by Menger (1883) and, subsequently, the Austrian political economists who influenced the work of Hayek and Popper (Hayek, 1942; Popper, 1944. See also Merton, 1936 and the overview in Hayek,

1967). According to these writers, social phenomena such as market relations and divisions of labour are the joint products of the actions of many individuals, their actions intertwining to form complex structures. The organization that these structures exhibit reflects regularities in the actions that produce them, but they are not the results of conscious individual design.

This view has been stated in a particularly clear and sophisticated form by Hayek, whose model of rational action rejects the simplistic assumption that short-term self-interest is the primary human motive. Rational individuals are, he claimed, rule-followers. They follow technical or moral rules that evolve through practical experience as individuals learn to act in ways that bring them the greatest rewards. These rules may be unconscious or only partly conscious, but they comprise the 'skills' through which individuals 'know how' to do particular things: 'the "know how" consists in the capacity to act according to rules which we may be able to discover but which we need not be able to state in order to obey them' (Hayek, 1962: 44. See also Hayek, 1965).[21] Through rationally-oriented rule-following, complex and organized social structures emerge as 'spontaneous', unplanned consequences.

What is particularly striking in Hayek's argument – despite his apparent influence on the New Right that dominated the political discourse of the 1980s – is that he firmly rejects any assumption that the structures that result from individual action will necessarily produce the greatest possible collective welfare. Smith's 'invisible hand', Hayek argues, is a fiction. Thus the market is not a self-legitimating mechanism that produces the best possible outcome for all individuals, and it certainly does not produce a distribution of rewards that corresponds to 'merit' or to individual needs. A market:

> operates on the principle of a combined game of skill and chance in which the results for each individual may be as much determined by circumstances wholly beyond his [*sic*] control as by his skill and effort. Each is remunerated according to the value his particular services have ... and this value ... stands in no necessary relation to anything which we could appropriately call his merits and still less his needs (Hayek, 1966: 172).

Hayek's political opposition to planning and state intervention is not based on any assumed *outcome* of rational individual action. It is justified, instead, on the grounds that *all* actions, including those of the state, have unintended and unforeseen consequences, and that individual freedom is preferable to state control. Individual freedom, he argued, is its own justification.

In Hayek's work, then, is found a highly sophisticated extension of the Hobbesian model of action that provides the basis for integrating the works of a wide range of rational choice theorists. Even those who question his political conclusions – such as Elster – have formulated models of rational actions and their unintended consequences that are quite compatible with

Hayek's argument (see also Coleman, 1973: 34). Despite the emphasis on unconscious, taken-for-granted 'rules', Hayek's model still lacks an awareness of the role of normative factors in structuring rational action. As Elster and Heath have shown, values and social norms cannot themselves be explained in terms of rational action, and the 'ends' or 'goals' that individuals pursue and the 'rules' that they follow are the product of cultural processes that do not figure in the rational choice model of action. Indeed, some commentators have gone so far as to suggest that 'no adequate theory of preference formation exists in social science' (Friedman and Hechter, 1990: 226).

This conclusion does, perhaps, overstate the case, as a number of important theories of cultural symbols and socialization have been formulated by sociologists and are discussed in other parts of this book. The statement does, however, reinforce the initial point made by Parsons 60 years ago: the ends of rational action cannot be explained from within a theory of rational action itself.

The various theories that have been discussed in this Chapter have made a number of competing claims. First, and least contentiously, there is the widely held view that all social actions can be understood in terms of a concept of rationality. For some of the writers who have been considered, action is exclusively rational; for others rationality is simply one aspect of action that is to be considered alongside normative factors. Talcott Parsons would not, of course, have demurred from the latter point. Those who argue that action is exclusively rational, however, would reject any concept of 'ritual' or 'expressive' action if this implied a form of action that had no rational, instrumental structure. A second claim that is made by many writers is that rational, instrumental action can be understood as being both self-interested and 'maximizing' or 'optimizing'. This is a far more contentious assumption, and it is difficult to reconcile with the idea that normative elements operate alongside rationality in the structuring of action.

A third – and most contentious – claim is that the maximization of self-interest in rational action follows a very particular logic: actors are assumed to have full knowledge of their situation and to adopt a scientific stance towards the appraisal of means and ends. Such an assumption makes no allowance for the possession of less than complete knowledge or for the influence of normative considerations in determining what might be 'efficient' or 'optimal'. Those who argue this 'strong' thesis of rationality are set sharply apart from others who have argued that actions are, indeed, rational, but that the exercise of rationality occurs with respect to specific *subjective* definitions of the situation. For these latter writers, rational action follows the 'logic of the situation' as it appears to the actors, and not as it appears to an external scientific observer (Popper, 1944; Jarvie, 1972).

Mainstream economic theorists seem to espouse all three claims in their strongest form, at least so far as economic actions are concerned. Homans adopted a similar point of view and extended this to other forms of action. Elster, on the other hand, recognizes the limitations of rationality and sees normative elements playing a significant part in a fully rounded social theory. None of the advocates of rational choice, however, have properly recognized the importance of the type of action that Parsons termed 'expressive' – action in which means–end rationality is subordinated to the expression of emotional and value commitments (but see Barry, 1970). This is, perhaps, the major limitation of these approaches as *general* theories. They do not encompass, as they claim, the full range of social actions. A truly general theory of action, as Parsons argued, would recognize the interplay of rationality and emotion in the structuring of action, and it would see instrumental action as simply one, extremely important, ideal type of action.

NOTES

1. Homans had actually called for 'men' to be brought back into sociological analysis, reflecting the sexist assumptions of his time. He was actually arguing for 'people' to be brought back in.
2. But see Blaug (1972) for a reconsideration of the continuity between classical and marginalist economics.
3. See the elaboration of this view in Mises (1949).
4. The early work of Emerson adopted a similar behavioural model. See Emerson (1972a and 1972b).
5. Coleman's most recent work in this area is his *Foundations of Social Theory* (1990).
6. I have greatly simplified the economic analysis of 'opportunity costs' and competitive markets in order to highlight the central contention of Homans himself.
7. Parsons's analysis of money, power and influence as generalized media of exchange was an attempt from within structural functionalist theory to produce a model of how such comparisons are made.
8. The laws of supply and demand were seen by Parsons as the paradigm for the analytical laws that he sought.
9. This type of situation has been described in 'games theory' as the 'prisoners' dilemma'.
10. Ekeh (1974: 111–19) questions the parallels between behavioural psychology and classical economics. He argues that they were not equated with one another but independently guided Homans's work, the incompatibilities between them creating contradictions in his work.
11. Homans uses 'he' and 'man' throughout, though the argument is intended to apply to both males and females. A fifth proposition relates to a different aspect of Homans's argument and will be introduced later in this Chapter.
12. Coleman's work showed that rational choice theories could explain the formation of voting coalitions *within* organizations, as individuals exchange support for one another, but he did not extend this to the formation of organizations or to citizen support for public goods. See Coleman (1966).

13. This provides a basis for holding that enterprise unions, as found in Japan, can never pose an effective challenge to employers, despite the fact that they have a virtually complete membership.
14. Offe and Wiesenthal gloss the distinction between the 'concentration' of capital and labour, on the one hand, and the 'organization' of capitalists and workers, on the other.
15. As I have shown in Chapter 2, Parsons made the further point that 'utilitarian' models of action could not even explain the origins of individual wants and goals themselves.
16. See also the arguments of Scheff (1990) and Barnes (1992) discussed in the following Chapter.
17. Elster tries, unsuccessfully, to distinguish legal and moral norms from 'social' norms. It is, I think, preferable to see legal and moral injunctions as specific forms of social norm, which can also take a traditional, religious or other form. Such an approach is certainly not incompatible with Elster's argument.
18. Some internalized norms may, of course, engender an *absolute* obligation to conform. A person may, for example, believe that it is absolutely wrong to steal or to murder, whatever the circumstances. The discussion of norms in situations of rational choice is further explored in Elster (1989b: Chapter 6), which looks at norms in bargaining situations. Rational choice theories have been applied to collective bargaining in industry in Crouch (1982).
19. On social network analysis see Scott (1991b).
20. Elster follows Cohen (1978) in seeing Marx as having employed 'functionalist' ideas to explain social structures through unintended consequences. Elster himself rejects any resort to functional explanation. These issues are explored in relation to the general question of functional explanations in Chapter 6.
21. Hayek's analysis of 'rules' has certain similarities with the argument of Giddens that will be discussed in Chapter 9.

4. Symbolic interaction and social constructs

Subjective meaning and its role in the structuring of social action had been a central theme in Parsons's synthesis of 19th century thought, but many of his critics pointed to the fact that the Parsonian theory of action was, in fact, deterministic rather than voluntaristic. It was held that Parsons gave insufficient attention to the fact that meanings are created by individuals and have constantly to be recreated if a stable social order is to be reproduced. The inspiration for such claims came from the so-called 'symbolic interactionist' approach to sociology, an approach whose origins were to be found in the work of Mead at the University of Chicago prior to the Second World War. It was in the intellectual ferment of Chicago in the first 30 years of the century that the basis of the 'interactionist' critique of Parsons was to be laid (Rock, 1979).

The dominant framework for sociological work at Chicago was provided by Small's theories of the conflict of groups and their struggle for resources. This 'conflict' perspective on the social process was, however, allied with a social psychological concern for individual attitudes and experience that was developed in the work of Thomas in the Sociology Department and Mead in the Psychology Department. Thomas had studied philosophy under William James and Charles Peirce, whose 'pragmatism' emphasized the meanings and definitions that individuals give to the situations in which they act. Often seen as a characteristically 'American' school of philosophy, pragmatism in fact shows many continuities with 19th century European romanticism and with the German schools of philosophy that flowed from this. Mead had studied psychology under Cooley and Dewey, also firmly committed to the pragmatist philosophy, and when Mead (together with Dewey) arrived at Chicago a fruitful period of collaboration with the sociologists began.

The translation of these ideas into an empirical research programme involved a focusing-down of Small's conflict theory to a concern for urban social processes and, in particular, for the city of Chicago itself. Not the nation state or the market, but particular localities within the city became objects of sociological investigation. Crucial to this reorientation was Robert Park, who had studied under James and Simmel. Under the influence of their ideas, Park was concerned to explore the subjective attitudes and experiences of individuals within small-scale social settings such as families, schools, gangs, work places and neighbourhoods. The city itself was seen as an ecological system of conflict relations among small groups. This orientation shaped the developing ideas of Mead, for whom 'society' and collective action had always to be seen in terms of such specific tangible realities.

Mead's work on subjective meaning and its role in the formation of the 'self' was incorporated into Park's framework of sociological research and was carried into the post-war period by his student Herbert Blumer, who taught at Chicago until the 1950s. During his final years at Chicago, Blumer supervised the early research of Erving Goffman. Blumer and Goffman became the leading figures in the development of symbolic interactionism, especially during the many years that they spent together at Berkeley in California. Their works were, in many respects, complementary to one another. Mead's concerns have been summarized in the phrase 'mind, self and society': in the post-war period, Blumer's work on 'mind and self' can be said to have been complemented by Goffman's work on 'self and society'. Thus Goffman undertook a series of studies of social encounters, while Blumer drew out the social psychological implications of these studies.[1]

Blumer mounted an increasingly vociferous challenge to structural functionalism, but his arguments had their greatest impact in the wake of a new challenge from Chicago. After Park, the influence of the Chicago Department of Sociology had waned and its research programme had fragmented. Everett Hughes and his student Howard Becker produced a number of important studies in the 1940s and 1950s, but Becker's work of the 1960s was the spearhead of the challenge to structural functionalism. Becker's sociology of deviance became the basis for others to draw on Blumer's work to counterpose symbolic interactionism to this orthodox consensus.

Pragmatism was not the only school of philosophy to generate a theory of action and subjective meaning. Similar ideas were derived from phenomenology by Alfred Schutz, whose work was taken up by Peter Berger during the 1950s and 1960s. Taken together, the pragmatist and phenomenological critiques of conventional sociology and of the structural concerns of Parsons posed a major challenge and led to a major reorientation of social thought.

INTERACTION, SELF AND SOCIAL ORDER

Pragmatism shared with Kantian philosophy the idea that the meaning of the world depends upon its selection and interpretation by human beings. Its particular contribution was to stress that the selective attention that people gave to the world was rooted in their practical problems and purposes, and that possible meanings were constrained by the nature of the world itself.

This element of realism – one is tempted to say of 'analytical realism' – led the pragmatists to conclude that the validity of meanings was to be gauged by the success of the actions that were based on them.

Mead's work drew on pragmatist ideas, but also on Hegel, to construct a social theory that stressed the communication of meaning in interaction. His work was originally described – though not by Mead himself – as 'social behaviourism', a term which now seems seriously misleading following the rapid development of the very different behaviourist psychology of Skinner. His work was, nevertheless, influenced by evolutionary biology and by the behaviourist ideas of his day.[2] In 1937, Herbert Blumer gave the name 'symbolic interactionism' to Mead's ideas, admitting that it was 'a somewhat barbarous neologism' (Blumer, 1969a: 1). It is, however, under the name of symbolic interactionism that Mead's legacy has come down to the present day.[3]

Human life, according to Mead, is a continual process of ongoing *activity*. This active, practical involvement in the world is escapable only through death. Humans do not, therefore, react in an automatic or mechanistic way to 'stimuli' or to objective circumstances, but must enter into a process of 'definition' or 'interpretation'. The active involvement and intervention of people in their own circumstances requires the informed use of practical knowledge, a fact that separates them from other animals. In order to pursue their plans, individuals must construct a meaningful definition of their situation and act on the basis of this definition. The starting point for sociological analysis must always be the meanings that objects have for individuals – the ways in which they are defined and constructed as meaningful objects of human action: 'in order to understand the action of people it is necessary to identify their world of objects' (Blumer, 1969a: 11).

This quite radical position holds, then, that the objects of the world in which people act are not mere brute facts of the physical environment, but are mental constructions. Individuals identify objects in their environment as means for their actions, as consequences of their actions, or as supporting elements in the ongoing framework of their activities. The process of interpretation that is inherent in all interaction involves the actor, first, indicating to her or himself those objects in the environment that are regarded as meaningful, and, second, combining these objects in an appropriate way. In undertaking the normal routine tasks of daily life, for example, a person must get up, wash, eat, travel to work, undertake a job and so on. In the course of these activities they identify their bed, their clothes, the bathroom sink, the bus, their work colleagues and so on. While each of these phenomena in their experience of the world may have a physical existence, their relevance as meaningful phenomena consists in the ways in which they have been constructed symbolically. The *cultural* significance of the bus, for example, consists in the expectation that it will stop at particular places, that it will follow a specific timetable, and that people may travel by handing over that symbolic object that we call money. There is nothing in the physical reality of the bus that requires any of these things. Indeed, redundant buses can and have been reconstructed as social centres, chicken coops and works of art. The cultural character of the world is even clearer in the case of those phenomena that have no direct physical reality. A 'career', for example, is a symbolic construction that orients much professional activity, but it has no physical reality or existence.

Mead did not subscribe to the Cartesian view of the isolated individual encountering the world without preconceptions. Language is the vehicle of symbolic construction and so plays a central part in the defining of situations. Mead argued that:

> Language does not simply symbolise a situation or object which is already there in advance; it makes possible the existence or the appearance of that situation or object, for it is a part of the mechanism whereby that situation or object is created (Mead, 1927: 78; see also Blumer, 1966: 68–70).

The language that people use to construct their world is a part of their culture and, like all cultural phenomena, it is social in character. Words and the ideas that they signify are elements in the shared cultural heritage of social groups. It is impossible for people to define their situations in anything other than social terms. In arriving at a definition of the situation, people employ symbols – and it is symbolic constructions that mediate between actions and objective circumstances.

The most important elements of the external world that actors must interpret are other people and their actions. As the significance of others is constructed through the use of symbols, social interaction is symbolically mediated: it is 'symbolic interaction'. At its most fundamental, however, interaction takes the form of a 'conversation of gestures', in which each participant's behaviour is a direct stimulus to the behaviour of the other. When dogs bark and snarl at one another, for example, they stimulate one another to respond in a similarly aggressive way and a spiral of mutual aggression leads to a fight. In a similar way, the crying of a baby directly triggers a caring response from its parent. Truly *social* interaction, however, does not involve such physical gestures, it involves their conversion into *symbols*. Behaviour becomes symbolic when people ascribe *meaning* to it and this meaning becomes the basis of their actions.[4] A vocal utterance becomes a greeting rather than a mere sound, for example, when speaker and listener understand that there is an intention to greet. Such a vocal utterance is symbolic in a way that the barking of a dog is not. Mead held that:

> Gestures become significant symbols when they implicitly arouse in the individual making them the same response which they explicitly arouse, or are supposed to arouse, in other individuals ... to whom they are addressed (Mead, 1927: 47).

Gestures become symbols only within specific social groups. The symbolic mediation of interaction arises through a social process of *communication* in which meanings are produced, reproduced and transformed. It is this process of communication that makes possible the very objects in terms of which people act. It does this by allowing them to construct and define one another *as* objects (Mead, 1927: 79).

The social process comprises a differentiated pattern of interactions, a diversity of distinct and specialized social groups. Each social group will possess symbols that are specific to it, but they also participate in wider processes of symbolic communication that draw them into particular 'universes of discourse'. The culture of a whole society comprises a diversity of such universes – religious, political, economic and so on – each with its specific sets of symbols and shared understandings. Discourse is, however, structured by language, and Mead held that this would give all discourse a common logical character. Behind the specialized discourse stands a common framework of logical discourse that is inherent in the very use of language.

Blumer's outline of symbolic interactionism stressed that definitions tend to form part of an accepted and taken-for-granted stock of knowledge that is shared by all members of a society. People do not invent symbols anew each time that they act; they acquire them through learning the common stock of symbols that is available in their culture. Their culture provides them with a cognitive 'map', a conceptual orientation that smoothes the course of their actions:

> Usually, most of the situations encountered by people in a given society are defined or 'structured' by them in the same way. Through previous interaction they develop and acquire common understandings or definitions of how to act in this or that situation. These common definitions enable people to act alike (Blumer, 1962: 86).

The construction of objects and the definition of situations, then, involves a continual process of interpretation in which actors may normally rely upon accepted and taken-for-granted interpretations that have become established in their society. A bus service, for example, can operate because most members of the society that it serves share particular definitions of timetabling, queuing, payment of fares and so on. These matters do not, typically, need to become the objects of new interpretations every time that they use a bus.

Scheff (1967) has shown that consensual collective representations exist where there is both an agreement among the members of a group about the meaning of a situation and an infinite series of 'reciprocated understandings' about this agreement. In such a situation, each participant knows that others agree, knows that they know that they agree, knows that they know that they know, and so on. The reality of consensus is solidified in the same way as an image in a hall of mirrors.

In many situations, of course, there will be no consensus, and the available stock of definitions may be of only limited guidance. In new or rapidly changing circumstances conflict and confusion may arise, and actions will not mesh together unless new interpretations can be arrived at and some kind of accommodation achieved: 'In the case of such "undefined" situations, it is necessary to trace and study the emerging process of definition which is brought into play' (Blumer, 1962: 86).

The need for a constant monitoring of established meanings and the peri-odic creation of new meanings ensures that the process of interpretation contains the everpresent possibility of change. In the very process of using symbols, individuals may contribute to their transformation; the outcomes of interaction are open, not determined:

> The actor selects, checks, suspends, regroups, and transforms the meanings in the light of the situation in which he is placed and the direction of his action. Accord-ingly, interpretation should not be regarded as a mere automatic application of established meanings but as a formative process in which meanings are used and revised as instruments for the guidance and formation of action (Blumer, 1969a: 5).

Symbolic interactionism adopts a stance of methodological individualism, seeing the social process as an outcome of individual action and denying any reality to social 'structures'. This does not rule out the possibility of collec-tive action. The action of groups, Blumer has argued, is an important social phenomenon, but it is to be seen as 'the collective or concerted actions of individuals seeking to meet their life situations' (Blumer, 1962: 84). Indi-viduals interpret one another's actions in an attempt to align their actions with one another, and group action can be seen as a particular form of aligned individual action. The actions of families, friendship groups and even busi-ness enterprises and political parties can be interpreted in this way, Blumer argued, and this requires that sociologists recognize that these groups have no reality over and above the actions of the individuals that form them. Thus Blumer argued that:

> Human society is to be seen as consisting of acting people, and the life of society is to be seen as consisting of their actions. The acting units may be separate

individuals, collectivities whose members are acting together on a common quest, or organisations acting on behalf of a constituency (1962: 85).

Despite their rejection of the idea that social structures have properties separate from those of individuals, symbolic interactionists do, nevertheless, see social action as being organized in relation to social *institutions*. According to Mead, an institution is 'a common response on the part of all members of the community to a particular situation'. It is the 'organized form of group or social activity' (Mead, 1927: 261). Institutions, then, are *general* phenomena in a Durkheimian sense. The institution of property, for example, involves a generalized attitude towards its maintenance by the members of the society. This is not, however, expressed in any collective reality. It is expressed only in the attitudes and responses of particular individuals and groups. The institution of property is manifested in the actions of the police officers, lawyers, judges and others who play various roles in enacting the defence of property.

Acting individuals assume that social institutions will remain relevant to their actions. They assume that any breach of expectations on their part will meet with a specific response from other people. In their minds they anticipate the likely actions of others, and this anticipation constrains their actions. This anticipation is achieved by trying to see the situation from the standpoint of the other. People take the attitude of others towards their own actions and so act accordingly. They refrain from theft, for example, because they expect that the various activities that define the institution of property will come into play if they breach it. In the same way, an individual whose home is burgled will call the police as he or she believes that this will be the most appropriate and effective course of action to defend their property rights.

Central to the idea of a social institution, then, is the idea of the *social reaction* of others to an action (Mead, 1927: 263). This organized social response is not an external factor in individual action, but is a directly internalized feature of action. In addition to taking the attitudes of specific others to their actions and intended actions, individuals also take the attitude of the 'generalized other'. Mead (1927: 154) held that:

> The organised community or social group which gives to the individual his unity of self may be called 'the generalised other'. The attitude of the generalised other is the attitude of the whole community.

This occurs through a process of *education,* or socialization, in which people take over the organized response of people in general and so are able to respond to themselves in the same way as the majority of the other members of their society. Through this internalization of the attitudes of the generalized other, the mind is structured socially and the person becomes a 'member' of society. Mead held that, 'It is the ability of the person to put himself [*sic.*] in other people's places that gives him his cues as to what he is to do under a specific situation' (1927: 270).

Socialization is a process through which a *self* is formed. The self reflects the structure of the generalized attitudes of the members of the society and it comprises what Cooley termed a 'looking glass self'. That is to say, the self 'reflects' the attitudes of others. As Mead (1927: 169) put it:

> The individual possesses a self only in relation to the selves of the other members of his social group; and the structure of his self expresses or reflects a general behaviour pattern of this social group to which he belongs.

Mead's emphasis on education and the internalization of the attitude of the generalized other inclined him towards an 'oversocialized' conception of the actor of the kind that is often seen as characteristic of Parsons's work. Mead did not assume a monolithic normative consensus in society, but he did assume that individuals took on the values of the social groups of which they were members. True to this pluralistic view of society, Mead held that there might, for example, be differences between the social institutions of a small clique or community and those of the larger society of which it is a part. Individuals will act in terms of the norms of their small group if they have not been educated into the ways of the larger society. Deviance, therefore, results from a clash of values:

> The criminal ... is the individual who lives in a very small group, and then makes depredations upon the larger community of which he is not a member. He is taking the property that belongs to others, but he himself does not belong to the community that recognizes and preserves the rights of property (Mead, 1927: 265).

The nature of deviance was central to the massive growth of interest in symbolic interactionism during the 1960s, largely due to the work of Becker (1963). While he did not ignore the fact that variations in behaviour may result from a clash of values, Becker stressed that deviance should not be seen as an attribute of individuals, but as a definition or 'label' that is applied to the actions of individuals by the others with whom they interact. The others who are the audience of actions judge them in terms of their values and norms, in terms of their own preferred rules of behaviour. 'Social groups create deviance by making the rules ... and by applying those rules to particular people' (Becker, 1963: 9). Mere deviation from a rule is not, however, sufficient for someone to become publicly defined as a 'deviant' – that is, as a 'thief', as 'mad', as 'gay' or whatever. The rule-breaking must be observed by an audience – or an audience must assume it to have occurred – and the audience must feel strongly enough about it to react in an overt and concerted way. As a self-image is shaped by its reflection in the attitudes of others, the social reaction – an act of labelling or stigmatization – is likely to lead people to reassess their motivation and identity. As more and more people come to act towards an individual in terms of their public definition as a deviant, so the individual will come to see him or herself as being a deviant.

Social reaction may be informal (through the attitudes of family, friends and public opinion) or it may involve the formal intervention of public agencies such as the police, doctors or priests. It is the collective action of official agencies that is likely to be especially fateful for people. The official reaction may lead to them being imprisoned, hospitalized or 'treated' in some other way, and it may lead to the closing-off of opportunities to them. They may, for example, be denied employment opportunities or the chance of living in particular areas. In these circumstances, people are likely to be forced into 'career deviance': they become locked-in to deviant sub-worlds and find it difficult to follow a normal life (Lemert, 1967).

This view of the relationship between social reaction and self-image depends heavily on the work of Goffman, who elaborated Mead's work on the self in a series of important studies. According to Goffman, social life must be seen as a 'theatrical' performance in which people give creative interpretations to their 'roles'. They employ particular 'props' and 'scenery' to support the impression of their self that they seek to convey to others (Goffman, 1959). Much self-presentation and 'impression management' goes on in public settings, and individuals may treat their private, domestic world as a 'backstage' area that they can withdraw to and prepare themselves for their next public performance. Where the self is being presented to a family audience in the domestic setting itself, other backstage regions must be used – people may withdraw to a bedroom or even a lavatory where they can 'be themselves' free of the need to act in front of an external audience. Even in these circumstances, however, symbolic interactionists emphasize that the individual's view of self – how he or she presents this self in isolation – depends upon the internalized attitudes of others. The individual self cannot escape 'society'.

Self-presentation, according to Goffman, is contrived and manipulated for an audience, whether the audience is physically present or not, and Goffman gave great attention to the ways in which self-conceptions are shaped by the attitudes and reactions of others. In *Asylums*, for example, he showed how organizational routines are employed to repress and control individuals and lead to definite shifts in their self-identity (Goffman, 1961; see also Goffman, 1963).

The works of Becker and Goffman have explored the impact of social organization on the individual self, and they have maintained the rejection of 'structural' concepts that Blumer also rejected. Becker, for example, focused his attention on specific agencies of control – the 'gatekeepers' of deviance – and not on such large-scale structures as the nation state or the world system. While Goffman (1983) held that an 'institutional order' existed alongside the 'interaction order' of face-to-face relations, his work did not examine the nature of social institutions themselves.

What, then, is the nature of the large-scale social institutions of society? While Mead (1927: 263) held that institutions are 'organically related to each other' in a systematic way, Blumer was particularly forceful in rejecting the idea that 'society', 'social structure' or 'social organization' were abstract and impersonal forces with the capacity to determine or constrain individual actions. These social institutions consist, he insisted, merely in individual and joint actions (Blumer, 1969a: 17). Large-scale social phenomena such as social classes, divisions of labour, authority arrangements and other 'institutions' are merely arrangements of people that are connected to one another through the intermeshing of their actions.[5] These social aggregates are:

> large complex networks of action involving an interlinkage and interdependency of diverse people. ... A network ... functions because people at different points do something, and what they do is a result of how they define the situation in which they are called on to act (Blumer, 1969a: 19).

The image that is suggested here is that 'society' exists as a network of connections among interacting individuals. However, Blumer and other symbolic interactionists have shown little inclination to pursue the possibilities that social network analysis offers for the mapping of the 'structural' features of interaction (Scott, 1991b). In this respect it contrasts sharply with recent trends in exchange theory, where network concepts have been used as ways of moving from the analysis of face-to-face interaction to larger-scale social entities (Cook and Whitmeyer, 1992). Blumer did not take this step.

Social networks as 'concatenations' of intermeshed actions are not to be understood as entities that exist separately from individuals – they are not social 'systems' with 'imperatives' or 'functional prerequisites'. They are a result of the processes through which people define and interpret their situations, and they may have an influence on people's actions only in so far as they are taken into account by them. Organized human society 'is the framework inside of which social action takes place' (Blumer, 1962: 87). It may 'set conditions for their action' only by making certain definitions available and precluding the use of others:

> Social organisation enters into action only to the extent to which it shapes situations in which people act, and to the extent to which it supplies fixed sets of symbols which people use in interpreting their situations (Blumer, 1962: 88).

To the extent that any pattern of social organization does exist, it does so only as a precarious 'negotiated order' (Strauss, *et al.*, 1963). Participants in a locale – a factory, a school, a hospital and so on – collectively negotiate an understanding of the social order that will govern their actions, but this remains a *product* of individual agreement and, therefore, is always subject to renegotiation. Blumer (1966: 72) concluded that 'society' is nothing but 'a diversified social process in which people ... [are] engaged in forming joint actions to deal with situations confronting them'. All in social life is, ultimately, flux, and the 'structures' that individuals – and some sociologists – identify in their social world are merely temporary routinizations of this process. Society comprises acting individuals and groups whose actions are structured by the institutional concepts that they share with one another.

CONSTRUCTING REALITY

Symbolic interactionism provided a sophisticated theoretical programme for the analysis of social action, and it posed a major challenge to the Parsonian viewpoint and to all forms of structural sociology. During the 1960s, however, a related view of action, rooted in the phenomenological philosophy of Edmund Husserl, appeared to offer a more radical challenge to conventional sociology. Phenomenological sociologists shared many ideas with symbolic interactionism, but they sought to provide a more fundamental reconstruction of the basis for a theory of action. The leading figure in the development of a phenomenological basis for sociology was Alfred Schutz, an Austrian who had undertaken an elaborate reconstruction of Weberian theory. Schutz migrated to the United States in the 1930s, where he influenced a number of post-war theorists. It was in the work of Peter Berger and his associates that phenomenological sociology was brought to a wider audience. In such work as *The Social Construction of Reality* (Berger and Luckmann, 1966) and a series of studies in the sociology of religion (Berger, 1969a, 1969b), Berger outlined a 'dialectical' theory rooted in phenomenological assumptions.[6] In a similar vein, Douglas developed a phenomenologically informed approach to sociology which shared many of Berger's concerns (Douglas, 1967, 1971a).

Husserl's works of the 1920s had set out a novel basis for theoretical work in science. Husserl adopted a stance of radical doubt, rejecting all theoretical presuppositions in order to get back to a bedrock of certain and indisputable knowledge. He therefore rejected all previous philosophical positions and sought to uncover the ordinary, everyday world of experience. Schutz allied Husserl's ideas with a Weberian approach to sociology, which he saw as comprising a comprehensive attempt to reduce 'all kinds of social relationships and structures ... to the most elementary forms of individual behaviour' (Schutz, 1932:

6). Schutz argued that it is only through a phenomenological investigation of meaning that it is possible to show that Weber's comparative and historical studies comprised a viable theoretical strategy.[7] Where the Kantian position involved starting out from the categories and concepts through which experience is organized, the phenomenological standpoint involved starting out from the phenomena of experience themselves. The aim of phenomenology is to describe things as they appear in conscious experience. The external world, Schutz argued, is known *only* through our consciousness of it: the external world is known as a phenomenon. The aim of a phenomenological sociology, then, is to study how a meaningful world is constructed.

The meaningful world of phenomena is the world of everyday life, the world in which people live on a day-to-day basis, and it is this world that is the centre of attention in the phenomenological sociology of Berger and his colleagues. The everyday world appears to people to have a reality and an autonomy of its own, and the objects and routines of this world are 'taken-for-granted' as 'natural', as constituting 'the way things are'. This world is the same, or similar, for thousands and perhaps millions of people, and it pre-dates any particular individual's involvement with it. The way in which a father and a child interact with one another, for example, is shaped by taken-for-granted assumptions about the appropriate actions of parents and children. The objects and routines of the social world appear to people as Durkheimian 'social facts', external to them and constraining them. For phenomenological sociology, however, this taken-for-granted objectivity is not what it seems. It is not external to individuals: 'It is a world that originates in their thoughts and actions, and is maintained as real by these' (Berger and Luckmann, 1966: 33).

The social world is the product of human subjectivity, but it takes on a factual 'objective' appearance because people externalize or 'objectify' meanings and definitions through their actions. Social reality, Berger and Luckmann argue, is *objectivated*, made into an object. This objectification occurs principally through language. Through the use of language, people objectivate their ideas and make them available to others as typifications, as categories of meaning that can be used to organize and to order their experiences. People use words and phrases such as 'husband', 'mother', 'child', 'going to work', 'wheeler dealer', 'boss', 'school run', 'time of the month' and so on, so making available a vocabulary of motives and meanings that define a social world of interlocking objects. When individuals give a name to something they make it appear as something separate from and external to them. In domestic life, for example, they may describe their social relations in terms of the idea of a 'family'. Those with whom they live may use the same terminology and so 'the family' comes to be seen as a thing, an object that exists independently of the individual members.

Social objects appear to acquire a life of their own, an independent reality, whenever people lose sight of the fact that they are human products. When children are born into a family they learn the habits and practices of their parents and accept them as being every bit as objective as the things of the natural world. The parents, too, come to see these habits and practices as being more real because of the way that they are accepted as normal by their children. They 'forget' that they invented or modified many of these ways of behaving in the first place. The idea of the family is widespread in modern society and many people employ the word to describe their domestic life. As a result, the family and 'family life' come to acquire an objective meaning as part of the taken-for-granted social world and may become the object of wider social action. Politicians, for example, may feel that 'the family' is under threat and in need of legislative and policy changes to protect it.

When objectivations come to acquire such a reality in large collectivities, Berger and Luckmann argue, they become *institutionalized* and acquire a fixity and solidity. Marriage and parenthood, for example, are institutions that define specific roles and ways of behaving that are rarely regarded as being mere conventions or human products:

> An institutional world, then, is experienced as an objective reality. It has a history that antedates the individual's birth and is not accessible to his [*sic.*] biographical recollection. It was there before he was born, and it will be there after his death. ... The institutions, as historical and objective facticities, confront the individual as undeniable facts. The institutions are *there*, external to him, persistent in their reality, whether he likes it or not. He cannot wish them away. They resist his attempts to change or evade them (Berger and Luckmann, 1966: 77–8).

Once objectivated, institutions acquire a reality and autonomy that leads people to lose sight of the fact that they are human products. They are shared by other people and come to be seen as natural and inevitable features of the world over which individuals have little or no control. They come to be seen as unavoidable constraints on social actions. This objectivity is, Berger and Luckmann argue, merely an appearance. Institutions do not actually possess a different ontological status from human action. People produce a world through action, but they come to experience that world as being something other than a human product. The objective reality of society is reinforced by socialization. People create social meanings that they pass on to subsequent generations who accept them as part of the natural order of things. Through primary and secondary socialization 'society' becomes a subjective reality as well as an objective reality. It is internalized within the self-identity of each individual member of the society.

Through these processes, then, individuals produce a social world that does, indeed, constrain their actions. The case of language illustrates this well:

> I encounter language as a facticity external to myself and it is coercive in its effect on me. Language forces me into its patterns. I cannot use the rules of German syntax when I speak English; I cannot use words invented by my three-year old son if I want to communicate outside the family; I must take into account prevailing standards of speech for various occasions, even if I would prefer my private 'improper' ones (Berger and Luckmann, 1966: 53).

Institutions and typifications together comprise a shared world of common sense experience and knowledge that has been 'sedimented' as what Schutz, following Husserl, termed the 'lifeworld' (*Lebenswelt*). The lifeworld is the world that people live in on a day-to-day basis – the everyday world, or everyday life. It is the foundation of all experience. The lifeworld is so natural to people that it is 'taken-for-granted' by them as a normal, inevitable and objective feature of existence.

The institutions of the lifeworld are surrounded by a particular framework of meaning, a body of knowledge that accounts for the nature of the institution and thereby legitimizes it. In some circumstances, people may assume that all the various institutions of their society are integrated in some way, and they will produce a 'universe of meaning' that describes and legitimizes this integrated structure. In other circumstances, however, various institutions may be seen as separate and distinct from one another, each associated with 'socially segregated sub-universes of meaning'. In general, Berger and Luckmann suggest, modern societies are pluralistic and involve the coexistence of segregated sub-universes within an overarching universe of meaning that integrates the whole institutional structure of the society (Berger and Luckmann, 1966: 142). While the overarching universe of meaning is a property of all members of a society, the sub-universes will be 'carried' by particular social groups. Such groups might include scientists, accountants, doctors, sociologists and so on. These groups produce the specific meanings that comprise the sub-universe, and these meanings have a particular reality for them. Each group tends to produce an alternative way of viewing the world, a worldview that is rooted in its specific interests, and this allows a variety of different views of the society to emerge.[8] This pluralism of worldviews in modern societies 'greatly increases the problem of establishing a stable symbolic canopy for the entire society' (Berger and Luckmann, 1966: 103; emphasis removed).

Berger and Luckmann rejected much of the Parsonian position, as did the symbolic interactionists. The objective reality of society and its institutions is not seen as a reflection of functional requirements, and systems are not seen as having a separate ontological existence apart from individuals. Social systems and social institutions are social constructions, objectivations of cultural meanings that people may reify but which, nevertheless, remain human products. Despite this, however, Berger and Luckmann remained remarkably close to many of the central tenets of the Parsonian position. The phenomenological account of society and social institutions retained an important place for *consensus* and the mechanisms of *socialization* in social life. Berger and Luckmann can be seen as 'pluralists' within the Parsonian tradition, phenomenological counterparts to Clark Kerr and Martin Lipset. This is, indeed, very clear in Douglas's phenomenological interpretation of American society (Douglas, 1971a).

A THEORY OF EXPRESSIVE ACTION

Predominant within symbolic interactionism and phenomenological sociology has been an emphasis on the cognitive aspects of interaction. Despite its focus on the impact of the attitudes of others on a person's self-conception, and despite some important work by Goffman (1967), the emotional aspects of this process have rarely been theorized. Indeed, Mead and Dewey made no mention of emotion and affect in their works.

This gap in symbolic interactionism was recognized by Hochschild (1979) and Shott (1979), and was explored at length in a major work by Hochschild (1983) that employed insights from Goffman and Freud to construct a concept of 'emotional labour'. This term is used to refer to paid work in which feelings are managed in order to achieve a particular public display. It takes the private activities of 'emotional management' into the public sphere of the market. Hochschild shows, for example, how airline flight attendants (stewards and stewardesses) are required to adopt a particular manner and to display specific feelings towards passengers. Discrepancies between actual and displayed emotions, she argues, lead to feelings of 'emotive dissonance' analogous to those found in studies of 'cognitive dissonance'. Such dissonance is resolved through changing what is felt or changing what is displayed: people either come to accept the emotions that they display, or they reject them and give an inadequate performance.

Scheff (1990) has recently set out a powerful and more generalized account that starts from Cooley's (1909, 1922) recognition of the emotional content of the primary group and uses an analysis of emotions as the basis of a reconstruction of social theory. In addition to seeing his recognition of emotion as the recovering of a suppressed dimension of symbolic interactionism, Scheff uses it to undertake a phenomenological reconstruction of Durkheim's concept of the social fact. Social facts are characterized by their externality and constraint with respect to individuals (Durkheim, 1895). Scheff argues that the externality of social facts derives from the cognitive mechanisms of consensus formation through which individuals develop an awareness of collective symbolic representations that are experienced as external to themselves. Building on his earlier work (Scheff, 1967), he argues that the establishment of consensus in interaction is not simply a cognitive process. Although cognitive processes of mutual understanding may allow people to recognize and to understand the 'external' social norms of their society, this cannot explain how social facts acquire a constraining power that results in conformity to these norms. The constraining power of social facts, Scheff argues, can be understood only on the basis of the emotional mechanisms of consensus formation that he calls 'attunement'.

The conventional answer to the problem of conformity and constraint has been to highlight the process of socialization through which people come to internalize norms and values and so come to accept them as their own. Scheff argues that this solution, as found in Parsons and in Berger and Luckmann, makes sense only if the emotional aspects of internalization are taken seriously. It is through their socialization that people learn to anticipate the sanctioning reactions of others and so come to acquire an emotional system that controls their actions. To understand this, Scheff builds on the insights of Freud and psychoanalytic writers into the role of emotional commitments in motivating social action.[9] To this end, he constructs a 'deference-emotion' model of social interaction in which people are seen as motivated by the maintenance or enhancement of their standing in the eyes of others. Guilt and anxiety are seen as the psychological correlates of the emotions of pride and shame that Scheff holds to be central to social order.

People are motivated, he argues, by a concern for status or prestige, and their conformity to social norms is a consequence of the pursuit of social standing. In many situations formal sanctions such as public acclaim or disgrace will be used to ensure conformity, but much conforming behaviour occurs in the absence of formal sanctions and in private situations where public sanctions are inappropriate. For this reason Scheff holds that informal, interpersonal sanctions are frequently more important. Such sanctions as interpersonal deference and derogation produce internal sentiments of pride and shame.

Scheff's analysis of these informal sanctions draws especially on the work of Goffman on 'face' and 'impression management' in social interaction (Goffman, 1959, 1967). Claims to social status and esteem are continuously reviewed and contested, with each action affirming or denying a claim. People are concerned with the respect and disrespect that is given by others and so are motivated by the pursuit of deference and the avoidance of derogation. In face-to-face encounters this is manifested in the seeking of approval and the avoidance of embarrassment, in the maintaining of 'face'. Rejection by others may be expressed in minor and subtle forms – an inflexion of the voice, a lapse of attention and so on. The experiencing of such rejection leads to feelings of shame at 'failure' or 'incompetence' in social interaction.

Similarly, acceptance by others leads to feelings of pride in one's success. Specifically, Scheff stresses the anticipation of pride and shame as crucial aspects of the self-monitoring of behaviour.

For Scheff, then, status or prestige is a fundamental interest for people, and the pursuit of money and power is often a reflection of a deeper motive of enhancing their prestige. The striving for 'respectability', for example, is often manifested in the pursuit of high value consumer goods: the desire for the consumer goods is not a pursuit of money *per se*, but of the status that the goods signify.

It is through these mechanisms that Scheff sees enduring social bonds being established, and he highlights the need for social bonds to be constantly built, protected or repaired if they are to persist. It is through the network of social bonds that people acquire 'a sense of belonging' (Scheff, 1990: 12). Social bonds are the basis of social solidarity, as Durkheim argued, and Scheff connects this argument with Tönnies's (1889) distinction between community and society. By 'community' Scheff means the primary groups of family and locality that Cooley emphasized as involving relations between identified persons. The sphere of 'society', on the other hand, consists of the secondary associations in which individuals relate to one another only through specific roles. Community involves Durkheim's 'mechanical solidarity', where individuals are 'engulfed' by their group memberships. In 'society', on the other hand, the individual is 'isolated': social bonds are weakened and people are less attached to social groups.[10]

The rise of modern society destroyed the communal structure of social bonds and left people increasingly isolated from one another. 'Individualism' rationalizes this loss of community by denying the need for social bonds and the emotions that sustain them. People deny any need for social bonds and see themselves as self-subsistent 'individuals'. This involves repression of their emotions. Although the emotions continue to make themselves felt, their reality is denied. Scheff holds that if the emotions that are generated by conformity and deviance are not acknowledged, a 'chain reaction of shame and anger' may result (Scheff, 1990: 76; emphasis removed). Shame is 'recursive'. Because feelings of pride and shame are repressed, people feel further shame whenever their pride or shame makes itself felt. People become angry at their own feelings of shame, they make inappropriate responses that lead to further rejection by others, and so the cycle begins again and the chain reaction takes place.

Scheff has suggested that his approach can effectively handle large-scale social processes as well as situations of face-to-face interaction, but his arguments are not yet compelling on this point. He makes the valid point that the emotional responses of political leaders will have significant structural consequences for their nation states and for the international systems, but he is less convincing when he refers to 'national' feelings of shame (Scheff, 1990: 78–9). Such arguments invoke an assumed national consensus and must be seriously questioned. More successful in extending Scheff's analysis beyond the face-to-face level are the related arguments of Barnes (1992), who sees a potential in the works of Goffman and Scheff for resolving the problem of collective agency.[11] The structure of communicative interaction, Barnes argues, occurs through the symbolic sanctioning of action, and it is the sanctions of praise and blame, approval and disapproval, recognition and rejection, and honour and contempt that are used to motivate people to engage in collective action. Barnes links this argument with Weber's analysis of status group formation, pointing the way to an effective link between Scheff's analysis of face-to-face interaction and the historical and comparative concerns of structural sociologists.

The symbolic interactionism of Mead, Blumer and Goffman, together with its phenomenological reconstruction in Berger and Douglas, has provided a powerful general perspective on action and interaction, grasping both the 'instrumental' and the 'expressive' dimensions of action from the standpoint of communication processes in social life.[12] It provides a way of examining the social integration of the 'interaction order', but its conception of social integration gives only a partial view of collective agency. The formation of small groups, business enterprises and political parties is recognized, but not explained, and they are seen as having only a shadowy existence as part of the 'framework' of social life.[13] In terms of the question of system integration – or institutional integration – symbolic interactionism appears as an approach that denies the independent reality of systems and structures above the level of the individual. Social institutions, for Mead and for Blumer, exist in the minds of individuals as what Durkheim called collective representations. They may constrain individual action, but only in so far as individuals take account of them and act accordingly. They exist only as anticipated patterns of reaction by specific individuals and groups. In the work of Berger there is a recognition of the 'externality' and facticity of social institutions, but he too claims that this is, ultimately, a cognitive illusion, an aspect of reification.

NOTES

1. For a useful account of Goffman's work see Burns (1992).
2. The principal work by which Mead is known (Mead, 1927) is a posthumous compilation

of lecture notes and student transcripts. It is based on a lecture series of 1927, with some additional material from 1930. Much of his work was concerned with individual psychology, rather than social psychology, and I shall not discuss that work in detail.

3.   There is some dispute over Blumer's interpretation of Mead, which minimizes the influence of behavioural and biological ideas and ignores the relevance of Hegel (Joas, 1980). Nevertheless, it is through Blumer that Mead's work has had its major impact on sociology.

4.   Mead's position on this was very close to Weber's distinction between behaviour and action.

5.   A related view can be found in the work of Harré (1979, 1981). Although Harré set out a powerful statement of realism as a general principle in scientific investigation, he refuses to accord any reality to emergent properties of interaction other than small groups and organizations. Bhaskar (1979) has used realist ideas to counter this suggestion and to defend the reality of social classes and other 'social wholes'.

6.   Related studies include Berger and Kellner (1970) and Luckman (1967). The work of Berger epitomizes what Wilson (1970) has called 'the interpretive paradigm'.

7.   Schutz's concern was to give a firm underpinning to Weberian and marginalist theories of rational action.

8.   Berger and Luckmann's arguments on the nature of groups as carriers of worldviews is an attempt to restate the arguments of Mannheim (1929) in phenomenological terms.

9.   Scheff draws, in fact, on the Freudian heretic Alfred Adler (1956) and, more particularly, on the recent work of Helen Lewis (1971).

10.   Scheff misleadingly sees the situation of 'egoism' as equivalent to Durkheim's 'organic solidarity'. In fact, Durkheim (1893, 1897) saw organic solidarity as a reconstitution of social order around forms of individualism that avoided isolation and egoism.

11.   Barnes had, in fact, put forward a parallel argument of his own in Barnes (1988).

12.   For an interesting attempt to unite symbolic interactionism and exchange theory see Fine (1990).

13.   The work of Randall Collins (1975, 1981) is, perhaps, one of the most fruitful directions in which a solution to this problem might be pursued.

5. Conflict and collective agency

Conflict and collective action were central themes in the theories of Gumplowicz and Mosca and, of course, they also formed a fundamental element in Marxist theory. These early theorists explored the role of conflict in large scale historical change, paying particular attention to the conflict of social strata, the power of ruling minorities, and the economic and ethnic bases of social divisions. 'Classes' and 'elites' were the principal collective agents, the driving forces in history. These ideas received far less attention during the long ascendancy of Parsons and the orthodox consensus to which he gave birth. Growing dissatisfaction with an orthodoxy that stressed consensus, however, led many sociologists to return to an emphasis on the role of conflict in social life.

This debate has frequently been seen in a rather stereotyped way, but the battle lines were never as clear-cut as some discussions of the 'consensus-versus-conflict' debate often supposed. It was undoubtedly the case, however, that Parsons and the structural functionalists had focused their attention on normative order, seeing this as something to which people were attached by their commitment to the core values that they held in common. This normative order was seen as leading to co-operation in social action, to integration in social relations and to stability in social structures. Those who advocated a greater emphasis on conflict stressed that the consensus model embodied a highly unrealistic set of assumptions and that a more realistic approach to sociological analysis was needed. This alternative theoretical framework had to begin from the existence of fundamental divergencies of interest between organized groups that entered into conflict with one another, established frameworks of coercive control over one another, and employed norms and values as elements in ideologies that masked and legitimated their power (Gluckman, 1955; Coser, 1956; Lockwood, 1956; Mills, 1956, 1963; Dahrendorf, 1957; Gouldner, 1959; Rex, 1961; van den Berghe, 1963).

'Conflict theory', as Collins (1990) has noted, 'is something of a misnomer'. The theories that have been given this label are, in fact, theories of collective agency and competition for resources. While the various theories centre around conflicts of interests and the social divisions that they create, they do not see the overt expression of conflict as being the normal state of affairs. Conflict is seen as an endemic but intermittent feature of collective action, as an ever present possibility in social life.

The modern theorists of conflict carried forward many of the central tenets of the Austrian, Italian and early American writers on conflict. Dahrendorf, for example, explicitly rooted his concerns in the arguments of Pareto and Mosca, though he and Coser both moved towards a 'pluralist' rather than an 'elitist' model of conflict. Coser developed his ideas through a reconsideration of Simmel – who was never in the mainstream of historical conflict theory – while Rex developed a more radical approach that owed much to both Marx and Weber.

Recent conflict theorists have set out powerful and important theories of groups and organizations in and around the struggle for power and resources, but they have been less successful in conceptualizing the agency of large-scale collectivities of the kind that figured in the works of the earlier writers. Dahrendorf did, indeed, use the language of class, but he shows a marked reluctance to see social classes as agencies of large-scale historical change. In Dahrendorf, class action is largely reduced to the actions of organized interest groups. Rex retains a concern for long-term historical processes and for the agency of large-scale collectivities, though he too has tended to see classes as organized groups. These concerns have, however, been given a renewed focus in recent work on 'social movements' which has returned conflict theory to the analysis of the historical agency of classes and other collectivities.

AUTHORITY AND CONFLICT GROUPS

Dahrendorf's work on conflict took shape during his time at the London School of Economics, and a paper by one of his colleagues at that time, David Lockwood (1956), set the scene for subsequent debates on conflict. In this paper, Lockwood holds that there are two distinct aspects of sociological analysis, the 'normative' and the 'material'. The normative aspect comprises the moral standards of evaluation in a social system; they make up the core or dominant values that Parsons had emphasized in his work. This 'normative order', Lockwood argues, is the sphere of socialization and of social control. The material level – Lockwood terms it the 'substratum' – comprises the 'factual disposition of means', the structure of 'differential access to scarce resources' that generates differential life chances and interests. This 'factual order' is the sphere of power. Lockwood's argument is that Parsons's work, especially that in *The Social System* (Parsons, 1951), had concentrated on the normative to the exclusion of the material and that this imbalance of attention must be rectified (see also the related argument in Gouldner, 1959).

Dahrendorf pursues a similar line. He identifies a long-standing theoretical differentiation in social thought between those approaches that stress value consensus and those that place greater emphasis on force and coercion. Parsons, as the latest advocate of the integration or coercion theory, played a major constructive role in the advancement of sociological knowledge. The dominance of this theory, however, meant that non-normative, material factors were underemphasized, and Dahrendorf seeks to develop the theoretical understanding of this other side of social reality. He does not, however, feel that it is fruitful to search for a synthesis of the two positions or to advocate the absolute value of one over and against the other. Rather, each theory is appropriate to a different set of problems. Through a critique of Marx – an earlier representative of the coercion tradition and whose empirical arguments Dahrendorf feels to have been overtaken by events – he outlines his own theory of conflict and coercion.[1]

Dahrendorf's starting point is the differential distribution of 'authority' among social roles. All socially structured associations, he argues, involve the granting of rights of control to the occupants of certain positions, so allowing them to coerce the other members of these associations. Social roles involve varying 'expectations of domination or subjection', and this distribution of authority is the structural basis for the formation of 'conflict groups' (Dahrendorf, 1957: 165). States, churches, business enterprises, political parties and trades unions all involve a distribution of authority and may, therefore, be the bases of structured conflicts between rulers and ruled: citizens and slaves, capitalists and workers, party officials and members, and so on.[2] The distribution of authority in any association is necessarily dichotomous, dividing the dominant from the subjected. A particular association can generate two – and only two – conflict groups: 'Authority implies both domination and subjection, and it therefore implies the coexistence of two distinct sets of positions or persons' (Dahrendorf, 1957: 173).

There may, of course, be a great difference between those with much and those with little authority, but Dahrendorf holds that the gulf is much greater between those with some authority and those with none.

The next step in his argument is to show that positions of dominance and subjection are characterized by distinct and conflicting *interests*. Interests are 'structurally generated orientations of the actions of incumbents of defined positions' (Dahrendorf, 1957: 175). That is to say, interests are *role expectations*. By virtue of their authority, or their lack of it, people are constrained to act in certain ways, and these actions express their objective interests in the maintenance or the modification of the structure of authority itself. Of the two authority positions in an association:

> one – that of domination – is characterised by an interest in the maintenance of a social structure that for them conveys authority, whereas the other – that of subjection – involves an interest in changing a social condition that deprives its incumbents of authority. The two interests are in conflict (Dahrendorf, 1957: 176).

The occupants of a particular authority position have certain interests in common and so they share a potential for united action. They are a collectivity united by their 'latent', structural interests and by a potential for action. This constitutes them as a 'quasi-group' rather than an actual organized social group. A quasi-group is transformed into one or more social organizations or *interest groups* when its members establish a programme of action, a structure of decision-making, and enter into action in pursuit of their interests. A political party, for example, is an interest group in this sense. Employed manual workers in a business enterprise form a quasi-group of people subject to the authority of the managers of the enterprise and may, as a collectivity, be designated 'working class'. The trades unions and political parties of which these workers are members are interest groups that seek to give voice to their interests.

A quasi-group may be the recruiting ground for a number of different interest groups, and it is rarely the case that the whole of a quasi-group will be transformed into a single unified interest group. There may be, for example, both Christian and socialist trades unions recruiting from the working class. Nor can it always be said that a particular interest group unambiguously 'represents' a particular quasi-group. Interest groups may be formed around latent interests in the distribution of authority, but they may also combine these concerns with 'a multitude of other and independent goals and orientations' (Dahrendorf, 1957: 182). Interests in the distribution of authority may, for example, be associated with ethnic or gender concerns. It follows that such phrases as 'the organized working class' must be used with extreme caution, and it should not be assumed that the whole of the working class is organized into a single interest group that unambiguously and single-mindedly pursues its class interests.

There is nothing inevitable about the formation of interest groups from quasi-groups, and Dahrendorf tried to identify the conditions that must exist for this to occur. He identifies three sets of conditions that he terms the technical, the political and the social conditions of organization. The *technical* conditions of organization include the existence of a *cadre* of activists who make the formation of an interest group one of their goals. This *cadre* will forge an interest group into being and will provide its founders and its first generation of leaders. A second technical condition is the existence of a 'charter', programme or 'ideology' that expresses the interests of the quasi-group in a systematic way. A charter allows the objective interests that are associated with structural positions to be translated into subjective orientations of organized action. The *political* condition of organization that is mentioned by Dahrendorf is the existence of a framework of civil and political citizenship rights that allow for freedom of association and for the expression of opposition. Without such rights, interest groups are unlikely to form. Finally, the *social* conditions of organization include the existence of a degree of communication among the members of the quasi-group, as this allows them to develop a common awareness and outlook on life. It is also important that there be a systematic, rather than a random, pattern of recruitment to the quasi-group, as this also reinforces the homogeneity of its members (Dahrendorf, 1957: 184–8). Where the members of a quasi-group are homogeneous and cohesive, they are most likely to form an interest group. It is, however, only when all three sets of conditions exist that a quasi-group comes to be organized into one or more interest groups.

Conflict groups, according to Dahrendorf, can exist as both 'quasi-groups' and 'interest groups': a quasi-group is a potential conflict group, while an interest group is an actual conflict group. This distinction is analogous to Marx's distinction between a class 'in itself' and a class 'for itself', and it is not surprising that Dahrendorf stresses the conceptual links between his own work and that of Marx. While rejecting the empirical content of Marx's predictions about the development of capitalism, Dahrendorf accepts the validity and the usefulness of the 'class' category itself, though his stress on 'authority' rather than 'property' gives the concept a very specific redefinition. 'Class', Dahrendorf argues, is simply another word for conflict groups rooted in the social distribution of authority (Dahrendorf, 1957: 204). Hence the struggle of conflict groups is class struggle.

THE FUNCTIONS OF SOCIAL CONFLICT

Having set out a general model of conflict groups, Dahrendorf sought to examine the consequences of their conflict for larger social structures. His starting point was the analysis of the 'functions' of social conflict that had been presented by Coser. Rejecting the Parsonian emphasis on consensus and stability, Coser (1956) returned to Simmel for ideas that would help to build his own model of conflict.[3] Coser's focus on the 'positive functions' of conflict involves only a partial departure from Parsonian assumptions, and Dahrendorf attempts to push beyond Coser. Coser's work, therefore, forms an essential part of Dahrendorf's argument.

Coser gives some attention to group formation, but he does not look at the factors that are responsible for the emergence of the social positions on which groups are based. His argument does, however, complement Dahrendorf's discussion of the technical, political and social conditions of group formation. Coser assumes that societies contain various groups that are organized around the distribution of resources – wealth, status and political power – and that these groups range from the 'positively privileged' to the 'negatively privileged'. Classes, status groups, ethnic groups and bureaucratic strata within societies, and nations in the international system are the groups to which he gives greatest attention, and he sees societies as being organized around the social relations between these groups. The members of these groups can adopt various emotional attitudes towards one another – acceptance, emulation, hostility and so on – and Coser is particularly concerned with hostility and with the conditions under which this comes to be expressed in overt conflict. This group conflict is seen as having important consequences for the groups themselves and for the societies to which they belong.

The translation of hostility into overt conflict is most likely to occur when there is a decline in the perceived legitimacy of the social distribution of resources. When the members of a negatively privileged group come to feel that their subordination is due to an illegitimate pattern of distribution that involves processes of denial and exclusion, their hostility is likely to be expressed in open conflict. In these circumstances, Coser argues, conflict forges the members of the group into a truly cohesive collective agent, a 'struggle group'. The group's identity is reinforced and it achieves a high degree of solidarity and cohesion.[4] In Marxian terms, it ceases to be a group 'in itself' and becomes a group 'for itself':

> When a social structure is no longer considered legitimate, individuals with similar objective positions will come, through conflict, to constitute themselves into self-conscious groups with common interests (Coser, 1956: 37–8).

Struggle groups are more likely to persist over time if they have a structure of representation or leadership. 'Representation' occurs when individuals engage in conflict in the name of, or on behalf of, the collectivity (Coser, 1956: 113). Representation may be more or less formal, the establishment of an official structure of leadership being the most formal pattern. Indeed, the establishment of a leadership structure is an important hallmark of the organization of a struggle group:

> Part of what is meant by the concept of 'group consciousness' ... is the transformation of individuals with their own specific life situations into conscious representatives of the group (Coser, 1956: 115).

Those who believe themselves to be the representatives of a struggle group are likely to be more radical and merciless in their demands than are those who feel themselves to be acting in a purely personal capacity. Coser sees intellectuals as being especially important in this representative role. Where intellectuals become the leaders of a group, they give voice to the struggle group's purposes and interests and formulate them into an ideology.

Overt and protracted conflict is costly, and struggle groups may seek to minimize the amount of conflict that they become involved in. Conflict can be minimized most effectively if the competing struggle groups are each aware of their relative power and can match their responses in appropriately limited ways. A carefully balanced response to a group that is unable to pose a serious challenge is less costly than all-out conflict. As the appraisal of the relative power of groups is often possible only *after* a period of actual conflict, struggle groups may engage in trials of strength that allow them to gauge one another's strength and to establish a stable balance of power. For the same reason, struggle groups prefer to face a unified opponent with a clear structure of leadership than they do a disorganized and chaotic enemy. With a unified opponent they can more easily establish a stable *modus vivendi*.

Struggle groups may find that their antagonists disappear or cease to be the objects of conflict: they may be successful in achieving their aims, or their circumstances may change. It is likely, however, that they will have developed a vested interest in maintaining their existing structure. Leaders, for example, will not wish to lose their position of leadership. In these circumstances they may search for new enemies – real or imagined – that would allow them to maintain their organization and cohesion:

> Disappearance of the original enemy leads to a search for new enemies so that the group may continue to engage in conflict, thereby maintaining a structure that it would be in danger of losing were there no longer an enemy (Coser, 1956: 105).

Identification of a new enemy may involve a self-fulfilling prophecy: by reacting to the enemy in terms of preconceptions or stereotypes, a dominant group may shape the enemy's behaviour in such a way that it comes to conform to the image that is held by the dominant group and its representatives. Conversely, unsuccessful struggle groups may search for internal enemies – traitors, dissenters and so on – on whose actions the failure can be blamed. The group re-establishes its solidarity by scapegoating some of its own members.

In many situations, Coser argues, hostility between negatively and positively privileged groups will not be directly and openly expressed. In particularly 'rigid' societies, hostility may be difficult to express and it may find its outlet only in regulated or ritualized 'safety valve' forms. Duels and ritual revenge, for example, can allow a controlled release of hostility that does not threaten the basic structure of group relations. In some cases, hostility may be displaced onto a 'scapegoat' group, and conflict may arise with this group rather than with the real object of resentment. Prejudice against ethnic and religious minorities, for example, involves the channelling of hostility onto weaker and more vulnerable targets and so may help to stabilize the structure of relations among the positively and negatively privileged groups that form the majority (Coser, 1956: 68). When hostilities are suppressed or partially displaced, however, 'the accumulation of such feelings is likely to further intensify the conflict once it breaks out' (*ibid.*). Scapegoating may build up a pool of latent hostility against the real target, and this may eventually break through into open conflict.

Coser's main concern, nevertheless, is with the positive effects of conflict – its positive functions – and he pays most attention to those situations in which 'flexible' or 'open' societies allow a certain degree of overt conflict to be expressed. Flexible societies, such as modern America, Coser holds, are marked by numerous lines of intersecting division and allow conflicts to offset and counterbalance one another without undermining the stability of the whole society. In such societies no single division becomes the basis of an all-out conflict between struggle groups:

> It may be that one reason for the relative absence of 'class struggle' in this country is the fact that the American worker, far from restricting his allegiance to class-conflict groupings and associations, is a member of a number of associations and groupings which represent him in diverse conflicts with different religious, ethnic, status and political groups. Since the lines of conflict between all these groups do not converge, the cleavage along class lines does not draw the total energies and allegiance of the worker into a single area of conflict (Coser, 1956: 77)

Thus the class structure of the United States is fairly stable and socialist beliefs are relatively weak. Cross-cutting cleavages undermine the class solidarity that would sustain political opposition to the structure of class privileges. Criss-crossing divisions 'sew the social system together' and prevent serious attack on its core values (Coser, 1956: 80). In the American system, political parties are formal associations or coalitions rather than communally organized groups with all-embracing ideologies. American politics involves the struggle of pressure groups, each concerned with a specific issue but forged into temporary coalitions in order to influence political parties and the government:

> The pressure group, formed to fight specific antagonists or to defend special interests against other interests, is typical of a society in which a general individualistic emphasis makes difficult the formation of more enduring groups which are so much more 'demanding' of involvement and participation on their members (Coser, 1956: 143).

Coalitions of pressure groups are not forged into single, cohesive struggle groups, and they remain concerned with purely instrumental ends. The formation of an overarching struggle group involves a sharing of fundamental values that override sectional differences. Thus Coser's position is akin to the pluralist tradition of political sociology, in which cross-cutting cleavages and pressure group politics serve as guarantors of *stable* political democracy (Lipset, 1959).[5]

Dahrendorf adopts a similar pluralistic image of cross-cutting cleavages in modern American society. His model of conflict relations within associations, it will be recalled, is dichotomous. Within particular associations, the distribution of authority must always involve a division between the dominant and the subordinate. Whole societies, on the other hand, comprise a number of associations, and the divisions within each may cross-cut one another in complex ways. For this reason, the dichotomy that exists within each association may not be translated into a dichotomy within the whole society. There is, for example, no necessary correspondence between the distribution of authority in different types of association. Those who hold authority in the modern state may not be dominant in business, and those who prevail in the army are unlikely to hold positions of authority in the Church. In these circumstances, there will be a plurality of conflict groups, and not a single dichotomy. Dahrendorf holds, in particular, that there is no evidence that modern industrial societies are organized around a simple dichotomous structure of authority: there are a number of separate and distinct hierarchies of authority, and so these societies can be seen as comprising 'a plurality of competing dominant ... aggregates' (Dahrendorf, 1957: 171–2). Business leaders compete with Church leaders, who compete with state leaders, and so on. There *may* be social conditions under which there is, indeed, a close association among different forms of authority, but this is not universal and its existence, or otherwise, must always be investigated empirically. Whenever the conflicts in different associations are superimposed, there will not be the stabilizing effects that occur with cross-cutting cleavages. There will be a small number of lines of intense class conflict. In the most extreme case, there will be a polarization of society into two great hostile camps:

> When conflict groups encounter each other in several associations and in several clashes, the energies expended in all of them will be combined and one overriding conflict of interests will emerge (Dahrendorf, 1957: 215).

STRATIFICATION AND CONFLICT GROUPS

Where Dahrendorf sees authority relations as the basis of conflict groups, John Rex (1961) has constructed a more general model in which authority appears as only one of the bases of social stratification. Rex's work draws heavily on Weber's recognition of class, status and authority as three separate but interdependent sources of social conflict. He starts out from similar assumptions as Lockwood (1956), arguing that norms and values always rest upon a 'balance of power' among social groups. The 'substructure of power' derives from the distribution of resources or facilities and involves a particular structure of scarcity that generates conflicts of interests between the groups. For this reason, argues Rex, sociological analysis must always begin with an identification of the major social groups that are involved in the power structure and with the conflicts in which they are engaged. Although relations *within* social groups might be explained in terms of normative factors, the relations *between* social groups will involve both value patterns and power relations. More generally, Rex recognizes a range of social situations that vary from normative consensus, where the balance of power is fully legitimized, to the pluralistic situation of competing normative systems (ideologies and counter-ideologies), where the exercise of power is likely to involve a resort to coercion or violence.

Where Dahrendorf sees 'conflict' and 'consensus' models as complementary, illuminating different aspects of reality, Rex argues that the consensus model describes a particular form of power relations and that the conflict model provides a general analysis of power relations. The Parsonian scheme is not rejected, it is to be reinterpreted as a special case of the conflict model. The perfectly integrated social system, Rex argues, is the outcome of a particular – and highly unusual – pattern of group conflict in which there is a long-standing 'truce' and a framework of mutual accommodation. The conflict model, then, is the more general model. Whereas Coser's model of conflict formed an *extension* to the consensus model and Dahrendorf's model was intended as a *supplement* to it, Rex's model is a full-scale *alternative* to the consensus model.

Rex constructs a typology of social relations that is intended to relativize the Parsonian view of institutionalized role expectations organized through shared values.[6] Although he shares the basic assumptions of Parsons's action frame of reference, Rex believes that the consensual social relation should be seen as an ideal type that describes situations 'in which there is an agreement over legitimate ends and of norms governing appropriate means for the attainment of ends' (Rex, 1981: 6). Consensus exists where there is perfect communication and agreement over values. Parsons himself had recognized a second ideal type of 'anomie', in which 'there is no community of ends or normative consensus about appropriate means', and Rex holds that 'conflict' is a third ideal type in which there is complete communicative understanding but a disagreement over the ends and means that should be pursued (*ibid.*). *Consensus, anomie* and *conflict* comprise the three-fold typology of social relations that must be employed to analyse real social situations.[7] This typology is summarized in Figure 5.1.

Parsons had recognized the unreality of the consensus assumption as a concrete description of actual societies, but he had held that a complete

	Communication	Shared values
Consensus	+	+
Anomie	−	−
Conflict	+	−

Figure 5.1   A typology of social relations

understanding of the consensual relation could provide an appropriate yard-stick for the analysis of more complex real social settings. Rex rejects this view, holding that the conflict model provides a far better yardstick because of the ubiquity of conflict in social life. With the conflict model as a point of departure, he argues, consensus and anomie can be understood as relatively unusual departures from the situation described in the general model.[8]

Like Coser, Rex turned to Simmel for insights into the construction of a sociology of conflict, though he recognizes that Simmel's particular *forte* had been the analysis of dyadic, face-to-face relations. A sociology of conflict that goes beyond the dyadic level to 'multi-person structures', Rex argues, must draw equally heavily on Weber. Rex's model of conflict assumes that actors seek allies with whom they can co-operate in order to achieve their goals, even against the actions of other actors and *their* allies that might oppose them. Each side of a conflict enhances its ability to mobilize sanctions if it can bring together allies that have a similar social situation. Allies form groups that are structured for conflict, and Rex terms these 'conflict groups'. Conflict groups, then, are collectivities 'the activities of whose members contribute to the attainment of the group's aims' (Rex, 1961: 123).

In place of Parsons's model of the integrated social system, Rex puts a model of competing conflict groups characterized by an unequal balance of power. In many situations, he argues, an established ruling group will domi-nate the society. Its institutions, ideas and values will prevail over those of the subordinate group. In yet other situations, a newly emergent 'revolution-ary' group might achieve dominance and seek to transform the society. A third pattern of relations between conflict groups is what Rex calls 'the truce situation': each group accommodates its aims to those of others in order to establish a balance of power that is more rewarding to all concerned than would be outright conflict. A limited area of co-operation can be established, and new institutions of compromise and reform may bridge the gulf that separates the conflict groups (Rex, 1961: 124–9).

The struggle of conflict groups results also in 'system conflicts' – those failures of system integration that Marxists have termed 'contradictions'.

Each conflict group espouses distinct goals and purposes that may become embodied in specific and distinct social institutions. The struggle of conflict groups, then, may come to involve a clash of institutions or of whole ways of life. Rex argues that there is, therefore, an interdependence of 'action' and 'system': the conflict of groups at the action level implies contradictions between institutions at the system level.[9]

Rex's general model of conflict groups, taken along with Dahrendorf's general arguments on group formation and Coser's arguments of the 'functions' of group conflict, provides a powerful perspective on social life. It offers a theory of collective agency and social integration that complements the theories of individual agency that were considered in the previous chapters, and it suggests the kinds of links that exist between social integration and system integration. Rex does not, however, leave his analysis at this general level. Like Dahrendorf, he considers the structural bases of conflict group formation. Where Dahrendorf sees conflict groups as originating in the social distribution of authority, Rex relates conflict groups to wider patterns of social stratification.

In complex modern societies, Rex argues, social stratification arises in three distinct spheres of action: the economic, the political and the value spheres. The *economic sphere* concerns action in relation to the means of life and the allocation of scarce resources. It is the sphere of market and property relations, including access to, and control over, these social relations. The *political sphere* is concerned with action in relation to patterns of domination and, in particular, with control over legitimate power. The *value sphere* involves action that is related to control over cultural ideas and values and to conceptions of superiority and inferiority. It operates through such institutions as education and religion (Rex, 1961: 123; Rex, 1974b).[10] These three spheres of action and the social institutions with which they are associated are the bases of social stratification and, therefore, they are the bases of conflict group formation.

Of the three spheres, Rex sees the economic sphere as fundamental, and he accords it the greatest attention. Productive institutions are fundamental to all societies, and hence the analysis of the economic sphere has a general priority. It is only for the last 400 years, however, that the economic sphere has been organized as a system of market transactions and that the market mechanism has, therefore, been the principal force in the organization of production. Market relations are, of course, relations of exchange, but Rex rejects a pure rational choice model of markets. Rational, economizing action is always embedded in a structure of property and power that constrains rational choices, and it is only under very specific historical circumstances that rational economic action achieves the degree of autonomy as a structuring element that it has achieved in modern capitalist societies. This pattern of market production results from particular patterns of political organization, and Rex holds that market processes can never be detached from their political context (Rex, 1981: 32).

The market is, then, the central social institution in all advanced societies. It is the principal 'multi-person structure' of the economic sphere, and the conflict groups that arise in the market are basic to the whole social structure. Rex focuses his attention on capitalist societies, where the distribution of property gives rise to specific 'bargaining situations': capitalist societies 'are property structured and provide for unequal bargaining' (Rex, 1981: 32). When bargaining over the control and use of property involves competition among pluralities of actors in specific bargaining situations, these economic exchange relations take the form of 'market relations'. In this situation the bargaining situation becomes a 'market' situation:

> A market situation exists ... where there is a plurality of 'buyers' seeking to make advantageous bargains with a plurality of 'suppliers' subject to the condition that both buyers and suppliers compete with one another (Rex, 1981: 35).

To the extent that 'buyers' or 'sellers' are able to form monopolies, the free play of pure market forces is limited and economic relations become, even more clearly, relations of conflict. This conflict occurs between the 'collectivities' or organized groups that constitute the monopoly buyers and sellers.

For Rex, then, market relations are the origin of those conflicts of interest that motivate the economically based conflict groups that Weber and Marx termed social classes. The classes described in the Marxian model of capitalist society are conflict groups that are formed on the basis of the distribution of property in and through a market and whose organized actions limit the operation of pure market processes. 'Collective bargaining' between trades unions and employers associations, for example, is a system of conflict relations and not simply of 'rational' market transactions.

Rex sees Marx's model of class conflict as a specific form of a general theory of social conflict. For Marx, Rex holds, classes were conflict groups that were organized around access to the means of production in a system which separates owners and non-owners in a labour market. While recognizing the power of this view, Rex prefers Weber's wider view, according to which classes can occur not only in relation to the means of production but in relation to *any* form of property. Rex, for example, argues that there may be 'housing classes' as well as employment classes (Rex and Moore, 1969). Weber also recognized that property relations are not necessarily dichotomous and that there may be a plurality of classes formed in relation to any particular type of property. There can, for example, be various 'middle classes'.

Market relations, then, generate latent conflicts and differential life chances that define classes as what Dahrendorf termed 'quasi-groups' – the Marxian 'classes-in-themselves'. Where the occupants of a class situation ally themselves with one another in order to pursue common aims and interests through conflict with other classes, they have been forged into a true conflict group, becoming a Marxian class-for-itself. Though the distinction between class-in-itself and class-for-itself is said to be 'Hegelian', Rex recognizes its value for sociological analysis: 'The former term refers to a group with a common class-situation only, and the latter to a group which is organized for conflict' (Rex, 1961: 140).

The transformation of an economic quasi-group into an organized conflict group occurs only if three conditions of organization are met.[11] First, there must be the establishment of leadership and organization. Trades unions exemplify this: they have a structure of leaders, officers, representatives and supporters that provides the basis for collective action. Political parties are also important in forging the unity of a conflict group. Second, the class must achieve a degree of internal normative order, as solidarity arises from specific norms and values that are rooted in working conditions.[12] Third, there is the emergence of group identification and 'class consciousness', through which people identify themselves as members of a particular class with specific political goals. In his discussion of elites and the ruling class, Rex has further explored the links between economic and political factors in the formation of classes as conflict groups (Rex, 1974a, 1974b).

Rex has also looked at nation states as conflict groups, demonstrating the close relationship between political and cultural factors in conflict. The global system of the modern world, he argues, is a system of nation states in which a particular balance of power has been established. This is organized through alliances and through satellite/client relations, and it structures international economic, political and cultural relations. International conflict may take the relatively peaceful form of diplomacy, the overt form of warfare or any of a number of intermediate forms, including the balance of nuclear threats that characterized East–West relations from the 1940s to the 1990s. The 'nations' that are associated with particular nation states are seen by Rex in the context of the wider issue of *ethnic* conflict groups. 'Primordial' feelings of ethnic identity and solidarity, rooted in language, kinship, religion and common history, and in a sense of place and community, may be mobilized to form ideas of nationhood:

> Nations ... only exist to the extent to which they have been mobilised. The entity, the nation, is something which is posited and brought into being by ideologists (Rex, 1981: 83).

In many situations, however, ethnic solidarities are not expressed in national-ist ideas but lead, instead, to the formation of ethnic group conflicts *within* nations. Ethnic conflicts are not seen as purely 'cultural' processes, but as conflicts in which cultural, political and economic factors intertwine to shape the struggles of groups. Rex has seen 'race relations' situations in precisely these terms (Rex, 1970; Rex and Moore, 1969).

Rex's analysis of conflict group formation in relation to the spheres of economics, politics and values has suggested a fruitful way in which the analyses of conflict and collective agency can be pursued. He has shown how conflict groups that originate within the economic sphere can be understood as 'classes', conflict groups that originate within the political sphere can be seen as states and elites, and he has analysed ethnic groups as one type of conflict group that originates within the cultural sphere of values. He has also shown how each of these types of conflict group must be seen in terms of the interdependence of economic, political and cultural processes. His analysis must, however, be judged as failing to incorporate gender relations. The division of societies along lines of gender and the differential valuation of men and women is a fundamental feature of the cultural sphere, and must be seen as a fundamental element in social stratification and in conflict group formation.[13] Rex would recognize this fact, and he makes no pretence that his discussion of stratification and the spheres of action exhausts all that can be said on the subject. He would, however, correctly insist that the underlying model of conflict group formation is a truly general and all-embracing ana-lytical theory, and that it must figure as a central element in the development of social theory.

PROBLEMS OF COLLECTIVE AGENCY

Both Dahrendorf and Rex have used the Marxian distinction between collectivities that exist 'in-themselves' and active, struggling groups that exist 'for-themselves' by virtue of their consciousness and organization. Their use of this distinction has, however, carried over an ambiguity from the original Marxian formulation. This ambiguity concerns the question of whether both collectivities (quasi-groups) and interest groups can be considered as *agents* of social action. Collectivities, in the sense that I am using that word, are systems of action with demographically defined boundaries and whose conditions of existence generate certain common orientations and concerns among their members. Social classes are collectivities in this sense (Scott, 1994b). Collective agents are those groups and collectivities that have deci-sion-making and leadership structures that make them capable of unified collective action.

While the case of organized interest groups and their struggles seems a clear-cut case of collective agency, this is by no means clear for quasi-groups as they lack a formal structure of leadership and decision-making. In the Marxist tradition itself collective agency is ascribed to trades unions and political parties as aspects of the organized class-for-itself, but also to classes as elements in the mode of production. The discussion of collective agency in Chapters 3 and 4 has shown how difficult it is to apply the idea of collective agency to anything other than organizations and small groups, but the problem of quasi-groups as collective agents has not properly been addressed by mainstream conflict theorists themselves.

One of the strongest arguments in favour of the idea of collectivities as agents comes from the work of the French theorist Alain Touraine on social action. Touraine has returned to an almost Hegelian position, emphasizing what he calls the 'historical subject' as the transformative agency in social change. The meanings and values that are embodied in individual action, he argues, are not the creations of the acting individuals themselves, but are the products of the collectivities of which they are members. The true authors of social change, then, are the collectivities and not the individuals or groups that merely carry forward the values of the collectivities. The crucial collectivities in a society are its social classes, whose positions are defined by the structure of a particular mode of production and that must be seen as participants in a wider 'social movement' that expresses the logic of a particular class as a historical subject. A social movement, as an all-embracing collectivity, embodies the collective agency of a historical subject (Touraine, 1964, 1965, 1981).

This can be illustrated in the case of the working class and the labour movement. According to Touraine, individual workers and their work place struggles, trades union bargaining over wages, and socialist political parties and their programmes of social transformation can all be seen as participants in a 'labour movement' that expresses the historical role of the working class. The working class is a historical subject that makes itself felt through the actions that constitute the labour movement.

Touraine, then, would cast the arguments of Rex and Dahrendorf in a much wider framework of collective agency. He holds that we must not reduce the analysis of conflict groups to the mere interplay of organized interest groups. Conflict groups must be seen as the core elements in social movements that give expression to class relations.

Touraine's position remains, however, highly metaphysical, as he does not demonstrate any sense in which it is legitimate to extend the idea of agency from interest groups to collectivities, let alone from collectivities to 'historical subjects'. Many of those who have followed his suggestions have, nevertheless, set out an important research programme that points the way forward for a broader framework of conflict analysis. This work has centred on the argument that modern societies have undergone a fundamental transformation and that, in consequence, social classes are no longer the principal collective agents. Instead of focusing its attention on the labour movement and its struggles with organized capital, they argue, sociology must concern itself with the 'new social movements' that are such a striking feature of contemporary politics: the women's movement, the gay movement, the black movement, the ecological movement, the peace movement and other new social movements that express the cultural concerns of a 'post-industrial', or even 'post-modern' society.

Klaus Eder (1993) has recently crystallized these concerns.[14] Eder rejects the idea of the 'historical subject' as having no contemporary relevance. The concept reflects the specific features of the 18th and 19th century discourse on progress and historical development that influenced Marx and the early conflict theorists. Instead, Eder seeks to formulate a theory of collective agency that recognizes the mediation of class relations through a complex set of social determinants that give rise to a diversity of 'social movements'. Collective actors, for Eder, are of three types: *groups* that emerge from face-to-face interaction, *organizations* that involve more extended networks of relations and a 'formal' structure, and *movements* that act on the societal level.[15]

Collective actors arise when the participants in collective action define boundaries around their actions and establish a reproducible identity for their bounded action. Once established in this way, collective actors may become agents of social action and are able to restructure themselves through collective learning processes. Explanation of the formation of groups, Eder argues, has been the principal achievement of symbolic interactionist and rational choice theories, as these have found it difficult to advance beyond the interactional level that results from a similarity in motivation among individuals.[16] Explaining the formation of organizations, on the other hand, Eder sees as being the achievement of 'resource mobilization' theorists in their studies of formal organizations (Zald and McCarthy, 1979, 1987; see also Perrucci and Potter, 1989).[17] To this can be added the works of Dahrendorf, Coser and Rex that have been discussed in this Chapter and that concentrate their attention on the formation of 'organizations' for conflict and struggle.

Social movements have, so far, been the least well theorized of the collective actors distinguished by Eder, and he fails to develop a comprehensive explanation of the formation of social movements capable of action on a societal scale. An early attempt to advance such theorization was undertaken by Castells (1970, 1976, 1977), who saw the societal focus of social movements in terms of their orientation towards structural change in a mode of production or apparatus of domination. Castells saw urban social movements as articulating class divisions in and through a number of specifically 'urban' issues that allow the social movement to draw support from beyond the bounds of a single social class. Despite his recognition that specific organizations give voice to the concerns of individuals and that social movements comprise a number of conjoined organizations, Castells does not show how it is possible to move from the organizational level to a conception of a social movement as a collective actor.

Such research is beginning to address the questions that must be resolved if conflict theory is to be broadened into a larger theory of collective agency. Two questions seem to be critical. First is the question of whether individuals or organized groups can be seen as 'representatives' of social movements and other collectivities. In what sense, for example, is it possible to say that a particular trades union 'represents' the interests of the working class, or that a particular feminist group 'represents' the interests of women? Second is the question of whether social movements, as large-scale collectivities, can in fact be seen as collective agents in the strict sense, given that they have no formal structure, no centralized decision-making apparatus, and no acknowledged leadership. Social movements are clearly *not* collective agents in the same sense as 'interest groups' and other formal organizations, but they can be considered as foci of action; and there does seem to be a sense in which it is possible to link the 'objective interests' of collectivities with the 'subjective interests' of individuals and groups.

On this basis, a social movement can most usefully be seen as a network of groups and organizations that are unified by a shared conception that they *do* form part of a single 'movement' with specific goals, by deliberate attempts on the part of the groups and organizations to ally themselves with one another through joint action, coalitions, umbrella groups and so forth, and by shared beliefs and ideals among the members of the groups and organizations.[18] Such a definition recognizes that 'groups' are collective actors on the interactional level, 'organizations' are collective actors on a more distanciated level of social relations, and that 'social movements' are networks of collective actors that may, under certain circumstances, be able to forge themselves into a single large-scale organization. The social movement as such is not a collective actor. Clearly, many issues remain to be resolved, and a full resolution of these issues awaits further theoretical research.[19] One thing seems certain: it does not yet seem plausible to recognize collectivities such as social classes, ethnic groups or gender categories as collective actors *per* se, although it is entirely plausible to discuss the 'emergent properties' of these collectivities and to analyse the groups, organizations and social movements with which they are associated.

Conflict theory has produced a powerful analysis of social integration in terms of collective agency, and Rex, at least, has shown how the conflict of groups and organizations involves issues of system integration. This work has also shown, however, that the very formation of conflict groups *presupposes* the existence of a structural framework in which groups are located and that their actions reproduce or transform. Conflict theory, then, points beyond its own concerns and towards the need for a more comprehensive understanding of the structural aspects of social systems.

NOTES

1. The critique of Marx can be found in Dahrendorf (1957), Chapters I to IV.
2. There is a significant confusion in Dahrendorf's argument on this point. The state and the established church correspond closely to his idea of an 'imperatively coordinated association', a social grouping that is structured by and for the exercise of authority. Political parties and trades unions, on the other hand, are closer to the 'interest groups' or social organizations that he later defines as arising from within the authority relations of associations. In practice, Dahrendorf's work emphasizes only states, churches and business enterprises as the bases of conflicts of authority.
3. I am not here concerned with the accuracy of his interpretation of Simmel; I am simply concerned with Coser's own position.
4. Coser (1974) has undertaken a separate analysis of the nature of closed and exclusive groups with a high degree of solidarity.
5. This view has been formulated into conflict theories of crime by Quinney (1970) and Turk (1969). While Quinney draws on an explicitly pluralistic model, Turk attempts to derive his argument from Dahrendorf's dichotomous model. Aho (1975) has claimed that Bentley (1908) is an early expression of the conversion of conflict theory into pluralism.
6. Rex grounds his analysis of social relations in concepts of social action, but he makes it clear that the fundamental concept is that of the social relation.
7. Where Parsons recognized the existence of the 'fully institutionalized' and the 'anomic' social relations, and Dahrendorf recognized the 'fully institutionalized' and the 'coercive', Rex has combined these into a three-fold typology of consensus, anomie and conflict.
8. Various formulations of this general position can be found, but see in particular Rex (1974b: 74–5).
9. Lockwood (1964) incorrectly holds that Rex fails to consider the question of system integration. Although Rex does not consider the problem at great length, it is recognized as a central element in sociological analysis.
10. Rex derives these three 'problem areas' from the structural functionalist work of Kingsley Davis (1955: Chapter 5; see Rex, 1961: 90–91). In view of this, it is not surprising that Rex's three spheres of action correspond rather closely to the three structurally differentiated systems of action that were identified in Parsons's work: the economy, the polity and the societal community.
11. On this point compare Dahrendorf's account of the technical, political and social conditions of organization.
12. Rex points to Hoggart's (1957) work on this point.
13. Some of the principal issues surrounding this question have been explored in the various contributions to Crompton and Mann (1986).
14. Unfortunately, Eder's book is very poorly written and his arguments are frequently unclear.
15. I have slightly reformulated Eder's claims in order to clarify what I take to be his intended argument.
16. The conflict theory of Collins (1975, 1981) may form an important link here. Collins has

focused on conflict relations in everyday life, drawing especially on Goffman's work, in an attempt to build up from the interactional to the organizational level.

17. I have discussed some aspects of this in the sphere of business relations in Scott (1991a). The distinctions in that paper among 'people', 'enterprises' and 'sectors' as units of analysis has an affinity with Eder's typology of groups, organizations and movements.
18. This definition is based on the argument of Diani (1992).
19. Collins (1990) has suggested that the large-scale historical studies of Mann (1986) and Tilly (1978) point the direction in which conflict theory must move.

6.   Structure, function and system

Structural functionalism, the sociological orthodoxy of the 1940s and 1950s, has often been identified with the work of Talcott Parsons and, indeed, as a product of his intellectual imagination. Parsons was, of course, a major influence on the development of structural functionalism, but his theoretical work was itself shaped by independent and autonomous developments in structural functionalist theory. The 'organismic' model from which many structural functionalist ideas were derived had a very long history in sociology, but it was the revolution in social anthropology of the 1920s and 1930s that led to its systematization as a distinct set of theoretical ideas (Jarvie, 1964).

Malinowski advocated the 'functional' analysis of culture, while Radcliffe Brown espoused a 'structural' version of functionalism that owed much to his reading of Durkheim.[1] Radcliffe Brown set out the idea of societies as organized structures whose parts were connected through 'functional' relations, and his idea became the cornerstone of subsequent anthropology. It was this form of structural functionalist theory that, during the 1940s, influenced Parsons and, independently, a number of other American sociologists. The mainstream of structural functionalism in sociology developed as a joint result of this early structural functionalism and the evolving framework of Parsonian theory.

The orthodoxy of the 1950s was a looser form of structural functionalism than the scheme that Parsons and his co-workers were formulating. In the hands of Merton, Davis, Levy and other leading sociologists it rapidly became the *lingua franca* of international sociology. It never crystallized into a closed doctrine and was beset by many internal differences. Indeed, there was not even a complete consensus about the meaning of the key word 'function'. In its most general sense, 'function' referred to the contribution or connection that one part of a society had with another, but more philosophically inclined writers sought to give it a precise meaning by drawing on mathematics or biology. It was through these debates and, again, through the influence of Parsons, that 'system' concepts came to figure more prominently in sociological discourse. Societies were seen as systems of mutually dependent parts that are combined into a whole with emergent properties that were irreducible to the properties of the constituent parts.

With the demise of Parsons's dominance and the rise of exchange theory, symbolic interactionism, phenomenological sociology and forms of conflict theory, structural functionalism went into decline. Its decline was, however, matched by the growing significance throughout the social sciences of general systems theory, with its ideas of 'open systems' operating in complex environments. A number of sociologists undertook work in this broad 'systems' framework that continued many of the themes of structural functionalism.

During the 1980s, systems theories of a more radical kind began to develop as many sociologists began to draw on the critical perspectives of the 1960s and 1970s in order to undertake a reconstruction of Parsonian theory. Niklas Luhmann in Germany and Jeffrey Alexander in the United States have been the leading figures in this movement of thought, which Alexander has even named 'neo-functionalism'. Structural functionalist ideas are, once more, in vogue, and they are beginning to have a significant influence on other theoretical approaches.

FUNCTION, CAUSE AND PURPOSE

Radcliffe Brown (1952) and Malinowski (1944) rejected the evolutionary conceptions and speculative historical reconstructions that were undertaken by their predecessors, and constructed 'functionalist' frameworks of analysis to handle their fieldwork observations. Small-scale village and tribal societies could be studied as self-sustaining 'wholes', with their various elements working together in a harmonious way. Their ideas were influential among American anthropologists who were involved in similar forms of ethnographic fieldwork. When Radcliffe Brown spent some time at the University of Chicago, he influenced the sociological studies of small American cities that were being undertaken by Lloyd Warner and his colleagues (1941, 1942), and the success of these studies helped to popularize functionalist ideas among sociologists. Parsons had encountered Malinowski during an early visit to London, but it was some time before he began to see structural functionalism as an integral part of his theoretical programme. It was largely through the work of Merton (1936, 1949) that functionalist ideas came to play a significant part in sociological studies, as Merton tried to remove those elements of functionalism that were specific to isolated, small-scale societies and to reconstruct a defensible functionalist method for sociology. During the 1940s, functionalist ideas became the basis of the leading sociology textbook of the day (Davis, 1948), and the author of this text subsequently proclaimed that there was no other way of doing sociology (Davis, 1959).

Merton rejected the tightly integrated view of society that generally formed a part of anthropological functionalism, and he outlined a looser conception of functional analysis. The concept of 'function' was seen as a way of conceptualizing the relationship between the actions and institutions that comprised the elements of societies. These were seen in terms of their 'functions' in maintaining or altering one another or the overall structure of a society. It is in this sense that 'function' and 'structure' have been such closely linked concepts that the functionalist position has also been termed 'structural functionalism'.

According to Merton, the function of an action or pattern of action is the *consequence* that it has for other activities in the social system of which it is a part. These consequences are often, though not always, *unintended*. For this reason, Merton argues, it is important to distinguish between the subjective meaning (the 'purpose') of an action and its objective consequence (its 'function'). People may intend to do one thing but may produce actions whose unintended repercussions result in a quite different outcome. Consequences – functions – of actions can be analysed quite independently of purposes.

Merton also held that the analysis of the consequences of actions was an empirical matter. Sociologists must not assume that all actions will have positive, 'beneficial' consequences for other activities, nor must they assume that consequences will all work in the same direction and produce a high level of 'integration' in the social system. The degree of functional integration in a society is always a matter for empirical investigation. To clarify these points, he distinguishes 'functional', 'eufunctional' and 'dysfunctional' consequences. Some actions will have no consequences for a particular institution or for the larger system, and these Merton terms 'eufunctional' or non-functional. Those actions that are consequential for the larger system have consequences that reinforce its structure or that undermine it. The former are the 'functional' and the latter are the 'dysfunctional' elements of the system.

The concept of function has generally been linked to the idea of the persistence or survival of a system, and Merton goes on to argue that an activity is functional, rather than dysfunctional, when its consequences help the 'adaptation', 'adjustment', or 'survival' of a system. The idea of the survival of a system is associated with the claim that systems have definite 'requirements' or 'needs'. Radcliffe Brown held that the concept of 'need' could be seen as referring to the 'necessary conditions of existence' for particular social structures and activities. He argued that the survival of the basic structures that comprised a society required the performance of those specific activities that were able to maintain these structures. This idea led to the search for 'functional prerequisites'. These were seen as being the fundamental requirements for any form of sustained social life: all societies depend upon biological reproduction, the provision of food and shelter, a degree of socialization and so on. If a list of such prerequisites could be produced, sociologists would know the basic survival requirements of any society and could go on to show *how* these requirements were actually being met in a particular society (Aberle *et al.*, 1950; Levy, 1966). Parsons, for example, regarded his four-fold functional scheme in just this way. In addition to identifying these basic requirements of social life, structural functionalists held that it was possible to identify the specific requirements for any particular form of social life. The survival of a particular form of government, for example, may depend upon the continuing availability of tax revenue from the economic units of the society. Showing how an activity contributed to the maintenance of the structure of the society or institution was a demonstration of its 'function'. By showing the existence of a requirement, it was held, the existence of the activity that sustained it was thereby explained.

Giddens (1976c) has argued against the idea of system 'needs', on the grounds that this involves an illegitimate recourse to the idea of system 'wants' or 'interests'. This does not, however, seem to be an essential feature of the idea of system requirements. Self-regulating mechanisms in biology, for example, involve no such reference to wants or interests. There is, of course, a sense in which an organism may be said to have an interest in its own survival: a dog, for example, has an 'interest', a definite stake, in having the level of its blood sugar regulated. But this is a very special sense of the word 'interest'. It is not a conscious, or even an unconscious, want or need; nor need the dog recognize that it requires such regulation if it is to survive.[2] Giddens puts forward no arguments to substantiate his view that social systems do not have 'interests' in exactly this sense. He is correct, however, to see the concept of 'interest' as somewhat misleading in this context. Where he is wrong is in his claim that it is completely illegitimate to talk of system needs or prerequisites in this general sense.

A system need is a *logical* requirement. It involves a recognition by the scientist of those conditions upon which the present state of the system depends for its survival – its 'necessary conditions of existence'. To refer to a system need is to claim that *if* a system is to survive, *then* it requires that certain processes occur. It is perfectly legitimate to say that wherever a system has actually survived, then these conditions must actually have been met in some way. It is illegitimate, in both biology and sociology, to assert that a system will *necessarily* be able to secure its own conditions of survival.

Giddens goes some way towards recognizing this, but he argues that such claims are frequently tautological. To say, for example, that a society requires a language may be to invoke a particular definition of society: the 'condition' is part of the definition. Even where tautology is avoided, however, Giddens holds that systems theorists have identified 'adaptive advantages' rather than essential 'prerequisites'. Here Giddens is, perhaps, correct. A society that actually survives major changes in its environment must have evolved some particular pattern of activities that has enhanced its chances of survival. It does not, however, seem wrong to hold that these are 'prerequisites' of survival.[3]

Merton did not deny that it was possible to identify the functional require-ments of a system, but he rejected the idea that they could be used to explain activities. Needs and requirements, defined in terms of the facilitation of the survival capacity of the system, are the point of reference from which *alter-native* ways of meeting these requirements can be identified. It is possible, he holds, to identify the survival requirements of any social system, and sociolo-gists may then search for any activities that might currently be meeting them. It is a mistake, he argues, to assume that only one kind of activity can fulfil a particular requirement, and it is, equally, a mistake to assume that any re-quirements will necessarily be met. There are always 'functional alternatives' – different and equally appropriate ways of meeting any particular need – and in any particular situation none of those alternatives may actually be present. No activity may be currently meeting the identified requirement, and in these circumstances the system might be expected, sooner or later, to change or to disintegrate.

This point of view involves a fundamental shift in the approach to func-tional explanation. If it is the case that there is no necessity that requirements be met, then they can play no role in the explanation of those activities that may, nevertheless, be performing a function. The fact that economic units are producing the tax revenue that is required by a government cannot be ex-plained by the government's requirement itself. Merton is here seeking to avoid the problem of 'teleology' in functional explanation. He holds that requirements can play an explanatory role only if it is assumed that societies have 'goals' and that they strive consciously to achieve them by calling forth those activities that will meet their needs. Merton rejects such a reified view, holding that only individuals can have purposes. Whole societies do not have goals or purposes. This conclusion, however, leaves Merton unable to defend the idea of functional *explanation*, as opposed to functional description.

The logical problems of functional explanation at which Merton arrived were explored in methodological papers by Nagel (1956) and Hempel (1959), who tried to show that functional explanation need not be seen as any differ-ent from causal explanation. Functional explanations *are* causal explanations of a particular type. If religious activity in a particular society actually has the function of increasing social solidarity, then this can be regarded as an explanation of the existence of the level of solidarity that is found in that society. But the existence of the functional consequence (social solidarity) does not give an explanation for the existence of the religious activity itself. Nagel and Hempel argue that activities can be explained by their conse-quences only under certain definite conditions. The demonstration of a func-tional connection between religion and social solidarity can be regarded as an explanation of the religious activity only if the social solidarity that results from it has effects which themselves promote religious practice. The solidarity that is generated by religion, for example, might be shown to encourage, among other things, higher levels of communal participation in a shared religion. In these circumstances, solidarity has the consequence (the function) of promoting religion, and so religious practice can be explained by the solidarity. Functional *explanation*, then, is that particular kind of causal explanation that occurs where there are 'causal loops' – chains of reciprocal causation (Cohen, 1968: 47–51). These kinds of causal relations are shown in Figure 6.1

Figure 6.1   A simple causal loop

Nagel's and Hempel's view that functional explanation is linked to the idea of causal loops converges with developments in general systems theory, where circular causation, 'feedback' processes and 'self-regulation' have figured centrally. General systems theory sees systems as characterized by self-regulating, or 'homeostatic', processes in which causal loops can ensure that the consequences of an activity 'feed back' into the activity itself. The causal connection that loops back from social solidarity to religion in Figure 6.1 is a simple example of such a feedback loop. General systems theorists have taken the concept of 'homeostatic', system-maintaining processes into the more general concept of 'cybernetic' processes. From this point of view, there may be system-changing as well as system-maintaining processes.[4]

Figure 6.2 shows two cybernetic models, one sociological and the other non-sociological. The first model is that of a simple thermostatically controlled central heating system. A heater operates (functions) to increase the temperature in a room. When the thermostat senses that the temperature is higher than is required, it switches off the heater. The consequence of the lack of heating is that the temperature falls. When the thermostat senses that the temperature is lower than is required, it switches on the heater. This increases the temperature, and so the process continues. In this mechanical system, the room temperature is maintained between the minimum and maximum levels set on the thermostat.

This example might not appear to have any relevance to sociology, but consider the second model in Figure 6.2, which shows a revised and more realistic version of the model shown in Figure 6.1. Religious observance increases the level of social solidarity in the society. When social solidarity is

(a) A domestic heating system

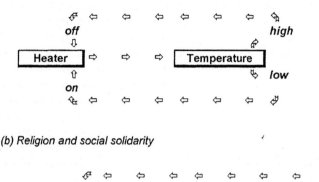

(b) Religion and social solidarity

Figure 6.2   Complex causal loops

too great and individual autonomy is stifled, the level of religious observance is reduced. The consequence of reduced religious observance is that the level of social solidarity declines. When social solidarity falls too low and individual, egoistic impulses threaten the survival of the society, religious observance is increased, and so the process continues. In this social system the level of social solidarity is maintained at a 'normal' level.[5]

There would, then, appear to be a precise logical parallel between the cybernetic processes of a mechanical system and those of a social system. Matters are not, however, this straightforward. In the case of the mechanical system, a specific control mechanism – a thermostat – was present. A thermostat contains a thermometer and a switching mechanism and, once it has been set, it will monitor and control the temperature of the room. No similar control mechanism was mentioned for the social system. Indeed, it is difficult to imagine what kind of mechanism could measure social solidarity and adjust the level of religious observance.

Recognition of this has led Giddens to argue that functional, cybernetic processes occur in social systems only where purposive, intentional action is involved. This is apparent even in the case of the mechanical system: it is assumed that a human agent has set the required temperature. In the case of a social system, human intervention is even more obvious. This point should not, however, be overemphasized. In the biological world, for example, there are control mechanisms that exist and operate quite independently of human intervention. The survival of an animal occurs because of a 'blind', 'unintended' process of adjustment that takes place through its interlocking organs. At no point is it necessary to invoke any conscious action on the part of the animal.[6] It is not impossible to imagine such mechanisms existing in the social world. What is undoubtedly the case, however, is that processes of adjustment in social systems can work only in and through the actions of individuals and groups – they depend upon consciousness and deliberate human agency at crucial points. Actors may not 'intend' the survival of a social system or even have any recognition of the wider implications of what is going on, but they must monitor their situation and act on the basis of this monitoring. This occurs, argues Giddens, through self-conscious *reflexive* monitoring.

It is not necessary, however, that actors engage in purposive action that is directly aimed at altering the circumstances under which they are acting. The functional relations may be the *unintended* consequences of actions undertaken with only a partial awareness of the immediate circumstances. High levels of social solidarity may, for example, lead people to engage in a wider range of communal and co-operative activities than previously, leaving them with less time for church-going. The increase in social solidarity, then, results in reduced levels of religious observance, despite the fact that actors may have little awareness of either the state of social solidarity or the level of religiosity.

It is clear, nevertheless, that such processes cannot occur without the existence of conscious, purposive actors, and these actors may often act on the basis of an intention to modify their own social circumstances. This can be illustrated by considering the model in Figure 6.3. In this model, the level of policing is seen as influencing the amount of crime in a society. When the level of crime becomes too high, the level of policing is increased. This increased policing results in a fall in the amount of crime. If the level of crime is very low, then the level of policing will be reduced. Reduced policing results in a rise in the amount of crime, and so the process continues. In

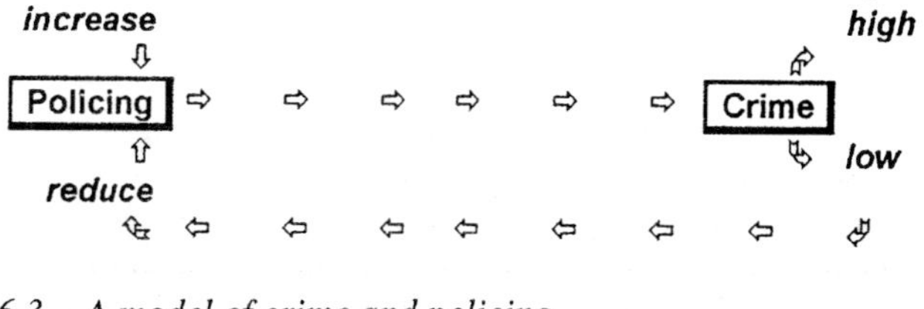

Figure 6.3   A model of crime and policing

this model the control mechanisms involve the conscious, purposive activity of politicians and chief constables and others who monitor the level of crime. When crime is high, for example, they may feel that 'something must be done': politicians will grant more money to the police and chief constables will intensify the policing of particular areas. When crime is low, politicians may feel that fewer police are needed because the 'war against crime' has been won.

Studies in the sociology of deviance have shown that the relationship between crime and policing is more complex than depicted in this simple model: citizens and criminals also monitor the levels of policing and crime, the mass media play a role through 'amplification' processes (themselves cybernetic processes) and so on.[7] The central point, however, is clear. It is sensible to construct 'functional' or 'cybernetic' models of social processes, but only where reflexive monitoring by purposive human actors enters into the suggested control mechanisms.

SYSTEMS, TRANSFORMATION AND DIFFERENTIATION

I have already referred to the influence of ideas from general systems theory on Parsons and other functionalist writers. Until the 1980s, however, few sociologists followed Parsons's lead in building a sociological theory around the idea of open systems and their environments. One of the few earlier writers was Walter Buckley (1967), who constructed a powerful theory that sought to integrate cybernetic ideas with an emphasis on cultural meanings that owed much to symbolic interactionism (see also Burns *et al.*, 1985a, 1985b). In Germany, Niklas Luhmann (1964, 1965; Luhmann and Habermas, 1971) worked in a similar direction, seeking to ally systems theory with hermeneutic analyses of cultural meanings, but his work did not appear in English for many years. During the 1980s there was a renewed interest in systems ideas as a number of theorists began to reconstruct Parsonian theory and to convert it into a more adequate research programme. Early intimations of this 'neofunctionalism' can be found in the work of Jeffrey Alexander (1982–3), whose *Theoretical Logic in Sociology* paralleled the attempt of Parsons (1937) in *The Structure of Social Action* to reconstruct the heritage of 19th century sociology. Alexander was in broad sympathy with Parsons's project, but he produced very different readings of Weber and Durkheim, and he considered Marx a more important precursor than Pareto. Alexander's work culminated in a critique of Parsons himself.[8]

The work of Alexander had been inspired by the important work that Eisenstadt had undertaken from within functionalism itself. At the same time that writers such as Coser, Dahrendorf and Rex had been developing their ideas on conflict theory, Eisenstadt had attempted to incorporate a conflict dimension into mainstream functionalism. His *Political Systems of Empires* (1963) used a materialist interpretation of Weber – similar to that of Bendix (1963) – to complement the normative focus of Parsonian theory. Power, interests and conflict became central mechanisms in the functional analysis of aspects of social systems that Eisenstadt produced during the 1970s (Eisenstadt, 1973, 1978).

Alexander's book served as a rallying point for others who wanted to develop rather than to reject the functionalist approach, and it pointed in a similar direction to the works of Buckley and Luhmann. Some of these new works were brought together by Alexander (1985) and by Colomy (1990) and were given the name 'neofunctionalist' in the mid-1980s.[9] The growth of this work coincided with more critical reconsiderations of Parsons that tried, nevertheless, to take his theoretical project seriously (Holton and Turner, 1986; Robertson and Turner, 1991).[10] Alexander (1988) himself produced a systematic statement of this neofunctionalism.

The key ideas in Buckley's work set the scene for these more recent theoretical developments. He starts out by clarifying the distinctions between physical, biological and social systems. These are not based in differences of substance, the various systems are not composed of different kinds of 'things'. Societies are, in a fundamental sense, composed only of biological individuals, and these are, in turn, composed only of particular chemical molecules. They are, however, concerned with different forms of organization. What gives a distinct object of analysis to the biological sciences is the fact that the chemicals that comprise human beings and other animals are organized in such a way that a new and distinctively 'organic' level of reality is produced. Similarly, social phenomena represent the organization of human beings in such a way that a 'social' reality is produced. These various types of organization are characterized by different levels of *complexity*.

In all systems, the links between system parts involve both 'energy' and 'information'. In mechanical systems it is energy exchange that is the dominant element, while in social systems it is information exchange that is dominant. The parts of a social system are linked through communicative processes of information exchange. This 'information' depends on some physical flow of energy (the electricity, for example, through which the television works and the human energy that is involved in the effort of talking), but the content of the information is independent of its base. Thus the same message can be conveyed through a number of different channels of communication: a person can speak directly to someone, who telephones someone else, who writes a script for a television show, that is videotaped and so on. Information conveys what Weber termed 'meaning', and Buckley sees social systems as structures of meaningful relations.

Buckley's central concept is *morphogenesis*, the process through which structures are not merely reproduced but also transformed. Change is an ever present possibility in social systems. The communication of meaning is central to the production and reproduction of definitions of the situation and, therefore, of structures that, by virtue of their 'negotiated' reality, are themselves subject to transformation. Social systems are 'open systems' within complex and uncertain environments, the systems being shaped by processes of 'uncertainty reduction'. Systems develop an internal structure in response to the constraints that are imposed by their environments. These environmental factors are constantly changing, in uncertain ways, and so systems that persist over time must have evolved mechanisms for handling these sources of strain and disruption. Through the selective response to its environment, a system is shaped over time. This is the nature of morphogenesis.

The method that Buckley uses to analyse social systems involves the construction of models in the form of flowcharts such as those in Figure 6.1. The causal interdependencies between the structural parts of a system are represented by arrowed flow lines, which are able to show such things as feedback paths and causal loops. Buckley (1967) outlines a number of extended examples, and Blalock (1970) has shown how such models can be formalized and analysed in mathematical terms. The possibility for this kind of formalization is somewhat limited in sociology, where quantitative measures are not always possible. While many areas of macro-economics might be modelled in a quantitative way, applications in sociology have been limited to such areas as occupational mobility (Blau and Duncan, 1967).

A related view of social systems has been set out by Luhmann, whose work developed as a critical debate with the ideas of Parsons. Luhmann (1977, 1979) contends that Parsons's work represents the most concerted attempt to move beyond the classic tradition in sociology, and it is necessary to carry through this project in a more satisfactory way. More specifically, he claims that Parsons failed to recognize that 'structural differentiation' takes analytical primacy over 'functional' differentiation.[11]

Socio-cultural evolution has led, argues Luhmann, to the structural differentiation of three levels of action: the *interactional*, the *organizational* and the *societal* levels (1975a, 1975b).[12] These have become relatively autonomous systems of action, each being subject to distinct mechanisms and processes and each following its own 'system laws'. The levels remain connected to one another by virtue of the fact that the larger and more 'impersonal' structures at the organizational and societal level are produced, reproduced and transformed in and through the everyday structures of face-to-face interaction. At the same time, however, the larger systems set the structural framework within which these interactions take place.[13] Many of the problems faced by differentiated societies arise from dislocations between these levels.

At the level of the societal system, Luhmann (1977) sees structural differentiation taking place in relation to functional problems. Distinct realms of action and structure have emerged in relation to such functional areas as economics, politics, religion, law, science, education and so on. The economic system, for example, includes those roles that are specialized in instrumental rationality and scarcity. The structures of the economy are organized around instrumental need satisfaction through rational market actions and the 'generalized medium' of money. The economic system in modern societies has, in turn, been internally differentiated into three sub-systems: 'markets' (concerned with distribution), 'firms' (concerned with production) and 'households' (concerned with consumption). On this basis, Luhmann (1970) reconceptualizes the subject matter of economic theory as the outcome of a long-term process of structural differentiation: the 'economy' emerges as a distinct system only under certain specific historical conditions.

Luhmann's (1968) political system is concerned with collectively binding decision-making. As a system, it generates 'power' – seen as analogous to money in the economy – and it produces certain distinctive regulative standards. The constituent sub-systems of the political system that have tended to become differentiated from one another in the modern period are the 'bureaucratic administration' (governments, ministries, parliament and the courts), 'party politics' (mechanisms of interest representation) and the 'public' (seen as tax-payers, voters, campaigners and so on, and not merely as undifferentiated 'citizens').

Luhmann's model of the societal system is, in the end, distinctly Parsonian. An institutionally undifferentiated societal system is seen as undergoing a historical process of structural differentiation in which specialized economic and political systems emerge, while the rest of the societal system remains more diffusely structured. Certain institutional areas of the societal system may be differentiated, but these do not seem to have the autonomy that characterizes the economic and the political systems.[14]

STRUCTURAL AUTONOMY AND SYSTEM INTEGRATION

Structural differentiation highlights a long-standing question in structural functional sociology: to what extent are the structural parts that make up a system actually integrated with one another? This problem of 'system integration' concerns the extent to which functional interchanges and feedback processes produce a tight correspondence between the various systems and their parts. In the works of many writers, especially those influenced by Parsons, this is not seen as a problem. The maintenance of the integrity of the system is seen as a fundamental pre-condition for social life. Critics of this assumption have produced compelling arguments in favour of treating system integration as a *problem*. Merton, for example, held that functional unity or integration must not be taken-for-granted.

Gouldner (1959) has argued that functional interchanges among the parts of a system involve varying degrees of 'reciprocity'. Much structural functional analysis, argued Gouldner, assumed that reciprocity would occur, but it is, in fact, a variable matter. Where the contribution of one part to another is not reciprocated, there will be a tendency for the relation to break down or change in some way unless there are 'compensating contributions' from elsewhere. Sociologists must investigate, rather than assume, the degree of reciprocity that characterizes functional interchanges: 'the notion of interdependence, so crucial to the concept of a system, needs to be taken as problematic rather than as given' (Gouldner, 1959: 203).

Systems, therefore, will show varying degrees of overall 'integration', because their parts have varying degrees of functional 'autonomy'. A system whose parts have a substantial autonomy from one another has a greater capacity for change than does a fully integrated system. Disruptions from inside or outside the system are less likely to lead to its complete collapse, as their effects – 'strains' and 'tensions' – can be localized and the system can undergo a structural differentiation and regrouping around the constituent parts (Gouldner, 1959: 214–17).[15]

Lockwood (1964) has pushed this argument one step further. In a highly sophisticated paper he has distinguished between 'social integration' and 'system integration' as specific levels of analysis. Social integration concerns the relations between the individuals and collectivities that act within a social system; system integration concerns the relations between the institutional and other parts of the system. The degree of integration or mal-integration that exists between the parts of a system is the crucial factor that underlies the pattern of order or conflict that exists in the relationships between individuals and groups.

The mistake made by many structural functionalists, argues Lockwood, has been to assume that there is a direct one-to-one relationship between these two levels. They have assumed, for example, that an integrated institutional pattern at the level of system integration would necessarily be expressed in consensus and cohesion between groups at the level of social integration. The work of the conflict theorists, he argues, has recaptured the autonomy of social integration by recognizing the existence of both order and conflict at this level. These theorists, however, have underemphasized the issue of system integration.

If social integration is to be seen in terms of the cohesion and consensus between the individuals and groups that comprise a particular social system, the integration of the 'parts' that make up the system are to be seen in terms similar to those described by Gouldner. Lockwood also points to parallels with Marx's analysis of the 'contradictions' that occur between the structural elements of social systems. Lockwood argues that the analysis of the material and normative aspects of group relations (social integration) that was produced by the conflict theorists must be complemented by an analysis of the material and normative aspects of system integration. Parsons's analysis of system integration, and that of the great bulk of structural functionalists, has been concerned almost exclusively with normative matters, and Lockwood characterizes the approach as 'normative functionalism'. This normative bias has been apparent from the very earliest days of systematic structural functionalism in the work of Radcliffe Brown.

Radcliffe Brown (1940, expanded in 1952) saw 'social structure' as an ordered arrangement of the parts of a society. These parts were the social positions that individuals occupied in their interactions with one another. These positions are uncovered through observation of the networks of interactions in which people are involved, the sociologist inferring, through a process of abstraction, the structural arrangement of the positions that it involves. If it is observed that Jack and Jill are involved in particular types of activity with one another, it might be inferred, for example, that they are acting towards one another in terms of an institutionally defined relationship of 'marriage'. The actual social relation between Jack and Jill is a marriage relation. But sociology is not concerned with particular individuals *per se*; it is concerned with the *general* features that are found in societies. If the actions of Jack and Jill are observed over a long period of time, along with the actions of Bill and Beth, David and Diana, and numerous other pairs of men and women, a structural form common to all the relations might be inferred. This structural form is a relation between *positions*: the structural relation of marriage involves the positions of 'husband' and 'wife'. The latter is an ordered arrangement that is stable and enduring in a society, both over time and across space. These ideas are summarized in Figure 6.4.

These ideas were extended in an influential essay by Merton (1957) that summarized the structural functionalist approach to positions and roles. People are seen as occupying numerous culturally defined positions – a family position, an occupational position and so on.[16] Each position is defined by the specific rights and obligations that are attached to it, and by the 'role' relationships in which its incumbents are involved with other people. The occupant of the occupational position of 'teacher' in American society, for example, is expected to interact with pupils, colleagues, head teachers, parents and others. Each relationship involves the enactment of a specific role, and Merton argues that each position can be seen as having an associated 'role set'. The role relationships are not actual networks of social relations, but are underly-

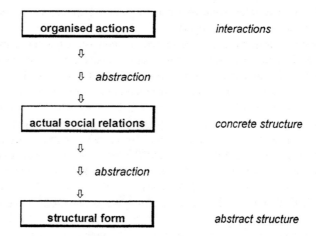

Figure 6.4   Social relations and structural forms

ing structural forms of relations. As structural forms they are patterns of normative expectations that define the character of the specific relationships.

This formulation by Merton captures the central features of structural analysis for the principal structural functionalist theorists. Social positions and their associated role sets are *normative* elements, as are the social institutions through which the positions and roles are organized. Lockwood argues that this is a peculiarly one-sided view of social structure. In addition to the normative aspects of social systems there are the 'material' aspects, and these barely figure in structural functionalism. The framework of functional analysis needs to be broadened out to a consideration of these material elements. People can be seen as occupying positions that are *not* culturally defined but are equally structural in character. Class positions, for example, are constituted by specific causal components in people's life chances, and while the market relations that comprise this causal component cannot be understood in isolation from cultural meanings, the structure of class positions in a society exists as a 'material' factor independent of its normative structure.

Marx's analysis of class conflict, for example, saw it as a phenomenon of social integration that was rooted in a lack of integration (a contradiction) at the system level. The changing state of system integration – the growing contradiction between the relations of production and the forces of production – results in increasing levels of class conflict. Lockwood is not, here, concerned with the empirical validity of this claim, but merely with the logic of the theoretical position that he sees in Marx. He attempts to generalize this idea by arguing that the overall structure of a social system can be understood in terms of the integration, or lack of integration, among its constitutive normative and material elements.

At its simplest, he argues, any society consists of a 'core institutional order' and a 'material substratum'. The core institutional order comprises such institutional patterns as its constitutional framework, its relations of production,[17] criminal law, religious beliefs and so on. The material substratum comprises its forces of production and means of organization and violence (Lockwood, 1956). The core institutional order and the material substratum together shape the distinct parts or elements that make up the structure of a society. What Lockwood calls the 'dominant political structure', for example, is one such cluster of normative (constitutional) and material (means of organization and violence) elements, and the 'production system' is another (comprising the normative relations of production and the material forces of production).

Analysis of system integration proceeds by identifying the structural parts that actually exist in a social system and then examining their internal (intra-system) and external (inter-system) integration. Analysis can then proceed to relate the observable state of group relations (social integration) to this understanding of the state of system integration. The examples that Lockwood gives of this approach are Weber's discussion of the contradiction between a patrimonial state (dominant political system) and a subsistence economy (production system), and a parallel suggestion of a contradiction between a totalitarian state and an industrial economy in the former Soviet Union. These are, however, very limited examples, and are no more than illustrative.[18]

Lockwood's distinction between social integration and system integration is fundamental to sociological analysis, as is his contention that system integration must be seen in relation to both normative and non-normative elements. If his own examples of such work are not completely convincing, this does not detract from his fundamental analytical points. Indeed, his work forms an essential part of any attempt to build on the contributions of structural functionalism, systems theory and neofunctionalism, and to link these with analyses of conflict and collective agency. In the following Chapter I will show that it is also central to understanding the significance of structuralist theories.

NOTES

1. 'Functionalism' and 'structural functionalism' are now used as virtually interchangeable words, though they originally signified the theoretical contrast between the ideas of Malinowski and of Radcliffe Brown.
2. But note the debate on power and interests which has discussed exactly these issues in

relation to the social sciences. See Lukes (1974) and the subsequent debate, all reprinted in Scott (1994b, Volume 2).

3. Runciman (1989) has recently argued for the return to such explicitly evolutionary ideas.
4. In the cybernetic view, the word 'function' becomes almost redundant, and is replaced by words referring to more specific system processes.
5. This discussion might be recognized as a rather free interpretation of a Durkheimian view of social solidarity.
6. In some cases, of course, such as eating to avoid hunger, it may be necessary to invoke instinctive mechanisms, but this is rather a different matter from asserting conscious intentionality on the part of the animal.
7. A particularly striking example is Young (1971). This whole area is reviewed in Downes and Rock (1988).
8. Similar arguments were put forward in the early 1980s by Münch (1981, 1982a, 1982b). Münch (1982b) has been translated as Münch (1982c, 1982d).
9. In some sources the word is 'neofunctionalism', in others it is 'neo-functionalism'.
10. Compare these with the very different style of Loubser *et al.* (1976), a last-ditch attempt to defend unreconstructed Parsonian systems theory. Other favourable views of Parsons can be found in Bourricaud (1977) and Leakey (1987), while a far more critical account is given in Savage (1981).
11. Luhmann also sees the functional categories (AGIL) and their input–output relations as being over-simple. He feels that Parsons's work correctly identified the general relevance of the temporal aspect of action (instrumental–consummatory) and the system–environment distinction (internal–external), but Parsons illegitimately combined these into an intellectually constraining set of boxes.
12. Compare the three levels identified by Eder (1993) that I discussed in Chapter 5.
13. This is Luhmann's formulation of what Giddens would later call the 'duality of structure'.
14. Other examples of societal sub-systems mentioned by Luhmann are the science system, organized around the generalized medium of 'truth', and the familial system organized around the generalized medium of 'love'. The latter is explored in Luhmann (1986).
15. Gouldner fails to make a satisfactory distinction between social integration and system integration, as defined by Lockwood (see below). Most of Gouldner's examples concern aspects of social integration.
16. Following Linton (1936), Merton misleadingly labels the positions as 'statuses'. This term is best restricted to the context of social stratification.
17. The relations of production have a strongly normative character, by virtue of their legal form as relations of ownership, but they go beyond the normative. The actual relations of production – relations of effective control over the means of production – may diverge from the purely legal relations. I have used Lockwood's argument, derived from the work of Renner (1904), to characterize relations of production in Scott (1990).
18. These arguments are applied to the Soviet case in Parkin (1972).

7.   Deep structures and causal mechanisms

While structural functionalist theorists recognized that actions are shaped by people's structural circumstances, some of their critics have claimed that these theorists have been insufficiently radical in their understanding of 'social structure'. This criticism, coming from 'structuralist' writers, holds that structural functionalists have limited their attention to relatively superficial features of social life – observable social relations, social organizations and social institutions – and have ignored the 'deep structures' that are responsible for them. These deep structures, it is held, have causal priority over the 'surface structures' studied by structural functionalism, and sociologists should focus their attention on the discovery of the deep structure of social life.

Structuralism has its roots in the linguistic analyses of Saussure, who held that speech patterns reflected the system of linguistic relations that speakers draw upon. Saussure set out a method for understanding the surface features of speech in terms of the deeper language structures that underlie it. The object of investigation for linguistics, he held, was not the flow of *speech* but the structure of the *language*. By analogy – so structuralists argue – the interactions and social relations into which people enter can be understood in relation to the deep structure of social relations that produce them. Just as there is a grammatical structure to speech, so there is also a 'grammar' to social interaction.

The work of Lévi-Strauss has been central to the structuralist tradition, but it gave birth to two quite distinct research programmes. In the work that he undertook on totemism and myth he remained very close to Saussure's original arguments. In this work he explored the structure of what Durkheim called 'collective representations', and he inspired a research programme into the analysis of cultural codes. In his work on kinship, on the other hand, and in the Marxist structuralism that it inspired, there was a move away from cultural codes *per se* and towards the *material* structures of social relations.

Lévi-Strauss' cultural analysis of collective representations contributed to, and was influenced by, structuralist approaches in literary and cultural studies that were concerned with the collective representations found in literature, television and film, and with the forms of knowledge found in such areas as science and medicine. His analysis of material structures of social relations, on the other hand, was taken up within Marxism, and came to be especially associated with the work of Althusser, Poulantzas and Wright. In the analysis of material structures of social relations, the linguistic ideas of Saussure are used in a fairly loose way. Only in the study of collective representations did the linguistic analogy become a central point of reference for the analysis of cultural signs and codes. In this Chapter I will concentrate on structuralist approaches to material structures, leaving the analysis of cultural structures to the following Chapter.

STRUCTURALIST METHODOLOGY

The methodological starting point for Lévi-Strauss is the Kantian separation of thought and reality. According to this position, the objects of the world that exist outside of human consciousness are unknowable: the only world that can truly be known is the world that is constituted through the words and concepts of a culture. The world that people experience is organized by the concepts and ideas of their culture. The meaning of a concept, then, is not determined by its correspondence with any concrete object external to thought. Concepts acquire their meaning from the cultural relations that specify the ways in which they can be used. These cultural relations are elements in systems that are separate from, and independent of, particular individual agents. People are born into a particular culture and they find its specific concepts already defined for them and available for them to learn and to use. It follows that the meaning of concepts is determined quite independently of the wishes, interests and intentions of individuals. If individuals wish to be understood they must use concepts in the ways defined by their culture. The analysis of social life, then, may begin and end with the analysis of cultural relations and need make no reference to individual consciousness and action. It is the structure of the cultural system that is all-important. It is in this sense that structuralism is seen as involving the 'disappearance of the subject' and as being in fundamental opposition to individualistic theories.

According to Lévi-Strauss, the culture of a society provides a set of concepts for the construction of a sense of reality. He pays particular attention to the systems of classification through which the world is divided into distinguishable items such as animal species, types of food, colours and social groups. The task of the anthropologist – and of the sociologist – is to study these systems of classification and the relations among them. In this way, it is possible to understand the articulation of systems of classification into cultural wholes.

Althusser (1965; Althusser and Balibar, 1968)[1] elaborated on the implications of this point of view for science itself. Scientific concepts, he argued, are elements in theoretical systems: they are 'theoretical objects' that can be used only in certain specific ways and that can be combined in various determinate ways to produce other, more complex theoretical objects. Individual concepts acquire their meanings only from their location within a 'problematic', the specific cluster of problems that is defined by the structure of the theoretical system. For this reason, he argues, concepts have an indeterminate relationship to the objects of the 'real' world that they nevertheless 'appropriate' in thought. What Althusser seems to mean by this is that scientific concepts are attempts to grasp and to understand the real world, but their actual relationship to this world can never be known because of the unbridgeable gulf that exists between concepts and reality. The objects of knowledge in a scientific investigation are *internal* to thought: they derive from the problematic and they are completely separate from any real objects that may exist in the external world. To lose sight of this crucial feature of scientific knowledge is to be guilty of what Althusser called 'empiricism'.

For both Lévi-Strauss and Althusser, then, the validity of scientific knowledge is not decided by any 'correspondence' between thought objects and real objects. Scientific investigation is concerned with the plausibility of the explanations that scientists construct, where this plausibility is assessed by the logical rigour and conceptual coherence of the explanation. Lévi-Strauss, trained in techniques of anthropological fieldwork, respected the role of empirical evidence in science, but his methodological reflections failed to explicate the relationship between theoretical concepts and real objects. Althusser, on the other hand, denied that there could be any knowable relationship between theory and empirical evidence. These methodological reflections have led many to conclude that Althusser's position is 'idealist' in character: in rejecting naive empiricism he also rejected any idea of a connection between thought and reality and confined his attention to that between thought and language (Pickvance, 1973). While Lévi-Strauss and Althusser may have denied that the label 'idealist' could apply to them, they did not provide an account of knowledge that would make this charge unwarranted.[2]

In applying these methodological ideas in specific sociological studies, Lévi-Strauss drew on Durkheim's work, albeit in a highly critical way. Durkheim's analysis of 'social morphology' was concerned with the structuring of social relations, and was seen as a basis on which actual structures of social relations arose. Collective representations are, in turn, a reflection of these social relations. Those who followed in Durkheim's own tradition pushed his structural analysis to deeper levels. Marcel Mauss (1925), for example, examined patterns of gift relations and disclosed an underlying structure of 'reciprocity' that he saw as a fundamental feature of social life. This kind of structural analysis complemented the Durkheimian analysis of collective representations, and Durkheimian writers sought to disclose not

only the structure of categories and relations embodied in these representations, but also the underlying structures of social relations. Radcliffe Brown's
work had also used Durkheim's arguments to explore the connections between actual social relations and their 'structural forms' (Radcliffe Brown,
1952).[3] Structural forms are the general and more pervasive relational patterns that characterize societies and that fit together to constitute a systematic
whole. The structural forms are, in a sense, the underlying structure.[4]

Lévi-Strauss was very critical of the direction in which Radcliffe Brown
had taken social anthropology. The structural functionalist concept of 'structure' did not go deep enough and failed to grasp the full complexity of social
life. Drawing on Saussure's linguistic ideas, Lévi-Strauss sought to enlarge
and to clarify the original Durkheimian approach. He accepted the strategy of
pushing the concept of 'structure' to a deeper level than that of the actual
pattern of social relations among people, and he aimed to uncover the underlying structures of both the collective representations and the material social
relations of a particular society. The geological metaphor of an 'underlying'
structure was very important for Lévi-Strauss, and it points to his awareness
of the existence of distinct levels of social reality. He allied this awareness,
however, with a Saussurian separation of concepts from reality. 'Structures'
are concepts, or 'models' as he generally termed them. They are not to be
seen as actual and empirically observable realities. Lévi-Strauss retained,
nevertheless, the belief that structures are, indeed, 'real' and that theoretical
models are means by which scientists can understand and explain the observable reality of actual social relations. Structural models grasp unobservable,
but real, structures, and these real structures are causally responsible for the
surface structures of actual relations and 'structural forms'.

The Saussurian strain towards idealism makes it difficult for Lévi-Strauss
to conceptualize properly the relationship between structures and reality. His
implicit assumption, albeit inadequately grounded in his methodology, is that
structures are idealized models – one might almost say 'ideal types' – of the
underlying principles on which a particular set of social relations actually
operates. 'Structures', then, are not the actual social relations of a society, nor
are they the obvious, 'surface' features of systems of classification and collective representation. They are the model forms that are embodied in these
phenomena.

STRUCTURES OF SOCIAL RELATIONS

Lévi-Strauss sees the aims of a structuralist analysis as to identify the elements from which social relations are built and to construct models of their
logically possible permutations. These models are to be grouped into a sys-

tem or 'table' of permutations. A system of permutations comprises a series of related structural models, each being a precise mathematical transformation of each of the others. A simple example can make this clear. The three elements A, B and C can be combined through positive or negative relations, such as those of love and hate, to generate, purely mathematically, a table of eight structures. There are eight, and only eight, ways of combining the three elements (see Figure 7.1).

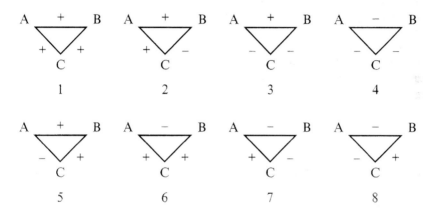

Figure 7.1   A table of structures

The search for logical, mathematical combinations of elements means that comparative research is an essential feature of social science, though the kinds of comparison made by Lévi-Strauss differ considerably from those made by mainstream structural functionalists. Lévi-Strauss holds that the anthropologist must use data from several societies as raw material for the construction of structural models. Comparison of four settings might, for example, uncover evidence that leads the researcher to construct models 1, 2, 3 and 4 in Figure 7.1. An investigation of the logical properties of these models, using algebraic and statistical techniques,[5] would show these models to be logical transformations of one another. It would also point to models 5, 6, 7 and 8 as further possible combinations. This logical analysis of data would suggest a search for social settings that might produce evidence to fit the further, mathematically derived, models. Two interpretations can be given to this procedure. The Althusserian position would imply that the 'evidence' is itself 'theoretical' in character and so the whole process is 'internal' to theory. A realist interpretation, of the kind suggested by Lévi-Strauss himself, would see the evidence as grasping certain features of the external world and the models as, therefore, explaining some of the variations observed. In this way, theory constructed from comparative research provides a guiding framework for further research.

Lévi-Strauss' earliest work on social relations had explored kinship relations in various tribal societies. To study kinship, anthropologists must study the categories that cultures provide for interpreting the facts of biological relatedness and the regulation of sexuality. The starting point for any investigation, therefore, is the system of kinship terminology.[6] These conceptual systems specify the rights and duties that are attached to kinship roles, and they can be treated as indicators of the actual social relations that are entered into by occupants of the roles that the kinship terminology defines. Lévi-Strauss (1949) sees a principal task for anthropology as that of going beyond the kinship terminology to the actual kinship relations themselves. From there it is possible to move to the underlying structures that generate the kinship relations.

Each kinship system, argues Lévi-Strauss, can be described as a system of 'surface' relations among the various roles that make up the system. This surface structure involves a number of distinct role relations, of which Lévi-Strauss identifies four as being elementary. These elementary kinship relations are marriage relations between husbands and wives, sibling relations among brothers and sisters, filiation relations between parents and their children, and avuncular relations between children and their parents' siblings. These four elementary kinship relations are shown in Figure 7.2.

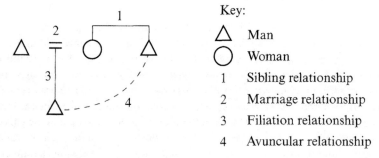

Key:

△   Man
◯   Woman
1   Sibling relationship
2   Marriage relationship
3   Filiation relationship
4   Avuncular relationship

Figure 7.2   Basic kinship relations

Lévi-Strauss claimed that the ethnographic research of earlier social anthropologists had shown that the kinship systems of primitive tribal societies fell into a limited number of types. Comparison of these known systems, he held, could disclose the underlying structures that generate each system, and would allow the researcher to see whether these structures are 'transformations' of one another. Looking at evidence from a number of societies, Lévi-Strauss concluded that their differences could be described by models built from the four elementary kinship relations. In the structural descriptions that he produced, each relation is defined as positive or negative in terms of two deep structure elements. The deep structure element of 'mutuality' characterizes sibling and marriage relations, while the deep structure element of 'familiarity' characterizes filiation and avuncular relations.[7] Figure 7.3 shows some of the 'elementary structures of kinship' that Lévi-Strauss analysed.

		Structural relation			
		Mutuality		Familiarity	
	Tribal group	Sibling	Marriage	Filiation	Avuncular
A.	Trobriand	–	+	+	–
B.	Dobu	+	–	+	–
C.	Kubutu	+	–	+	–
D.	Cherkess	+	–	–	+
E.	Tonga	–	+	–	+

Note: The sibling relations considered are those of brother to sister; the filiation relations are father–son relations only; and the avuncular relations are those of the mother's brother to his sister's son. A negative sign for mutuality indicates 'separation' and a negative sign for familiarity indicates respect.

Figure 7.3 Elementary structures of kinship

The cases in Figure 7.3 can be seen as more complex – and therefore more realistic – versions of the artificial diagrams in Figure 7.1. The table of elementary structures shows the known permutations of the mutuality and familiarity relations. It might appear, to the mathematically inclined, that there ought to be 16 possible combinations of the positive and negative values on these relations.[8] Lévi-Strauss holds, however, that the values within each relation must always be opposite: if the brother/sister relation of mutuality is positive, for example, then the husband/wife relation must be negative, and *vice versa*. For this reason, only four combinations are actually expected to occur. Lévi-Strauss' study of fieldwork evidence produces data supporting all four of these combinations, and these are the cases shown in Figure 7.3.[9] These five cases are also shown to be related to the system of descent that prevails in a society. Matrilineal and patrilineal relations are systems of descent that govern the transmission of rights and obligations from one generation to the next. Systems A and B (the Trobrianders and the Dobu) occur in matrilineal societies, while systems C, D and E (the Kubutu, the Cherkess and the Tongans) occur in patrilineal societies.[10]

The relations set out in Figure 7.3 can be made a little more concrete by considering the Trobriand case. In the Trobriands there is a separation (a negative value on the sibling relation) between brothers and sisters, and there is a corresponding mutuality (a positive value for the marriage relation) between husband and wife. Boys are involved in familiar and friendly relations with their fathers, but more distant and negative relations of 'respect' with their maternal uncles. The negative character of the avuncular relation follows from the 'separation' that exists between a married woman and her brother. In the Tongan case, on the other hand, patrilineal descent operates, and similar sibling and marital relations are associated with positive relations of familiarity between boys and their uncles.

Lévi-Strauss' method for constructing models of the deep structure of social relations established a paradigm for subsequent structuralist investigations, many being studies of cultural representations. The main area of advance in the structuralist investigation of social relations occurred under the influence of Althusser, who combined Lévi-Strauss' method with concepts drawn from Marxist theory.

STRUCTURES OF PRODUCTION, DOMINATION AND IDEOLOGY

I have shown how Althusser's structuralist methodology holds that all scientific activity takes place within specific theoretical 'problematics'. The objects of investigation for scientific Marxism, for example, do not come from the direct objective experience of the real world, they are derived from the internal logic of the Marxian conceptual system. This Marxian problematic had, Althusser felt, been distorted by those who had taken it in an 'empiricist' or positivist direction. These writers, he held, had misunderstood or misrepresented the true nature of the Marxian problematic, and Althusser held that it was necessary to return to the conceptual system set out in *Capital* (Marx, 1867) – Marx's most mature and complete work. The task of Marxism, Althusser said, is to develop the logic of this system and to break completely with contemporary distortions of Marx and with Marx's own early and immature work.

Althusser's first task, then, was to clarify the Marxian problematic itself: to identify the system of theoretical concepts that structured the questions that Marxists must investigate. At the heart of the Marxian conceptual system, he argued, is the concept of surplus value. It is from this fundamental concept that all other theoretical concepts are derived and in terms of which their theoretical differentiation can be understood. Concepts such as the commodity, exchange value and use value, wages and profit, capital and labour, class, relations of production and forces of production, mode of production and so on can all be logically interrelated to form a coherent theoretical system. Social scientists work on this conceptual scheme and, in so doing, they both reproduce and transform it.

Althusser also drew on the structuralist method in a second respect. Not only did he reject the 'empiricist' distortion of Marxism, he also rejected its 'subjectivist' distortion. Subjectivist approaches to social theory reduce social reality to the actions of individuals and groups, and to the subjective experiences that give them 'meaning'. In doing so they fail to understand that science is concerned with *structures*. Human action, for Althusser, comprises sets of *structured practices*. The true objects of social scientific investigation are not intentions or subjective meanings, they are the structural 'places' or 'positions' that are produced by these practices. The intentional subjects that play such an important part in rational choice and symbolic interactionist theories are, therefore, of secondary importance for Althusser. Individuals are mere 'supports' or 'bearers' of the social relations that define the places that they occupy in a social structure. The relations of production, for example, define the class places of the capitalist and worker, and these places are filled by particular individuals endowed with the appropriate skills and abilities. The true driving force in structural transformations are the structures themselves:

> The structure of the relations of production determines the places and functions occupied and adopted by the agents of production, who are never anything more than the occupants of these places, in so far as they are the supports of these functions. The true 'subjects' (in the sense of constitutive subjects of the process) are therefore not these occupants or functionaries, are not, despite all appearances … 'concrete individuals', 'real men' – but the definition and distribution of these places and functions (Althusser and Balibar, 1968: 180; emphasis removed).[11]

The practices that make up a society – or, more strictly, a 'social formation' – appear as a set of social organizations and agencies: business enterprises, trades unions, political parties, the mass media, families, schools, Churches and so on. Beneath the 'surface structure' of organizations, however, is a deeper structure of social relations. Althusser and Balibar (1968: 319) followed Marx's statement in his 1859 *Preface* and saw this deep structure as comprising three elements: an economic base, a political and ideological superstructure, and the corresponding 'forms of consciousness'.[12] Althusser reworked this argument in terms of three 'levels' of practice: the economic, the political and the ideological. These three levels together constitute the

deep structure that underlies the observable surface structure of social organizations.[13] Each of these levels of practice was seen by Althusser as forming a
distinct structure, but they each combine equivalent elements. These structures are, in structuralist terms, 'transformations' of one another. This is
illustrated in Figure 7.4, where each structure is seen to involve a relation
between objects, means of production and products.[14]

		Element of Practice		
		Objects	Means of production	Product
	Economic	Natural materials	Labour power	Products
Level of practice	Political	Social relations	Class struggle	Transformed social relations
	Ideological	Consciousness	Ideological struggle	Representations
	Theoretical	Practical concepts	Conceptual problematics, scientific methods	Knowledge

Figure 7.4   The deep structure of social practices

Economic practice comprises a set of structures through which labour
power works on nature, in the form of its raw materials, and produces
products with a use value. In a capitalist system the products of economic
practice take the form of commodities with an exchange value in the market.
Political practice is defined as those activities through which class struggle
transforms existing social relations into new relations. Finally, ideological
practice works on people's consciousness and produces collective representations that organize people's relations to their lived world. Formal religions
and philosophical ideas are codified systematizations of these ideological
representations (Althusser, 1965: 167). An analysis of a social formation
requires an analysis of these three interrelated levels of practice.

Althusser claimed that Marx's major contribution to social theory was to
have analysed the economic level of deep structural relations. His conceptual

system was concerned principally with economic concepts, and it suggests in only a sketchy way the links that these have with political and ideological concepts. Marx completely failed to analyse the structure of political and ideological relations in as much detail as he did the structure of the economy, and Althusser saw his own work as being a first step towards overcoming this gap in Marxist theory. This is possible, he held, because of the structural transformations that exist among the three levels of practice: the Marxian analysis of the economic level can serve as a model for similar analyses of the political and ideological levels.

According to Althusser, Marx had analysed the structure of the economic level as a *mode of production*, a specific and determinate way of ensuring the material reproduction of human life. With a colleague, Althusser set out the basics of his understanding of the mode of production (Althusser and Balibar, 1968). According to this position, the various modes of production that characterize human history – the ancient, the feudal, the capitalist and similar modes of production – can be seen as specific combinations of certain fundamental and invariant elements. The three basic elements of the labourer, the non-labourer and the means of production, he argued, can be combined in various ways by two distinct types of social relation. These social relations are the property relation of class exploitation and the technical relation of control over the labour process (Althusser and Balibar, 1968: 215). These are, it might be said, the 'elementary structures' of economic life.

This can be illustrated by referring to the use of these elements to form a table of modes of production (see Figure 7.5). The '+' and '−' entries in the table are used to indicate whether the occupants of a particular class position have or do not have the particular relationship to the means of production. In the capitalist mode of production, the labourer has neither ownership nor technical control of the means of production, while the non-labourer has

	Structural relation			
	Property ownership		Technical control	
Mode of production	Labourer	Non-labourer	Labourer	Non-labourer
A. Feudal	−	+	+	−
B. Capitalist	−	+	−	+
C. Socialist	+	−	+	−

Figure 7.5   Modes of production

both. This specific combination defines the class relations of capitalist and worker. In the socialist mode of production, on the other hand, both property ownership and technical control are in the hands of labourers, and non-labourers are excluded from any participation in the direction of the means of production. The class relations of the feudal mode of production are, in some respects, a more complex structure in that the non-labourer (the lord) is the property-owner, but the labourer (the serf) retains considerable technical control over the means of production.[15]

The economic structure, therefore, can be understood as a mode of production in which specific relations and forces of production are combined. This can be seen, in some respects, in purely economic terms, although the economic relations of the mode of production have specific political and ideological conditions of existence.[16] For this reason, a full account of a mode of production can be given only as a specific combination of economic, political and ideological elements (Althusser and Balibar, 1968: 177–8). The mode of production is an 'economic' concept, but it does, nevertheless, involve economic, political and ideological elements.[17] The economic element is always the *determinant* element in a mode of production and, therefore, in a social formation, but politics or ideology may, in some modes of production, be the *dominant* element in shaping its characteristics (Althusser and Balibar, 1968: 220ff). By this is meant that economic relations are such that they require the existence of certain dominant political or ideological elements if they are themselves to persist and to be reproduced. The feudal mode of production, for example, involves the dominance of ideology (religion) in shaping the economic relation of lord and serf.

The various modes of production, according to Althusser and Balibar, are merely different combinations of the same elements. They are 'transformations' of one another. The periodization of history in Marxism is not an empirical generalization, it is the result of the theoretical work that produces the table of structural transformations. For this reason, Althusser's Marxism is radically anti-evolutionist. A structural analysis gives priority to the construction of models rather than to the description of a chronological sequence:

> There is neither a progressive movement of differentiation of the forms, nor even a line of progress with a logic akin to a destiny. Marx does tell us that all the modes of production are historical moments, but he does not tell us that these moments descend one from the other ... Marx's aim was to show that the distinction between different modes is necessarily and sufficiently based on a variation of the connexions between a small number of elements which are always the same (Althusser and Balibar, 1968: 225; emphasis removed).

Given the starting point of Althusser – that the analysis of the economic level provides a model for the analysis of the political and ideological levels – it might be expected that he would have offered a comparable analysis of these two levels. In fact, the political and ideological levels were not analysed to the same 'depth' as the economic level. Balibar had argued that the political and ideological levels of the structure of a social formation could be understood as 'specific complex combinations' (Althusser and Balibar, 1968: 220). The mode of production is a concept for understanding the combination of elements that make up the economic level, and there must be similar concepts for understanding political and ideological relations. Althusser's discussions of the state and ideology, however, made no use of the tripartite distinction between objects, means and products that he and Balibar suggested as the core elements of *all* levels of practice. There was no attempt to construct models of 'modes of political production' ('modes of domination') or 'modes of ideological production' ('modes of ideation') to correspond to their analyses of the various modes of production.[18] Instead, Althusser's analysis of ideology pointed in a radically different direction.

The particular combination of elements that constitutes the structure of the ideological level is what Althusser termed the 'ideological state apparatuses'. A mode of production might be said to consist of such apparatuses and organs as markets, divisions of labour, enterprises and so on, all of which are unified through their function in economic production and by the structural unity that derives from the relations of production. The ideological state apparatuses, on the other hand, include such apparatuses as families, schools, the mass media and Churches that Althusser saw as unified through their function in reproducing the dominant relations of production (Althusser, 1971: 135ff). The ideological state apparatuses have only a functional unity, and not a structural unity. They are also, it will be apparent, designated as elements within the state, which Althusser saw as a complex of elements that represent and defend class relations. This does not mean, however, that the ideological state apparatuses are part of the formal, legal apparatus of the state. As Hirst puts it in his critical summary: 'They are organs of the state but are not necessarily institutions within the constitutional form of the state' (Hirst, 1979: 42).

The other aspect of the state is the political level, which Althusser saw as comprising the *repressive* apparatuses of the state. Through such apparatuses as the government, the civil service, the military, the courts, the police and the prisons, the political conditions of the reproduction of the relations of production are secured. The repressive apparatuses are concerned with the maintenance of order and cohesion (Poulantzas, 1968: 44, 52; Althusser, 1971: 131–2, 142). The state, then, comprises both the ideological and the repressive apparatuses that serve to maintain and to reproduce the relations of production that structure a particular mode of production.

This viewpoint reflects the novel conception of ideology that Althusser set out. The real social conditions under which people live, he argued, are not directly given to them in their experience: they are not immediately 'observable' phenomena that present themselves to their minds. Instead, people construct images of these social conditions, and these images are separate and distinct from the real conditions. In Althusser's methodology, I have shown, the 'theoretical object' is distinct from the 'real object', and Althusser generalized this point in his discussion of ideology. In ideology there is a separation between the *representations* that people employ and the real conditions under which they live. Ideology, then, is a system of relations under which are constructed the representations that allow people to 'imagine' their real social circumstances. The sphere of ideology generates an imaginary lived existence that constitutes the common sense world in which people live their everyday lives.[19] Ideology is said to be imaginary not because it is 'false', but because it is possible *only* to imagine what real objects are like.

To this general conception of ideology Althusser added a second, distinct element. Ideology, he said, has a specific *function*, and this function is to reproduce the dominant relations of production. By this he meant that ideology produces individual agents with particular values and skills and that it distributes them to the class positions that require these values and skills. Ideology, then, centres on the processes of socialization, selection and recruitment of agents. Individuals as 'subjects' or 'agents' are the products of the social practices that are reproduced in their actions. The specific attributes and forms of subjectivity (self-conception, intentional orientation and so on) are a consequence of the specific ideological apparatuses that shape people's lived experiences and that ensure that they meet the requirements of the relations of production.[20] What Althusser failed to provide was any account of the mechanisms through which the fulfilment of this function is secured: he failed to observe the basic principles of functional explanation that were discussed in the previous Chapter.

The three structural levels of practice – the economy, the polity and ideology – comprise distinct levels of a social formation. Whereas the general structuralist method holds simply that there are rules of transformation that govern the relations among these levels, Althusser held that the rules of transformation must be seen as reflecting *causal relations*. To understand this, he introduced the idea of 'structural causality'. The structure of each level conditions the structure of each of the other levels: they set limits and opportunities for one another. At the same time, each level has a 'relative autonomy' and so is able to develop, to a greater or lesser extent, according to its own principles. Within this structure of causal relations, the economic level has a fundamental importance – although the political and ideological levels have a relative autonomy, they are, 'in the last instance', determined by the structure of the economy (see Figure 7.6).

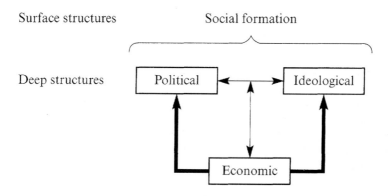

Figure 7.6 Structural causality

Structural causality involves complex processes of causation, as none of the three levels of practice ever occur in their pure form. The economic level, for example, rarely consists of a single mode of production. More typically, a social formation will include a number of modes of production, one of which predominates over the others. A capitalist mode of production, for example, may be the dominant mode of production in a social formation in which there are also elements of petty commodity production, slavery and other modes of production. The contradictions of the mode of production, then, do not operate in a direct way but alongside and interdependently with those of other modes of production. Similar considerations apply to the political and ideological levels, and the whole 'structure in dominance' is characterized by complex and intersecting causal processes. Particular historical events are never the simple expression of a fundamental contradiction. They must, instead, be seen as the outcome of a complex articulation of structures. They are, said Althusser, 'overdetermined'. The intersecting combination of causal processes results in an 'accumulation of effective determinations', an intensity of causal effects (Althusser, 1965, for: 106, 113). For these reasons, historical events must be seen as uniquely determined by the specific combination of causal mechanisms that are in operation. There are always, 'innumerable intersecting forces, an infinite series of parallelograms of forces which give rise to one resultant' (Althusser, 1965: 120, quoting Engels).

Subsequent writers, such as Poulantzas and Wright, have sought to elaborate on this basic idea and to introduce more complex typologies. Wright, in particular, has attempted to overcome the idealist implications of Althusser's work and to demonstrate its relevance to empirical research. Wright has rephrased Balibar's distinction between property and technical control as that between the relations of 'ownership' and 'possession', and he used these relations to construct a class schema for contemporary capitalism (Wright, 1978: 68–9). Similar, though less successful, attempts to use the Althusserian concept of relations of production in class analysis can be found in Carchedi (1975a, 1975b) and Poulantzas (1975).[21] The relations of ownership and possession coincide with one another in the pure model of capitalism and create a fundamental class division between the bourgeois owner-possessors and the proletarian non-owner-possessors. But the capitalist mode of production rarely appears in this pure form, and the class divisions that are found in actual societies will be more complex. Capitalist and non-capitalist modes of production may co-exist in the same social formation, and the development of the capitalist mode of production itself creates more complex forms of combination in the fundamental relations. 'Petty bourgeois', self-employed producers, managers and others arise as classes 'between' the fundamental classes. Many of these intermediate class positions are 'contradictory' class locations because of the specific social relations that they combine. The unambiguous and the contradictory class locations are the building blocks of Wright's class schema for modern capitalist society.

THE LIMITS OF STRUCTURALISM

Lévi-Strauss, in his empirical work, had been convinced that structural models were theoretical devices that could be used to understand real structures that are at work in the social world. The empirical evidence that is collected by fieldworkers allows them to describe the surface features of societies and provides them with the raw materials for constructing structural models. Althusser pushed the structuralist method in an idealist direction, arguing that the logic of the structuralist theory of knowledge requires the recognition of a sharp and unbridgeable gulf between theory and reality. Structural models of modes of production and ideological state apparatuses are 'theoretical objects' and they must be understood purely within the realm of theoretical discourse. There is, according to Althusser, no direct correspondence between these theoretical objects and any 'real objects'. If the latter do indeed exist, they must always remain beyond thought and, therefore, unknowable. Scientists, like all other individuals, may only 'imagine' the realities that they try to study.

If this is indeed the case, then the problem that Althusser has to face is that of how scientific theories and concepts are to be distinguished from ideology. He argued that ideology is the more general process through which representations and, thereby, the imaginary world in which people live are produced, reproduced and transformed. If theoretical objects are imagined objects, the question arises whether the distinction between science and ideology may not be artificial. Althusser argued that this was not the case and that the theoretical objects of science are not mere imaginings: they are 'knowledge'. He had, however, rejected the 'empiricist' idea of a correspondence between theoretical object and real object, and so the knowledge claims of science could not be justified on the basis of any theory of empirical 'truth' (Althusser and Balibar, 1968: 35–40). The knowledge produced by science, he concluded, is more than mere ideology because of the specific methods that are followed by the scientist. These methods define the practices of scientists.

Science is seen by Althusser as a particular form of practice: 'theoretical practice' (see Figure 7.4). Theoretical practice involves the use of a scientific problematic and scientific techniques to transform the practical concepts that ideological practices produce as ways of imagining the unknowable economic and political practices of a social formation. Theoretical practice converts these practical concepts and representations into knowledge. This knowledge may itself become an element in the raw material of further theoretical practice. Indeed, the normal pattern of scientific activity requires the establishment of the kind of autonomy from social circumstances that allows its raw materials to be drawn exclusively from the sphere of knowledge and not from ideology.

The theoretical practice of a science emerges initially within the sphere of ideology, and it is in constant danger of falling back into this sphere if its autonomy is weakened. If this is to be avoided, theoretical practice must make the crucial 'epistemological break' from ideology and detach itself completely from all social constraints. Only then can it follow a purely internal, theoretical logic of development that is uncontaminated by ideological concerns or practical interests. Theoretical practice has the same structural form as other practices, but it is not itself a part of the social formation. It is detached from all social determination.

This leads Althusser to reject the framework of the sociology of knowledge, according to which *all* thought is relative to the social circumstances in which it is produced. Science can escape the social determination of knowledge, and the consequent relativism that this involves, by mastering the epistemological break and by establishing the autonomy of its theoretical practice. Historically, the breakthrough from ideology to science occurs in a particular area of study whenever social conditioning gives way to an autonomous theoretical logic. Althusser regarded Marx's break with the immature theories of his youth as a crucial turning point – an epistemological break – in the development of a science of social formations (Althusser, 1965: Chapter 2).

Unfortunately, Althusser did not show *how* such detachment and autonomy could be achieved, and he failed to see that the relative autonomy of science requires the existence of specific social conditions (Geras, 1972). In consequence, he did not attempt to specify what social conditions or which social groups might further the autonomy of science from ideology. The orthodox Marxist position has always posited the standpoint of the proletariat as a guarantee of objective knowledge, while Mannheim (1929) had put his faith in the 'relatively unattached intelligentsia' whom he believed were more likely to overcome some of the consequences of the social determination of knowledge. Althusser would allow neither of these positions. Indeed, he held that the ideological distortions that characterized many strands of Marxism were the products of intellectuals. Althusser was left, then, with a mere empty gesture in the direction of the detachment and autonomy of theoretical practice.

In his *Essays in Self-Criticism* (Althusser, 1974) he recognized some of the problems of this idealist position and embraced some of its consequences. The position at which he arrived was that the distinction between science and ideology must itself, as an idea, be the result of ideological practice. This left him in a vicious circle of relativism from which he could find no escape. Science may, after all, be merely a form of ideological practice, and there could be no grounds for accepting the 'knowledge' of science in preference to the practical concepts and collective representations of ideology.

The only way out of this vicious circle is to abandon Althusser's contention that the relation between theoretical objects and real objects is completely indeterminate and that real objects are unknowable. While Althusser may have been correct to reject the empiricist view of this relation, he overshot the mark and ended with an unsustainable relativistic idealism.

Althusser's rejection of the 'empiricist' idea of a correspondence between the 'theoretical object' and the 'real object' was seemingly allied with a rejection of any *empirical* criteria in the assessment of knowledge. The truth and objectivity of knowledge could not, for Althusser, be assessed in relation to empirical evidence. The only basis on which bodies of theory could be compared with one another was in terms of the degree of logical coherence that they exhibit. An explanation that is more tightly structured in its logic and that has a greater degree of conceptual coherence is to be counted as more scientific than an explanation that contains logical contradictions and inconsistencies (see Hindess, 1973, 1977). The obvious difficulty with this position is that it provides no basis on which a theorist is able to determine his or her theoretical object in the first place. Why should a scientist construct a logical concept of the 'capitalist mode of production' rather than, say, the 'social system', 'symbolic interaction' or even the 'kingdom of God'? Althusser attempted to avoid this problem by claiming that real objects remain the absolute point of reference for the construction of theoretical objects. However, he provided no grounds for believing this to be a viable strategy without recourse to the very 'empiricism' that he had rejected (Glucksmann, 1972).

The answer to Althusser's dilemma must surely be to recognize the proper role of empirical evidence in science. While he was correct to recognize that theoretical frameworks and conceptual schemes enter into the construction of theoretical objects, it must not be assumed that this proceeds in total disregard of the real objects. Engels – a principal source of inspiration for Althusser – clearly stated the problem of any idealist theory of knowledge: 'If I include a shoe-brush under the unity mammals, this does not help it to get mammary glands' (Engels, 1876: 63–4).

There are definite limits to the freedom that scientists have in the construction of theoretical objects, and these limits are defined by the nature of the real objects themselves. This realist position can be defended without a resort to 'empiricism'. Indeed, Keat and Urry (1975) have claimed that a realist interpretation of Althusser's methodology can provide an effective basis for incorporating his substantive arguments into a more comprehensive social theory. They claim, furthermore, that Marx himself followed a realist approach to science and that a realist reconstruction of Althusser will be more compatible with the thrust of Marx's own work.

According to the realist position, science is concerned with uncovering the properties of the real causal mechanisms that are at work in the world. Science as an activity – as theoretical practice – makes sense only if such objects exist and if they exert their influence independently of the theories that scientists are currently using to investigate them.[22] Knowledge is a socially and historically specific attempt to grasp the structures of these real objects. Science consists in the construction of a theoretical model of a real causal mechanism that, if it operated as specified in the model, could explain the observations that have been made. Once such a task has been achieved, the scientist can proceed to a 'deeper' level of analysis and can construct a model of a mechanism that is capable of explaining the initial mechanism. Science, then, consists in the progressive uncovering of ever deeper causal mechanisms.[23]

In real situations, numerous casual mechanisms operate simultaneously, and scientists may construct models only of a few of these. It is very unlikely, as Althusser recognized, that there will be a one-to-one correspondence between observed events and the predictions derived from theoretical models. Causal mechanisms both reinforce and undermine one another, they operate alongside other (as yet) unknown mechanisms, and the combination of mechanisms differs from situation to situation. As a result, actual events are never simple consequences of a particular mechanism: they are always 'overdetermined'. The task of science is to comprehend this overdetermination by extending the scope of its knowledge of the causal mechanisms operating in the world.

From the standpoint of epistemological realism, structural descriptions are models of real causal mechanisms. Althusser's conception of the theoretical object failed to comprehend this distinction between models of structures and the real structures themselves. Keat and Urry (1975) have illustrated this point by considering the 'structure' of a building. The real structure of the building, they argue, is not the actual arrangement of the physical fabric of the building, nor is it a conceptual model of that fabric. It is the underlying pattern of forces that maintains the arrangement of the fabric and that architects and engineers try to represent in their models:

> The structure of a building may be taken to consist of the way in which building materials are assembled and combined together to produce an object constructed for particular purposes and serving certain functions. In our representation of such a structure we may use arrows, for example, to symbolize the pressures exerted by one element upon other elements. If our model of that structure is correct then each arrow will represent a set of given physical facts. We picture these physical facts by means of the arrow. However, they are nonetheless physical realities which comprise the structure of the building. That structure is not immediately visible to us but it is nevertheless present. We have a model of that structure pictorially symbolized by the arrow; the structure is the concealed, physically real relations between certain elements comprising that building (Keat and Urry, 1975: 120–21).

On this basis, the insights of Lévi-Strauss, Althusser and other structuralist writers can be articulated and elaborated. Without such a realist interpretation, the structuralist approach ceases to have any connection with the analysis of material structures of social relations and their causal powers.

A realist reconstruction of the structuralist method provides the basis on which the arguments of Lockwood (1964) can be restated. In the previous Chapter I showed that Lockwood had argued that sociological analysis must recognize the existence of non-normative structural elements alongside the normative elements on which structural functionalism had concentrated. The Althusserian approach complements the Parsonian analysis of 'institutions' with an analysis of 'practices'. These practices, in their most general sense, are those patterns of activity that have become regular or recurrent features of a social system. Institutions are the patterns of normative expectations – clusters of culturally defined positions – that may enter into the formation of practices but remain distinct from them. Practices are structures of actual social relations.

The relations of production, I showed in Chapter 6, are an element in the structuring of the economic practices of a society, but they are only partially structured by legal norms. As Renner (1904) showed, legal relations are embedded in a larger system of practices and so the relations of production must be seen as relations of effective control rather than merely of legal ownership. These relations of effective control enter into the formation of specific class locations that exert a causal influence on the life chances of individuals. The structuralist analyses of class relations that have been produced by Poulantzas and Wright can be seen as attempts to comprehend these real structures as objects of sociological investigation in their own right. The investigation of material structures is essential in the analysis of system integration.

NOTES

1. All of Althusser's books consist of collections of essays and lectures. As they are known principally in their reprinted form rather than as originally published or delivered, I refer only to the relevant collections.
2. I shall argue later in this Chapter that the structuralist programme can be rescued only on the basis of a realist epistemology.
3. A clear discussion of Radcliffe Brown's link to Durkheim can be found in Glucksmann (1974).
4. The relation between actual networks of social relations and the underlying structural forms has been extensively discussed in the tradition of network analysis. See Wellman and Berkowitz (1988) and Scott (1991b).
5. In statistical theory 'combination' and 'permutation' are used to refer to different ways of selecting and ordering elements. The words are used interchangeably in this Chapter.
6. Lévi-Strauss' analysis of kinship terminology is an analysis of collective representations and therefore forms a continuous thread with the wider analysis of cultural structures that is discussed in the following Chapter.
7. This summary draws on Leach's (1970) discussion.
8. There are four combinations of the mutuality relation and four combinations of the familiarity relation, and each of the first four combinations could be combined with each of the second four to generate the 16 cases.
9. As there can be only two 'balanced' forms of each relation, the number of combinations is two times two. It can be seen from Figure 7.3 that the Dobu and the Kubutu are structurally identical cases, if their patterns of descent – to be discussed shortly – are ignored. If the matrilineal/patrilineal relation is built into the table there would be eight possible combinations, of which only five appear in the table.
10. Lévi-Strauss limits his attention to systems of unilineal descent.
11. Clarke (1980: 49) holds that an emphasis on the *distribution* of people to places involves a departure from Marx's emphasis on the determining role of *production*.
12. Here and elsewhere I treat the arguments of Balibar in *Reading Capital* (Althusser and Balibar, 1968) as equivalent to those of Althusser himself.
13. Althusser tends to use the word 'institution', in its loosest sense, to refer to the organizations and agencies of the surface level. In order to avoid any confusion with the structural functionalist concept of the social institution, I have tried to avoid the word in connection with Althusser.
14. Althusser sometimes recognizes or implies that there are more than three levels of prac-

tice. This is particularly clear in his methodological discussions, where he contrasts the 'scientific' form of 'theoretical practice' with mere ideological practices. I have indicated this in Figure 7.4.

15. It is possible to construct other combinations of these elements, though Balibar gave little attention to this task. He recognized, for example, the historical importance of a mode of production 'transitional' between the feudal and the capitalist (Althusser and Balibar, 1968: Chapter 4). For further work in this tradition see Hindess and Hirst (1975). Balibar did make a rather half-hearted attempt to distinguish his method from Lévi-Strauss' structuralism, but this does not affect his basic argument (Althusser and Balibar, 1968: 226).

16. Compare the idea of 'functional prerequisites' discussed in the previous Chapter.

17. Benton (1984: 74) claims that the involvement of political and ideological elements in the constitution of modes of production makes it impossible for Althusser clearly to distinguish the mode of production from the social formation. This claim rests on the false assumption that the social formation is to be equated with the 'superstructure'.

18. The works of Jessop (1972), Urry (1973), Runciman (1989) and, above all, Lockwood (1992) do attempt such analyses, though from radically different assumptions.

19. Althusser's concept of the 'lived world' of experience has obvious affinities with the phenomenological concept of the 'lifeworld'.

20. This argument has, of course, many similarities with Parsons's oversocialized view of the human actor.

21. See also dos Santos (1970).

22. This is not, of course, to deny that existing scientific knowledge in the social sciences may, through its policy application or its appropriation by actors, influence the social world. The point is that causal mechanisms exist and operate independently of the current investigation.

23. For further sources on contemporary realism see Bhaskar (1975, 1979), Harré (1961, 1964, 1970) and Harré and Madden (1975).

8. Collective representations and cultural codes

Two distinct programmes of research were inspired by structuralist ideas. The research programme that was discussed in the preceding Chapter was centred on the investigation of material structures of social relations. The second programme was concerned with cultural structures of collective representations and remained much closer to Saussure's original studies of language. This approach to social life was expressed in 'semiotic' approaches to cultural codes and discourse, and from these ideas emerged so-called 'post-structuralist' and, subsequently, 'post-modernist' approaches.

Saussure had established semiotics – the science of signs – as the logical development of his own linguistic analysis. The central concept in his analysis of language was that of the *sign*,[1] and he held that 'language is a system of signs that express ideas' (Saussure, 1916: 16). Linguistic signs comprise two elements that Saussure termed the 'signifier' and the 'signified': the spoken sounds or written words of a language comprise the 'signifiers', while the conceptual elements to which these words refer are the 'signifieds'.

The English word 'dog', for example, is associated with the concept of a particular kind of furry, four-legged animal. The relation between the word and the concept – between signifier and signified – is, Saussure argued, 'arbitrary'. The same concept could equally well have been associated with the words *chien* or *hund*. Indeed, it has been associated with these words in French and German, respectively.[2] There is no necessary reason why this concept should be represented by 'dog', '*chien*', '*hund*', 'splodge', 'xyz' or any other combination of letters or sounds. There is no natural or inevitable connection between signifier and signified; the connection is purely contingent. Within the established vocabulary of a particular language, however, a speaker has no choice of signifiers. An English speaker *must* use the word 'dog' if he or she wishes to be understood by other English speakers.

A language, then, comprises a conventional system of relations among signs. It is a social institution that specifies the 'correct' or appropriate relationships between words (or sounds) and concepts. A sign is the unity of sound and concept, and, 'a linguistic system is a series of differences of sounds combined with a series of differences of ideas' (Saussure, 1916: 16).[3]

This idea of 'difference' is central to Saussure's view of language. The meaning of any particular sign is not something that can be understood in isolation. Each sign acquires its meaning from the position that it occupies within a system of signs, its meaning deriving from the ways in which it is *differentiated* from the other signs that make up the system. 'Dog' acquires its specific meaning by virtue of its differentiation from other 'animals' such as 'cat', 'hamster' and 'pony', and by the ways in which 'animals' are differentiated from 'people', 'toys' and 'plants'. This can easily be demonstrated by consulting a dictionary, where no absolute definitions are given: each word is defined in relation to other words. Thus, Saussure concluded that signs are defined in relation to the other signs from which they are differentiated.

Saussure's science of semiotics extended its concerns from the relatively familiar area of spoken and written language to all forms of communication in which signs are used. The 'sign language' of the deaf, the road signs of the Highway Code, and the visual signs and gestures of everyday interaction, for example, can all be analysed in the same way as spoken and written language. All cultural systems can be seen as systems of differentiations among related signs. In extending semiotics from language to *communication*, the analysis of linguistic codes is extended into that of *cultural codes*.

CULTURAL PRODUCTS AND CULTURAL CODES

Lévi-Strauss saw societies as systems of communication among individuals and groups. Social interaction, whether conversation, the exchange of goods and services or the transfer of women between kinship groups, is symbolically mediated and so may be analysed through the methods of semiotics. Saussure's linguistic model of the relationship between 'language' and 'speech' was transformed by Lévi-Strauss into a communication model of the relationship between 'code' and 'message'. Each process of interaction carries a message that is constructed through the use of signs drawn from the cultural codes available to the participants. Whole societies, in turn, can be interpreted as complex, intersecting combinations of cultural codes. Lévi-Strauss employed the methods of Saussure to investigate societies and social processes, but his work suggested one crucial extension to the position of Saussure. Where Saussure wrote of language as a system of *relations* among signs, Lévi-Strauss' work has inspired later structuralists to see language as a system of *rules* that specify how signs are to be used.[4] In most recent variants of structuralism, 'culture is basically a set of rules for the communication of signs' (Rossi, 1983, signs: 142).

This concern for cultural codes was demonstrated in an early study of totemism (Lévi-Strauss, 1962b), where Lévi-Strauss followed in the footsteps of Durkheim's work in this area (Durkheim and Mauss, 1903). Totemic religions use animal names to designate social groups, and certain animal characteristics are attributed to the members of these groups. Lévi-Strauss argued that this practice involved a correspondence between two separate conceptual systems or cultural codes: the system of animal species and the system of social groups. In more formal terms, one system is 'mapped' onto the other (see Figure 8.1). When animal species are used to represent social groups, the relations of the animals to one another can be used to represent the relations of the groups to one another. Thus joking relations between groups can be based on the characteristic relations that are imputed to animals. Totemism strengthens and reinforces social differences by describing them in terms of accepted and understood animal differences.

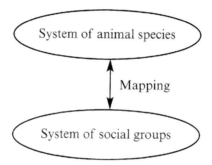

Figure 8.1   Lévi-Strauss' view of totemic classification

Totemism serves Lévi-Strauss as a model for the analysis of the various classification systems that are used to organize social activities. There may be, for example, classifications of animals according to their means of movement (flying, swimming, crawling and so on) or their availability for eating, classifications of colours and sounds, classifications of foods, classifications of illness and so on. A structuralist analysis of these classifications involves uncovering their structures and disclosing the connections, or 'mappings', that exist between them in order to uncover the 'transformations' that exist among the various structures.

As with systems of classification, so with the other collective representations that comprise the cultural sphere. Lévi-Strauss showed, for example, that mythologies could be subjected to structural analysis and that the logic of mythical thought is comparable to the logic of social classification. Myths were seen by Lévi-Strauss as being central to the conceptual aspects of 'primitive' culture. The concepts that appear in the myths of a society are the means through which their members engage in more 'abstract' thought of various kinds. In societies where there are no established and institutionalized mechanisms of abstract thought such as religion, philosophy and science, mythical thought allows people to conceptualize and to attempt to comprehend their conditions and social relations. Because they are such free forms of human creativity, myths are especially powerful vehicles for exploratory and abstract thinking.

In Lévi-Strauss' method, the investigation of myths begins with the collection of a large number of myth stories to use as the materials for structural analysis. These myths can then be grouped into categories on the basis of similarities in their narratives, and they can then be reconstructed into simplified 'surface structure' accounts, each structural account corresponding to a particular category of narratives. From the surface structure narratives, deeper structural models can be constructed and the anthropologist can uncover the logical transformations that convert one structural model into another and one narrative into another. The example of structural linguistics was, again, uppermost in Lévi-Strauss' mind. Linguists had classified languages into groups and had used structural methods to show that apparently disparate language groups could be traced back to a common origin: the Celtic and Germanic languages of Europe and the many languages of India, for example, were traced back to an original 'Indo-European' language.

In the same way, an analysis of all the known variants of a particular myth, regardless of the societies and settings from which they come, will uncover any common structure that they have and may suggest the existence of a prototypical myth of which the actual myths are variants. This prototype is the deep structure that lies behind the various mythical narratives that are found at the surface level of social life. The variants are differing cultural transformations of the prototype, although this may exist nowhere in its pure form. Lévi-Strauss (1960) looked, for example, at all the known variants of the myth of Asdiwal that could be found in the area inhabited by the Tsimshin Indians of South America. This yielded knowledge of a wider cultural code that was not apparent from an analysis of only one variant of the myth. The prototype myth that he discovered was interpreted in relation to the particular structure of social relations that characterized these societies. It expresses the contradictions and tensions that exist between lineages that are connected into a system of patrilocal, matrilineal cross-cousin marriage. The real problems in actual marriages, Lévi-Strauss argued, were contrasted in the myths with the far worse problems faced by the inhabitants of the imaginary worlds. In this way, practical problems could be defused. People think through their actual problems in mythical form. The myth serves as a critical recognition of the shortcomings of real life, but it is also a way of accommodating people to their circumstances, which are depicted as better than the conceivable alternatives.

In some of his final work Lévi-Strauss applied this same structuralist method to cookery, which he saw as yet another form of 'communication'.

By studying the systems of classification that surround cookery practices, he argued, social anthropologists could uncover the rules and relations on which they rest (Lévi-Strauss, 1964). These systems of classification, he argued, can be understood as structures that are built from three elements – the 'raw', the 'cooked' and the 'rotted' – that are themselves transformations of one another. The raw is the natural state of food, the cooked is a cultural transformation of raw food, and the rotted is its natural transformation. Lévi-Strauss represents these transformations in an underlying structural model that has come to be known as 'the culinary triangle' (see Figure 8.2).

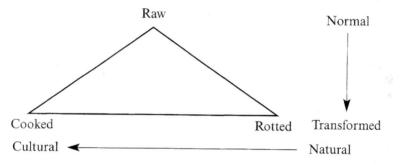

Figure 8.2   The culinary triangle

In the culinary triangle there are three binary oppositions – raw/cooked, raw/rotted and cooked/rotted – that are combinations of deeper binary oppositions between the normal and the transformed and between nature and culture. Roasting, smoking and boiling are different means of transforming the normally found items of raw food. Thus some types of cooking are closer to natural processes and others are more distinctively cultural.

The analyses of totemism, myth and cookery are different exemplifications of the same structuralist method. In each case, processes of communication are seen to lie at the heart of the production of collective representations and the social practices that they inform. Language, myth, music, cookery, table manners (Lévi-Strauss, 1968b), art, architecture and all the other cultural forms of human social life involve the use of specific cultural codes – systems of signs whose relations structure human activities.

THE STRUCTURES OF THE HUMAN MIND

The task of any structuralist analysis is the production of 'tables' of the structural transformations that are exhibited in systems of collective representations. However, Lévi-Strauss argued that structural analysis could proceed even further than this. He held that comparing the tables produced for different kinds of phenomena – tables of kinship structures, tables of totemic structures, tables of mythic structures and so on – made it possible to move to the deeper structures of the human mind itself. A structuralist analysis can, then, produce knowledge that goes beyond the confines of a particular cultural code to the universal and invariant structures of human thought. If the structures of myth narratives, for example, can disclose the structures of underlying prototype myths, then a structuralist analysis of prototypes and of other deep structures can disclose the even deeper structures of the human mind, independent of all cultural peculiarities. These structures are 'unconscious', 'innate' characteristics of all human mental processes. They form the genetically conditioned structuring capacity that is possessed by all human beings, and they underlie all the various collective representations and social relations that are produced by human beings. They are the most fundamental objects of investigation in the human sciences. Social relations and collective representations are ultimately reducible to the structures of the human mind (Lévi-Strauss, 1962a).

Lévi-Strauss justified this strong claim on the grounds of the results produced in the linguistic studies that had been undertaken by Jakobson, who showed that the patterns of sounds that are found in the various languages of the world could be understood as relatively simple elaborations of the basic sounds that are producible by the human speech apparatus. A young child can, for example, initially make a vocal distinction between 'loud' vowel sounds and 'soft' consonant sounds, and these are subsequently refined into more specific speech sounds on the basis of variations in their pitch. At each stage in the learning of a language, 'binary oppositions' are made – loud/soft, high pitch/low pitch and so on. This making of binary oppositions, said Jakobson, is a universal characteristic of human linguistic abilities.

For Lévi-Strauss this points to the conclusion that the human mind operates through binary oppositions, and it is for this reason that kinship, totemism, myths and cookery all exhibit binary structures. Kinship relations and cooking practices, for example, can be seen as involving a number of binary oppositions with positive or negative values. These empirical data, according to Lévi-Strauss, offered clear evidence for seeing the universal properties of the human mind as involving the mathematical handling of binary oppositions. Leach has summarized this argument in the following terms:

> In the course of human evolution man [*sic*.] has developed the unique capacity to communicate by means of language and signs. ... In order that he should be able to do this it is necessary that the mechanisms of the human brain ... should embody certain capacities for making +/– distinctions, for treating the binary pairs thus formed as related couples, and for manipulating these 'relations' in a matrix algebra (Leach, 1970: 51–2).[5]

The mind operates in algebraic terms, and this is a necessary *biological* condition of human social life. Anthropology yields evidence not simply on the human mind but, more particularly, on the human *brain*:

> The structure of relations which can be discovered by analysing materials drawn from any one culture is an algebraic transformation of other possible structures belonging to a common set and this common set constitutes a pattern which reflects an attribute of the mechanism of all human brains (Leach, 1970: 53).

Few other structuralists have followed Lévi-Strauss in his excursions into the structure of the human mind. Instead, they have remained at the cultural level and have sought to explore the binary oppositions and other devices that occur in cultural codes concerned with the collective representations of science, literary texts and mass media output. This has not, however, involved a simple extension of Lévi-Strauss' work from tribal societies to modern societies. The investigation of cultural structures has increasingly been marked by a move away from structuralism as Lévi-Strauss conceived it, and towards so-called 'post-structuralist' schools of thought.

ABANDONING STRUCTURES?

Lévi-Strauss' structural anthropology embodies a monolithic view of primitive societies. These societies were seen as structured by integrated systems of signs that give them their unity. In this respect, his view is similar to Parsons's structural functionalist view of modern societies, according to which a value consensus ensures the coherent structural unity of a society. Althusser had argued that many Marxists adopted a similar holistic view, albeit one that saw the unity of a social formation as an expression of its economic structure rather than its cultural structure. In Marxist writing, Althusser claimed, there was a strong tendency towards essentialism. Althusser sought to recover the core of Marx's own view, which he saw as eschewing essentialist methods and developing a 'de-centred' concept of structure.

In Althusser's own work, and in that of Poulantzas and of other structural Marxists influenced by Althusser, social formations were seen as comprising a number of relatively autonomous levels. Economic, political and ideological levels had an autonomy from one another, and their interrelations could not be reduced to an overall structure of expressive causality. The Althusserian view of these levels as forming a 'structure in dominance', however, shows clearly that he did not completely abandon the idea that social structures were necessarily integrated in some way. According to Althusser, one level is *dominant* in any mode of production, and this dominance is *determined*, in the last instance, by the economic level. The structure of the economy shapes the overall structure of the social formation.

It was in the Althusserian analysis of ideology that the move away from the idea of holistic, integrated structures became more apparent. Unlike the mode of production, which has a structural unity that results from its specific relations of production, the ideological state apparatuses have only a functional unity. Indeed, the use of the plural term – ideological state apparatuses – is significant, as it points to Althusser's recognition that the ideological level comprises a diversity of agencies and organizations that are integrated only through the function that he attributed to them. Althusser recognized, then, a structural diversity of ideological phenomena, a 'de-centring' of ideology, but he sought to retain the problematic idea of the functional unity of the ideological state apparatuses.

The work of Michel Foucault, heavily influenced by the whole structuralist tradition, attempted a complete break with all forms of essentialism. Foucault rejected all holistic, functionalist and systemic conceptions of social and cultural phenomena and, in particular, he rejected the Althusserian idea of the 'totality' structured in dominance. He broke with the mainstream of materialist structuralist views on the social formation and, more crucially, he broke with semiotic structuralist views of an integrated culture, aiming to develop a fully de-centred concept of social reality. In his initial studies, Foucault set out what he called an 'archaeology' of discourse, an approach that he later extended into a 'genealogy' of discourse. Through these ideas Foucault stresses the need to dig deep and to uncover the structures that underlie discourses and to disclose the ways in which one discourse gives way to another. Foucault's genealogical method required a historical approach to knowledge, and he eschewed any suggestion that there was a universal or ahistorical basis to human thought. The generative processes that underlie a discourse are not universal and innate, as held by Lévi-Strauss: they are historical. Historical processes were themselves seen in a de-centred way, Foucault rejecting evolutionary models of historical development. He emphasized, instead, the discontinuity of successive discourses, each being structured by a distinct cultural code.[6]

Foucault's view of the 'social' was organized around two elements: the material phenomena of power and the cultural phenomena of discourse. Each of these dimensions of social reality is understood in a de-centred way, as diverse and autonomous agencies and organizations, and the combination of power and discourse is seen in similarly kaleidoscopic terms. While the phenomena of power and discourse are 'structured' and 'structuring', they are not to be seen as structural wholes. In stressing the plurality and diversity ('difference') in material and cultural forms of social life, Foucault rejected the idea that there is an essence or purpose behind society, culture or history.

It is for this reason that Foucault saw himself as being a 'post-structuralist' rather than a structuralist. He abandoned the conception of 'structure' as being too bound up with integrationist styles of thought, and he replaced concepts of material and cultural structures with those of power and discourse.

Power and discourse are interdependent elements in the organization of social life. While Foucault focused his attention on changing discourses and their impact on the formation of individuals, discourses were seen as effected in and through power relations. As Foucault rejected the idea of the causal role of active individual subjects, power was not seen in Weberian terms but as the result of mechanisms that operate independently of particular individuals (Foucault, 1982). It is through power that forms of discourse are produced and transformed, but it is also through discourse that structures of power are produced and reproduced. Indeed, discourse, knowledge and power are so clearly related that Foucault often wrote of 'power/knowledge'.

Social reality constitutes a highly diverse collection of discourses, of structures of power/knowledge, but there is no overall integration of these into a single 'culture' or 'social system'. Social reality is a 'dispersed regularity of unevenly developing levels of discourse' (Best and Kellner, 1991: 39). It comprises intellectual discourses, social organizations, architectural forms, laws and regulations, administrative processes, scientific statements and so on, each having its own specific and distinctive features. Each discourse is carried by a specific social group, and it reflects their particular perspectives and interests. The clash of discourses reflects the struggle of these groups for power and domination over one another, and the consequent fragmentation of discourse means that there is an incommensurability among the various discourses that make up the social world.[7]

Foucault's earliest empirical works were in the tradition of Durkheim's analysis of social classification, which had also inspired Lévi-Strauss (Durkheim and Mauss, 1903; Lévi-Strauss, 1962b). In these studies he argued that it is through the emergence of new forms of discourse and their associated bodies of 'experts' that new classifications are produced. Experts produce the classifications and knowledge claims of a discourse, but they are, at the same time, the products of that discourse. They acquire their status as 'experts' only because they are defined by a discourse as the possessors of its specific forms of knowledge. The idea of 'madness', for example, was constructed in an emergent psychiatric discourse during the early 19th century, at the same time as there was occurring a reconceptualization of 'medicine' and of medical practice (Foucault, 1961, 1963). Through these discourses, new categories of 'insanity', 'illness' and 'criminality' began to emerge and to become embodied in the power struggles of organized experts such as 'doctors' and 'psychiatrists'. In a series of studies Foucault explored the ways in which the 'power/knowledge' of experts could establish organizational and disciplinary practices that shape individuals and their actions. Prisons, schools, asylums, hospitals and factories can be considered as distinct and autonomous organizations of power/knowledge within which specific discourses structure the actions of experts and 'inmates' in relation to the human body and mind (Foucault, 1975).

The discourses of the human sciences themselves figured in Foucault's general studies in methodology. Psychology, sociology, economics, linguistics and other social sciences were all seen as contributing to the construction of the modern concept of 'man' (Foucault, 1966, 1971). Indeed, Foucault stressed that the conception of the individual human subject was the product of a very specific set of discourses and that there is, therefore, no warrant for positing 'the individual' as the fundamental unit of analysis in social theory. It is not the case that social processes are the result of individual action. Rather, individuals are the result of social practices rooted in specific forms of discourse. Individual subjects are the bearers and the results of power relations. Even such an apparently individual and personal matter as intimate sexual behaviour was seen as the result of a specific discourse of sexuality (Foucault, 1976).[8]

The principal form of power with which Foucault was concerned in his analysis of modernity is what he called 'bio-power'. This is the form of power/knowledge that operates through norms and technologies that shape the human body and mind through processes of *administration* and *discipline*. Administrative practices of surveillance and regulation create the 'populations' that may then be subjected to disciplinary practices through which a direct control over bodies can be exercised in processes of exclusion and confinement. These modern mechanisms of social control crystallized during the 19th century with the emergence of the clinic, the asylum, the prison, the factory and various other social organizations that Foucault analysed.

Modern societies control their populations through knowledge claims generated in the human sciences, which allow the establishment and enforcement of standards of 'normality' and 'deviance' in all areas of human life. This position has been summarized by one commentator in the following terms:

> The normal child, the healthy body, the stable mind, the good citizen, the perfect wife and the proper man – such concepts haunt our ideas about ourselves, and are reproduced and legitimated through the practices of teachers, social workers, doctors, judges, policemen and administrators (Philp, 1985: 67).

Through the establishment of such organizations of power/knowledge, people are locked into the complex network of power relations that Foucault termed the 'carceral archipelago'. This concept of the carceral archipelago shows that Foucault recognized that it is possible to move beyond the logical diversity and plurality of power and discourse to examine whether, in a concrete situation, there is a degree of interdependence or coherence among social practices. He did not hold that large-scale social structures do not exist, merely that they must not be *assumed* to exist. Social investigation begins with studies of specific practices, and only then moves on to any larger 'structures' that might arise from the connections that exist among practices. Such structures, if they exist, may be more or less integrated, and may often contain contradictory practices.[9] There are, for example, numerous centres of power, areas where domination is produced. Power circulates through these specific networks of institutions, organizations and discourses, but it may occasionally crystallize into larger structures of 'class' or 'state' relations.

Foucault did, however, reject such totalizing ideas as 'history' and 'society', a rejection that aligns him with Lyotard's rejection of 'grand narratives' such as that of 'progress'. He rejected all attempts to impose an overarching pattern on the discontinuities and struggles of social life. The future is always 'open', never determined, and so there can be no development, no evolution and, in short, no history. The emphasis on plurality and diversity leads Foucault to repudiate the very possibility that social theorists might establish an impartial and objective framework of theory. Indeed, the ideas of rationality and objectivity, generally seen as constitutive of scientific thought, are seen as products of discourse rather than as absolute and universal standards for knowledge. The 'truth' of knowledge is relative to discourse, as it is the rules of a particular discourse that specify what is to count as 'truth' and 'falsity'. Foucault's post-structuralism, then, emphasized the role of discourse in the constitution of social relations and, therefore, of science itself. Like his teacher, Foucault's methodology implies idealism and relativism.

Foucault's analysis of social life embraces the material relations of power and the cultural relations of discourse. It approaches these matters through the struggles and conflicts of collectively organized groups of experts and the larger structures that they produce. The determining element in his analysis, however, is not the actions of these groups, but the discourses through which their power relations are structured. Cultural codes and the forms of discourse in which they are embodied have a causal priority. Although Foucault's work lies outside the mainstream of structuralist writings, his interest in decentred cultural codes converges with certain other developments within the structuralist tradition.

REALITY AND HYPERREALITY

Myths are the dominant cultural products of tribal societies, and it is natural that myth analysis should play such an important part in social anthropology. Prominent among the cultural products of the modern societies with which sociologists are principally concerned is the output of the media of mass communications – novels, newspapers, films, television programmes and so on – and sociologists influenced by semiotic ideas have seen these cultural items as particularly appropriate subjects for structural analysis. For the same reason, literary theorists have also made great use of semiotic ideas as supplements to the traditional tools of literary criticism for the analysis of texts. Although I will not be concerned with the work of literary theorists, it is important to understand the shared body of ideas that structuralist-influenced theorists in literature and sociology have drawn upon.

A key figure in developing structural analyses of modern culture is Barthes, who held that any text could be analysed in terms of the discourse through which its author organizes a sequence of events or descriptions into a 'narrative'. The structure of a discourse is defined by the particular conventions of style and *genre* that specify the ways in which the elements can be combined into a narrative, and the task of literary analysis is to uncover the rules and relations of the discourses that underlie the narratives.

Literary texts are merely one kind of cultural product among many, and Barthes proposed that his ideas could be extended to such cultural products as fashion and advertising. The significance of advertising for Barthes was that it replaces the reality of particular consumer goods with 'images'. Consumers orient themselves towards the images rather than towards the reality; advertising images drive the processes of production and consumption. Barthes concluded that, far from making rational choices about their purchases on the basis of the utilities of particular goods, people are swayed by image and by fashion to consume particular items. An adequate understanding of the operation of markets for consumer goods requires that the discourses that structure advertising narratives be deciphered (Barthes, 1967).

These concerns pushed Barthes's analyses closer to the post-structuralist writings of Derrida (1967), himself influenced by Foucault. Derrida transformed Saussure's argument, moving semiotics closer to hermeneutics and to the work of Wittgenstein. His method for the analysis of texts centres around the idea of 'deconstruction'. Any text, he argued, is internally inconsistent, and the aim of textual interpretation is to deconstruct the text by showing how its inconsistencies are an integral part of its production. A discrepancy between what the language of the text constrains the author to say and what he or she meant to say will be apparent in the internal contradictions and inconsistencies of the text. Textual analysis, then, involves the deconstruction of texts into their contradictory elements. Derrida implies that any collective representation can be deconstructed in the same way as a literary text, but there have been few direct applications of his work in sociology. Instead, this strand of post-structuralism has made itself felt through the work of Baudrillard, whose work involves a break with the residual materialism of Foucault in that he eschews any talk of 'power'. Baudrillard's work is, instead, concerned solely with discourse and with the cultural images that it produces. Social reality for Baudrillard is simply those de-centred products of discourse that he calls 'simulations', and these cultural images are the products of the media of mass consumption.

The starting point for Baudrillard, however, was the cultural analyses that had been developed by Lukács and the Frankfurt school of critical theory. In his early work on mass consumption, Baudrillard saw these Marxist writings as a useful complement to semiotic ideas. He accepted the Marxist claim that the objects of everyday life had been 'commodified', but he added to this the semiotic view that these objects could also be regarded as 'signs' that are organized into systems of signification (Baudrillard, 1968). In addition to use value and exchange value, Baudrillard argued, a commodity has a 'sign value' that represents the prestige and power that it confers on its possessor. This sign value is apparent, at its simplest, in mass media advertisements: cigarettes can be presented as signs of sexual success, vacuum cleaners as signs of domesticity and so on. The various commodities that are consumed in everyday life are systematically linked to one another through mass media advertising and, as cultural objects, they are able to shape consumer wants and behaviour (Baudrillard, 1970, 1972). Baudrillard saw this as integral to the whole pattern of everyday life in contemporary society, and he later came to characterize this contemporary society as 'post-modern' society.

The Mirror of Production (Baudrillard, 1973) marked a change in this argument and a break with the whole Marxian tradition of cultural analysis. Marxism, Baudrillard argues, provided the key to understanding pre-modern and modern societies, but it cannot grasp the distinctive features of the emergent post-modern societies. In these societies, differences of class, rooted in the sphere of production, cease to have any great significance for social action. Blacks, women and gays organized into social movements that affirm their own significance and identity and that challenge the dominant cultural order are the source of radical change that points to a society 'beyond' modern capitalism.[10] As a result, Baudrillard argues, class analysis and the paradigm of production have been superseded by status analysis and the system of consumption. Although he initially saw new foci of revolutionary action arising in the private spheres of lifestyle and sexuality, Baudrillard increasingly abandoned any overtly political stance (Baudrillard, 1977). Those whose societies have entered the post-modern era live in a world of 'simulation' that defuses and diverts political action. The world of signs and simulations acquires a sense of 'reality'. They acquire a life of their own independent of any external reality. The world of everyday life is a world of interlocking and self-reinforcing images that constitute a new sphere of 'hyperreality' (Baudrillard 1981, 1983).

The whole social world of post-modern society is a chaotic and fragmentary interplay of simulations: it is a simulated reality. 'Reality' is fragmentary, chaotic and disorganized, it is a complex of often contradictory images behind which there is no source of unity. All is indeterminate and relative, creating an all-pervasive sense of 'vertigo'. Baudrillard's argument can be seen in the tradition of earlier theories of 'mass society' (Giner, 1976), according to which the strengthening of media images leads people to become apathetic: in Baudrillard's terminology, the apathetic mass is described as a 'silent majority' (Baudrillard, 1978).

In the post-modern world, signs have become completely separated from any external referent.[11] They are elements in free-floating systems of images that are produced by the mass media. Media images acquire a 'reality' that is 'more real' – hyperreal – than the reality that is conventionally ascribed to the 'real world'. The images that are conveyed in television dramas, soap operas, advertisements and films constitute the bulk of the information that people have about their own society. Media simulations lie at the heart of the 'imagined' world that Althusser described in his discussion of ideology. The media images come to be seen *as* reality: something must be real because it was on the television. People have no external and independent evidence to which they can turn in order to assess the validity of the media images, and so they accept them as real.[12]

Baudrillard is not arguing that people treat particular soap opera characters as if they were real, although there would be evidence to support this claim and also some evidence that some viewers actually believe them to *be* real. Baudrillard's argument concerns, rather, the *general* imagery of the media rather than the actuality of particular characters. People may not believe that the characters in *Neighbours* actually exist, but they may believe that the programme tells them something about what life is 'really' like in Australia and, indeed, in other contemporary societies. It is not particular characters and events that people believe in; it is the images of their lifestyle and their ways of behaviour. 'Documentary' and factual images are incorporated into the same cultural pattern as fictional images, and it is through all these simulations that people come to know about particular individuals and places.

All the information that most people have about the British royal family, for example, comes from the mass media. People believe that the royal family actually are as they are depicted on television, a fact of considerable importance as the royal family becomes the subject of soap operas and entertainment in television programmes such as *Pallas* and *Spitting Image*. Documentary, soap operas and gossip columns fuse together into a seamless web of images from which viewers derive their sense of reality.

Under these circumstances, the cultural codes that structure everyday experience create images that can no longer be related to any external 'reality'. Where Saussure had avoided the question of the connection between signs and reality, Baudrillard argues that in the post-modern world signs *are* reality.[13] Cultural signs and images are 'simulations' that have acquired a reality of their own; it is no longer possible to know 'reality' other than through these cultural images. There can be no independent assessment of the 'truth' or 'falsity' of images. It is possible only to compare and combine different but equally valid images. Theorists such as Foucault can no longer serve as guides to the understanding of this post-modern world, as their arguments are wedded to such 'modernist' views as the idea that 'power' relations really exist outside of discourse. For Baudrillard, power itself must be recognized as a simulation.

Theory can no longer be seen as an attempt to describe, analyse or explain reality in an objective or scientific way. Theorizing is itself simply the creation of simulations. For this reason, the boundaries between theory, art and entertainment break down. Epistemology cannot privilege theory over everyday common sense. Baudrillard makes the further and even more contentious point that every possible theoretical, artistic or political form has already been produced: there is nothing 'new' to say. All that theorists, artists and politicians can do is to combine and recombine existing forms. Theorizing in a post-modern world, then, consists of 'playing with the pieces'. Fragmentation and pastiche is the form taken by intellectual activity in post-modern society. This conclusion has led Baudrillard to abandon all sociological and explanatory goals. He now undertakes theory as a form of art or of poetry, and his hugely popular book *America* (Baudrillard, 1988), for example, consists of playful commentary and superficial generalizations, not of sociological analysis. The 'post-modern' is not simply an object of theoretical analysis, it is itself a style of theoretical activity. Baudrillard's work has transformed post-structuralist ideas into post-modern theorizing.

Baudrillard has, in some respects, come to a similar position to that of Weber, though he draws very different conclusions from this. Weber held that reality was a complex and infinite variety of sense impressions that can be constituted as meaningful or significant only by its selective grasping through cultural concepts and values. Social life for Weber is a kaleidoscope of value-relevant conceptualizations among which there is no overarching 'system'. Weber's view of modernity was that of a world that had abandoned metaphysical narratives and had become 'disenchanted'. Modern cultural reality was chaotic and fragmentary, and individuals had to make their own choices among the competing values that produced this chaos. Baudrillard ascribed these characteristics to post-modernity, and he made the final break with the idea that concepts could grasp aspects of an external reality. Concepts – simulations – *are* reality. In this situation, individuals no longer face the existential anxiety depicted by Weber, as the connection between their ideas and an external reality is no longer a problem. Individuals can, instead, respond to the 'vertigo' of chaotic images in a relatively detached way. They can 'play' with various images, rather than having to choose one of them.

Weber had concluded that sociologists conceptualize reality from particular, value-relevant standpoints, but seek to test these conceptualizations through objective methods of scientific investigation. Baudrillard abandons all attempts at 'science' and sees theory as a form of playful 'poetry'. A dispassionate observer would recognize the inadequacy of Baudrillard's position, as it is premised on the contention that there is no way of connecting signifiers and signified with a world that is external to, and independent of, experience. Weber's position, especially as it was developed in Parsons's 'analytical realism', provides a firmer basis for sociological activity that allows Baudrillard's substantive claims about the mass media to be explored without falling into chaotic relativism.

NOTES

1. Saussure himself described his approach as 'semiology', but Peirce's term 'semiotics' is now more widely used.
2. The relation between signifier and signified can be seen as Saussure's formulation of the question of the relation between language and thought. He concerned himself solely with the relationship between words and concepts and made no assumptions about any relationship between concepts and the 'real' world. Thus it is not strictly correct to say that 'dog' and '*chien*' refer to the *same* signified. Each language defines its own concepts and they cannot be compared by relating them to some presumed 'real object' in the external world.
3. I ignore here the slight, but important, distinction between 'sounds' and 'words' in order to concentrate on the general thrust of Saussure's argument.
4. Lévi-Strauss did not himself distinguish strictly between 'rules' and 'relations'. Clarification of this distinction is, perhaps, rather more due to Chomsky's (1957) structural linguistics, which used the idea of 'rule' as its central explanatory mechanism.
5. Leach himself had strongly disagreed with Lévi-Strauss on this point.
6. Foucault was a student of Althusser and, like his teacher, his work has some similarities with the works of Bachelard, Canguilheim and, more distantly, Kuhn (1962). Unlike these writers, however, Foucault pointed to continuity as well as discontinuity in the production of discourse: new codes emerge from pre-existing codes.
7. A common link to Schopenhauer and Nietzsche connects Foucault's discussion on this point with the otherwise different arguments of Gumplowicz, Mosca and other conflict theorists.
8. Foucault's final works pursued this theme through an examination of the idea of the 'self', but he increasingly abandoned any attempt at social theory *per se*. Two books (Foucault,

1984a and 1984b) were presented as the second and third volumes of *The History of Sexuality*, but they departed from the social themes of the first volume.

9. In terms of the terminology introduced in previous Chapters, Foucault could be seen to hold that 'system integration' is to be demonstrated empirically rather than assumed *a priori*.

10. On this point compare the argument of Eder (1993), discussed in Chapter 5.

11. Baudrillard is himself ambivalent about the term 'post-modern' as a description for the social forms that came after the phase of modernity, but commentators on his work – both critical and sympathetic – have tended to identify his views with those now commonly termed 'post-modern'.

12. A related view can be found in the work of Castoriadis (1975) in his idea of the 'imaginary institution' of society.

13. Indeed, Baudrillard, like Kristeva and the *Tel Quel* group, rejects even the distinction between signifier and signified.

9. Interpretation, structuration and rules

Recent work by Anthony Giddens has highlighted the importance of 'rules' in the production of social action. Through a critical reconsideration of Saussure's linguistics, Giddens came to recognize the importance of speech as a paradigm for understanding action. Just as human speech is structured by specific rules of grammar, so action must be seen as structured by distinctive systems of rules. This recognition of the importance of rules in social life is shared by the theoretical approach that has come to be known as ethnomethodology. This particular approach to theory had, however, originated in the phenomenological explorations of Harold Garfinkel, who took up the work of Schutz as a way of exploring the taken-for-granted procedures of everyday life.

Schutz had, of course, also inspired the work of Berger and Luckmann (1966), but Garfinkel moved Schutz's work in a radically divergent direction. Though sharing many assumptions with Berger's phenomenological sociology, Garfinkel and his followers saw their task as the investigation of the deep structure of rules and interpretative procedures used in everyday life. This investigation was seen as a crucial pre-condition for any further explorations of social life. Where symbolic interactionism and phenomenological sociology focused their attention on the moving picture of social life, ethnomethodology attempted to give a frame-by-frame account of how such a moving picture was possible.

Garfinkel's ethnomethodology posed a radical challenge to many of the taken-for-granted assumptions of orthodox sociology itself. Whether concerned with 'action' or 'system', orthodox sociology was seen as having failed to understand the most fundamental features of social life. This challenge was especially strong during the 1960s and early 1970s, but the claims of ethnomethodology were largely ignored by orthodox sociology until they were taken up by Giddens. It is through Giddens's work that ethnomethodology has been brought into the mainstream of sociological analysis. Giddens's combination of ethnomethodology with structuralist and post-structuralist ideas has allowed him to construct a novel approach to the structuring of action through taken-for-granted rules. He has used this approach as the basis for a powerful attempt to reconcile the analysis of action with that of structure and system.

RULES, ROLES AND REASONS

Harold Garfinkel had studied under Parsons in the late 1940s, but he became increasingly critical of Parsons's approach to social order and social structure. He turned, like Berger, to the work of Alfred Schutz, which he saw as offering the starting point for a critical reformulation of Parsons's central ideas. His own ideas were developed in a series of essays written during the 1950s and 1960s; these had a major impact on sociological thought when they were republished in 1967, a year after Berger and Luckmann's (1966) principal work (Garfinkel, 1967b). Garfinkel's work was, implicitly, as critical of Berger and Luckmann as it was of Parsons, as both approaches remained wedded to assumptions of consensus and socialization. Indeed, the distinctiveness of Garfinkel's approach was signalled by the label 'ethnomethodology' that he gave to it. The word, whose meaning will be given shortly, was intended to indicate that Garfinkel initially saw himself not as a 'sociologist' but as a practitioner of a discipline that was separate and distinct from sociology. The phenomenological discipline of ethnomethodology was an attempt to elucidate the presuppositions of sociology (Mehan and Wood, 1975; Heritage, 1984).

Ethnomethodology became a rallying point for a number of writers who sought to develop a radical critique of Parsons and orthodox sociology that went beyond the arguments of symbolic interactionism and abandoned the assumptions of consensus and socialization that characterized Berger and Luckmann. The fundamental theoretical programme was set out by Garfinkel, and these ideas were elaborated by Harvey Sacks and by Aaron Cicourel (1964, 1967).[1]

Garfinkel's starting point is Parsons's explanation of social order in terms of socialized normative commitments. Parsons held that individuals learn the norms that define the particular social relations that they enact. The actions of doctors and their patients, for example, mesh together in an orderly way because the participants have been socialized into a common culture. Garfinkel held that this view presented people as 'cultural dopes': they were mere passive containers for cultural norms. The contrary view that Garfinkel set out was that the orderliness of social life was a practical *achievement* of people in their everyday life. Social meaning and social order are problematic, and they have to be created and sustained through the ongoing activities of actors.

Garfinkel does not, however, reject the view that social order is *experienced* as an objective reality. Indeed, he sees the perception of its objectivity as a central feature of social life. Garfinkel, following Schutz, wanted to examine the ways in which people sustain a sense of social structure. In order to achieve a smooth meshing of their everyday activities, people need to create a sense of social order: they need to demonstrate to other people that their actions conform to certain rules or follow certain principles. To this end, they employ various ways of reporting and accounting for their actions, so helping to create the impression of social order. The orderly structure of the social world is 'an accomplishment of the accounting processes through and by which it is described and explained' (Zimmerman and Wieder, 1970: 293–4). The task of ethnomethodology, then, is to explore the 'practices of investigating and reporting' that people employ to make sense of their own and of other's actions.

Central to this task is the question of *how* people make sense of what others are doing. This emphasis on activities was crucial to Garfinkel's whole project. Activities aimed at the collecting and processing of information involve the use of specific 'methodologies'. The natural sciences, for example, involve the use of laboratory and mathematical methods for making sense of the physical world. Garfinkel argues that lay people, too, follow specific methodologies for making sense of their observations and experiences in everyday life. The task that he set himself, therefore, was the study of the everyday methodologies that are used by ordinary people. By analogy with the disciplines of 'ethnobotany' and 'ethnomedicine' that study ordinary people's classifications of plant life and diseases, Garfinkel termed his investigations 'ethnomethodology'. This discipline, he argued, is concerned with studying the ordinary, everyday methodologies that are used to make sense of the social world. Practical, everyday methodologies are specific bodies of knowledge, definitions and rules whose organized application produces a sense of social structure. The objectivity of the social world is a result of the accounting practices that people use in applying their methodologies.

The elements in practical methodologies – knowledge, definitions and rules – are normally unconscious or only partly conscious. They are 'taken-for-granted' and become so deeply embedded in day-to-day activities that they rarely need to be made explicit. The use of these methodologies is a *skill* that individuals possess and, like any skill, the individuals may be unable to describe, in any detail, exactly what they are doing. Someone who has the skill of riding a bicycle, for example, applies a complex body of taken-for-granted knowledge and rules of behaviour, but is unlikely to be able to describe exactly what they need to do in order to maintain their balance. Virtually all human skills, including such skills as speaking a language, have this same taken-for-granted character. Thus Garfinkel concludes that everyday methodological skills, though rule-governed, are not typically accessible to individual consciousness. They are applied routinely and virtually without thought in normal situations, and there is no need for people to reflect upon their skills. The everyday world is, under normal conditions, reconstructed as an objective, structured reality in a thoroughly routine way, without individuals having to give any serious thought to what they are doing. Social reality, like the skills that produce and reproduce it, is a taken-for-granted phenomenon.

In order to make these implicit methodologies available for study, Garfinkel devised an experimental approach that would force people to make them explicit. He aimed to create situations that would disrupt their expectations by presenting them with unanticipated or 'non-sensical' experiences. When faced with such experiences, Garfinkel showed, the taken-for-granted world does not collapse. People reconstruct its meaning, re-establishing a sense of structure and so allowing their actions to continue as before. By investigating the ways that people respond to those experiences, it is possible to uncover the knowledge, definitions and rules that comprise the taken-for-granted methodologies. Garfinkel shows that people draw on common-sense understandings of what others are expected or likely to do. These understandings are used to interpret the strange or unusual occurrences and so to 'normalize' them. To make sense of something is to see it as part of a normal, everyday reality that, until it was disrupted, was taken-for-granted and unproblematic.

Cicourel (1968, 1970, 1972) has presented what must rank as the most sophisticated attempt to use Garfinkel's ideas to uncover the basic rules that are involved in *all* interaction. Such basic rules, he argues, are invariant features of social life and are used to provide a sense of social order that underpins any normative order. Cicourel bases his account of these rules on the arguments of Chomsky, and a small digression into Chomsky's work will help to illuminate the whole issue of the part that is played by 'rules' in social life.[2]

Chomsky's analysis of language is, of course, rooted in structural linguistics, and it might appear to be totally alien to the concerns of the ethnomethodologists. This is not, however, the case. Chomsky begins from a distinction between actual speech (which he calls 'linguistic performance') and the underlying 'linguistic competence' that allows speech to be produced. Speech comprises a phonetic utterance (a pattern of sentences) that conveys meaning. The meaning of an utterance is the deep structure that is embedded in the surface structure of the utterance. Chomsky's work was intended to elucidate the rules that produce both the meaning and the utterance. Linguistic competence consists of a system of rules that provides the capacity for people to produce speech: rules of phonology (specifying the possible connections of sounds), rules of semantics (specifying the connections of meaning), and rules of syntax (specifying how sentences can be formed). These three types of rule comprise the *grammar* of a language (Chomsky, 1957). Each language, then, has its own grammar, and those normally socialized individuals who learn the rules of their grammar can be said to possess a linguistic competence.

Syntax involves two sub-types of rule: 'phrase structure rules' and 'transformation rules'. Phrase structure rules specify how verbs, nouns and other parts of speech can be combined into phrases that constitute a 'deep structure' of meaning. In his later work, Chomsky (1965) added that phrase structure rules operate along with a 'lexicon' (or 'dictionary') of words to produce the deep structure. Transformation rules specify how the deep, phrase structures can be converted into the actual sentences that constitute a 'surface structure' of meaning (see Figure 9.1).

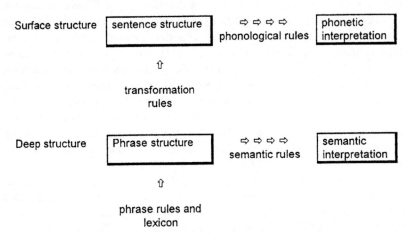

Figure 9.1   Chomsky's model of linguistic competence

The deep structure comprises the phrase structure and its semantic interpretation; the surface structure comprises the sentence structure and its phonetic interpretation. The transformation rules are the *generative* element in language: they generate surface structures from deep structures. Thus a particular deep structure meaning might be converted into two or more distinct, but equivalent, meaningful utterances. The two sentences, 'Cats chase mice' and 'Mice are chased by cats' have a different surface structure, but the same deep structure. It is also possible for two quite distinct deep structures to be transformed into the same surface structure. The two deep structure meanings, 'Planes that fly can be dangerous' and 'To fly planes can be dangerous', could both be converted into the same sentence, 'Flying planes can be dangerous'.

It is the ambiguity of meaning in the latter case of an utterance with two possible interpretations that forms Cicourel's starting point for his critical extension of Chomsky. Cicourel's argument is that such ambiguity can be resolved only by reference to the *social context* in which the speech occurs. A proper theory of semantics would need to go beyond linguistic competence to a consideration of linguistic performance. Linguistic performance, as a social process, involves a different, but related, set of rules. Speech, Cicourel (1970) argues, depends upon a system of basic rules – or 'interpretative procedures' – that establish the context for speech. Only when context has been established can the question of meaning be resolved.

Cicourel's purpose in making these extensions to Chomsky's work was to use them as a basis of a model of actors' performance in social interaction (see Figure 9.2). The establishment of a 'surface structure' of normative order – such as, for example, a consensually defined pattern of role expectations and definition of the situation – is a complex process. People do not 'know' which norms are to apply in a particular situation unless they have arrived at an understanding of the kind of situation that they are involved in. The interpretative procedures that people use allow them to build up a sense of the social structure in which they are operating and, therefore, to identify the nature of the situation and the relevant norms that are to be employed. Once a sense of social structure has been acquired, people are able to account for what they are doing by incorporating it under some normative description.[3]

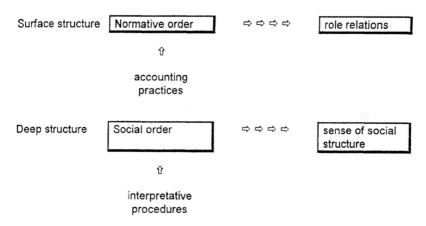

Figure 9.2   Cicourel's model of interactional performance

The model that Cicourel has constructed is complex and is built at a highly general level. He has attempted to sketch out the fundamental interpretative procedures of social interaction, but the import of his work is best seen by taking it as a framework for understanding more concrete ethnomethodological studies of interaction.[4] Conversation – verbal interaction – is one of the best-researched areas in ethnomethodology, and conversational analysis provides a critical insight into the nature of social rules. The leading contributor to the development of conversational analysis was Harvey Sacks, who set out an account of the methodologies that individuals use to make sense of what each other is saying and to manage talk. An orderly, structured conversation requires that each participant has a chance to speak and that there be a smooth 'transition' from one speaker to another. Individuals must know when one person's 'turn' is finished and another's can begin. Conversation, then, involves the exercise of 'skill'.

The task that Sacks set himself was to use transcriptions of ordinary, natural conversations to uncover the rules that govern turn-taking. His formulation of the rules is somewhat complex, but can be simplified as follows:

Rule 1:   The current speaker may designate the next speaker.
Rule 2:   If no one is designated, then anyone may speak when the current speaker finishes; or the current speaker may continue.
Rule 3:   If the current speaker continues, return to Rule 1.[5]

The participants in a conversation, Sacks argued, apply this set of rules to their actions. They are 'skilled' conversationalists and can produce an orderly transition from one speaker to the next. These rules are what 'everybody knows' – people 'know' the rules in the sense that they 'know how' to take turns. They are the basis of orderly conversation and they also govern reactions to interruptions, silences and other forms of 'deviance'. It is unlikely, however, that any conversationalist would be able to state the rules in the formal way that they were set out by Sacks.

This approach to the analysis of conversation can, and has, been extended through the discovery of rules governing other aspects of conversation: 'openings' and 'closings'; the 'sequencing' of conversations into beginnings, middles and ends; the introduction of new topics for discussion; the distribution of participants over the course of the conversation; gender differences in contributions to conversations (Fishman, 1978), and so on (see also Boden, 1990; Boden and Zimmerman, 1990). Putting all of these studies together would yield a comprehensive account of the orderly characteristics of conversation.[6]

Ethnomethodology's most lasting successes have been made in the area of conversational analysis, but the approach has been applied in many other areas. Ethnomethodologists have investigated the rules used by doctors in making diagnoses and producing medical records; the rules used by laboratory scientists in producing 'data' and undertaking replications; the rules used by jurors in coming to decisions; how women use rules that demonstrate their femininity and reinforce the dominance of men (Garfinkel, 1967a); how inmates of a hostel use rules of a 'convict code' to control one another's behaviour (Wieder, 1974); how nurses, patients and administrators use rules concerning death to organize hospital routines and to construct medical records and statistics (Sudnow, 1967); the rules used by the police in producing arrests and criminal statistics (Cicourel, 1967); and the rules used by teachers and counsellors in educational decision-making (Cicourel and Kitsuse, 1963). To these might be added the suggestion that a fruitful area for investigation would be the rules of consumer optimization (Hayek, 1962, 1965) discussed in Chapter 3.

THE THEORY OF STRUCTURATION

Anthony Giddens developed a novel and independent approach to theory. Its origins are to be found in his reinterpretation of the work of the founding generation of sociologists, but it has increasingly been shaped by the work of Garfinkel and other ethnomethodologists. The principal target of Giddens's early explorations in social theory had been Parsons's interpretation of Weber and Durkheim (Parsons, 1937) and his neglect of Marx. Giddens believed that before social theory can be developed further, it must recast its understanding of its own history. Sociology arose, he argues, as an attempt to understand the specific features of the *modern* society that had begun to emerge by the 19th century:

> Modernity is the core concern of sociology. Sociology was established as an endeavour to understand the massive changes that, from about the eighteenth century onwards, disrupted traditional modes of life and introduced quite novel forms of social organization (Giddens, 1991b: 207).

Weber and Durkheim – not to mention Marx – were, in their varying ways, grappling with this same problem. Giddens holds that an adequate understanding of modernity and its consequences can be achieved only if sociologists return to the classic interpretations of modernity. The purpose of this return, however, is not to take over the writings of the founding sociologists in an uncritical way. The need is for a critique and reconstruction of their works. Such a reconstruction requires that they be understood in their historical context and in the context of the rise of sociology as a discipline.

The orthodox interpretation of sociology saw its history in terms of a 'great divide' that separated the pre-scientific and philosophical ideas of the 18th and 19th centuries from the scientific ideas of the founding sociologists who wrote in the period between 1890 and 1920. Giddens rejects this view of the history of the discipline (Giddens, 1971, 1972, 1976a). He relates the tremendous influence of this interpretation to its presence in Parsons's *The Structure of Social Action*, and he traces its impact to the continuing influence of that book. Parsons (1937), as I have shown, saw Durkheim, Weber and Pareto, together with other writers such as Simmel, Tönnies and Freud, as having brought about a revolutionary reorientation of social thought. Giddens's own view is that this view has had an almost completely negative impact on the attempt to develop an adequate social theory.

Giddens has attempted to achieve such a reconsideration at the level of general theory and to apply these ideas to the understanding of modernity. His reconstruction begins with a recognition that the writings of the classical theorists, as filtered through the influence of Parsons, has spawned two contrasting theoretical stances. One of these has emphasized the individual and social action; the other has emphasized society and 'social facts'.

Sociological approaches that focus their attention on the individual and social action have emphasized a concept of the 'subject', the knowledgeable human agent. These approaches adopt the characteristically 'subjectivist' stance that is found in interpretative, interactionist and hermeneutic approaches to social theory. The strongest intellectual roots of this theoretical stance are to be found in the writings of Dilthey and the German historical school of social thought, and it found its classic expression in the works of Weber and Mead. The common thread in these subjectivist approaches is to see social organization – social institutions and 'society' itself – as the direct creations of individual acting subjects. Individual actions and their subjective meanings are accorded theoretical primacy in the 'understanding' of human conduct and, therefore, in its explanation.

Those who focus their attention on society and the social system, on the other hand, have emphasized external and constraining forces that are supposed to exist over and above the individual members of society. This 'objectivist' approach had its immediate roots in the work of Comte, and it found its classic expression in the work of Durkheim. It is also the principal characteristic of the 'orthodox consensus' in social theory that was established in the works of Parsons and his followers. Both American functionalism and French structuralism, according to Giddens, embody this objectivist standpoint. They accord the social system a primacy in the explanation of human conduct, seeing it as a constraining or even a determining force in human life.

Giddens holds that this dualism between individual action and the social system, between agency and determination, has continued to bedevil social theory because writers on each side have failed to understand properly the interdependence of individual actors and social systems. Misconceptions of their nature have led to a reification of the supposed opposition between them. Giddens's argument is that in place of the *dualism* of the individual and the society must be recognized a *duality* of 'structure'. Individual actions are shaped by social 'structure', but the structured elements of social systems are the outcome of human action. Actors and social systems have to be seen as interdependent elements in a duality: the object of investigation for the social sciences 'is neither the experience of the individual actor, nor the existence of any form of social totality, but social practices ordered across space and time' (Giddens, 1984a: 2). These practices are reproduced in and through the activities of conscious human actors, but they are, at the same time, the very conditions which make such activities possible. Neither individual actions nor social systems can be isolated from the larger social process.

For this reason, Giddens argues, social practices can be studied from two different, but complementary, points of view. Each point of view is achieved by 'bracketing' – putting to one side – the issues and concerns of the other. Individual action and interaction can be studied if the researcher 'brackets' the institutions and collectivities that comprise the systemic features of social life. This methodological procedure of bracketing allows the researcher to analyse 'strategic action' and 'social integration' without having to take account of the complexities of the system level of analysis. If, on the other hand, individual action is 'bracketed', researchers can engage in 'institutional analysis' and the investigation of 'system integration' without having to take account of individual action. The analysis of action and the analysis of system are not opposed to one another; they are distinct but complementary aspects of sociological investigation. Action and system are not different 'things', they are, rather, different ways of looking at the same social practices. A recognition of the centrality of practices to social life allows sociologists to analyse both action and system without reifying either side of this methodological distinction.

Giddens aims to show how action and system, individual and society, can be integrated within a single theoretical framework centred around the idea of social practices. This can be achieved, he argues, through a proper understanding of the concept of structure. The word 'structure' has tended to be used in the same way as the word 'system', and many objectivist writers have, indeed, contrasted 'structure' and 'action'. 'Structure', in this sense, refers to the institutionalized features of social systems – kinship structures, class structures, political structures and so on (Giddens, 1984a: 185). Giddens argues that this usage may be legitimate for many descriptive purposes, but it is too loose and ambiguous to serve as the basis of an adequate theoretical synthesis.

'Structure', he believes, must be sharply distinguished from 'system'. Structures in the narrower technical sense that is preferred by Giddens are the sets of rules and resources that individual actors draw upon in the practices that reproduce social systems. Systematically organized social practices embody structures and they constitute actors. The 'duality of structure' arises from the role that is played by structures in linking the systemic features of practices with the actions of the individuals who produce and reproduce them. Structure is involved in both system and action, but it is reducible to neither of them. Structures, therefore, are both the *medium* and the *outcome* of the actions that they organize; they are the *means* through which actions are made possible, and they are the *consequences* of these same actions.

Giddens's concept of 'structure' is most unusual, and it has led to much criticism and confusion. His basic meaning can be grasped, however, if the distinction between structure and system is observed. Social systems are seen as the actual patterns of social relations that are formed into interdependent social institutions and collectivities. Social structures, on the other hand, are sets of rules and resources that are involved in the production and reproduction of social systems by individual actors. 'Structuration' is Giddens's name for the process by which systems are produced and reproduced through the interactions of actors who draw upon structural rules and resources.

Unlike actions and systems, structures have no real existence: they exist 'out of time and space' and have merely a 'virtual' existence in the practices that they organize (Giddens, 1976b: 127; 1981: 26). Actions are governed by structures; but structures exist only in and through actions. Structures do not literally exist as 'things' that can be pointed to (like the physical skeleton of the human body). They exist only in and through interaction. Giddens illustrates this idea through a parallel with speech and grammar. Speech embodies certain rules of grammar, but these rules exist only in and through human speech. The rules of grammar exist nowhere outside the speech of the members of a particular linguistic community. When the pattern of speech in a community alters, the existing grammatical rules may no longer be reproduced and a new set of rules may come into being as a condition for subsequent speech.[7] This idea is complex and difficult to grasp. The important point is Giddens's claim that the dualism of 'action' and 'system' can be transcended through an awareness of the role of 'structure' as a linking concept between the two levels of analysis.

ACTION, INTERACTION AND AGENCY

How, then, does Giddens understand individual action? His analysis of agency stresses openness and choice, but it departs from traditional ideas of 'free will' as well as from Parsonian 'voluntarism' and means–ends models of action. His starting point is the claim that human action must be seen as a continuous flow of activities which it is not possible to divide into separate and discrete elements such as 'means' and 'ends'. Individuals do, however, reflect upon their actions in an attempt to understand and to control them. While involved in their actions, people are engaged in a continual 'monitoring' of these activities and their consequences. This monitoring involves a reflection upon what has happened and an anticipation of what might happen in the future. On this basis, individual actors are able to modify their current actions in the light of the results of their past actions. Giddens sees this process of monitoring as central to the 'reflexivity' of human action.

Reflexivity, then, involves the monitoring of actions – one's own actions and those of others – and of the wider context within which these actions occur. This is rarely undertaken in a fully conscious way. It is, typically, undertaken in a state of 'practical consciousness' that involves many taken-for-granted assumptions. Practical consciousness does, however, involve an attempt by actors to arrive at an understanding of action that enables them to 'account' for it to themselves and to others. Such accounts are attempts to reconstruct the 'reasons' that led to the action, and Giddens sees actors as involved in a continual 'rationalization' of action. This rationalization – the producing of reasons – involves the interpretative process of accounting for action and the normative process of being accountable. Together, these elements constitute the 'accountability' of action.

Giddens builds this view of action into a model of individual personality (see Figure 9.3). In this model, there are three levels of consciousness – unconsciousness, practical consciousness and discursive consciousness. Unconscious 'wants' and 'needs' are the motives that drive action, but they do not do this in a deterministic way. Wants and needs must be consciously taken into account and acted on before they can impinge on social action. Practical and discursive consciousness enter into the shaping of action through the formulation of a definition of the situation facing the actor. This may occur purely at the level of practical consciousness, where the action is

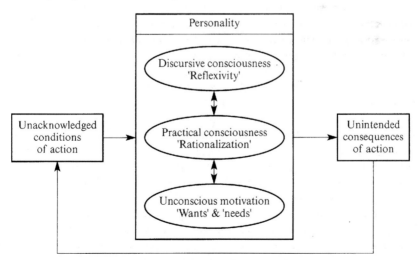

Figure 9.3   Giddens's model of personality and action

organized in routine ways, or it may involve a form of discursive reflexivity whereby acts are monitored in relation to a moral 'conscience' that enables the person to justify or ground their reasons for acting. Discursive consciousness involves a systematic reflection on action and produces a rational reconstruction of it. Models of the rational actor and rational choice have tended to overstate the significance of discursive consciousness. Much action in everyday life, argues Giddens, involves only the practical consciousness of actors: they know things in a tacit, taken-for-granted way, in the same sense that individuals 'know' the rules of grammar. Such practical knowledge is routinized and taken-for-granted, rather than being systematic and formalized in discursive terms. Actors know *how* to do things, but they may not be able to formulate this knowledge discursively.[8]

A central aspect of the reflexive monitoring in which actors are continually involved is the monitoring of the *consequences* of their actions. Action involves agency and, therefore, has effects on the world. An actor or agent[9] is one who has the power or capacity to make things happen. However, not all of the effects that are achieved are intended by the actor: as Merton showed, unintended consequences play a crucial role in social life. As shown in Figure 9.3, actions result in unintended consequences that then become conditions for future actions. While Giddens rejects the general framework of functionalist theory, he accepts the validity of its stress on the unintended consequences of action. The unintended consequences of action and their entwining ramifications are the crucial element in social reproduction.[10] To the extent that individual actors are unaware of the ramifying unintended consequences of their actions, they may be faced with unknown and unacknowledged conditions in their subsequent actions. That is to say, while actors always know what they are doing, their knowledge may not accurately describe the actual conditions that are responsible for their actions, and they may know very little about the wider ramifications of their actions. They may know what they are doing, but they may not know what they have actually done.

From considering action, Giddens proceeds to interaction, where two or more actors are involved together. Interaction is normally a face-to-face encounter in which the actors are physically co-present. Each actor, by virtue of his or her physical presence, has to handle problems of self-presentation and has to interpret the meanings of the self-presentations of others.[11] In early stages of human history and in pre-history, argues Giddens, almost all interaction was of this face-to-face kind, though the invention of writing, the spread of literacy and the introduction of postal systems allowed more 'mediated' forms of interaction to occur without the actors having to be physically co-present. Correspondence through the post, for example, is a form of interaction that does not involve bodily co-presence. In modern societies, the opportunities for such mediated interaction have grown considerably, as electrical and electronic media have allowed interaction to take place through the use of telephones, televisions and computers.

Actors occupy 'positions' within the institutions and collectivities that make up their society: interaction always involves actors who are 'positioned' relative to one another and to other actors. Each position involves a normatively sanctioned 'identity' that actors can draw upon in their interactions. Thus two people may act towards one another as 'doctor' and 'patient' or as 'man' and 'woman', and their interactions will be patterned by the identities that have been imputed to the occupants of these positions. Doctors, for example, are likely to be expected to behave in certain distinctive ways.

Behind the diversity of interactional encounters is the common feature that they all involve the handling of time and space, and Giddens sees this as a fundamental feature of human life. Time is handled through the adoption of routines such as turn-taking in conversations and the avoidance of interruption to those who are already engaged in interaction. Space is handled through spacing or 'regionalization', a process through which particular areas are defined as 'public' or 'private' – 'front' or 'back' areas in Goffman's terminology – each area having its own appropriate forms of behaviour.

These features of interaction define what Giddens terms *social integration*. This latter term refers to the reciprocity between individual actors in their face-to-face encounters, and is achieved through the reflexive monitoring of action.[12] Actors define their situations from the standpoint of the positions that they occupy, and they negotiate an agreed definition of the situation on the basis of their relative power to make their own definition stick. Berger and Kellner, for example, analysed the negotiation of reality in marriage in these terms (Berger and Kellner, 1970). Where an agreed definition of the situation is negotiated, there is a high degree of 'social integration' in the encounters of the actors.

The 'structural' features of interaction and the state of social integration are the consequences of the use of specific 'rules' by those who are involved in the interaction. Giddens sees this structuring of interaction as occurring in three dimensions: these are the *communication* of meaning, the justification of action through normative *sanctions* such as the creation of expectations and 'moral' obligations, and the exercise of *power*. Communication and sanction are cultural processes through which meanings and norms are established and enforced, while power is seen as the 'transformative capacity' that allows actors to achieve or to change things. As Giddens argues, 'All social interaction involves the use of power, as a necessary implication of the logical connections between human action and *transformative capacity*' (Giddens, 1981: 28). Power, communication and sanctioning are integral features of all human action and interaction. They are central to human agency. The communication of a diagnosis between doctor and patient, for example, is shaped by the normatively sanctioned identities that are attached to these positions and by the relative power of the participants to define the conditions of the encounter.

The relationship between interaction and structure is similar to the relationship between speech and language. 'Speech' comprises a pattern of connections among words that embody meanings; 'language' comprises the syntactic and semantic rules that 'structure' speech. Systems of action are, in the same way, structured by generative rules of interaction. In emphasizing the structuring capacity of rules, Giddens has retraced the steps through which Garfinkel and Cicourel welded Chomsky's linguistic analyses into a model of social interaction.[13]

The distinction between communication and sanction centres on a distinction between two types of rule: semantic and moral rules. Semantic rules are involved in the interpretation of meaning through processes of communicative action. Moral rules are involved in the establishment and validation of norms through processes of moral sanctioning. In his later work, however, Giddens argues that it is wrong to draw a sharp distinction between 'constitutive' (or semantic) and 'regulative' (or moral) rules (Giddens, 1979: 83). The distinction between communication and sanction should be seen as pointing not to different *types* of rule, but to different *aspects* of rules. All rules involve both interpretative and normative aspects. Thus it is not possible to divide rules neatly into two exhaustive categories, the semantic and the moral.

Power is less clearly analysed by Giddens. He links power with 'resources', but it is clear from his discussion that power arises not from resources *per se* but from the ways in which resources are controlled and used. What seems to be implied – though never made clear – is that a third aspect of rules must be considered alongside the semantic and the moral. This 'resource aspect' of rules refers to the ways in which access to and control over particular objects allows them to be used as means or facilities in interaction. Giddens's statement that 'structure' is concerned with rules and resources, then, can be rephrased as a statement that structure is concerned with rules that relate to the semantic, moral and resourceful aspects of interaction. Seen in this way, it can be seen as an attempt to theorize the material features of the 'substratum' of action alongside the cognitive and normative features of social life (Lockwood, 1956). This argument is summarized in Figure 9.4.

In *The Constitution of Society* (Giddens, 1984a), Giddens further specifies the idea of 'rule' that is involved in his conception of structure. A rule, he says, is a formula for reproducing a particular set or pattern of activities. The rules of grammar, for example, are formulae for reproducing particular pat-

Dimension of interaction	Structural rule
Communication	Semantic
Sanction	Moral
Power	Resourceful

Figure 9.4   Structure and interaction

terns of speech: the speech embodies these rules and it is only when others share these rules that they can understand, or decode, the speech. The rules that make up a structure are, in Cicourel's sense, procedural rules.

Actors are generally unaware, or only partially aware, of the rules that are involved in their actions. People are not normally conscious of the grammatical rules that are embodied in their speech and writing, for example. Where people learn how to speak, how to drive a car, how to cook and so on, the rules that comprise these skills are retained in their memory. They are retained, however, only as 'memory traces' in their brains: these memory traces allow them to perform the skills, but the rules that they constitute are typically available to conscious recall in only a partial or distorted form.[14] These skills are normally exercised 'automatically', in a routinized way, and actors need neither recall the rules to consciousness nor formulate them in a discursive way. They do, nevertheless, 'know' how to do those things that they have learned, even if they cannot recall this knowledge to consciousness or codify it in a formal way.

In speaking to one another, for example, people routinely employ grammatical rules, but they will attempt to specify these rules only when someone makes a 'mistake'. When speaking to a foreigner, for example, they may tell them that 'the object follows the verb' in order to clarify a mistake in word order. Such verbalizations of rules, however, are not the actual rules themselves: they are discursive *interpretations* of the procedural rules. When people reflect upon the procedural rules that they use, or when they attempt to codify them, they are already interpreting them discursively. Codified rules, such as legal statutes, written rules for games and so on, are not true 'rules' in Giddens's sense: they are interpretations of the procedural rules that are produced by actors who attempt discursively to summarize them.

This idea might be clarified by an analogy with computing. The rules or procedures by which a computer operates comprise its programmed instructions. These are coded into its memory in the form of patterns of binary digits. These procedures can be formulated (in this case quite accurately) in a programming language such as Basic or Fortran. The computer does not follow the actual statements that are written down in the programming language – these must be translated by a compiler or interpreter into a symbolic code that is held electronically in the computer's memory. In the same way, the rules or procedures that are followed in action have been coded into the memories of actors, who may become consciously aware of them only after they have been interpreted discursively. Giddens is not, of course, holding that actors are programmed automata – indeed, the terminology of being 'programmed' is mine and not his. Actors reflexively 'program' themselves, as well as being programmed by the circumstances in which they act. The defining characteristic of a human 'program' such as the grammar of a language, is its 'openness', a characteristic that results from the capacity for deliberation and choice that human actors possess.[15]

It is important to recall that Giddens is not talking about structure as it is conventionally understood in structural functionalism, where it refers to a pattern of social relations. He is referring to the *structuring capacity* of rules. It is, in many respects, confusing of Giddens to term this capacity a 'structure'. He would have caused less confusion if he had retained the word 'structure' in its conventional sense to refer to the surface pattern of social institutions and practices (the 'system' in Giddens's terminology) and then referred simply to the 'grammar' of rules that generates it. In his later work he does, in fact, allow the use of 'structural' terms to describe features of systems of social relations. If Giddens's term 'structure' is understood as 'grammar', his meaning becomes much clearer.[16]

SYSTEM, INSTITUTION AND COLLECTIVITY

I have suggested that Giddens's concept of 'structure' is far removed from the structural concerns of most other approaches to sociology and that he is best seen as using an idea of structure as 'grammar'. Giddens does not deny the importance of the kind of 'structural' questions that are explored in structural functionalism and Marxism, but he holds that these concerns must be understood as aspects of the 'system' of social life. Social systems are sets of interdependent institutions and collectivities. Institutions and collectivities are not structures, but they do *have* structures. Giddens introduces a whole range of concepts to help with the analysis of social systems.

'Institutional analysis', it will be recalled, is Giddens's method for handling the 'objective' issues of 'society' and the social system after action processes have been 'bracketed'. *Institutions* are those practices that are most deeply embedded in time and space: an example might be the institution of marriage. *Collectivities*, on the other hand, are collective actors such as associations, organizations and social movements. It is organizations and social movements that Giddens sees as the characteristic collective actors of modern society. Unlike the 'associations' that are tied to traditional ways of doing things, organizations and social movements are concerned with changing the conditions of their own reproduction. Institutions and collectivities are the building blocks of social systems, which are seen as sets of interdependent institutions and collectivities characterized by a particular degree of 'system integration'. Unlike the social integration that characterizes face-to-face interaction, 'system integration' arises from the reciprocity across time and space that characterizes the institutions and organizations that comprise the system.[17]

Giddens also defines a concept of 'society', though he has some reservations about its usefulness. A society, he argues, is a systematic clustering of institutions and collectivities within a particular territorial locale that is sustained by processes of social and system integration and by a sense of 'community' and common membership. Only those systems that meet these criteria can be described as 'societies'.

Societies and other social systems can be analysed in terms of their 'structural principles', 'structural sets' and 'elements/axes of structuration'. Thompson has pointed out that these are not structural phenomena in the narrow sense that Giddens has given to that term (Thompson, 1989). They are not, that is to say, grammatical structures of rules. In his reply to Thompson, Giddens recognized that he had been unclear on this, but said that he had not meant to imply that they were 'structures' in his narrow sense. While recognizing that they are not 'structural' in the sense that he has used this word, Giddens holds, nevertheless, that in so far as they are 'structured' by social rules it is acceptable to adopt conventional terminology and to describe them in terms of the language of 'structure'. They are phenomena at the social system level that describe the mode of articulation of institutions and, like all systemic phenomena, they are produced and reproduced as actors draw upon rules. This qualification to his argument brings Giddens closer to conventional structural functionalism, at least so far as the concept of 'structure' is concerned, as it stretches the idea of structure to the 'looser' sense of the pattern or form of social relations (Craib, 1992: 148). He approaches these more conventional matters, however, through considering, first, the structural aspects of social systems in the narrower sense.

Giddens holds that there are three aspects or dimensions of the structure of social systems, and these correspond to the interactional elements of communication, sanction and power. These three structural dimensions are signification, legitimation and domination (Giddens, 1976b: 104–113; 1979: 81–111). These structural properties of social systems, Giddens argues, are analogous to the 'levels' of structure that were identified by Althusser, but he rejects the Althusserian concept as unclear and as ungrounded in a larger framework of appropriate theory (Giddens, 1981: 46–7). He feels that his own concepts are

more firmly grounded by virtue of their connection with specific aspects of
the rule-governed nature of human action.[18] His argument is summarized in
Figure 9.5, which extends the initial model set out in Figure 9.4.

Dimension of system	Structural rule	Dimension of interaction
Signification	Semantic	Communication
Legitimation	Moral	Sanction
Domination	Resourceful	Power

Source: Modified from Giddens, 1976: 122; Giddens,1984: 29.

Figure 9.5   System, structure and interaction

Structures of *signification* involve sets of semantic rules, or the semantic
aspects of rules, that are formed into a cognitive order from which interpretative schema are derived. Signification, therefore, comprises the rules or procedures through which signs are established for use in the communication of
meaning. Structures of *legitimation* involve sets of moral rules, or the moral
aspects of rules, that are formed into a legitimate order from which norms are
derived. Legitimation, therefore, comprises the rules or procedures through
which validity is established for use in the assertion of obligations in the
normative sanctioning of actions. Structures of *domination* involve sets of
rules that concern the use of resources.[19] It is through structures of domination that facilities and means of action can be mobilized for use in power
relations.

The basic outline of Giddens's argument should be clear. Signification
structures the communication of meaning, legitimation structures the constitution of moral judgements, and domination structures the exercise of power.
Thus communication, morality and power are integral features of interaction;
signification, legitimation and domination are integral features of social systems.

The three structural aspects of social systems – signification, legitimation
and domination – are distinguishable from one another only in an analytical
sense, as they are generally found entwined together in concrete settings.
Where the semantic and moral aspects of rules are fused into a cohesive
framework, the structure comprises a 'common culture' or 'form of life'.
Such consensus is, however, unusual. Unlike the rules of language, which are
widely shared throughout a speech community, other social rules do not
normally involve such wide consensus. More typically, rules are characterized by ambiguity and dissensus, and there may be distinct 'sub-cultures'.

For this reason, Giddens argues, orderly interaction is generally likely to occur only if resources are used to underpin the relations of power through which particular rules are imposed on one individual or group by another.

Giddens rejects, as has been seen, the sharp distinction between semantic rules and moral rules. Signification and legitimation are seen as two aspects or dimensions of rule-following – the semantic and the moral aspects. What he is saying is that specific rules will always comprise both 'cultural codes' and 'moral norms'. The basic element in signification is the *sign*, and the paradigm for all cultural signs is the linguistic sign. For this reason, structures of signification can best be analysed, Giddens believes, through the ideas developed within semiotic approaches to social theory. Hence a critical examination of structuralist writings provides Giddens with the basis for understanding this process. Signification, the use of interpretative schema for the communication of meaning, involves actors drawing on those 'typifications' and 'standardised elements of stocks of knowledge' which are the basis of the 'mutual knowledge' through which a 'universe of meaning' is sustained (Giddens, 1979: 83). Signification is, therefore, central to what Garfinkel called the 'accountability' of action.

Legitimation, on the other hand, centres around normative sanctions. At the interactional level, this involves the enactment of rights and obligations, as depicted in Parsons's analysis of the 'double contingency' of interaction – the mutual sanctioning of reciprocal sets of normative expectations. At the system level, therefore, legitimation through norms involves the *establishment* of rights and obligations, such as institutionalized role expectations. Rules are here seen as modes of normative regulation. Role expectations may be objects of moral commitment or they may be rooted simply in a rational, pragmatic acceptance.[20] It is not necessary to assume a moral consensus or perfect 'internalization'. Giddens argues that it is necessary to re-examine critically the central legacy of Durkheim and Parsons on this question, taking account also of the more active 'negotiation of reality' depicted in symbolic interactionist theories.[21] In terms reminiscent of a famous critique of the 'dominant ideology' thesis (Abercrombie *et al.*, 1979), Giddens holds that:

> The level of normative integration of dominant groups within social systems may be a more important influence upon the overall continuity of those systems than how far the majority have 'internalised' the same value-standards (Giddens, 1979: 103).

The centrality of domination to social systems reflects the centrality of power in interaction. Power involves relations of autonomy and dependence among actors, and it depends upon their drawing on, and reproducing structures of, domination:

> Resources treated as structural elements of social systems are drawn upon by
> actors in the instantiation of interaction. The power relations sustained in the
> regularised practices constituting social systems can be considered as reproduced
> relations of autonomy and dependence in interaction. Domination refers to struc-
> tured asymmetries of resources drawn upon and reconstituted in such power
> relations (Giddens, 1981: 50; emphasis removed).

Domination also plays an important part in structures of signification and
legitimation, but it is in the discussion of domination and resources that
Giddens's early work was at its weakest. Giddens's early writings on structure emphasized 'rules' rather than 'resources', but in his later work he
clarified both his concept of 'structure' and his concept of resources (Giddens,
1979, 1981). It is significant that he invariably writes of structure as 'rules
(and resources)', the placing of the brackets suggesting that resources are,
almost, an untheorized afterthought. This neglect is paradoxical in view of
the centrality that Giddens has accorded to power in his theoretical schema.

These structural dimensions of social systems enter into the production
and reproduction of the social institutions and collectivities that form the
surface features studied in much contemporary sociology. While Giddens
allows that these phenomena may be loosely described as 'structural', he
holds that they must be clearly distinguished from the narrower structural
concept of generative rules. This was recognized by a number of Giddens's
critics (Urry, 1982; Layder 1985; Thompson 1989). The institutional features
of social systems must not be identified with the 'grammatical' features of
social systems.

Structure-as-grammar has a 'virtual existence', while structures-as-sys-
tems have a 'real' existence (Bhaskar, 1975). Class relations, for example,
are causal mechanisms that constrain the actions of individual actors in ways
that are quite separate from the impact that structural rules have on them.
Giddens is reluctant to go too far in this direction, preferring to concentrate
his attention on action and its grammatical structuring. This reluctance has
led some (Craib, 1992) to hold that Giddens is, in fact, a highly sophisticated
action theorist who has failed properly to synthesize or to transcend the
dualism of action and system.

Giddens does, however, suggest an outline for system and institutional
analysis, albeit rather underdeveloped. He first shows how the structural
dimensions of social systems are involved in the generation of specific social
institutions. Signification is the primary element in the formation of the
symbolic orders and modes of discourse that form the *Weltanschaungen* –
worldviews – of societies and collectivities. Legitimation, on the other hand,
is the primary element in the formation of legal institutions and modes of
normative regulation. Political and economic institutions are formed, respectively, through the authoritative and allocative control over resources. An

important issue in the analysis of societies is the formation of institutions and the differentiation of specialized 'institutional orders' such as the economy and the polity (Giddens, 1981: 48). Giddens holds that each aspect of rule use operates alongside others in the constitution of particular institutions. The constitution of symbolic orders and modes of discourse through signification, for example, involves secondary processes of domination and legitimation (Giddens, 1981: 47). Similarly, the formation through authoritative domination of political institutions such as the nation state involves secondary processes of signification and legitimation. This argument is summarized in Figure 9.6, and it allows Giddens to develop his analysis of the political (authoritative) and economic (allocative) processes that comprise the forms of social domination.

	Primary structural dimension	Secondary structural dimension	Institutional forms	Parsonian parallels
1.	Signification	Domination Legitimation	Symbolic orders, modes of discourse	L
2.	Authoritative domination	Legitimation Signification	Political institutions	G
3.	Allocative domination	Legitimation Signification	Economic institutions	A
4.	Legitimation	Domination Signification	Law, modes of regulation	I

Source: Modified from Giddens 1979: 107; 1981: 47.

Figure 9.6   Structural dimensions and social institutions

The authoritative use of resources in concrete social situations involves also processes of signification and legitimation that constitute it as 'authority'. This generates 'command over persons', over the social world. Giddens holds that this involves control over the spatio-temporal organization of social life, the socially organized human body and the organization of life chances (Giddens, 1981: 47, 52). Some 'locales' – the spatio-temporal settings in which people interact – permit the concentration of resources in such a way that they become 'power containers' that allow groups a greater degree of control over the spatial and temporal organization of their actions. Giddens's view is that the accumulation and 'containment' of resources is the material basis for relations of domination. This is true, for example, of castles and cities in pre-industrial societies, and of formal organizations and nation states in modern societies. The accumulation and containment of resources is the material basis of relations of domination.

This form of domination is particularly achieved through *surveillance*, which is seen as the collection, storage and control of information concerning other people in order to use it in the direct superintendence of their activities. Surveillance is the 'collation and integration of information put to administrative purposes' (Giddens, 1985: 46). Writing and electronic means of communication are the principal forms of information storage. They allow mediated interaction across large expanses of time and space, and so break with the patterns of face-to-face communication that prevail in non-literate societies. In this way, communication is severed from its direct link with the body in immediate personal encounters. Cities and formal organizations are among the most effective means of allowing such stored information to be used in the direct superintendence of others, and this superintendence is enhanced by the establishment of a body of specialized administrative officials. Authoritative control over resources can, therefore, be regarded as the basis of power in administrative organizations (Giddens, 1985: 19). Administrative power, such as that found in bureaucratic organizations, gives control over the timing and spacing of human activities through its facilitation of surveillance and superintendence.

The allocative use of resources involves command over the material objects of the 'object world' – raw materials, sources of energy, technologies of production and produced goods. It is, says Giddens, 'human dominion over nature' (Giddens, 1981: 51). In concrete situations, the structuring of allocation also involves processes of signification and legitimation that constitute it as 'property'. In modern capitalist societies, the 'economy' is structurally differentiated from the rest of society and from the 'political' system, and an institutionally autonomous market mechanism structures property as forms of 'market capacity'. It is through capital and labour markets that a structured class differential between 'capital' and 'wage labour' is established (Giddens, 1981: 113ff, 121). Allocative domination, then, is linked to class divisions.

In his *New Rules*, Giddens (1976b) had tried to illustrate his approach to structure by reconsidering his earlier views on class structure (Giddens, 1973). In the analysis of class, he argued, processes of legitimation structure private property relations as legally defined sets of rights sanctioned by the state. These institutions legitimate, and thereby regulate, class relations. Domination, on the other hand, he left rather unclear. He simply said that 'these [property] rights are also elements of the structure of class domination' (Giddens, 1973: 123). This would seem to imply that private property rights bring about a distribution of resources that constitute the 'market capacities' that are the basis of class divisions. What was left unclear, however, were the mechanisms through which legal institutions are transformed into material structures of domination. Signification is seen as relating principally to the worldviews that underlie class awareness or 'class consciousness'. This was clearly inadequate as an exemplification of Giddens's approach, but he gave no more.

Clarifying somewhat these remarks on class domination in *New Rules*, Giddens holds in *Contemporary Critique* that class relations are intrinsically exploitative (involving the appropriation of surplus by the class of non-producers) and, therefore, necessarily involve domination: 'exploitation may be regarded as domination which is harnessed to sectional interests' (Giddens, 1981: 60; emphasis removed). Similarly, 'ideology consists of structures of signification which are harnessed to the legitimation of the sectional interests of dominant groups' (Giddens, 1981: 61). As all signification involves domination, ideology arises when structures of signification serve the interests of dominant classes (and other dominant groups). The objective interests of a class concern those social conditions that enable its members to realise their capacities as members of the class. In the case of a dominant class, the overriding interest is the interest that it has in maintaining its own power. Thus exploitation and ideology are particular expressions of, and aspects of, domination.

The principal concepts that Giddens introduces for analysing systemic structures have already been mentioned: structural principles, structural sets and axes of structuration. Although these general concepts are introduced at various points in Giddens's work, they are barely discussed. Only 'structural sets' are accorded any extended discussion, and this is illustrative rather than definitive. Structural sets are illustrated through an extension of Marx's view of the circuit of capital. A capitalist system involves, Giddens claims, the three structural sets shown in Figure 9.7.

1.	Private property:	Money:	Capital:	Labour contract:	Profit
2.	Private property:	Money:	Capital:	Labour contract:	Industrial authority
3.	Private property:	Money:	Educational advantage:	Occupational position	

Source: Giddens, 1979: 104.

Figure 9.7 A structural set: the circuit of capital

The meaning of the colon in the diagram of structural sets is never speci-fied, though Giddens's commentary shows that it must be seen as involving the idea of the 'transformation' or convertibility of resources. Money allows private property to be converted into capital, and it allows the 'commodification' of labour power. The relation of capital to labour, through the production and appropriation of surplus value, allows private property, ultimately, to be converted into profit. Similarly, the labour contract is the basis of the legitimation of authority in the capitalist enterprise. The third set is a simplified statement of the arguments of Bourdieu that the conversion of money into a privileged education (through private schooling) is the basis for a further conversion into occupational positions through such mechanisms as the old boy network (Giddens, 1979: 105). This convertibility is structured by a specific cluster of rules and involves the institutions of allocative domi-nation such as the market, property and contract.

Giddens has gone no further in the analysis of social institutions and systemic structures, giving much support to the claim that he must be seen as constructing a synthesis that is biased towards the analysis of the actions of individuals. He has, however, undertaken substantive investigations at the system level. Those who seek to discover Giddens's 'institutional analysis' must attempt to uncover it from his substantive account of the development of modernity.

MODERNITY AND LATE MODERNITY

The view of modernity found in much contemporary sociology, Giddens argues, remains wedded to the inadequate viewpoint constructed by Parsons and those who were influenced by him. Parsons's interpretation of the history of sociology and his reconstruction, in particular, of Durkheim's ideas, had led to the view of modern society as an 'industrial' society. This orthodox view, Giddens believes, has obscured some of the key features of modernity. Found in the work of Parsons himself and epitomized in the influential work of Clark Kerr and his associates, the theory of industrial society holds that:

> The fundamental contrast in the modern world ... is between traditional agrarian society, normally based upon the dominance of land-owning elites, sanctioned by religion, though in reality often deriving from military power and co-ordinated within an authoritarian state; and industrial, urban society, fluid and 'meritocratic' in its structure, characteiised by a diffusion of power among competitive elites, in which social solidarity is based upon secular exchange transactions rather than upon religious ethics or coercive military power, in which government is trans-formed into a mass democratic state (Giddens, 1976a: 718–19).[22]

This theory, Giddens argues, must be abandoned, and contemporary sociologists must aim for a more adequate theoretical understanding of modern society. But this aim can be achieved only if a radical break is made with those past theories that are too closely tied to 19th century conditions. The world has changed since the 19th century, and it can be understood only on the basis of the systematic and comprehensive reconsideration of the 19th century legacy that Giddens has undertaken.

Giddens constructs his account of modernity through an extended model of social development. He constructs a classification of societies (Figure 9.8) in which there appears to be a development from tribal societies through 'traditional', class-divided societies to 'modern' class societies, but he is at pains to point out that he completely rejects evolutionary models of necessary and inevitable stages of social development. There is no inevitability in social development; nor is there a single, unilinear path of development.

Tribal societies	Band	Hunters, gatherers	Classless
	Village	Settled agriculture	
Traditional societies	City state Empire Feudal society		Class-divided
Modern societies	Capitalist		Class societies
	Socialist		

Figure 9.8   Giddens's schema of social development

The most basic forms of human society are the 'tribal' societies, of which Giddens recognizes two variants: the band society and the settled agricultural society. In the wandering band societies of hunters and gatherers, social processes are not extended over time and space. Social interactions are face-to-face and there is a low degree of 'time–space distanciation'. Such societies do not possess a conception of 'history' as directional change, and they operate only in 'reversible time'. Reversible time is time that is structured as repetition, rhythm and cycle; it involves no conception of the linear passage of time and, therefore, no conception of history (Lévi-Strauss, 1968a). These societies are, quite literally, pre-historic societies. Settled agricultural societies, where the tribes occupy fixed village locations, are similarly localized in time and space. In neither the band nor the village society is there any differentiation of 'economic' or 'political' institutions from the broader institutional framework of the tribe's social life. All social life is organized through kinship and is sanctioned by tradition (Giddens, 1981: 92–4; 1984b: 147).

Jary suggests that Giddens's view of the gulf that separates tribal from other societies is comparable with that of Mann, who holds that the Neolithic revolution marks a fundamental divide between pre-historic and historical societies (Jary, 1991: 121; Mann, 1986: 39). For Giddens, this divide marks a fundamental change in the organization of time and space. Historical societies are characterized by very specific structurings of time and space and by the emergence of the linear time of historical change. In these societies, time is organized as a measure of the flow of events. Linear, clock time is a formal, measurable and irreversible sequence of hours, days, months, years and centuries. Much of day-to-day life remains organized around the repetitions and routines of reversible time – getting up, going to work, eating meals and so on – but the public areas of life are organized in linear terms. The two levels of time are, however, mutually implicated. Institutions have the particular form that they do because they are continually reproduced in everyday encounters; and the historical continuity of institutions provides the framework for face-to-face interaction (Giddens, 1984b).

Pre-modern historical societies are 'traditional' or class-divided societies. They are agrarian societies in which a differentiation of economic and political institutions is produced by, and itself reproduces, class divisions (Giddens, 1981: 105–8; 1985: Chapter 2). They are marked by a structural separation of the 'countryside' from the 'city'. The countryside is the arena of agricultural production and is structured around autonomous village communities that show many similarities with those of the tribal societies. The city, however, is the specific locale in which differentiated economic and political structures have their focus. Structures of domination – based on both authoritative and allocative resources – are concentrated in the city, which becomes a 'power container' and serves as the basis of central control over the numerous village communities that lie within its territory. The city is both the central administrative body and the central market for its society, and it becomes the focus for the institutions of law and symbolic order. The life of the city is separate from that of the countryside, which remains the basis of the traditional and communal institutions of village society. It is in the villages that material resources are produced, but the economic surplus is channelled through the city and the systems of exchange around which the city is organized.

The city is the sphere of the public, political life of the society, though this sphere of public participation is confined to the dominant classes: the mass of the population is excluded from participation in the discursive sphere of politics. Thus politics and government are concerned with the handling of conflicts within the dominant class and within the city itself. The first great forms of traditional society, for example, were the city states of the ancient world, in which political and economic life was sharply divided by the division between 'citizens' and the rest of the population (including 'slaves').

The 'system integration' of traditional societies is generally very weak: the autonomous village communities remain subject to custom and kinship organization, and their members often subscribe to different religions and speak different languages from the inhabitants of the city. Traditional societies are class-divided, as they have massive divisions of wealth and privilege, but these class divisions differ from those of modern society. The absence of labour markets and the low degree of alienability in property contribute to this difference, but Giddens sees the more important factor as being the relative lack of face-to-face contact between the peasantry of the countryside and the members of the dominant classes. The principal link that exists between the city and the countryside results from the taxation that is levied on the agricultural product of the society. Thus class conflict does not become an important feature of these societies.

When cities fuse into larger imperial states another great breakthrough occurs, allowing even greater concentrations of resources to appear in the imperial centres. Imperial world systems such as the Roman Empire incorporated many of the surviving tribal societies into their orbit, and they exist as specific and very extensive inter-societal systems (Giddens, 1981: 102–4). Through the city and the empire, then, emerges the structural form of the *state*. Initially embodied in the city, the state is organized through, and for the use of, authoritative resources. The apparatus of the state allows information and knowledge to be collected, retained and controlled in ways that were hitherto impossible. The development of literacy is a crucial condition for this development of the state, as a written language – unlike the oral culture of the tribal societies – allows record-keeping, documentary archives and surveillance of all kinds. The reach of the state in traditional societies is, nevertheless, fairly limited. Its power is enhanced through its increased surveillance capacity, but this power is limited by the absence of any monopoly of the means of violence.

The breakthrough from tradition to modernity occurred in the West with the transition from feudalism to capitalism. It was in the West that the key institutions of modernity arose. Giddens recognizes four 'institutional dimensions' of modernity: capitalism, industrialism, surveillance and militarism. By capitalism he understands, following Marx, a system of commodity production through competitive markets for goods and labour power that centres on the *class* relation of privately owned capital to propertyless wage labour. Industrialism, on the other hand, was stressed by Durkheim and involves the

application of inanimate sources of energy and machine technology to organize and co-ordinate production. Taken together, capitalism and industrialism
relate to the 'economic' institutions through which resources are mobilized
and allocatively used. Surveillance relates to the enhanced capacity of nation
states and other political organizations to control information and to super-
vise their members. This institutional dimension has been particularly recognized in the work of Foucault, though Giddens recognizes Weber's analysis
of the state and bureaucracy as a precursor of contemporary analyses (see
also Dandecker, 1990). Militarism, the control over the means of violence,
becomes more organized and 'industrialized' as states achieve enhanced
capacities for coercion and violence. Surveillance and militarism together
relate specifically to the 'political' institutions through which resources are
mobilized and authoritatively used.

Capitalist societies are those in which capitalism is their main, though not
their only, structural principle. Capitalism is the epitome of a commercial
system and involves the *commodification* of allocative resources – of labour
power, land and the means of production. Central to this commodification is
money, a 'symbolic token' that allows social relations to be impersonalized
and 'disembedded' from local contexts on a scale not previously possible
(Giddens, 1990: 22–6, drawing on the arguments of Simmel). Social relations
become detached from their embeddedness in time and space and are organized in terms of the commodification of time and space themselves. Economic processes involving the allocative use of resources, then, acquire an
institutional autonomy that is historically unprecedented.

At the same time, class societies involve the emergence of the *nation state*.
Commodification and the autonomy of the economy was not possible without
the concurrent separation of the autonomous framework of political institutions
through which the population could be pacified and the law enforced. The
authoritative use of resources became concentrated in the nation state which, as
a power container, operates with greater intensity than city states and imperial
states. Nation states have more tightly defined and strongly defended boundaries than their traditional predecessors, and they exist within an inter-state
system in which warfare and international conflict are endemic. Such political
forms become apparent in the absolutist states that characterized the transition
period between feudalism and capitalism (Giddens, 1981: 184–6; 1985). In
these states, a more centralized and more strongly territorial political order was
built, and the idea of political sovereignty was established. The absolutist state
coincided with the emergence of early capitalism in Western Europe in the
period from the 16th century to the 18th century, and it was a crucial condition
for the establishment of autonomous commercial forms.

Modern 'societies' are co-existent with their nation states. The boundaries
of these societies are defined by the territorial claims of the nation state, and

it is within these boundaries that economic relations are concentrated. In the same way that states are involved in 'international relations', however, economies are embedded in 'world economies'. Economic relations stretch beyond the bounds of each nation state to create an international trading network and international flows of capital. Thus the modern world comprises a 'world system' (Wallerstein, 1974, 1980, 1989) of inter-state and inter-economy transactions in which national 'societies' have a declining autonomy (Giddens, 1985: 166; 1990: 65–9). The world system is – or it was prior to the East European upheavals since 1989 – divided into the capitalist and socialist geopolitical blocs and a 'third world' of 'developing' countries and surviving tribal and traditional societies whose development is constrained by their location within the world system.

Alongside the inter-state and inter-economy systems, Giddens also recognizes tendencies towards the globalization of industrialism and militarism. In the sphere of industrialism, an international division of labour arises as production in each part of the world becomes more closely integrated with that in all others. The spread of industrialism creates 'one world': the world comes to form a single 'created environment' in which ecological effects spread rapidly from one area to another. In the sphere of militarism, Giddens sees the establishment of an internationalization of violence that results from the 'industrialization' of warfare. A world military order arises as the means through which international agreements are enforced and international differences resolved. Taking these arguments together, it can be seen that Giddens identifies a process of 'globalization' that encompasses the processes of capitalism–industrialism and surveillance–militarism.

Giddens, it will be recalled, held that four institutional clusters could be identified for all societies: allocative domination, authoritative domination, legitimation and signification. The twin processes of capitalism–industrialism and surveillance–militarism are organized around the mobilization of, respectively, the allocative and the authoritative use of resources. These 'economic' and 'political' institutions also involve 'legal' institutions of legitimation, as they rest on such institutional patterns as legal ownership and citizenship. Behind all these processes, however, lies signification, as the communication of meaning enters into all social relations. Giddens recognizes, therefore, a corresponding tendency to globalization in the sphere of symbolic orders and cultural meanings:

> Mechanised technologies of communication have dramatically influenced all aspects of globalisation since the first introduction of mechanical printing into Europe. They form an essential element of the reflexivity of modernity and of the discontinuities which have torn the modern away from the traditional (Giddens, 1990: 77).

The global extension of the institutions of modernity would not have been possible without the globalization – or, at least, the 'internationalization' – of signification that allows the world-wide sharing of knowledge and meanings. The crucial economic and political processes of today, for example, depend upon the rapid and effective communication that has been made possible first by telegraphy and the telephone, and later by radio, television and satellite technology.[23]

The development of modernity through the 19th and 20th centuries has involved a subtle deepening and reinforcing of its characteristics, which has often been misdescribed, Giddens says, as the emergence of 'post-modernity'. No stage of post-modernity has been achieved, he argues. Instead, the late 20th century should be seen as a stage of 'radicalized', 'high' or 'late' modernity. In these conditions, some of the features of early modernity have been eclipsed by other features that were later to develop.

Individuals have, for example, become progressively 'de-skilled', not just in the industrial sphere but in all spheres of their everyday life. Everyday knowledge has been appropriated by 'experts' and transferred into 'expertise' and technical knowledge. The old 'professions' and expert occupations of doctors, lawyers and accountants are joined by the increasing number of experts concerned with the personal and intimate aspects of life: counsellors, therapists and consultants of all kinds. Individuals have 'lost' the knowledge that they formerly possessed, they become dependent upon experts for 'help' and 'advice'. At the same time, they have no basis for judging the expertise of those that they consult, it must be taken on trust. Patients, for example, are unable to appraise the medical knowledge of doctors and so must trust them to intervene in their lives in appropriate ways. There are great risks in this, and Giddens has made this a central theme of his latest investigations. He has given particular attention to the ways in which people attempt to reassert control over their own lives through constructing and reconstructing a sense of their own self-identity (Giddens, 1991a, 1992). Much of this work has been undertaken through a dialogue with the ideas of Beck concerning the increasing salience of 'risk' in people's lives (Beck, 1986).

The wider consequences of these trends have been traced in the decline of class politics and the rise of new social movements. The class politics of the labour movement was tied to the predominance of capitalism:

> Labour movements are the contestatory associations whose origins and field of action are bound up with the spread of capitalist enterprise. Whether reformist or revolutionary, they have roots in the economic order of capitalism, specifically in attempts to achieve defensive control of the work place through unionisation and to influence or seize state power through socialist political organisation (Giddens, 1990: 159–60).

In the early stages of modernity, opposition to industrialism tended to be allied with opposition to capitalism, and the 'romantic' rejection of industry in favour of the countryside tended to be aligned with the labour movement. The romantic anti-industrial values of William Morris, for example, were an important element in the formation of the British Labour Party. As industrialism has developed, however, the 'created environment' and its ecological problems have transformed these early reactions into more radical ecological and 'green' movements that see dangers in industry *per se* and not simply in industrial capitalism.

In the sphere of politics and the nation state the demand for civil rights and democracy that Marshall saw as a central feature of modern citizenship was also tied to the labour movement in its early stages (Marshall, 1949). The expansion of the surveillance capacities of states, however, has made more pressing the need to engage in struggle over surveillance itself. The late modern civil rights and democratic movements are oriented towards the exercise of control over the surveillance activities of modern states. Finally, the growth of militarism has encouraged the concomitant growth of 'peace' movements that go beyond the aims of the early pacifists (Giddens, 1990: 160–61).

Democratic, ecological and peace movements, therefore, complement, and to a considerable extent supplant, the labour movement as the principal focus of struggle in late modernity. Modern societies are no longer structured simply around the struggles of a labour movement rooted in class divisions; they are organized around the struggles of a variety of 'old' and 'new' social movements.

Giddens's discussion of the development of modernity uses many of the concepts that he has outlined in his general social theory, and he has made a major contribution to understanding contemporary social trends. The substantive theory, however, is separated from his general theory by something of a conceptual gap. His general theory sets out a sophisticated conceptualization of action and interaction, and a suggestive outline for the analysis of social systems, but neither level of analysis is developed into a comprehensive theoretical statement.

This is particularly clear in relation to his central concept of 'rule'. Critics have pointed out, for example, that Giddens gives no examples of actual rules and their operation in the reproduction of interactions and social systems. The central concept of rule is simply asserted and reasserted in the most general terms. This criticism is, I think, well founded, though it is not completely fair. A sympathetic reading of Giddens's work will show – perfectly clearly – that he invokes the work of ethnomethodologists in support of his central claims about the part played by rules in the production and reproduction of interaction. Garfinkel, Cicourel, Sacks and their followers, as I have shown, have constructed detailed empirical accounts of rules and rule use in a variety of interactional contexts. Giddens clearly believes that the mass of such work makes further exemplification on his own part unnecessary. He sees it, furthermore, as an essential underpinning for the work of Goffman and other symbolic interactionists. Giddens's analysis of action, then, must be understood alongside the contributions of ethnomethodology and symbolic interactionism.

So far as the analysis of social systems is concerned, the picture is less clear. He again sketches a framework for systems analysis, albeit more briefly than in his discussion of action, but it is not so clear which – if any – theoretical perspectives he would invoke to enlarge on his arguments. At the system level, no complementary theoretical framework can be identified in the same way as ethnomethodology and symbolic interactionism are at the action level. Giddens's substantive theory of modernity shows the extent of his intellectual debts to Marx and to Weber, and it is clearly to these writers that he would look for further exemplification of social systems analysis. But he will not borrow directly from Marxism. While he clearly owes much to Marx and the Marxist tradition, he is extremely critical of it and argues for its 'contemporary critique'. Similarly, he will not borrow directly from contemporary systems theory: while he accepts, and indeed stresses, the role of the unintended consequences of action in the reproduction of social systems, he rejects both functionalist and neofunctionalist analyses.

The duality of structure, then, remains a suggestive rather than a definitive solution to the dualism of action and social system. Giddens's work is far stronger in relation to the analysis of action than it is in relation to the analysis of social systems. If his attempt at synthesis must be judged a failure, it remains, nevertheless, a monumental landmark that may yet be developed to its full fruition.

NOTES

1. Sacks's principal work (1965–72) has only recently been published, but it was widely circulated in photocopied form. For additional sources on ethnomethodology see Sudnow (1972) and Turner (1974).
2. Despite Cicourel's use of Chomsky's arguments, Chomsky was not himself an ethnomethodologist.
3. Goffman (1974) has drawn a similar distinction between the 'surface' definition of the situation and the 'deep' 'frame' that organizes the experience. Frames are schemes of interpretation that make observed experiences and events meaningful.
4. Cicourel's work is also important in highlighting the differences between ethnomethodology and symbolic interactionism. Although the two approaches are often seen as similar to one another, there are many fundamental differences that separate them. See Denzin (1970) and the criticism in Zimmerman and Wieder (1970).

5. The original source is Sacks *et al.* (1974). I have simplified the position from the presentation given in Sharrock and Anderson (1986: 63).

6. Other forms of speech can be studied in the same way. Atkinson (1984), for example, has examined the rules used by politicians in public speeches.

7. A similar point of view was put forward, independently, by Clegg (1975: Chapter 5; see also 1989).

8. Giddens's model of personality derives from Freud's distinctions between id, ego and super ego, and his view of action relates these also to Weber's distinction between affectual, traditional and rational action.

9. Giddens uses the word 'agent' instead of 'actor' to emphasize the idea of agency. I have, for the sake of consistency with other approaches discussed in this book, generally used the word 'actor' when discussing his views.

10. See the discussion of this point in Chapter 6.

11. Giddens draws on Goffman (1959, 1961). The argument of Goffman (1983) is also relevant. See Giddens (1986).

12. Giddens claims to derive his concept of social integration from Lockwood (1964), but Lockwood did not limit the concept to individual, face-to-face interaction. Lockwood, unlike Giddens, saw collective actors as important elements in social integration.

13. Giddens's actual position is that structure involves both rules and 'resources'. I shall address this apparent complexity shortly.

14. I think it is important to appreciate that these 'memory traces' can only be understood as aspects of the biochemistry of the brain, although Giddens does not himself spell out these biological implications of his argument. It is because of this biological basis of memory that people who experience brain damage – for example, through a stroke – may lose the ability to perform such basic skills as talking and muscular co-ordination.

15. The biological interpretation of 'memory traces' and the conception of programming that I have used to interpret Giddens's view of rules owes a great deal to Chomsky's view of language and to research on 'artificial intelligence' and simulation. This view does not require an acceptance of Lévi-Strauss' view that all brain processes involve 'binary oppositions'. Psychologists and biologists are not yet advanced enough in their understanding of the brain to allow this step to be made. The 'Darwinian' model of learning that has been proposed by Edelman is an important advance that is in line with my suggestions here.

16. In linguistics, 'grammar' includes both 'syntax' (the rules governing the sequencing of words) and 'morphology' (the rules governing the inflection of words). Layder (1994: 143–4) has correctly shown that Giddens's grammatical model of structure has much in common with Bourdieu's (1977) concept of the 'habitus' and that much clarity would have resulted if Giddens had cast his analysis in these terms.

17. Giddens uses Lockwood's (1964) distinction between social integration and system integration, but fundamentally misconceives it. In Lockwood, as I have already noted, 'social integration' relates to the interdependencies of individual *and* collective actors.

18. Giddens also rejects any direct comparisons with Althusser's concepts. 'Signification', for example, is not the same as 'ideology'. Despite this, as will be seen, he ends up with a classification of institutions that is similar not only to Althusser but also to Parsons.

19. I have, again, rephrased Giddens on this point.

20. See the similar views about pragmatic acceptance in Mann (1970).

21. See, for example, Turner (1962) and interactionist theories of deviance. Compare Emerson's (1970) account of the doctor–patient relationship with that of Parsons (1951).

22. The main thesis of the theory of industrial society can be found in Kerr *et al.* (1960). This argument is discussed and criticized in Scott (1985).

23. Giddens specifically rejects Baudrillard's conclusions about the 'hyperreality' introduced by this process.

10. Jürgen Habermas: a new beginning?

Jürgen Habermas is the only contemporary sociologist to have undertaken a theoretical project with the same scope and purpose as that of Parsons. Following the post-Parsonian fragmentation of sociological theory, Habermas's work has extended the tentative steps towards synthesis that have marked some of the leading theoretical works produced during the 1980s. Habermas, like Parsons, is a theorist with the kind of encyclopaedic and systematic interests that marked the work of the founding generation of sociological theorists. With Habermas, sociology has, once again, been provided with a starting point for consolidation and advance.[1]

The work of Habermas has its roots in the 'critical theory' of Max Horkheimer and Theodor Adorno that was developed as a new basis for Marxist theory during the 1930s. Their work was undertaken at the Institute of Social Research in Frankfurt, a base for radical theoretical and empirical research that was headed by Horkheimer from 1931. The intellectual work of the Institute was interrupted by the Nazi rise to power just two years later, when Horkheimer and his colleagues migrated to the United States. Horkheimer continued as Director in exile, co-ordinating the work of Marcuse, Adorno and others into a critically oriented social theory whose purpose had been sharpened by the struggle against fascism. By the time that the principal members of the Institute were able to return to Frankfurt in the 1950s, a clearly identifiable school of social thought had been established.

The central tenets of this critical theory had been set out by Horkheimer (1937) in an early essay. Influenced by the attempts of Lukács and Korsch to renew Marxism by reconstructing its Hegelian foundations, Horkheimer had set out a critique of 'traditional' theory as a basis for his own 'critical' theory. Horkheimer rejected the 'empiricism' or 'positivism' of the established social theories, which he saw as extending an inappropriate natural science model to the study of the social world. Positivism makes too sharp a separation between human knowledge of the social world and the actual social world of human interests and values itself. Horkheimer held that no such separation is possible. Science is a social activity and knowledge is oriented by practical interests and concerns. The apparently detached and objective knowledge of the natural sciences was, in fact, oriented by a technical interest in controlling and manipulating the world. When extended to the social

228

world, this model of science led to a focus of attention on the superficial, more controllable phenomena of social life and to a failure to relate these surface features to their underlying and *essential* structures. Positivism was, then, specifically linked to a non-critical, 'bourgeois' standpoint.

The 'critical' theory that Horkheimer sought to put in place of this 'traditional' theory was oriented by the practical interests and concerns of the proletariat to achieve its emancipation. This was not, however, something that developed spontaneously within proletarian class consciousness. Members of the proletariat are subject to mystification and false consciousness. Left to its own devices, the working class is unable to penetrate surface appearances and uncover the essential features of the social world in which they live. For a critical understanding of society to develop, critical intellectuals must ally themselves with the working class and formulate a proper understanding of proletarian circumstances and interests. The aim of critical theory was to produce theory that would inform social action that was geared to social transformation and that would result in human emancipation.[2]

To develop his critical theory, Horkheimer looked to Nietzsche, Dilthey, Weber and Freudian psychoanalysis, which he sought to build into Marxism.[3] His intention was to develop an analysis of cultural processes and of socialization to complement Marxism's strengths in economic analysis. This concern for cultural issues was inspired by a recognition of the cultural changes that had been responsible for the rise of fascism during the 1930s. Members of the Institute had undertaken a number of empirical studies of the prejudice, anti-Semitism and authoritarianism that they felt had produced fascist support. These beliefs were seen as reflecting a growing conformist outlook, rooted in the family patterns and mass lifestyles of modern society. The growth of this 'mass' culture was seen as a central element in the expansion of modernity, and orthodox Marxism had little to say about it.

Together with Adorno, Horkheimer undertook a number of theoretical investigations in pursuit of critical theory. Their work traced mass culture back to certain deep-lying features of modern thought. They held that natural science and the scientific worldview of positivism, together with their associated forms of 'technology', were distorted, one-sided expressions of the 'rationality' of the Enlightenment (Adorno and Horkheimer, 1944). The 'instrumental reason' of this essentially technological form of consciousness had undermined alternative forms of cultural expression and had produced a uniform mass culture that had become a new basis of social domination. Aristocratic 'high' culture – literature, music, painting and poetry – had been debased and had been fused with the cultural products of mass entertainment and advertising to form an immense 'culture industry' that produces images that manipulate human desires and emotions in support of mass consumption.

These ideas appeared in a series of papers during the 1940s and 1950s, but they had their greatest influence through Herbert Marcuse's *One Dimensional Man* (Marcuse, 1964b; see also Marcuse, 1964a). In this book Marcuse saw technological rationality as eliminating any element of conscious human control over the development of modern society. In these circumstances, Marcuse argued, the working class could no longer be seen as a historical agent of revolutionary change, having been politically incorporated into the established system by the forces of mass culture and the logic of industrial technology. Marcuse saw this dominance of technological rationality as a feature of capitalist and Soviet society alike: it was a feature of *industrial society* rather than specifically of capitalist society. This conclusion brought Marcuse close to the theories of industrial and post-industrial society that were propounded by such writers as Aron (1967) and Bell (1961, 1973) in the 1960s and 1970s.

It was from this context that the work of Habermas sprung. He had begun to achieve prominence as the leading figure in a younger group of theorists – the group included Wellmer, Schmidt and Offe – who had trained at Frankfurt and who sought to develop the ideas of the first generation of critical theorists, who were then coming to the ends of their careers. Adorno died in 1969 and Horkheimer in 1973, shortly after Marcuse's formulation of critical theory had achieved its greatest influence.[4] Habermas's work began to have a significant influence on social thought at the same time that the early works of Horkheimer and Adorno were coming to be more widely known outside Germany as a result of the appearance of English language translations.

Habermas's earliest work (1963a, 1963b) was a reformulation of Horkheimer's critique of positivism. This position was summarized in Habermas's inaugural lecture at Frankfurt (Habermas, 1965a) and was subsequently much extended in other essays and in a book (Habermas, 1968, 1971). From this philosophical basis he built a methodology for the social sciences (Habermas, 1967b) and he undertook an impressive range of substantive studies in which he considerably expanded the framework of Marxian ideas (Habermas, 1968-9, 1973b). From the middle of the 1970s, however, he began to repudiate his early epistemological concerns, and he moved even further away from Marxism. His new theoretical strategy involved exploring the theoretical convergence of Marx with Weber, Parsons and other sociologists and psychologists. A 'reconstruction' of historical materialism (Habermas, 1976) was followed by a two volume study in substantive theory that summarized all the ideas that he had been developing over a 20 year period (Habermas, 1981a, 1981b).[5]

KNOWLEDGE AND INTERESTS

Habermas's initial aim was to reconstruct the principal philosophical traditions of the modern period in order to show how 'positivist' assumptions had
come to be established as the dominant set of assumptions about the nature of
knowledge.[6] He suggested, as had Horkheimer, that the positivist model of
science had set itself up as the sole paradigm and arbiter of claims to knowledge. Habermas's epistemological project aimed to show, on the contrary,
that positive science was merely *one* form of knowledge and that an adequate
theory of knowledge would have to recognize a variety of knowledge forms.

Kant's recognition that people were active participants in the construction
of knowledge was accepted by Habermas, but he adds that this is a *social
process*. The individual who acquires knowledge is not an isolated, pre-social
'ego', but a social being. This led Habermas to the Hegelian view, shared also
by Marx, that knowledge is an *historical* product. Habermas's earliest methodological reflections, then, began with Hegel's critique of Kant, and then
proceeded to Marx's critique of Hegel. The conclusion is that while Hegel
correctly added an historical dimension to Kant's theory of knowledge, Marx
had rightly transformed Hegel's idealism into an historical *materialism*. Knowledge, argues Habermas, is produced in, and through, historically specific
social relations. Habermas is concerned to emphasize, however, that Marx's
position needs to be modified as it reduces all forms of action to *labour*
(Giddens, 1977). A social theory of knowledge cannot rest solely upon the
economistic model of labour and productive activity to which Marx had
given so much attention. This must be enlarged into a more comprehensive
view of history.

The historical production of knowledge is structured by universal and *a
priori* 'cognitive interests' that are features of the human 'species being',
essential characteristics of human life. These cognitive interests, Habermas
claims, are transcendental 'knowledge-constitutive' interests that guide the
search for knowledge. They are fundamental and invariant orientations to
knowledge and action that are rooted in the universal conditions and circumstances of the evolution of the human species, understood as a process of 'self-
formation'.[7] Knowledge is possible only in a form that is structured by these
interests. It is embedded in experience and action, and the cognitive interests
are the links between action and the knowledge that it produces. Cognitive
interests are deep structure elements, in Chomsky's sense of that term (Chomsky,
1957). They are the procedures through which human beings constitute the
world of experience and through which the surface structures of knowledge
and action are possible. Habermas argues that there are three distinct cognitive
interests and, therefore, three forms of knowledge. Each of these interests is
rooted in a distinct sphere of action and experience (see Figure 10.1).

Sphere of action or experience	Cognitive interest	Form of knowledge
Labour in the material sphere	Technical control	Empirical-analytical (instrumental)
Interaction in the cultural sphere	Practical understanding	Historical-hermeneutic (communicative)
Domination	Emancipation	Critical-dialectical

Figure 10.1   Knowledge, action and interests

The interest in *technical control* arises from labour – action that is geared to manipulating the material environment and to ensuring successful outcomes. Habermas holds that this cognitive interest is the basis of the 'analytical-empirical' knowledge that is found in the natural sciences. This form of knowledge comprises 'information' that can be organized into 'explanations' and 'predictions' – it is technically utilizable knowledge that has the capacity to expand human powers of technical control and manipulation. This form of knowledge, like the cognitive interest that underlies it, is a universal and necessary feature of human existence. While recognizing the necessity for analytical-empirical knowledge, Habermas rejects the positivist view of science as a one-sided and historically specific distortion of it. Positivism presents an image of science as the detached apprehension of an inert external world, not as the conceptual construction of reality that it is. Positivism ignores the fact that analytical-empirical knowledge is produced by human action aimed at controlling people's material circumstances.

The interest in *practical understanding* arises from interaction – action that is concerned with attaining and extending mutual understanding, consensus and community in social relations. People's attempts to understand the social world in which they live involves grasping the pre-constituted meanings and definitions of those whose interactions make up that reality. This is a process of interpretation that works through the 'hermeneutic circle', or the 'cycle of interpretation', through which the meaning of each item of experience is related to the larger cultural context, and the nature of this cultural context is inferred from particular items of experience. This is the basis of the historical-hermeneutic knowledge that is found in the cultural sciences. This form of knowledge comprises 'interpretations' and meanings that can be organized into shared 'understandings' – it is practically relevant knowledge that has the capacity to increase 'mutual understanding in the conduct of life' (Habermas, 1968: 311).

Analytical-empirical and historical-hermeneutic knowledge together comprise the core of what Horkheimer called 'traditional theory'. The knowledge produced by critical theory, on the other hand, is rooted in the interest in emancipation. Whereas the technical and practical interests are 'primary' bases of knowledge production, the emancipatory interest is a derivative 'meta-interest'. It is rooted in forms of action that are 'distorted' as a result of the exercise of domination. Labour and interaction are systematically distorted when they are structured by ideology and illusory beliefs; emancipatory knowledge informs actions that are oriented to the liberation of people from ideology and error, and that can help them to achieve autonomy and self-development.

If human evolution is seen as a process of reflexive self-formation – a process in which people seek to acquire higher levels of self-understanding and self-determination – human life cannot be seen simply in terms of technical control and practical understanding. Reflexive awareness of the social conditions under which thoughts and actions are produced leads to a recognition of the technical and practical interests that shape knowledge. This reflection expands the self-knowledge of the species and contributes to its emancipation from historically formed constraints. The emancipatory interest is the basis of critical-dialectical knowledge. This form of knowledge comprises 'criticism' that can be organized into the rational self-knowledge of an individual or species. Critical theory, then, destroys ideology and restores to people an awareness of their historical location as actors under constraints that can be rationally appraised and can, therefore, be fully understood and brought under control.

Habermas's discussion of the cognitive interests and their grounding in the conditions of human evolution draws on a Hegelian view of evolution as a process of reflexive education leading to freedom. It takes over the Hegelian idea of the human species as a historical subject, a collective agency of social transformation. This focus on the 'anthropological' characteristics of the human species as a whole echoes many of Marx's early views on alienation, where social conditions are appraised in relation to the supposed characteristics of the 'species being'. Habermas has, then, cast his argument at the most general level imaginable: the social context for the production of knowledge is not the structure of class relations or any other historical pattern of social division, it is the human species as a whole. The theory is, for all this, a *social* theory of knowledge, and this introduces a circularity into the very heart of Habermas's position: social theory must provide the foundations for a theory of knowledge, but this theory of knowledge must itself provide the unassailable foundations for social theory. This circularity came to be seen as a major problem by Habermas, and his later work involved an attempt to recast his understanding of the grounding of social theory.

LABOUR, INTERACTION AND THE SOCIAL SYSTEM

At the same time as he was constructing his theory of knowledge, Habermas was elaborating the social theory that underpinned it and that, in turn, it underpinned. A consistent and coherent account of social action and social systems was developed in his early work (Habermas, 1963c, 1965a, 1965b, 1967a, 1968), and this formulation remained the cornerstone of his later work. Habermas developed his early account of action from a theory of social evolution that he rooted very firmly in Hegel's understanding of the development of the world spirit. Social evolution is a complex process that can be analysed in terms of its three dimensions: language (or symbolic representation), instrumental action and communicative action. These dimensions of evolution are seen as aspects of Hegel's 'absolute spirit' as they are fundamental and absolute analytical features of all concrete forms of human action. Language plays a key role in his work, as it enters into the constitution of both the instrumental and the communicative types action. Language is the medium through which meanings are discursively constructed. It is through language that empirical discourse establishes factual generalizations and practical discourse justifies normative claims in relation to values. Theoretical-empirical discourse enters into instrumental action, while practical discourse enters into communicative action. This theme became progressively more important in his later work.

Instrumental action, understood as an analytical dimension of all action, was described by Weber as *Zweckrationalität*. This form of action involves a strict means–end relationship and a strategic orientation to the choice of alternative actions. Actors orient themselves towards preference rules and decision rules, draw on analytical-empirical knowledge, and undertake a purely formal calculation of the various alternatives that are open to them. They make a rational choice of action. This kind of action is not necessarily based on 'perfect' information and accurate *scientific* knowledge, despite what Habermas sometimes claimed. What is crucial is that the subjective orientation of the action follows a rational means–ends relationship. Instrumental action is, in Parsonian terms, oriented through the pattern variables of neutrality, specificity, universalism and performance (Habermas, 1965a).

Communicative action, as an analytical ideal type, is structured by norms that define reciprocal role expectations and that are recognized as binding by those involved. This type of action draws upon historical-hermeneutic knowledge that is geared to the achievement of mutual understanding. It is orientated through the pattern variables of affectivity, diffuseness, particularism and quality. Where instrumental action is concerned with problem-solving situations and with the possibility of success or failure, communicative action is concerned with internalized motivations and with the possibility of conformity and deviance.

Instrumental and communicative processes enter into the formation of all concrete forms of social action. As aspects of absolute spirit, Habermas saw them as entering into the constitution of the two concrete forms of 'actual spirit' that he believes are to be found in particular historical settings. These concrete forms of social action are work (*Arbeit*) and speech (*Sprache*), which he subsequently generalized as, respectively, *social labour* (or productive activity) and *social interaction* (see Figure 10.2).[8] The actual patterns of social labour that are found in particular historical periods are primarily forms of instrumental action, but they are shaped also by communicative processes. Labour depends on the existence of a degree of co-operation, and Habermas holds that this must be reinforced by the framework of social norms that Durkheim described as the 'non-contractual' element of contract. These normative factors are non-instrumental elements that arise through communication. In the same way, concrete patterns of social interaction are primarily forms of communicative action, but they are shaped also by instrumental considerations. Interaction requires, for example, that the participants recognize one another's rights to the possession of the material means of action. Thus in any particular social situation, concrete forms of social labour and social interaction will be closely linked with one another.

	Analytical type of action	Concrete form of action	Social system
Language			
	Instrumental action	⇨ Social labour	⇨ Economy and state
	Communicative action	⇨ Social interaction	⇨ Institutional framework

Figure 10.2   Actions and the social system

Patterns of social labour and social interaction are, in turn, entwined in the formation of historically specific social systems. Systems of economic and political relations, for example, are differentiated clusterings of labour or purposive activity and can be understood as predominantly structured by instrumental action. Such social systems as those of family and kinship relations, on the other hand, are differentiated clusterings of social interaction and can be understood as being predominantly structured by processes of communicative action. The overall structure of a society, Habermas argued, comprises two interdependent sub-systems: the political economy and the 'institutional framework'. Paradoxically for a writer who had sought to re-

... basis of Marxist social theory, Habermas held
...mework of social norms has a priority in the overall
...ety, as it is only through this 'non-contractual' element
... actions will actually be constrained to follow technical

...e recalled that labour and interaction were seen by Habermas as
...ng, respectively, technical and practical interests. The emancipatory
...rest, on the other hand, was associated with 'domination', and Habermas
sees this as playing a particularly important part in social systems. Domination (*Herrschaft*) is a feature of the institutional framework of a society, but it can have consequences for both social labour and social interaction. Domination, for Habermas, refers to the specific historical distortions of institutionalized labour and interaction that occur in particular societies.

Habermas's understanding of 'systematically distorted communication' was based on Freud's psychoanalytical studies of neurotic behaviour and the many 'incomprehensible' acts and utterances of everyday life. Dreams and slips of the tongue, for example, were seen by Freud as distorted expressions of a 'deeper' meaning that could be uncovered through psychoanalysis. These distorted patterns of thought and behaviour involve the use of idiosyncratic rules of grammar and meaning, the undertaking of rigid and compulsive courses of conduct, and dislocations between speech, actions and gestures. They involve, in short, a disruption of the 'normal' pattern of meaningful communication, and even the individual author of these actions will fail properly to understand them. According to Freud, these distortions of communication arise from the repression of emotions, which results in their displacement from a normal expression to a distorted level of meaning. Freud's studies showed that the normal structure of non-distorted communication is systematically distorted through particular, deviant patterns of socialization (Habermas, 1970a: 209–10).

Generalizing this idea to the social sphere, Habermas argued that systematically distorted communication occurs wherever social interactions and systems of such actions are structured by domination and so depart from a pattern of 'undistorted' communication. When the institutional framework of a society is structured by patterns of domination, all the processes of social interaction that it regulates will be similarly distorted (Habermas, 1970a, 1970b). Wherever domination prevents free and open rational discourse, the interactions of individuals will be bound by 'ideological' conceptions and so can be regarded as 'systematically distorted'. This distortion involves reciprocal misunderstandings and failures of communication in role behaviour. Distortion can also arise in the economic and political processes of social labour that are shaped by the institutional framework. Labour occurs under specific, historically formed modes of production in which the forces of production (structures of instrumental action) are embedded in relations of production (institutionalized norms).[9] 'Exploitation' results wherever the relations of production establish a structure of domination through which social labour becomes 'alienated'. Marx's critique of exploitation, Habermas argued, was aimed at disclosing the non-rational constraints that restrict the expression of human creativity in truly free labour.

As a form of communicative action, undistorted communication was described by Habermas in terms of what he called the 'ideal speech community'. In an ideal speech community, consensus is achieved through free and unconstrained discussion that follows only the logic of rational argument. Differences of power, class and status, for example, do not influence the ability of a person to participate in the discourse and they do not affect the likelihood that his or her views will be accepted. Each participant is recognized as having an equal right to enter into dialogue as an autonomous contributor to the discourse. Systematically distorted communication occurs wherever these conditions do not exist. This idea served Habermas as a yardstick for assessing the degree of distortion that existed in any actual speech situation. Where discourse is shaped by considerations of power and other social divisions, the resulting structure of domination ensures that instead of autonomous and unconstrained communication, there is systematically distorted communication. The outcome of such communication is 'ideological', and the resulting framework of institutional norms has a correspondingly ideological character.

allows measurement of actual speech situation

A critical theory that is aimed at emancipation from domination – aimed at the creation of freedom and autonomy in discourse – will take the form of a critique of ideology and, thereby, of the social conditions that are responsible for it. Through the critique of ideology, Habermas believed, critical theorists can free people from the distorted social forms under which they live. It is through the critique of ideology, therefore, that people can be freed from exploitation and class division. The role of critical theory is to further this emancipation and to promote human autonomy.

PURPOSIVE AND COMMUNICATIVE ACTION: SYSTEM AND LIFEWORLD

After the theory above revised it.

In Habermas's work from the early 1970s he began to move away from the attempt to root social theory in a theory of knowledge. Although he held fast to earlier views on the three forms of knowledge and their relation to social interests, he no longer saw them as providing the foundations for social theory. Instead, social theory was seen as self-sufficient, not requiring epistemological underpinning. This strategy left Habermas's theory rather exposed:

if epistemological considerations provide no warrant for accepting the theory as valid, why should anyone subscribe to Habermas's theory in preference to any other? Habermas came to rely more completely on the idea of the ideal speech community. If conditions for theoretical discussion can be made to approximate those of the ideal speech community, and the resulting unconstrained discourse accepts the tenets and conclusions of critical theory, then critical theory is vindicated.

It is clear, however, that this argument smuggles epistemological considerations in through the back door. It involves an untheorized preference for 'undistorted' communication. Without epistemological arguments, there can be no way of grounding this preference: *why* should autonomous discourse, rather than discourse structured by domination, lead to objectivity and truth? This question requires epistemological investigation, but Habermas refuses to provide it. Habermas has, rightly, abandoned the circularity of his earlier position, according to which the epistemology that grounded social theory was itself justified by that theory. He has replaced it, however, with a different circularity, according to which the ideal speech community that grounds social theory is itself theorized by that social theory. I shall return to these epistemological difficulties later in the Chapter.

The core of Habermas's mature work consists of a thorough reformulation of his social theory (Habermas, 1981a, 1981b). To achieve this reformulation he has undertaken a systematic reconsideration not only of his own views but also of those of earlier sociologists. Having started his work in critical theory through a critical reconstruction of Marx, Habermas has subsequently paid more attention to the critical reconstruction of Weber, Mead and Parsons.

His starting point is, once again, a typology of action, and the two fundamental modes of action are now termed 'purposive action' and 'communicative action'. *Purposive action* is rational action that is oriented towards technical success in its outcome. It involves the instrumental or strategic use of means to attain ends under specific given conditions. When this type of action is concerned with the physical objects of the natural world it is 'instrumental action'; when it is also concerned with the anticipated reactions of others it is 'strategic action'. Thus the social form of purposive action is necessarily strategic in its orientation. Strategic social actions involve the rational, ego-centric calculation of the costs and benefits of alternative courses of action and the assessment of their likely success in relation to the actor's goals. Decisions are made on this rational, strategic basis.

Communicative action, on the other hand, is action that is oriented towards the establishment of mutual agreement in a social relationship. It involves the co-operative attainment of intersubjective understanding and consensus. Actors seek to establish a consensual definition of the situation as the basis of social order. They seek to reach mutual agreement about their situations and their plans for action in order to co-ordinate their activities in a solidaristic way. In practical social situations, then, communicative action takes the form of 'symbolic interaction'. This involves interpretative processes through which actors seek to negotiate agreed definitions through the establishment of shared norms. Symbolic interaction involves the cognitive element of communication and the normative element of agreement. Where strategic action follows the logic of rational, maximizing action, symbolic interaction involves 'communicative rationality' and a logic of unconstrained discourse.

Previous social theorists, Habermas argues, have produced only partial and one-sided accounts of these two modes of action. A particularly influential theoretical framework in the history of social thought, for example, has been what he calls 'teleological action'. The teleological theory of action originated in the classical economists and utilitarians, and the contemporary form of this rational choice theory is most clearly expressed in games theory. Habermas sees this theoretical tradition as providing a one-sided generalization of the model of purposive action. It mistakes one form of action for the totality of action. Theories of 'normatively regulated action', on the other hand, have sought to challenge such teleological models. Expressed most clearly in the works of Durkheim and Parsons, this approach to social theory sees social actions as structured by norms that are rooted in common values: norms generate legitimate expectations of compliance. This tradition of theory results in an oversocialized model of the human agent and an unwarranted generalization of the model of symbolic interaction to all action.[10]

With certain reservations, Habermas accepts the relevance of teleological theories for explaining many aspects of purposive action, but he firmly believes that this form of action cannot be understood in isolation from its interdependence with processes of communicative action. From this point of view, he believes, a priority must be to develop an adequate theory of communicative action that would be valid in its own terms and would also allow us to understand how strategic action is complemented and underpinned by structures of symbolic interaction.

In order to build this theory of communicative action, Habermas turns to Mead's symbolic interactionism. The model of communicative action that Habermas outlines complements Mead's framework with Wittgenstein's work on language games, Austin's work on speech acts, and Gadamer's work in hermeneutics. He also turns to ethnomethodology for insight into communicative action. Unlike Giddens, however, he sees the ethnomethodologists as providing merely a rather extreme formulation of Mead's ideas. Ethnomethodological ideas must be reined back and consolidated into the mainstream of symbolic interactionism.

Cross-cutting the various specific theories, Habermas argues, is the theoretical dualism that distinguishes 'subjective' from 'objective' concerns.[11] If a subjective point of view is adopted, the task of social theory is seen as being concerned with investigating the subjective meanings and *orientations* of actions. If an objective point of view is adopted, these tasks are, instead, seen as relating to an exploration of the systematic connections that exist among the *consequences* of actions, whether these are intended or unintended by the actors. Thus symbolic interactionist and phenomenological theories of action have tended to remain with a 'subjective' point of view, while structural functionalist theories have generally adopted an 'objective' point of view.

The subjective point of view sees societies as 'lifeworlds' – symbolic structures of taken-for-granted meanings – that are produced through communicative actions. An exclusive focus on these phenomena, Habermas argues, means that sociological analysis is tied:

> to the internal perspective of members of social groups and commits the investigator to hermeneutically connect up his own understandings with that of the participants, The reproduction of society then appears to be the maintenance of the symbolic structures of the lifeworld (Habermas, 1981b: 150–51).

The objective point of view, on the other hand, sees societies as 'systems' that are produced through rational, purposive action. An exclusive focus on these phenomena means that societies tend to be regarded as self-regulating systems, and sociological analysis is tied 'to the external perspective of the observer' in terms of which societies are:

> understood as open systems, which maintain themselves viz-à-viz an unstable and hyper complex environment through interchange processes across the boundaries. States of the system are viewed as fulfilling functions with respect to its maintenance (Habermas, 1981b: 151).

It is Habermas's contention that the dualism between subjective and objective points of view must be overcome through the use of a perspective that combines both into a single theoretical framework. Only a synthesis of the two points of view can overcome the limitations of each taken alone. The theory of communicative action, he argues, provides the only effective basis for achieving such a synthesis. Where Giddens sought to combine the analysis of action and the analysis of system through the 'bracketing' of one level while analysing the other, Habermas aims, like Parsons, to construct a model of social life in which the relations between the subjective and the objective levels are explicitly incorporated.

Habermas's concept of society comprises *both* patterns of meaningful communication among action orientations *and* patterns of systematic connections among action consequences. Society, understood as a 'totality', must be seen as having the characteristics of both a 'socio-cultural lifeworld' and a 'social system'. These two structural components are its analytically distinct elements.[12]

The concept of society as a *lifeworld* is seen as having been most thoroughly developed in the work of Schutz and his followers (Schutz and Luckmann, 1973; Berger and Luckmann, 1966).[13] In this theoretical tradition, there is a focus on interaction, seen as an interpretative process through which actors seek to understand one another. In so doing, the actors establish 'negotiated orders' through the constant construction and reconstruction of transient shared meanings. These negotiated realities are 'diffuse, fragile, continuously revised' (Habermas, 1981a: 100):

> Within every sequence of interaction, communicative actors renew the appearance of a normatively structured society; in fact they are groping from one problematic, momentary consensus to the next (Habermas, 1981a: 124).

Mutual understanding and argument are ongoing accomplishments that take place against the backdrop of the 'lifeworld' of taken-for-granted meanings that results from the production and reproduction of the negotiated order.

This form of analysis, then, has tended to focus its attention on the interaction level. Habermas argues that it must be broadened out from its interactional basis in order to consider the structural aspects of the lifeworld. He sees these structural issues as having been explored in a particularly illuminating way in Durkheim's concept of the *'conscience collective'* and collective representations. He also draws much from Parsons's analysis of the 'societal community', which Habermas sees as the structured set of norms and institutions that emerges from, and sustains the interaction order of, the everyday lifeworld. The lifeworld, understood as a societal community, is concerned with the 'integration' and 'pattern maintenance' processes that Parsons had highlighted as contributing to the 'internal' organization of societies.[14] Habermas holds that the lifeworld, understood as a 'socio-cultural' phenomenon, can be seen as comprising both symbolic meanings (its cultural aspect) and social institutions (its societal aspect).

This socio-cultural sphere of symbolic ordering and institutional integration is rooted in interpretative schema and principles of legitimation. It comprises 'a reservoir of taken-for-granteds, of unshaken convictions that participants in communication draw upon in cooperative processes' in order to negotiate a common definition of the situation (Habermas, 1981b: 124). It therefore provides the background of shared meanings that establish a degree of social solidarity and that make orderly social interaction possible through the definition of personal and collective identities and motives, of ideas of group boundaries and membership, and of norms of obligation. It comprises the shared stock of taken-for-granted knowledge, definitions and understandings that shape everyday actions, and it provides the 'roles' and 'identities' that can be enacted in order to ensure stability and cohesion in everyday social relationships. It is 'a culturally transmitted and linguistically organized stock of interpretive patterns' that is passed from generation to generation through processes of socialization. While the lifeworld is the source of conscious and systematic 'worldviews', its structures are so deeply embedded in human learning processes that they are normally unconscious or only partly conscious. Habermas does not, however, see this as implying that the lifeworld is fixed and unchanging. People elaborate and change their lifeworld, as well as reproduce it, through the communicative actions of everyday social interaction. At the same time, communicative actions are embedded in that lifeworld and are shaped by it.

The similarity that Habermas recognizes between his concept of the lifeworld and the Parsonian concept of the societal community is worth spelling out. This recognition indicates that Habermas sees structured social institutions as forming an important aspect of the lifeworld. Indeed, this was very clear in his earlier usage of the phrase 'institutional framework' to describe this sphere of social relations. Using the term 'lifeworld', however, highlights the realm of everyday, face-to-face experience that is neglected in Parsons's work. Both emphases are clearly required, and desired, by Habermas. From the standpoint of institutional analysis, communicative actions are formed into a societal community; from the standpoint of face-to-face interaction, it forms a lifeworld.

Communicative actions, then, create a socio-cultural lifeworld for members of a society. In 'primitive' and traditional societies virtually the whole of social life falls within the sphere of the lifeworld: 'society' and 'lifeworld' are virtually equivalent terms. As societies become more advanced, however, purposive forms of action become differentiated from the lifeworld. They come to be organized into 'systems' of action that are separate from the lifeworld. The economic and political systems, for example, are differentiated systems of strategic action that have achieved a considerable degree of autonomy from the formerly all-encompassing socio-cultural lifeworld.

To understand this differentiation of 'systems' of action from the 'lifeworld', Habermas turns to the work of the general systems theorists who have also inspired neofunctionalism.[15] The concept of the social system Habermas sees as centring around the organization of purposive actions, whose interconnections in a social division of labour – in relations of functional interdependence – enhance the capacity of a society to reproduce itself and to 'steer' its activities in relation to the complexities of its environment. This emphasis on the 'steering' or guiding functions of systems of purposive action was derived from Parsons's analysis of the 'adaptive' and 'goal attainment' processes concerned with the 'external' organization of a system in relation to its environment. Like Parsons, Habermas sees these processes as defining, respectively, the economic and political systems of action. The system aspect of social life, then, comprises the economic forces of production and the political forces of power that may, under certain historical circumstances, become differentiated from the rest of society and from one another (see Figure 10.3). Structural differentiation along functional lines is a central feature of the evolution of societies, and it is a primary basis for the expansion of the technical knowledge that is embodied in production and power.

Analytical type of action	Social form of action	Function	Social sphere	Differentiated sphere	Media
Purposive action	Strategic action	Steering	Social system	Economic system	Money
				Political system	Power
Communicative action	Symbolic interaction	Normative	Socio-cultural lifeworld	Societal community	Influence
				Domestic sphere	Commitments

Figure 10.3   Action, system and lifeworld

While Habermas uses the terminology of 'system' to describe those economic and political structures that have become differentiated from the lifeworld, he is not denying that the lifeworld is just as structured and systemic in character as the more narrowly defined 'system' of purposive action. The parallel that he makes between the lifeworld and the societal community makes this perfectly clear. Habermas's 'system' is a structure that is detached from the societal community around that particularly denuded form of action, purposive action, in which norms and social institutions play a secondary part.

Where Marx's model of society emphasized the distinction between an economic 'base' and a political and ideological 'superstructure', Habermas's model revolves around a distinction between an economic and political system and a socio-cultural lifeworld (see Figure 10.4). The lifeworld is the sphere of 'social integration' and the system is the sphere of 'system integration'.[16] Habermas also modifies the Marxian model by rejecting any conception of economic determinism. Marx, he argues, had developed a one-sided economic determinism, and later Marxists had simply added political factors to the economic relations of the base. Habermas seeks to recognize the

Sociological theory

Figure 10.4   Marx and Habermas

crucial and independent role of the lifeworld. He postulates not merely a reciprocal causation between system and lifeworld, but also a predominance of the lifeworld in shaping the purposive actions that comprise the system. This emphasis on the role of the normative elements of the lifeworld in shaping patterns of purposive action led Habermas to see the relations of production in normative terms. Where Marx had seen the social relations as actual relations of effective control over the means of production, Habermas sees them as defined solely in terms of the norms generated in the socio-cultural lifeworld. This relative neglect of 'material' factors, paradoxical for someone rooted in the Marxist tradition, brings Habermas even closer to the Parsonian overemphasis of normative elements.

Habermas's basic model of system and lifeworld is the conceptual framework within which he constructs a more detailed model of social structure. The system is seen as having two distinct elements within it, the political and the economic, and Habermas sees the changing relationship between economic and political structures as an important feature of the overall development of systems of purposive action. The lifeworld, in turn, is seen as having a number of partially distinguishable elements. The societal community, I have suggested, is the structural core of the lifeworld, and Habermas sees this as centring on a 'public sphere' within which, in modern societies, the mass media shape social identities and lifestyles. This public sphere emerged as a differentiated structure in the 18th century as a sphere of 'public opinion' shaped by newspapers and public discourse. The public sphere connects 'civil society' and the state, it is the part of the lifeworld that links the whole lifeworld with the state and the economy (Habermas, 1962). Partially distinct from this public sphere is the private, domestic sphere of family and household relations in which motivations and commitments are generated.[17] The lifeworld, then, comprises the public and private spheres in which norms and values are produced, reproduced and transformed. Where the structural ele-

ments of the 'system' tend to become sharply different
other, the lifeworld tends to remain more diffusely organi
differentiated only into the closely related public and priv

When structurally differentiated from one another, eacl
produces a particular medium of exchange that mediate:
other aspects of the society and ensures a degree of struct
The economy generates 'money', and the political system generates 'power',
and money and power are major mechanisms of system integration and
structural co-ordination. There are, however, other, analogous media. Within
the public sphere, for example, 'influence' is generated. Thus mass media
advertising influences consumption patterns and so enters into the process of
economic production. Influence is a mechanism of structural integration that
operates alongside money and power. The parallels with Parsons's argument
on the generalized media of exchange is obvious and deliberate, and Habermas,
in truth, adds little to Parsons's conceptualization of these media at the
abstract level.[18] He does, however, use them in a rather ingenious way in his
account of social evolution.

THE EVOLUTION OF MODERNITY

Social development has always been seen by Habermas as a process of
evolution, a directional process of change in which the human species achieves
its inherent potential by emancipating itself through its own actions. This
teleological view of social development differs sharply from the strictly anti-
evolutionist model outlined by Giddens, though his actual description of the
course taken by social development has considerable similarity to that given
by Giddens.

Social evolution is seen as a 'learning' process for the human species, a
process in which the species as a whole comes to appreciate its own powers
and capabilities. This learning process takes place along the two dimensions
of social action that Habermas has identified. In the sphere of purposive
action and the social system, Habermas sees it as involving an extension of
technical knowledge that results in enhanced productive and 'steering' capacity. In the sphere of communicative action and the lifeworld, he sees it as
involving the enhancement of reflexivity and awareness in practical consciousness as a result of growing individuation and self-knowledge. Social
evolution, then, involves the growth of technical knowledge and enhanced
reflexive awareness.

The action concepts and the concepts of social system and lifeworld are
used by Habermas to construct a model of social evolution as leading from
'primitive' societies through 'traditional' to 'modern' societies (see Figure

Societal type	Organizational principle	Examples
Primitive society	Kinship	Neolithic societies
Traditional society 1. Archaic civilizations 2. Developed civilizations	Political class domination	Egypt Greece, China, Rome
Modern society 1. Liberal capitalism 2. Organized capitalism	Market	19th century Europe mid 20th century Europe

Figure 10.5   Habermas's schema of social evolution

10.5). While Habermas has much to say about the specific features of each stage in social evolution, the principal purpose of his scheme is to illuminate the stage of modernity itself. The evolutionary typology defines each type of society by a particular 'organizational principle', a structural characteristic that determines the patterns of exploitation and systematically distorted communication around which the society is organized.

In 'primitive' societies, such as those of the Neolithic period, social organization centres on kinship. The social relations of kinship are the basis of tribal identity and of participation in subsistence production, and they structure the whole society around age, sex and lineage relations. All these social relations are embedded in a magical and animistic culture that gives meaning to them. Lifeworld and system, in these societies, are barely differentiated, the lifeworld is virtually co-extensive with the society. 'Traditional' societies, on the other hand, first become apparent in the historical record between the eighth and the fourth centuries BC. They involve a growing structural differentiation of the various elements of social life. Economic and political activities begin to acquire an autonomy from the lifeworld, and the socio-cultural lifeworld itself shows a move from magical religions to 'world religions' such as Buddhism, Hinduism and Christianity. The legitimation of the differentiated economic and political systems by a world religion takes the form described by Weber as 'traditionalism'. In these societies, class divisions become apparent for the first time as the basis of political domination: a bureaucratic state apparatus is the co-ordinating focus for the social dominance of a land-owning class.

'Modernity' is the crucial development that Habermas sees as resulting from the unique historical circumstances of the West. Following Weber, modernization is seen essentially as a process of 'rationalization', a process in which traditional culture is destroyed and the level of rationality in all spheres of social life increases. Societies become more sharply differentiated.

The basis for this rationalization was the emergence of the spirit of ascetic Protestantism in 17th century Europe. This had posed a fundamental challenge to all traditional ideas and had encouraged a specifically 'rational' outlook in everyday matters. The worldview of ascetic Protestants was the origin of the disciplined and methodical conduct of life through rationally organized social relations and the pursuit of a vocation. This new religious outlook and its associated social ethic had established a new cultural framework for the organization of economic activity, and the growth of a rational economic outlook had promoted the spread of rationality to other areas of the lifeworld. The lifeworld, no longer structured around an overarching traditional cosmology, exhibited a progressive 'disenchantment', a loss of integrative meaning.

This rationalization of the lifeworld created the conditions necessary for the expansion of the liberal capitalist societies to which Marx had directed his attention in his theoretical works. The organizational principle of liberal capitalism is the economic mechanism of the market, which is differentiated from the lifeworld and is also structurally separate from the state. The market mechanism is a self-regulating mechanism of 'system integration' that connects and co-ordinates individual actions without the need for any external intervention or control. The product market and the labour market operate on the principle that goods and services can be treated as commodities, and they ensure that both the suppliers and the purchasers of commodities experience an equally advantageous balance of rewards over costs. This 'exchange of equivalents' is the source of the legitimation of market relations. It is the belief in the exchange of equivalents that ensured the integration of early capitalist societies.

It is in the market that owners of capital and the wage labour that they employ come together. Class relations are detached from the apparatus of the state and, instead of being expressed in political form, they are expressed in a purely economic form as exchange relations on the market. Class relations are 'depoliticized' and come to appear simply as exchange relations in which monetary transactions yield benefits for all. Habermas accepts Marx's critique of the market, according to which the apparent exchange of equivalents is a mere 'appearance': it is an ideological form that masks the reality of the underlying relations of class exploitation. Unlike all other commodities, labour power is a source of value and the purchaser of labour power is able to appropriate the surplus value that is created in the process of production. What appears on the surface to be an exchange of equivalents is, in reality, the alienation and exploitation of labour by capital.[19] The class relations of liberal capitalism are, therefore, concealed in the ideological framework of the exchange of equivalents.

Habermas holds, however, that the liberal capitalism described by Marx has now been transformed by continuing rationalization. In the new stage of 'organized' or late capitalism, the relation between the state and the economy is transformed. Monopolization and concentration in the economy is associated with a growth of state intervention aimed at ensuring continued capital accumulation. Instead of existing as a separate apparatus that follows the principle of *laissez-faire*, the state becomes an essential element in the reproduction of capitalist production. The market mechanism is no longer self-sustaining, as market relations become increasingly subject to political regulation. The ideology of the exchange of equivalents can no longer be sustained, and class divisions lose their 'natural' economic expression and become 'repoliticized' (Schroyer, 1975). The differentiation of the economic from the political breaks down, and a single steering system – a political economy – emerges.

At the same time, the economic and political spheres – the spheres of purposive action – are themselves subject to the process of rationalization; all residual value elements are eliminated from them. These systems come to be organized in purely rational terms as impersonal, 'utilitarian' systems of social technology. Practical activities lose all 'meaning' as they become completely disengaged from the lifeworld. The economic and political systems – the market and the state – are the driving forces in social development, but they drive society in a blind, meaningless way. Purposive actions come to form 'an ever denser network of actions that do without directly normative steering and have to be co-ordinated in another way' (Habermas, 1981b: 181). The state and the market are differentiated from the lifeworld as 'norm free structures' that are co-ordinated only through the use of money and power:

> Media such as money and power ... encode a purposive rational attitude toward calculable amounts of value and make it possible to exert generalized, strategic influence on the decisions of other participants while *by passing* processes of consensus-oriented communication. ... Societal sub-systems differentiated out via media of this kind can make themselves independent of the lifeworld, which gets shunted aside into the system environment (Habermas, 1981b: 183).

Money and power co-ordinate actions in a 'norm free' way, there can be no discussion of the morality or justice of their outcomes. Habermas sees this as an emerging situation of 'anomie', or loss of meaning. This has a fateful impact on the lifeworld itself. Areas of the lifeworld become 'uncoupled' from the normative processes of communicative action and are co-ordinated, instead, through money and power (Pusey, 1987: 107). The public sphere, for example, is increasingly dominated by the state apparatus and ceases to be an arena of autonomous communication. Education, health, welfare and certain other aspects of the lifeworld are split off and are subjected to economic or political control through, respectively, the market and the state bureaucracy. These activities are guided solely by the utilitarian criteria of the technocratic worldview that prevails in the economic and political system. Where economic control occurs, Habermas, like other Marxists, has described this as a process of *commodification*. Where political control through bureaucratic administration prevails, he writes of *juridification*.[20] The treating of health as a commodity that can be purchased through systems of private medicine is, for example, a process of commodification; the determination of medical treatment through centrally planned bureaucratic procedures is a process of juridification. What Habermas is describing, then, is the polarity of 'privatization' and 'socialization' (through the state) that has characterized the provision of health, education and welfare in the second half of the 20th century.

In *Legitimation Crisis* Habermas (1973b) had tried to draw out the consequences of the growing role of the state in modern societies, looking particularly at the 'crisis tendencies' that resulted.[21] His latest work involves a reformulation of this argument in terms of his 'system' and 'lifeworld' model. Economic crises in late capitalism can be resolved through state action, but only by displacing them to the political level, where they result in those fiscal and administrative problems that Habermas has called 'rationality crises'. Such crises involve 'a hiatus in the administrative competence of the state and its affiliated agencies, an inability to cope' (Giddens, 1977: 209). The state must, therefore, seek to legitimize its activities, as it can no longer rely on the 'traditional' sources that were available in pre-capitalist societies. If the state fails to resolve its rationality crises, it may experience a withdrawal of popular support, a legitimation crisis. Legitimation crises result from the failure of the public sphere of the societal community to generate the 'influence' necessary to sustain economic and political relations. Where 'economic' and 'political' crises characterize the economic and political system – they are 'system crises' – legitimation and what Habermas calls 'motivational crises' involve the lifeworld and have their effects at the 'seam' between the system and the lifeworld. Legitimation and motivational crises are consequences of commodification and juridification.

In the long run, Habermas sees 'motivational crises' as fundamental to social order. The normative framework of the lifeworld has come increasingly to be organized around the calculative and utilitarian principles of the market mechanism. Motivational crises arise from a failure of the private sphere of family households to generate the necessary commitment to the performance of occupational and economic roles. They are crises of personal and collective identity that undermine the capacity of the system to mobilize people to sustain its activities.[22] In these circumstances, economic crises are directly translated into lifeworld crises, as there is no overarching framework of tradition that can provide a legitimation for any economic dislocations.

As part of the rationalized disenchantment of the lifeworld, the various spheres of life have come to be regulated by distinct and incommensurable bodies of values and norms. In the sphere of art and music, for example, autonomous aesthetic values disappear and a mass culture emerges in which the differences between various cultural products become mere matters of 'image' or 'style'. Habermas does recognize, however, the growth of formal rationality and universality in the sphere of the lifeworld, seeing this as opening-up opportunities for social change. Science and technology, for example, emerged as rational disciplines with their focus in autonomous academic institutions, and the establishment of an aesthetic sphere of art, music and literature with its own institutions of academies and galleries. Of particular importance to his argument is his recognition of the development of universal ethics and formal law. The legal sphere has achieved an autonomy from politics and religion, coming under the control of autonomous legal professions and institutions. No longer subject to the complete dominance of 'external' and arbitrary interests and powers, the law develops more and more in terms of the inner logic of legal norms and considerations. This has important implications for the kinds of activity that can be legitimated in modern society. The rationalization of the lifeworld leads to the production of moral forms that are incompatible with the purposive orientation of economic and political actions. The underlying motivational supports for the system are not produced, and legitimation becomes increasingly dependent upon the maintenance of material benefits that, by their very nature, are unsustainable during periods of rationality crisis.

Possibilities of change, then, are contained within the rationalization of the lifeworld itself. These changes cannot, however, be ushered in through the old-style politics of the labour movement. Class struggles among entrepreneurs, professionals and workers through the conflict of parties and trades unions are tied to the economic and political systems and are no longer sources of radical change. It is the disturbances of the lifeworld that provide the framework for the new politics of the young, women and students. New social movements, concerned with the 'cultural politics' of peace, the environment, sexual liberation, women's liberation and so on, are the principal sources of change in organized capitalism.

Habermas's work is, undoubtedly, a sophisticated attempt to reconstruct the insights of 19th and 20th century social theorists. In constructing his powerful synthesis he has brought contemporary sociology full-circle by returning to the principal themes of Parsonian sociology. While he has a firm grasp of the significance of the rival theoretical approaches that were spawned during the 1960s and 1970s, Habermas's work restates many of Parsons's leading ideas. Habermas has produced an analysis of action and social systems that explicitly parallels that of Parsons, and he has forged these into a theory of social evolution that broadens out Parsons's understanding of modernity. Habermas provides a framework for transcending the fragmentation of social theory that seemed such a danger in the 1970s and 1980s, and he points the way forward towards the possibility of a truly post-Parsonian theory.

One of the major problems in Habermas's work, however, is its insecure epistemological basis. Habermas has tried to steer an admirable course between absolutist and relativist approaches to knowledge, but he fails properly to establish his middle way. Absolutism and false objectivism are challenged through his consideration of 'foundationalism', the attempt to provide knowledge with a firm and unshakeable foundation. A foundationalist strategy lies behind the empiricist approach to science and is expressed most clearly, Habermas holds, in the work of Popper. This strategy was the core of 'traditional' theory, and it lay behind his own attempt in his early work to establish the ultimate grounds of knowledge in human interests. 'Anti-foundationalist' positions, on the other hand, reject the idea of a neutral world of 'facts' independent of theory and stress that knowledge is rooted in the values and interests of particular social groups. These arguments are today stated most clearly in the work of Richard Rorty, who denies the possibility of establishing any 'objective' knowledge on firm and unquestioned foundations.

Habermas sympathizes with much of the anti-foundationalist position, yet he also seeks to avoid the relativism that it implies. To avoid the relativism that results from the denial of empiricism, he attempts to pull himself up by his own bootstraps and to locate the guarantee of non-normative knowledge in the nature of rational discourse itself. Knowledge is secure, he argues, when it is arrived at through completely free and unconstrained rational discussion. This is, of course, the idea of the ideal speech community. Rational discourse – coherent, structured argument – results in a consensus among those who participate in the discourse.[23] The consensus is 'rationally motivated' rather than constrained, and so is a feature of discourse itself, uncontaminated by considerations of power and inequality. Rationally motivated agreement, then, results from an ideal speech community characterized by freedom, equality and justice in dialogue roles. The attempt to justify knowledge involves examining the structure of discourse within a particular science in order to assess the degree of its rationality and to uncover the conditions that would make it a purely rational enterprise.

This is a novel and interesting bootstrapping operation that requires only a commitment to rationality in order to underwrite a methodology for the social sciences. Yet there remains an epistemological gap in Habermas's work. Like Althusser, he has resorted to a methodology in which the rational, theoretical practice of a science becomes itself the sole criterion for judging the truth of the knowledge produced by the science. Recourse to factual evidence plays no significant part, and the position is in danger of embracing the very idealist relativism that it seeks to avoid. In seeking to learn from the anti-foundationalist position on the relativity of knowledge, Habermas fails to recognize that it is equally important to learn from the foundationalist position on the relationship between knowledge and the external world. It is here that he might, once more, learn from Parsons. It was in his reflections on Kantian epistemology that Parsons produced his arguments in support of 'analytical realism'. This position recognized the existence and the constraining power of real world processes and mechanisms, and it recognized also the impossibility of grasping these processes and mechanisms except as 'phenomena' of experience constituted within particular theoretical frameworks. Consideration of realist epistemology, then, might allow Habermas to provide himself with a more secure basis for his position while continuing to avoid the extremes of foundationalism and anti-foundationalism.

NOTES

1. Habermas's interests range more widely than sociological theory and, for the purposes of this Chapter, I have ignored his wider philosophical considerations.
2. A similar view to that of Horkheimer was set out in Marcuse (1941).
3. The early work of Erich Fromm was undertaken at the Institute, although he later broke away from it.
4. Marcuse died in 1979.
5. A good account of Habermas's early work can be found in McCarthy (1978).
6. Sources for this section include Habermas 1963a, 1963b, 1965a, 1968 and 1973a.
7. This discussion draws on Scott (1978).
8. The distinction between language and speech that Habermas makes is not exactly the same as that made in structural linguistics. Language is seen by Habermas as the capacity of symbolic representation that is constitutive of both speech and work.
9. Because of his emphasis on the role of norms in defining patterns of domination, Habermas might best be seen as describing patterns of 'authority' in Weber's sense. His emphasis on norms departs from the view of the relations of production that was taken by Althusser, for whom they were material structures. His concept of domination, like that of Giddens, needs to be detached from its anchorage in the institutional framework.
10. Habermas also recognizes a third tradition of thought associated with Goffman's 'dramaturgical' theory, but this plays a very minor part in his discussion.
11. The dualism of 'subjective' and 'objective' approaches is related to the dualism between 'action' and 'system' that Giddens identified, though it is not identical to it.
12. Habermas holds that lifeworld and social system involve the primacy of, respectively, communicative and instrumental actions, but he also points to the constitution of the lifeworld through the *meanings* of actions, and of the social system through the *consequences* of action.
13. Habermas also points to Wittgenstein's work on the 'form of life' as an important source. See Winch (1958).
14. Parsons uses the terminology of 'system' for all the sub-spheres of society, while Habermas – wrongly to my mind – wishes to distinguish the communal lifeworld from the 'system' of purposive actions.
15. Many of these ideas were developed in discussion with Luhmann in their jointly produced volume (Luhmann and Habermas, 1971).

16. This conception of social integration and system integration might appear to be logical, but it departs from the original usage of Lockwood that I have been stressing throughout this book. While Habermas's distinction has some similarities with Giddens's, it also departs from it in crucial ways.
17. Habermas sees a parallel between his 'private sphere' and Parsons's 'fiduciary' structures.
18. The Parsonian parallel is completed by Habermas's argument that 'commitments' are generated in the private (fiduciary) sphere of the household.
19. This was originally set out in Habermas (1968: 59–60) and (1968–9: 97).
20. Commodification and juridification are described by Habermas as expressing the 'colonization' of the lifeworld by the political and economic system.
21. His argument draws on Habermas (1962).
22. Habermas refers here to Luhmann's work on the lifeworld in Luhmann and Habermas (1971).
23. Habermas's use of 'consensus' is, perhaps, unusual. He does not mean by this a monolithic Parsonian consensus, but unconstrained agreement and mutual tolerance.

11. Coda

My aim in this book has been to present a comprehensive account of the principal theoretical positions that have contended with one another in sociology since the 1930s. I have tried to outline the strengths and the main weaknesses of each of these positions as they have emerged in the intellectual struggles that have arisen during this period. Although I have tried to present a sympathetic picture of each position, no description can be completely devoid of criticism. Throughout the book I have used the work of Lockwood (1956, 1964) as the basis for my critical considerations. His ideas on social integration and system integration, and on the relationship between the normative and the non-normative elements in human life, are fundamental to any adequate sociological theory. The accounts that I have presented have been constructed from the standpoint of a commitment to the need to synthesize the valid and useful elements in rival positions in order to overcome their various limitations, and I have tried to use Lockwood's arguments as the basis of my discussions. The kind of theoretical position that I see emerging from this synthesis has, however, remained largely implicit in the accounts of the contending positions. The full development of this alternative view would require a further book which may, one day, be written. It is necessary, however, for me to indicate, briefly, the general shape of this alternative theoretical framework.

The phenomena studied by sociology are those of the human world, understood as a world of experience that is distinct from the physical and biological worlds. Physical and biological phenomena are presupposed in any analysis of the human world, but the latter cannot be reduced to them. Human phenomena are irreducible to the mechanical and living systems of the worlds of 'matter' and 'life'.[1] The human world is the realm of agency, a level of reality that is distinct from the biological life of the body that it animates. It is through the creative powers of human agency that matter and life acquire 'meaning' in relation to human purposes and intentions.

All human phenomena are products of *action*. It is in and through actions that human phenomena are produced, reproduced and transformed. This was Weber's fundamental insight that Parsons had tried to elaborate – perhaps to over-elaborate – in his general theory of action. At the same time, human phenomena form *systems*, patterned relations of connections. The dualism of action and system has formed the point of reference for many of the writers that I have considered in this book. Human phenomena have *both* action *and* system characteristics, and neither can be ignored or exaggerated at the expense of the other. The dualism of action and system, therefore, is fundamental to all human phenomena, whether these be the *psychological* level of the mind and its mental and emotional faculties, the *social* level of relations among individuals and groups, or the *cultural* level of shared symbols, concepts and values.[2]

I have, of course, concentrated on the relation of action and system in the social world, but the dualism is a feature of the psychological and cultural levels as well. Indeed, the dualism of action and system has often appeared in the form of a supposed opposition of 'individual' and 'society', leading to a tendency misleadingly to equate 'action' with the 'individual' and the psychological world, and to conflate 'system' with 'society' and the social world. My argument is that the distinctiveness, but interdependence, of the psychological, social and cultural levels must be recognized, and that the dualism of action and system must be seen as integral to all three levels.[3] Paraphrasing Giddens, it might be concluded that the dualism of action and system embodies the duality of the human world.

Personality systems, social systems and cultural systems, then, are the outcomes of – and conditions for – human action. In so far as the human world is necessarily social, the social world is fundamental to the formation of personalities and the development of culture. It is through the analysis of socially structured action that it is possible to understand the production of personality systems and cultural systems as well as of social systems. Sociology is central to the understanding of human phenomena.

From the standpoint of action, sociological analysis is concerned with the investigation of what Lockwood (1964) termed 'social integration': the relations of order and conflict among individuals, groups and organizations.[4] The arguments of symbolic interactionism, phenomenological sociology and other theories of interaction are all relevant to analyses of the structural characteristics of social action. Symbolic interactionists and phenomenologists have explored the ways in which 'competent' actors enter into negotiation with one another and draw on cultural meanings to construct the particular social definitions that organize their interactions. They have explored those 'communicative' processes that Habermas held to be the foundation of all the more specialized forms of social action. Rational choice theories, however, have pointed to a radically different set of issues in the analysis of action, and it is necessary to see how these differing views relate to each other. Throughout the debates of contemporary sociology, two polar types of social action have been identified. On the one hand, there is the instrumental or purposive form of action highlighted in theories of rational choice and social exchange, and, on the other hand, there is the expressive form of action that has recently begun to be analysed as a structured expression of emotion, affect and sentiment. Scheff (1990) has been the principal theorist to return symbolic interactionism to the emotional issues that Parsons raised in his concept of expressive action and that he saw as fundamental to matters of human valuation. This suggests another area in which sociological concerns cannot be detached from psychological issues, and a critical examination of the work of Freud, in particular, may once again prove fruitful. The two polar types of action – expressive and instrumental – are rarely found in isolation from one another in concrete social situations. They are analytically distinct elements in all concrete forms of action.

Figure 11.1 sets out a conspectus of action concepts. I have tried to indicate the broad parallels and continuities that can be identified in some of the leading contributors to the theorizing of action. I must emphasize that I am not arguing that the various concepts proposed by different theorists are direct equivalents of one another. Rather, I want to suggest that sociological theorists have constantly returned to the exploration of similar sets of issues and that they have come to interestingly parallel conclusions about these issues. It is through an exploration of these parallels, and of the equally important differences, that sociology is most likely to advance its understanding of actions and interactions. It is through such an exploration that the contributions of symbolic interactionism and phenomenological sociology can be combined into a fuller understanding of communicative processes and the construction of meaning, and that a framework can be built for understanding both instrumental-purposive and expressive-emotional actions.[5]

Parsons		Giddens		Habermas	
	Instrumental	Power			Purposive
Moral			Language		
	Expressive	Communication			Communicative
		Sanction			

Figure 11.1   A conspectus of action concepts

Expressive action and the broader forms of communicative action generate the *moral expectations* that lie at the heart of a culture's normative expectations. These are culturally defined rights and obligations concerning what people 'ought' to do, and they rest on the sentiments of 'commitment' that people have to their underlying values. The normative expectations through which action is organized involve both these moral norms and factual norms, where the latter are *de facto* (as against *de jure*) expectations concerning behaviour. Together, the moral and factual norms define what is expected as 'normal', what is expected to occur 'as a rule' in a society or social situation. Instrumental or purposive forms of action, on the other hand, involve rationally anticipated and 'realistic' appraisals of what it is in a person's 'interest' to do. Actions are, then, structured by norms and by interests, and the great majority of concrete actions are structured by both elements operating together. In these circumstances, interests and norms may come into conflict with one another. Interests may frequently generate motivations that run counter to normative expectations, but people's value commitments, if they are strong enough, may ensure that they override the pull of interests and continue to act in conformity with the norms. If, however, the pull of interests is particularly strong, or their orientation to the norms is based on pragmatic acceptance (Mann, 1970) rather than value commitments, then they are more likely to act in conformity with their interests.

Actions of all kinds must draw on resources for their implementation. The resources that are involved in expressive forms of action are those that are involved in 'persuasion' and in the formation of commitments. These resources are especially likely to be intangible 'moral' claims and injunctions. The resources that are involved in instrumental and purposive forms of action are those involved in 'inducement' and in the formation of 'advantages'. These resources are especially likely to be tangible, 'material' facilities. Persuasion and inducement are forms of the exercise of power.

Such a synthesis of action concepts must explore both the fully institutionalized and the anomic types of social relations identified by Parsons. Too much sociology has limited its attention to situations of consensus and full institutionalization. It is important to take Parsons's remarks seriously and analyse both types of social relation. It is also important, however, to recognize with Rex the need to add a third type of social relation, that of conflict (see Figure 5.1). Rex holds that the analysis of institutionalized social relations can be combined with the analyses of anomie and deviance that have been produced in symbolic interactionism and the analysis of conflict relations that have been strongly linked with theories of rational action.[6]

My discussion of symbolic interactionism and rational action has shown how writers in both traditions have attempted to move beyond individual action in order to take account of collective action. It is striking, however, that analyses of action have tended to be resolutely individualistic and concerned with face-to-face interaction. It is true, of course, that collective actors may be 'reduced' to the actions of the individuals who are their members, but the distinctively 'collective' properties of these actors are lost in such a reduction. While recognizing that individual action provides the ultimate grounding for all social action, it is important not to lose sight of the emergent properties of collective actors. Only in the work of the conflict theorists was this made a central aspect of the investigation of social life. The conflict theorists of the 1950s and 1960s built on the looser formulations of their 19th century predecessors, but their arguments have been marginalized in the principal debates of the 1970s and 1980s. Empirical issues are beginning to force a change of theoretical direction. Giddens and Habermas have, in their different ways, suggested that class action has been supplemented or replaced by the struggles of new social movements, yet neither writer has properly recognized the need to theorize collective action with the same degree of rigour as they have individual action.[7] As I suggested in Chapter 5, the analysis of new social movements and the earlier work of the conflict theorists have much in common, and it is undoubtedly the case that the arguments of Rex and Dahrendorf must be returned to centre stage.

'Social integration', then, involves a focus on the activities of individuals, groups and other decision-making organizations. In the sphere of economic action this has taken the form of so-called micro-economics, which looks at the ways in which the actions of producers and consumers create market relations of co-operation and competition.[8] Although many writers have suggested the use of the equivalent term 'micro-sociology' (Alexander *et al.*, 1987; Layder, 1994), this term has generally been tied so closely to the level of individual face-to-face interaction that it ignores, or plays down, the actions of groups and organizations. For this reason, I have avoided the term 'micro-sociology' and the related idea of the micro–macro linkage in this book. The arguments can, I believe, be more clearly stated in the terminology that I have used.[9]

The central issue underlying social integration is the question of how action is to be conceptualized. Answers to this question point to a dualism of agency and determination. This dualism concerns the extent to which actors (individual and collective) are able to create or to shape their own circumstances; and the extent to which, on the other hand, they are the mere creatures of constraining social conditions that mould them and determine their actions. Giddens's concept of the duality of structure was an attempt to resolve this dualism and to avoid the polar positions of 'free will' and 'determinism' associated, respectively, with phenomenological sociology (especially its existential variants) and structuralism.

At the level of the social system it is possible to identify two distinct combinations of analytical elements, each corresponding to the analytical types of action. Expressive forms of action are especially closely involved in the formation of *institutions*: established and solidified patterns of normative expectations that define specific 'positions' and their associated 'roles'. Although moral norms are likely to be especially important in any established normative order, it must not be assumed that all social institutions are morally grounded. Institutions may, for example, be constructed from factual norms to which actors are oriented in a purely pragmatic way. Some institutionalized expectations refer to assumed social groups ('the family', 'the company', 'the school'), while others comprise generalized aspects of the assumed actions of individuals and groups ('contract', 'property', 'domesticity').[10] Instrumental forms of action, on the other hand, are involved in the formation of alignments of interlocking interests among actors. Such alignments of interests may lead them to form 'factions', 'coalitions' or other instrumentally structured relations.

Institutions and alignments of interests, it must be emphasized, are analytical elements that rarely occur in isolation from one another. Social systems are structures of positions and practices, and the various practices involved in the actual social relations of a system are the outcome of both institutionalized expectations and interest alignment, in varying combinations.[11] Functionalist and neofunctionalist theorists have highlighted the ways in which such practices are produced as the unintended consequences of action, but functionalists, in particular, have concentrated their attention on those practices that correspond closely to social institutions. In confining their attention to fully institutionalized social relations, they have often failed to distinguish between the institutions and the actual practices that they regulate, and this has led them to ignore the part played by the non-institutional and non-normative elements of interest alignment. Structuralist theorists influenced by Althusser have highlighted the importance of studying the actual practices of a society, and post-structuralist theorists such as Foucault have stressed the interdependence of normative and non-normative elements. Althusser's attempt, however, was vitiated by the idealist epistemology to which he was drawn, and the post-structuralists have increasingly focused on cultural systems rather than social systems.

Lockwood (1956) argued that the crucial issue in the analysis of social systems is that of their 'system integration' – the degree of compatibility or interdependence of their parts – and he recognized clearly the need to explore both the normative and the 'material' aspects of this problem.[12] Although Lockwood has begun this task himself, starting out from the issue of social integration (1992), an exploration of the interdependence of normative and non-normative structures remains to be worked out. No synthetic theory of the articulation of normative and non-normative elements has yet emerged to replace Parsons's programmatic statements on this.

Some of the dimensions along which this interdependence can be explored are apparent in the conspectus of system concepts shown in Figure 11.2. Institutional elements are especially important in those practices that Parsons

Parsons	Althusser	Giddens	Habermas
Economic system	Economic	Allocative domination	Economic system
Political system	Political	Authoritative domination	Political system
Societal community	Ideology	$\left(\begin{array}{l}\text{Signification}\\\text{Legitimation}\end{array}\right)$	Lifeworld

Figure 11.2 A conspectus of system concepts

termed the 'societal community'. This centrality of social institutions to communal practices was recognized by Habermas when he originally named this part of the social system the 'institutional framework'. Those structures that are differentiated from the societal community must also be seen as combining both normative and non-normative elements, though they may often exhibit the dominance of the non-normative elements of interests. In the differentiated 'economic' and 'political' systems, for example, practices are relatively detached from institutional elements and are more directly governed by alignments of interests. In an economy, for example, instrumental forms of action have a high degree of autonomy and there may be systematic contradictions between institutional patterns and actual practices.[13] Althusser's discussion of the ideological state apparatuses, and Luhmann's work on structural differentiation, have discussed the emergence of numerous specialized systems of relations in which there are greater or lesser degrees of autonomy of actual practices from institutional regulation.

This concluding statement faces the risk – indeed, the certainty – of being dissatisfying for both the reader and the writer. It is condensed and programmatic, and its length has not allowed the principal arguments to be given their due attention. I hope, however, that I have been able to indicate some of the theoretical commitments that underlie the argument in the main part of this book, and I hope that I have encouraged others to follow me in exploring and developing the contending positions in contemporary sociological theory.

NOTES

1. Barber (1992) has recently restated a Parsonian position on the distinction between 'matter', 'life' and 'action'. For reasons that will become clear, I prefer to use the more general term 'human' in preference to the term 'action' in this context.
2. At the risk of implying a Hegelian position, it might be pointed out that the psychological, social and cultural have an affinity with Hegel's categories of subjective spirit, objective

spirit and absolute spirit. More directly, they are related to Parsons's distinction between 'personality', 'society' and 'culture'.

3. See Archer (1988) for a discussion of dualism in relation to the cultural world.

4. As I have already emphasized, Giddens and Habermas misunderstand and misapply Lockwood's distinction between social integration and system integration.

5. On the development of a more general approach to interaction see Turner (1988).

6. Lockwood's (1992) reconstruction of the dominant and residual elements in Durkheim's theory of action points in a similar direction.

7. This need to bring back collective action has recently been stressed by Mouzelis (1991), who relates it to the 'hierarchical' structuring of social action. This view is similar to Bhaskar's (1979) stress on the 'stratification of reality'.

8. Unfortunately, contemporary micro-economics has become increasingly mathematical, at the expense of any concern for empirical investigation. Sociological investigations of economic life have not moved in this direction.

9. 'Social integration' might, nevertheless, be usefully seen as involving the two issues of 'interpersonal integration' (the sense in which Giddens uses the term) and 'collectivity integration'.

10. Institutionalized conceptions of assumed groups always involve the use of the definite article (as in *'the* family'), as they are invoking *general* concepts that are assumed to regulate the behaviour of those who are seen as members of *particular* groups (actual families, for example).

11. These actual social relations are, of course, also shaped by particular situational and environmental factors – by, for example, the limitations inherent in specific historical conjunctures or the availability of natural resources.

12. In Chapter 2 I suggested that Parsons equates system integration with 'institutional integration'. It might be remarked here, as suggested in Chapter 7, that system integration is, in fact, 'practice integration' rather than merely institutional integration.

13. This is the case, for example, with the relations of 'ownership' and 'control' that were discussed in Chapter 7.

Bibliography

Items are referenced in the text by their date of first publication or, in the case of posthumous publications, their date of composition. Where the date of an edition consulted differs from this date, it is indicated in the entry below by the inclusion of a second date. In the case of translations into English from foreign languages, the reference date is that of the original language edition.

Abel, Theodor (1929), *Systematic Sociology in Germany*, New York: Octagon Books, 1965.

Abercrombie, Nicholas, Bryan Turner and Stephen Hill (1979), *The Dominant Ideology Thesis*, London: George Allen and Unwin.

Aberle, David F., Albert K. Cohen, Alison K. Davis, Marion J. Levy and Francis X. Sutton (1950), 'The Functional Prerequisites of a Society', *Ethics*, **60**: 100–111.

Adler, Alfred (1956), *The Individual Psychology of Alfred Adler*, New York: Basic Books.

Adorno, Theodore (ed.) (1976), *The Positivist Dispute in German Sociology*, London: Heinemann, 1976.

Adorno, Theodore and Max Horkheimer (1944), *Dialectic of Enlightenment*, London: Verso, 1979.

Aho, James A. (1975), *German Realpolitik and American Sociology*, New Jersey: Associated University Presses.

Alexander, Jeffrey (1982–3), *Theoretical Logic in Sociology*, Four volumes, Berkeley: University of California Press.

Alexander, Jeffrey (ed.) (1985), *Neofunctionalism*, Beverley Hills: Sage.

Alexander, Jeffrey (1988), *Action and Its Environments*, New York: Columbia University Press.

Alexander, Jeffrey, B. Giesen, Richard Münch and Neil Smelser (eds) (1987), *The Macro–Micro Link*, Berkeley: University of California Press.

Althusser, Louis (1965), *For Marx*, Harmondsworth: Allen Lane, The Penguin Press.

Althusser, Louis (1971), *Lenin and Philosophy and Other Essays*, London: New Left Books.

Althusser, Louis (1974), *Essays in Self-Criticism*, London: New Left Books, 1976.

Althusser, Louis and Etienne Balibar (1968), *Reading Capital*, London: New Left Books, 1970.

Archer, Margaret Scotford (1988), *Culture and Agency*, Cambridge: Cambridge University Press.

Aron, Raymond (1936), *German Sociology*, New York: Free Press, 1964.

Aron, Raymond (1967), *The Industrial Society*, London: Weidenfeld and Nicolson.

Atkinson, J. Max (1984), *Our Masters' Voices: The Language and Body Language of Politics*, London: Methuen.

Avineri, Shlomo (1972), *Hegel's Theory of the Modern State*, Cambridge: Cambridge University Press.

Barber, Bernard (1992), 'Neofunctionalism and the Theory of the Social System', in Colomy (ed.) 1992.

Barnes, S. Barry (1988), *The Nature of Power*, Cambridge: Polity Press.

Barnes, S. Barry (1992), 'Status Groups and Collective Action', *Sociology*, **26**: 259–70.

Barry, Brian (1970), *Sociologists, Economists and Democracy*, London: Collier-Macmillan.

Barthes, Roland (1967), *Système de la Mode*, Paris: Editions du Seuil.

Baudrillard, Jean (1968), *The System of Objects*, Paris: Denoel-Gouthier.

Baudrillard, Jean (1970), *La Société de Consommation*, Paris: Gallimard.

Baudrillard, Jean (1972), *For a Critique of the Political Economy of the Sign*, St Louis: Telos Press, 1981.

Baudrillard, Jean (1973), *The Mirror of Production*, St Louis: Telos Press, 1975.

Baudrillard, Jean (1977), *Forget Foucault*, London: Routledge, 1992.

Baudrillard, Jean (1978), *In the Shadow of the Silent Majorities*, New York: Semiotext(e), 1983.

Baudrillard, Jean (1981), *Simulations*, New York: Semiotext(e), 1983.

Baudrillard, Jean (1983), *Les Stratégies Fatales*, Paris: Grasset.

Baudrillard, Jean (1988), *America*, London: Verso.

Beck, Ulrich (1986), *Risk Society: Towards a New Modernity*, London: Sage, 1992.

Becker, Gary S. (1976), *The Economic Approach to Human Behaviour*, Chicago: University of Chicago Press.

Becker, Gary S. (1981), *A Treatise on the Family*, Cambridge, Mass.: Harvard University Press.

Becker, Howard P. (1938), 'Sociology in the Germanic Language', in Becker and Barnes (eds) 1961.

Becker, Howard P. and Harry Elmer Barnes (eds) (1961), *Social Thought From Lore to Science*, New York: Dover, 1961.

Becker, Howard S. (1963), *Outsiders: Studies in the Sociology of Deviance*, New York: Free Press.

Bell, Daniel (ed.) (1961), *The End of Ideology*, New York: Collier-Macmillan.

Bell, Daniel (1973), *The Coming of Post Industrial Society*, London: Heinemann.

Bendix, Reinhard (1963), *Max Weber: An Intellectual Portrait*, London: Methuen.

Bentley, Arthur F. (1908), *The Process of Government*, Cambridge, Mass.: Harvard University Press, 1967.

Benton, Ted (1984), *The Rise and Fall of Structural Marxism*, London: Macmillan.

Berger, Peter (1969a), *A Rumour of Angels: Modern Society and the Redis-covery of the Supernatural*, Harmondsworth: Allen Lane The Penguin Press, 1970.

Berger, Peter (1969b), *The Social Reality of Religion [The Sacred Canopy]*, London: Faber and Faber.

Berger, Peter and Hansfried Kellner (1970), 'Marriage and the Construction of Reality', in Dreitzel (ed.) 1970.

Berger, Peter and Thomas Luckmann (1966), *The Social Construction of Reality*, Harmondsworth: Allen Lane, 1971.

Berger, Joseph, Morris Zelditch and Bo Anderson (eds) (1972), *Sociological Theories in Progress, Volume Two*, Boston: Houghton Mifflin Company.

Bernstein, Eduard (1899), *Evolutionary Socialism*, New York: Schocken Books, 1961.

Bershady, Harold (1973), *Ideology and Social Knowledge*, Oxford: Basil Blackwell.

Best, Steven and Douglas Kellner (1991), *Postmodern Theory*, London: Macmillan.

Bhaskar, Roy (1975), *The Realist Theory of Science*, Leeds: Leeds Books.

Bhaskar, Roy (1979), *The Possibility of Naturalism*, Brighton: Harvester.

Black, Max (ed.) (1961), *The Social Theories of Talcott Parsons*, Englewood Cliffs: Prentice-Hall.

Blalock, Hubert M. (1970), 'The Formalisation of Sociological Theory', in McKinney and Tiryakian (eds) 1970.

Blau, Peter M. (1964), *Exchange and Power in Social Life*, New York: John Wiley.

Blau, Peter M. and Otis D. Duncan (1967), *The American Occupational Structure*, New York: Wiley.

Blaug, Mark (1972), 'Was There a Marginal Revolution?', *History of Political Economy*, **4**.

Blumer, Herbert (1962), 'Society as Symbolic Interaction', in Blumer 1969b.

Blumer, Herbert (1966), 'Sociological Implications of the Thought of George Herbert Mead', in Blumer 1969b.

Blumer, Herbert (1969a), 'The Methodological Position of Symbolic Interactionism', in Blumer 1969b.

Blumer, Herbert (1969b), *Symbolic Interactionism*, Englewood Cliffs, New Jersey: Prentice-Hall.

Boden, Deirdre (1990), *The Business of Talk: Organisations in Action*, Cambridge: Polity Press.

Boden, Deirdre and Don H. Zimmerman (eds) (1990), *Talk and Social Structure: Studies in Ethnomethodology and Conversational Analysis*, Cambridge: Polity Press.

Bonald, Louis de (1796), 'La Théorie du Pouvoir', in *Ouevres Complètes, Volume 1*, Paris: Abbé Migne, 1859.

Bottomore, Tom (1975), *Marxist Sociology*, London: Macmillan.

Bottomore, Tom and Robert A. Nisbet (eds) (1979), *A History of Sociological Analysis*, London: Heinemann.

Bourdieu, Pierre (1977), *Outline of a Theory of Practice*, Cambridge: Cambridge University Press.

Bourricaud, François (1977), *The Sociological Theories of Talcott Parsons*, Chicago: University of Chicago Press, 1981.

Bourricaud, François (1984), *The Sociological Theories of Talcott Parsons*, Chicago: University of Chicago Press.

Bryant, Christopher A. G. and David Jary, (eds) (1991), *Giddens' Theory of Structuration: A Critical Appreciation*, London: Routledge.

Buchanan, J. M. and G. Tullock (1962), *The Calculus of Consent*, Ann Arbor: University of Michigan Press.

Buckley, Walter (1967), *Sociology and Modern Systems Theory*, Englewood Cliffs: Prentice-Hall.

Burke, Edmund (1790), *Reflections on the Revolution in France*, Harmondsworth: Penguin, 1968.

Burns, Tom (1992), *Erving Goffman*, London: Routledge.

Burns, Tom R., Thomas Baumgartner and Walter Buckley (1985a), *The Shaping of Society*, London: Wiley.

Burns, Tom R., Thomas Baumgartner and Philippe Deville (1985b) *Man, Decisions, Society*, New York: Gordon and Breach.

Buxton, William (1985), *Talcott Parsons and the Capitalist Nation State*, Toronto: University of Toronto Press.

Carchedi, Guglielmo (1975a), 'On the Economic Identification of the New Middle Class', *Economy and Society*, **4**.

Carchedi, Guglielmo (1975b), 'Reproduction of Social Classes at the Level of Production Relations', *Economy and Society*, **4**.

Carling, Alan (1992), *Social Divisions*, London: Verso.

Castells, Manuel (1970), 'Theoretical Propositions For an Experimantal Study of Urban Social Movements', in Pickvance (ed.) 1976.

Castells, Manuel (1976), 'On the Study of Urban Social Movements', in Pickvance (ed.) 1976.

Castells, Manuel (1977), *The Urban Question*, London: Edward Arnold.

Castoriadis, Carlos (1975), *The Imaginary Institution of Society*, Cambridge: Polity Press, 1988.

Chomsky, Noam (1957), *Syntactic Structures*, The Hague: Mouton.

Chomsky, Noam (1965), *Aspects of the Theory of Syntax*, Cambridge: M.I.T. Press.

Cicourel, Aaron V. (1964), *Method and Measurement in Sociology*, New York: Free Press.

Cicourel, Aaron V. (1967), *The Social Organisation of Juvenile Justice*, New York: Wiley.

Cicourel, Aaron V. (1968), 'The Acquisition of Social Structure: Towards a Developmental Sociology of Language and Meaning', in Cicourel (ed.) 1973.

Cicourel, Aaron V. (1970), 'Generative Semantics and the Structure of Social Interaction', in Cicourel (ed.) 1973.

Cicourel, Aaron V. (1972), 'Interpretive Procedures and Normative Rules in the Negotiation of Status and Role', in Cicourel, (ed.) 1973.

Cicourel, Aaron V. (ed.) (1973), *Cognitive Sociology*, Harmondsworth: Penguin.

Cicourel, Aaron V. and John I. Kitsuse (1963), *The Educational Decision-makers*, New York: Bobbs-Merrill.

Clarke, Simon (1980), 'Althusserian Marxism', in *One Dimensional Marxism*, edited by S. Clarke and others, Luton: Allison and Busby.

Clegg, Stewart R. (1975), *Power, Rule and Domination*, London: Routledge and Kegan Paul.

Clegg, Stewart R. (1989), *Frameworks of Power*, London: Sage.

Cohen, Gerry A. (1978), *Karl Marx's Theory of History*, Oxford: Oxford University Press.

Cohen, Percy S. (1968), *Modern Social Theory*, London: Heinemann.

Cohen, Stanley (ed.) (1971), *Images of Deviance*, Harmondsworth: Penguin.

Coleman, James S. (1966), 'Foundations For a Theory of Collective Decisions', *American Journal of Sociology*, 71: 615–27.

Coleman, James S. (1973), *The Mathematics of Collective Action*, London: Heinemann.

Coleman, James S. (1990), *Foundations of Social Theory*, Cambridge: Belknap.

Collins, Randall (1975), *Conflict Sociology: Toward An Explanatory Science*, New York: Academic Press.

Collins, Randall (1981), 'On the Microfoundations of Macrosociology', *American Sociological Review*, **86**: 925–42.

Collins, Randall (1990), 'Conflict Theory and the Advance of Macro-Historical Sociology', in Ritzer (ed.) 1990.

Colomy, Paul (ed.) (1990), *Neo-functionalist Sociology*, Aldershot: Edward Elgar.

Colomy, Paul (ed.) (1992), *The Dynamics of Social Systems*, London: Sage.

Comte, Auguste (1830–42), *Cours de Philosophie Positive*, Paris: Bachelier.

Comte, Auguste (1851–54), *System of Positive Polity*, London: 1875–77.

Condorcet, Antoine-Nicoles de (1794), *Sketch For a Historical Picture of the Progress of the Human Mind*, London: Weidenfeld and Nicolson, 1955.

Cook, Karen S. (1977), 'Exchange and Power in Networks of Inter-organisational Relations', *Sociological Quarterly*, **18**: 62–82.

Cook, Karen S. and Richard M. Emerson (1978), 'Power, Equity and Commitmant in Exchange Networks', *American Sociological Review*, **43**: 721–39.

Cook, Karen S. and J. M. Whitmeyer (1992), 'Two Approaches to Social Structure: Exchange Theory and Network Analysis', *Annual Review of Sociology*, **18**: 109–27.

Cook, Karen S., R. M. Emerson, M. R. Gillmore and T. Yamagishi (1983), 'The Distribution of Power in Exchange Networks: Theory and Experimental Results', *American Journal of Sociology*, **89**: 275–305.

Cook, Karen S., Jodie O'Brien and Peter Kollock (1990), 'Exchange Theory: A Blueprint For Structure and Process', in Ritzer (ed.) 1990.

Cooley, Charles H. (1909), *Social Organisation*, New York: Schocken.

Cooley, Charles H. (1922), *Human Nature and the Social Order*, New York: Scribner's.

Coser, Lewis (1956), *The Functions of Social Conflict*, London: Routledge and Kegan Paul.

Coser, Lewis (1974), *Greedy Institutions: Patterns of Undivided Commitments*, New York: Free Press.

Coser, Lewis and Bernard Rosenberg (1967), *Sociological Theory: A Book of Readings*, New York: Collier-Macmillan.

Craib, Ian (1992), *Anthony Giddens*, London: Routledge.

Crompton, Rosemary and Michael Mann (eds) (1986), *Gender and Stratification*, Cambridge: Polity Press.

Crouch, Colin (1982), *Trade Unions: The Logic of Collective Action*, Glasgow: Fontana.

Dahrendorf, Ralf (1957), *Class and Class Conflict in an Industrial Society*, London: Routledge and Kegan Paul, 1959.

Dandecker, Christopher (1990), *Surveillance, Power and Modernity*, Cambridge: Polity Press.

Davis, Kingsley (1948), *Human Society*, New York: Macmillan.

Davis, Kingsley (1959), 'The Myth of Functional Analysis as a Special Method of Sociology and Anthropology', *American Sociological Review*, **24**: 757–73.

Denzin, Norman K. (1970), 'Symbolic Interactionism and Ethnomethodology', in Douglas (ed.) 1971b.

Derrida, Jacques (1967), Writing and Difference, Chicago: University of Chicago Press, 1978.

Deutsch, Morton (1964), 'Homans in the Skinner Box', *Sociological Inquiry*, **34**: 156–65.

Diani, Mario (1992), 'The Concept of Social Movement', *Sociological Review*, **40**: 1–25.

Douglas, Jack (1967), *The Social Meanings of Suicide*, Princeton: Princeton University Press.

Douglas, Jack (1971a),*American Social Order*, New York: Free Press.

Douglas, Jack (ed.) (1971b), *Understanding Everyday Life*, London: Routledge and Kegan Paul.

Downes, David and Paul Rock (1988), *Understanding Deviance,* Second Edition, Oxford: Oxford University Press.

Downs, Anthony (1957), *An Economic Theory of Democracy*, New York: Harper and Brothers.

Dreitzel, Hans-Peter (ed.) (1970), *Recent Sociology, Number 2,* New York: Macmillan.

Durkheim, Emile (1893), *The Division of Labour in Society*, London: Macmillan, 1984.

Durkheim, Emile (1895), *The Rules of the Sociological Method*, London: Macmillan, 1982.

Durkheim, Emile (1897), *Suicide: A Study in Sociology*, London: Routledge and Kegan Paul, 1952.

Durkheim, Emile (1912), *Elementary Forms of the Religious Life*, London: George Allen and Unwin, 1915.

Durkheim, Emile and Marcel Mauss (1903), *Primitive Classification*, London: Cohen and West, 1963.

Eder, Klaus (1993), *The New Politics of Class: Social Movements and Cultural Dynamics in Advanced Societies*, London: Sage.

Eisenstadt, Shmuel (1963), *The Political Systems of Empires*, New York: Free Press.

Eisenstadt, Shmuel (1973), *Tradition, Change and Modernity*, New York: Free Press.

Eisenstadt, Shmuel (1978), *Revolution and the Transformation of Societies*, New York: Free Press.

Ekeh, Peter (1974), *Social Exchange Theory*, London: Heinemann.

Elster, Jon (1983), *Sour Grapes*, Cambridge: Cambridge University Press.

Elster, Jon (1985), *Making Sense of Marx*, Cambridge: Cambridge University Press.

Elster, Jon (1986a), *An Introduction to Karl Marx*, Cambridge: Cambridge University Press.

Elster, Jon (ed.) (1986b), *Rational Choice*, Oxford: Basil Blackwell.

Elster, Jon (1989a), *The Cement of Society*, Cambridge: Cambridge University Press.

Elster, Jon (1989b), *Nuts and Bolts For the Social Sciences*, Cambridge: Cambridge University Press.

Emerson, Joan (1970), 'Behaviour in Private Places: Sustaining Definitions of Reality in Gynaecological Examinations', in Dreitzel (ed.) 1970.

Emerson, R. M. (1962), 'Power–Dependence Relations', *American Sociological Review*, **27**: 692–703.

Emerson, Richard M. (1972a), 'Exchange Theory, Part I: A Psychological Basis For Social Exchange', in Berger *et al.* (eds) 1972.

Emerson, Richard M. (1972b), 'Exchange Theory, Part II: Exchange Relations and Network Structures', in Berger *et al.* (eds) 1972.

Engels, Friedrich (1876), *Anti-Dühring*, Moscow: Foreign Languages Publishing House, 1954.

Ferguson, Adam (1767), *An Essay on the History of Civil Society*, Edinburgh: Edinburgh University Press, 1966.

Fine, Gary (1990), 'Symbolic Interactionism in the Post-Blumerian Age', in Ritzer (ed.) 1990.

Fishman, Pamela M. (1978), 'Interaction: The Work Women Do', *Social Problems*, **25**.

Fortes, Meyer and Edward Evans-Pritchard (eds) (1940), *African Political Systems*, London: Oxford University Press.

Foucault, Michel (1961), *Madness and Civilization*, New York: Vintage Books, 1973.

Foucault, Michel (1963), *The Birth of the Clinic*, New York: Vintage Books, 1975.

Foucault, Michel (1966), *The Order of Things*, New York: Vintage Books, 1973.

Foucault, Michel (1971), *The Archaeology of Knowledge*, New York: Pantheon, 1972.

Foucault, Michel (1975), *Discipline and Punish*, London: Allen Lane, 1977.

Foucault, Michel (1976), *The History of Sexuality*, New York: Vintage Books, 1980.

Foucault, Michel (1982), 'The Subject and Power', in *Power, Volume 1*, edited by J. Scott, 208–26. London: Routledge, 1994.

Foucault, Michel (1984a), *The Care of the Self*, New York: Vintage Books, 1988.

Foucault, Michel (1984b), *The Use of Pleasure*, New York: Vintage Books, 1986.

Freund, Julien (1978), 'German Sociology in the Time of Max Weber', in Bottomore and Nisbet (eds) 1979.

Freyer, Hans (1930), *Soziologie als Wirklichkeitswissenschaft*, Leipzig: Duncker and Humblot.

Friedman, Debra and Michael Hechter (1990), 'The Comparative Advantages of Rational Choice Theory', in Ritzer (ed.) 1990.

Friedson, Eliot (ed.)(1963), *The Hospital in Modern Society*, New York: Free Press.

Garfinkel, Harold (1967a), 'Passing and the Managed Achievement of Sex Status in an Intersexed Person', in Garfinkel 1967b.

Garfinkel, Harold (1967b), *Studies in Ethnomethodology*, New Jersey: Prentice-Hall.

Geras, Norman (1972), 'Althusser's Marxism: An Account and Assessment', *New Left Review*, **71**.

Giddens, Anthony (1971), *Capitalism and Modern Social Theory*, Cambridge: Cambridge University Press.

Giddens, Anthony (1972), 'Four Myths in the History of Social Thought', *Economy and Society*, **1**.

Giddens, Anthony (1973), *The Class Structure of the Advanced Societies*, London: Hutchinson.

Giddens, Anthony (1976a), 'Classical Social Theory and the Origins of Modern Sociology', *American Journal of Sociology*, **81**: 703–29.

Giddens, Anthony (1976b), *New Rules of the Sociological Method*, London: Hutchinson.

Giddens, Anthony (1976c), 'Functionalism: Après la Lutte', in *Studies in Social and Political Theory*, by A. Giddens, London: Hutchinson, 1977.

Giddens, Anthony (1977), 'Review Essay: Habermas's Social and Political Theory', *American Journal of Sociology*, **83**.

Giddens, Anthony (1979), *Central Problems in Social Theory*, London: Macmillan.

Giddens, Anthony (1981), *A Contemporary Critique of Historical Materialism, Volume 1: Power, Property and the State*, London: Macmillan.

Giddens, Anthony (1984a), *The Constitution of Society*, Cambridge: Polity Press.

Giddens, Anthony (1984b), 'Time and Social Organisation', in *Social Theory and Modern Sociology*, by A. Giddens, Cambridge: Polity Press, 1987.

Giddens, Anthony (1985), *The Nation State and Violence, Volume 2 of A Contemporary Critique of Historical Materialism*, Cambridge: Polity Press.

Giddens, Anthony (1986), 'Erving Goffman as a Systematic Social Theorist', in *Social Theory and Modern Sociology*, by A. Giddens, Cambridge: Polity Press, 1987.

Giddens, Anthony (1990), *The Consequences of Modernity*, Cambridge: Polity Press.

Giddens, Anthony (1991a), *Modernity and Self-Identity*, Cambridge: Polity Press.

Giddens, Anthony (1991b), 'Structuration Theory: Past, Present and Future', in Bryant and Jary (eds) 1991.

Giddens, Anthony (1992), *The Transformation of Intimacy*, Cambridge: Polity Press.

Giner, Salvador (1976), *Mass Society*, London: Martin Robertson.

Gluckman, Max (1955), *Custom and Conflict in Africa*, Oxford: Basil Blackwell.

Glucksmann, André (1972), 'A Ventriloquist Structuralism', *New Left Review*, **72**.

Glucksmann, Miriam (1974), *Structuralist Analysis in Contemporary Social Thought*, London: Routledge and Kegan Paul.

Goffman, Erving (1959), *The Presentation of Self in Everyday Life*, Harmondsworth: Penguin.

Goffman, Erving (1961), *Asylums: Essays on the Social Situation of Mental Patients and Other Inmates*, New York: Doubleday.

Goffman, Erving (1963), *Stigma*, Englewood Cliffs: Prentice-Hall.

Goffman, Erving (1967), *Interaction Ritual: Essays on Face-to-Face Behaviour*, New York: Doubleday.

Goffman, Erving (1974), *Frame Analysis*, New York: Harper and Row.

Goffman, Erving (1983), 'The Interaction Order', *American Sociological Review*, **48**: 1–17.

Gouldner, Alvin W. (1959), 'Reciprocity and Autonomy in Functional Theory', in Gouldner 1973.

Gouldner, Alvin W. (1973), *For Sociology*, Harmondsworth: Allen Lane The Penguin Press.

Granovetter, Mark (1986), 'Economic Action and Social Structure: The Problem of Embeddedness', *American Journal of Sociology*, **81**: 481–510.

Gumplowicz, Ludwig (1875), *Rasse und Staat*, Innsbruck: Wagner.

Gumplowicz, Ludwig (1883), *Der Rassenkampf*, Innsbruck: Wagner.

Gumplowicz, Ludwig (1885), *Outlines of Sociology, First Edition*, Philadelphia: American Academy of Political and Social Science, 1899.

Gumplowicz, Ludwig (1905), *Outlines of Sociology, Second Edition*, New Brunswick: Transaction, 1980.

Habermas, Jürgen (1962), *Structural Change in the Public Sphere*, Cambridge: Polity Press.

Habermas, Jürgen (1963a), 'The Analytical Theory of Science and Dialectics', in Adorno (ed.) 1976.

Habermas, Jürgen (1963b), 'A Positivistically Bisected Rationalism', in Adorno (ed.) 1976.

Habermas, Jürgen (1963c), 'Between Philosophy and Science: Marxism as Critique', in *Theory and Practice*, edited by J. Habermas, London: Heinemann, 1974.

Habermas, Jürgen (1965a), 'Knowledge and Interests', in *Knowledge and Human Interests*, edited by J. Habermas, London: Heinemann, 1971.

Habermas, Jürgen (1965b), 'Technology and Science as "Ideology"', in *Towards a Rational Society*, edited by J. Habermas, London: Heinemann, 1971.

Habermas, Jürgen (1967a), 'Labour and Interaction: Remarks on Hegel's Jena Philosophy of Mind', in Habermas 1971.

Habermas, Jürgen (1967b), *On The Logic of the Social Sciences*, Cambridge: Polity Press, 1988.

Habermas, Jürgen (1968), *Knowledge and Human Interests*, London: Heinemann, 1972.

Habermas, Jürgen (1968–69), *Towards a Rational Society*, London: Heinemann, 1971.

Habermas, Jürgen (1970a), 'On Systematically Distorted Communication', *Inquiry*, **13**.

Habermas, Jürgen (1970b), 'Towards a Theory of Communicative Competence', in Dreitzel (ed.) 1970.

Habermas, Jürgen (1971), *Theory and Practice*, London: Heinemann, 1974.

Habermas, Jürgen (1973a), 'A Postscript to Knowledge and Human Interests', *Philosophy of the Social Sciences*, **3**.

Habermas, Jürgen (1973b), *Legitimation Crisis*, London: Heinemann, 1976.

Habermas, Jürgen (1976), *Communication and the Evolution of Society*, London: Heinemann, 1979.

Habermas, Jürgen (1981a),*The Theory of Communicative Action, Volume One: Reason and the Rationalisation of Society*, London: Heinemann, 1984.

Habermas, Jürgen (1981b), *The Theory of Communicative Action, Volume Two: The Critique of Functionalist Reason*, London: Heinemann, 1987.

Harré, Rom (1961), *Theories and Things*, London: Sheed and Ward.

Harré, Rom (1964), *Matter and Method*, London: Macmillan.

Harré, Rom (1970), *The Principles of Scientific Thinking*, London: Macmillan.

Harré, Rom (1979), *Social Being*, Oxford: Basil Blackwell.

Harré, Rom (1981), 'Philosophical Aspects of the Micro–Macro Problem', in Knorr-Cetina and Cicourel (eds) 1981.

Harré, Rom and E. H. Madden (1975), *Causal Powers*, Oxford: Oxford University Press.

Hawthorn, Geoffrey (1976), *Enlightenment and Despair*, Cambridge: Cambridge University Press.

Hayek, Friedrich von (1942), 'Scientism and the Study of Society', Economica, **10**.

Hayek, Friedrich von (1962), 'Rules, Perception and Intelligibility', in *Studies in Philosophy, Politics and Economics*, edited by F. von Hayek, London: Routledge and Kegan Paul, 1967.

Hayek, Friedrich von (1965), 'Kinds of Rationality', in *Studies in Philosophy, Politics and Economics*, edited by F. von Hayek, London: Routledge and Kegan Paul, 1967.

Hayek, Friedrich von (1966), 'The Principles of a Liberal Social Order', in *Studies in Philosophy, Politics and Economics*, edited by F. von Hayek, London: Routledge and Kegan Paul, 1967.

Hayek, Friedrich von (1967), 'The Results of Human Action But Not of Human Design', in *Studies in Philosophy, Politics and Economics*, edited by F. von Hayek. London: Routledge and Kegan Paul, 1967.

Heath, Anthony (1968), 'Economic Theory and Sociology: A Critique of P. M. Blau's Exchange and Power in Social Life', *Sociology*, **2**: 273–92.

Heath, Anthony (1976), *Rational Choice and Social Exchange*, Cambridge: Cambridge University Press.

Hechter, Michael (1987), *Principles of Group Solidarity*, Berkeley: University of California Press.

Hegel, Georg W. F. (1807), *Hegel's Philosophy of Mind [Die Philosophie des Geistes]*, Oxford: Oxford University Press, 1971.

Hegel, Georg W. F. (1821), *Hegel's Philosophy of Right [Naturrecht und Staatswissenschaft im Grundrisse. Grundlinien der Philosophie des Rechts]*, London: Oxford University Press, 1952.

Held, David and John B. Thompson (eds) (1989), *Social Theory of Modern Societies*, Cambridge: Cambridge University Press.

Hempel, Carl G. (1959), 'The Logic of Functional Analysis', in *Symposium on Sociological Theory*, edited by N. Gross, New York: Harper and Row.

Henderson, Lawrence J. (1935), *Pareto's General Sociology*, Cambridge, Mass.: Harvard University Press.

Herder, F. (1784–91), *Outlines of a Philosophy of the History of Man*, Chicago: University of Chicago Press, 1968.

Heritage, John (1984), *Garfinkel and Ethnomethodology*, Cambridge: Polity Press.

Hilferding, Rudolf (1910), *Finance Capital*, London: Routledge and Kegan Paul, 1981.

Hindess, Barry (1973), 'Models and Masks: Empiricist Conceptions of the Conditions of Scientific Knowledge', *Economy and Society*, **2**.

Hindess, Barry (1977), *Philosophy and Methodology in the Social Sciences*, Hassocks: Harvester.

Hindess, Barry (1988), *Choice, Rationality and Social Theory*. London: Unwin Hyman.

Hindess, Barry and Paul Q. Hirst (1975), *Pre-capitalist Modes of Production*, London: Routledge and Kegan Paul.

Hirst, Paul Q. (1979), *On Law and Ideology*, London: Macmillan.

Hobbes, Thomas (1651), *Leviathan*, Harmondsworth: Penguin, 1977.

Hochschild, Arlie Russell (1979), 'Emotion Work, Feeling Rules and Social Structure', *American Journal of Sociology*, **84**: 551–73.

Hochschild, Arlie Russell (1983), *The Managed Heart: Commercialization of Human Feeling*, Berkeley: University of California Press.

Hoggart, Richard (1957), *The Uses of Literacy*, London: Chatto and Windus.

Holton, Robert, and Bryan S. Turner (1986), *Talcott Parsons on Economy and Society*, London: Routledge and Kegan Paul.

Homans, George (1941), *English Villagers of the Thirteenth Century*, Cambridge, Mass.: Harvard University Press.

Homans, George (1950), *The Human Group*, London: Routledge and Kegan Paul, 1951.

Homans, George (1961), *Social Behaviour: Its Elementary Forms*, London: Routledge and Kegan Paul.

Homans, George C. (1964), 'Bringing Men Back In'. *American Sociological Review*, **29**: 809–18.

Homans, George C. and Charles P. Curtis (1934), *An Introduction to Pareto: His Sociology*, New York: Alfred A. Knopf.

Homans, George and David Schneider (1955), 'Marriage, Authority and Final Causes', in *Social Behaviour: Its Elementary Forms*, edited by G. Homans, London: Routledge and Kegan Paul, 1961.

Horkheimer, Max (1937), 'Traditional and Critical Theory', in *Critical Theory*, by M. Horkheimer, New York: Herder and Herder, 1972.

Jarvie, Ian C (1964), *The Revolution in Anthropology*, London: Routledge and Kegan Paul.

Jarvie, Ian C. (1972), *Concepts and Society*, London: Routledge and Kegan Paul.

Jary, David (1991), 'Society as Time Traveller: Giddens on Historical Change, Historical Materialism and the Nation State', in Bryant and Jary (eds) 1991.

Jessop, Robert D. (1972), *Social Order, Reform and Revolution*, London: Macmillan.

Joas, Hans (1980), *G. H. Mead*, Cambridge: Polity Press, 1985.

Keat, Russell and John Urry (1975), *Social Theory as Science*, London: Routledge and Kegan Paul.

Kerr, Clerk, John T. Dunlop, Frederick Harbison and C. A. Myers (1960), *Industrialism and Industrial Man*, Cambridge Mass.: Harvard University Press.

Knorr-Cetina, Karen and Aaron V. Cicourel (eds) (1981), *Advances in Social Theory and Methodology*, London: Routledge and Kegan Paul.

Korsch, Karl (1923), *Marxism and Philosophy*, London: New Left Books, 1970.

Kuhn, Thomas S. (1962), *The Structure of Scientific Revolutions*, Chicago: University of Chicago Press.

Layder, Derek (1985), 'Power, Structure and Agency', *Journal for the Theory of Social Behaviour*, **15**: 131–49.

Layder, Derek (1994), *Understanding Social Theory*, London: Sage.

Leach, Edmund R. (1970), *Lévi-Strauss*, Glasgow: Fontana Modern Masters.

Leakey, Pat N. (1987), *Invitation to Talcott Parsons' Theories*, Houston: Cap and Gown Press.

Lemert, Edwin (ed.) (1967), *Human Deviance, Social Problems and Social Control*, Englewood Cliffs: Prentice-Hall.

Lévi-Strauss, Claude (1949), *The Elementary Structures of Kinship*, Boston: Beacon Press, 1969.

Lévi-Strauss, Claude (1960), 'The Myth of Asdiwal', in *The Structural Study of Myth and Totemism*, edited by E. R. Leach, London: Tavistock, 1967.

Lévi-Strauss, Claude (1962a), *The Savage Mind*, Chicago: University of Chicage Press, 1966.

Lévi-Strauss, Claude (1962b), *Totemism*, London: Merlin Press.

Lévi-Strauss, Claude (1964), *The Raw and The Cooked [Mythologiques, Volume 1]*, London: Cape, 1969.

Lévi-Strauss, Claude (1968a), *Structural Anthropology*, London: Allen Lane The Penguin Press.

Lévi-Strauss, Claude (1968b), *The Origin of Table Manners [Mythologiques, Volume 3]*, London: Cape, 1978.

Levy, Marion J. (1966), *Modernization and the Structure of Societies*, Princeton: Princeton University Press.

Lewis, Helen (1971), *Shame and Guilt in Neurosis*, New York: International Universities Press.

Linton, Ralph (1936), *The Study of Man*, New York: Appleton Century.

Lipset, Seymour Martin (1959), *Political Man*, London: Heinemann, 1960.

Lockwood, David (1956), 'Some Remarks on The Social System', *British Journal of Sociology*, **7**.

Lockwood, David (1964), 'Social Integration and System Integration', in *System, Change and Conflict*, edited by G. Zollschan and W. Hirsch, 1976.

Lockwood, David (1992), *Solidarity and Schism*, Oxford: Clarendon Press.

Loubser, Jan J., R. C. Baum, A. Effrat, and Victor M. Lidz (eds) (1976), *Explorations in General Theory in Social Science, Two Volumes*, New York: Free Press.

Luckmann, Thomas (1967), *The Invisible Religion: The Problem of Religion in Modern Society*, New York: Macmillan.

Luhmann, Niklas (1964), *Funktionen und Folgen Formaler Organisationen*, Berlin: Duncker und Humblot.

Luhmann, Niklas (1965), *Grundrecht als Institution*, Berlin: Duncker und Humblot.

Luhmann, Niklas (1968), 'Politics as a Social System', in *The Differentiation of Society*, edited by N. Luhmann, New York: Coumbia University Press, 1982.

Luhmann, Niklas (1970), 'The Economy as a Social System', in Luhmann 1982.

Luhmann, Niklas (1975a), 'The Differentiation of Society', in Luhmann 1982.

Luhmann, Niklas (1975b), 'Interaction, Organisation and Society', in Luhmann 1982.

Luhmann, Niklas (1977), 'Systems Theory, Evolution Theory and Communication Theory', in Luhmann 1982.

Luhmann, Niklas (1979), 'Talcott Parsons: the Future of a Theory', in Luhmann 1982.

Luhmann, Niklas (1982), *The Differentiation of Society*, New York: Columbia University Press.

Luhmann, Niklas (1986), *Love as Passion*, Cambridge: Polity Press.

Luhmann, Niklas, and Jürgen Habermas (1971), *System Theorie oder Sozial Technologie*, Frankfurt: Suhrkamp.

Lukács, Gyorgy (1923), *History and Class Consciousness*, London: Merlin Press, 1971.

Lukes, Steven (1974), *Power: A Radical View*, London: Macmillan.

Luxemburg, Rosa (1913), *The Accumulation of Capital*, London: Routledge and Kegan Paul, 1951.

MacIntyre, Alasdair (1966), *A Short History of Ethics*, New York: Macmillan.

Macpherson, Crawford B. (1962), *The Political Theory of Possessive Individualism*, Oxford: Clarendon Press.

Malinowski, Bronislaw (1944), *A Scientific Theory of Culture*, New York: Oxford University Press, 1960.

Malthus, Thomas R. (1820), *Principles of Political Economy*, New York: Augustus Kelley, 1964.

Mann, Michael (1970), 'The Social Cohesion of Liberal Democracy', *American Sociological Review*, **35**: 423–39.

Mann, Michael (1986), *The Sources of Social Power, Volume 1: A History of Power from the Beginning to AD 1760*, Cambridge: Cambridge University Press.

Mannheim, Karl (1925), *Conservatism: A Contribution to the Sociology of Knowledge*, London: Routledge and Kegan Paul, 1986.

Mannheim, Karl (1929), 'Ideology and Utopia', in *Ideology and Utopia, Chapters II–IV*, edited by K. Mannheim, London: Routledge and Kegan Paul, 1936.

Marcuse, Herbert (1941), *Reason and Revolution*, New York: Humanities Press, Second Edition, 1954.

Marcuse, Herbert (1964a), 'Industrialization and Capitalism', *New Left Review*, **30**: 3–18.

Marcuse, Herbert (1964b), *One Dimensional Man*, London: Routledge and Kegan Paul.

Marshall, Thomas H. (1949), 'Citizenship and Social Class', in Marshall 1963.

Marshall, Thomas H. (1963), *Sociology at the Crossroads*, London: Heinemann.

Marwell, Gerald, Pamela E. Oliver and R Prahl (1989), 'Social Networks and Collective Action: A Theory of the Critical Mass, III', *American Journal of Sociology*, **94**: 502–35.

Marx, Karl (1844), *Economic and Philosophical Manuscripts*, London: Lawrence and Wishart, 1959.

Marx, Karl (1859), 'Preface to a Contribution to the Critique of Political Economy', in *Werke, Volume 13*, edited by K. Marx and F. Engels, Berlin: Dietz Verlag, 1964.

Marx, Karl (1867), *Capital, Volume 1*, London: Lawrence and Wishart, 1965.

Marx, Karl and Friedrich Engels (1846), *The German Ideology*, London: Lawrence and Wishart, 1970.

Mauss, Marcel (1925), *The Gift*, London: Routledge and Kegan Paul, 1966.

McCarthy, Thomas (1978), *The Critical Theory of Jürgen Habermas*, London: Hutchinson.

McKinney, John C. and Edward A. Tiryakian (eds) (1970), *Theoretical Sociology*, New York: Appleton-Century-Crofts.

Mead, George Herbert (1927), *Mind, Self and Society From the Standpoint of Social Behaviourism*, Chicago: University of Chicago Press, 1934.

Mehan, Hugh and Houston Wood (1975), *The Reality of Ethnomethodology*, New York: Wiley.

Menger, Carl (1883), *Investigations into the Methods of the Social Sciences [Untersuchungen über die Methode der socialwissenschaften und der Politischer Ökonomie insbesonre]*, New York: New York University Press, 1985.

278 *Sociological theory*

Menzies, Ken (1976), *Talcott Parsons and the Social Image of Man*, London: Routledge and Kegan Paul.

Merton, Robert K. (1936), 'The Unanticipated Consequences of Purposive Social Action', *American Sociological Review*, 1.

Merton, Robert K. (1949), 'Manifest and Latent Function', in *Social Theory and Social Structure*, by R. K. Merton,' New York: Harper and Row, 1949.

Merton, Robert K. (1957), 'The Role Set: Problems in Sociological Theory', *British Journal of Sociology*, 8.

Mill, James (1821), *Elements of Political Economy*, New York: Augustus Kelley, 1963.

Mill, John Stuart (1848), *Principles of Political Economy*, London: Parker and Co.

Mill, John Stuart (1869), *The Subjection of Women*, London: Longmans Green, 1949.

Millar, John (1779), *The Origin of the Distinction of Ranks*, reprinted in W. Lehmann (ed.), *John Millar of Glasgow*, Glasgow: Glasgow University Press, 1960.

Mills, C. W. (1956), *The Power Elite*, New York: Oxford University Press.

Mills, C. W. (ed.) (1963), *Power, Politics and People*, New York: Oxford University Press.

Mises, Ludwig von (1949), *Human Action*, New Haven: Yale University Press.

Montesquieu, Baron de (1748), *The Spirit of Laws*, New York: Haffner, 1948.

Mosca, Gaetano (1896), 'Elementi di Scienza Politica', in *Elementi di Scienza Politica*, First Edition, edited by G. Mosca, 1982.

Mouzelis, Nicos P. (1991), *Back To Sociological Theory: The Construction of Social Orders*, London: Macmillan.

Münch, Richard (1981), 'Talcott Parsons and the Theory of Action, I: The Structure of Kantian Lore', *American Journal of Sociology*, **86**: 709–39.

Münch, Richard (1982a), 'Talcott Parsons and the Theory of Action, II: The Continuity of Development', *American Journal of Sociology*, **87**: 771–826.

Münch, Richard (1982b), *Theorie des Handelns* [Translated as Two Volumes: *'Theory of Action' and 'Understanding Modernity'*].

Münch, Richard (1982c), *Theory of Action: Towards a New Synthesis Going Beyond Parsons* [Part translation of *Theorie des Handelns*], London: Routledge and Kegan Paul, 1987.

Münch, Richard (1982d), *Understanding Modernity: Towards a New Perspective Going Beyond Durkheim and Weber* [Part translation of *Theorie des Handelns*], London: Routledge and Kegan Paul, 1988.

Nagel, Ernest (1956), 'A Formalization of Functionalism', in *Explorations in Social Change*, edited by G. K. Zollschan and W. Hirsch, New York: Houghton Mifflin, 1964.

Nisbet, Robert A. (1966), *The Sociological Tradition*, New York: Basic Books.

Nisbet, Robert (1978), 'Conservatism', in Bottomore and Nisbet (eds.) 1979.

Offe, Claus and H. Wiesenthal (1980), 'Two Logics of Collective Action: Theoretical Notes on Social Class and Organizational Forms', *Political Power and Social Theory*, **1**.

Oliver, Pamela E. and Gerald Marwell (1988), 'The Paradox of Group Size in Collective Actors: A Theory of the Critical Mass, II', *American Sociological Review*, **53**: 1–8.

Oliver, Pamela E., Gerald Marwell and R. Teixeira (1985), 'Interdependence, Group Heterogeneity and the Production of Collective Goods: A Theory of the Critical Mass, I', *American Journal of Sociology*, **90**: 522–56.

Olson, Mancur (1965), *The Logic of Collective Action*, Cambridge, Mass.: Harvard University Press.

Oppenheimer, Franz (1914), *The State*, Montreal: Black Rose Books, 1975.

Oppenheimer, Franz (1922), *System der Soziologie*, Jena: Fischer.

Paine, Thomas (1792), *The Rights of Man*, London: Watts and Co., 1937.

Pareto, Vilfredo (1901), *The Rise and Fall of Elites*, New York: Bedminster Press, 1968.

Pareto, Vilfredo (1902), *Les Systèmes Socialistes, Two Volumes*, Paris: Marcel Giard.

Pareto, Vilfredo (1916), *A Treatise on General Sociology*, edited by A. Livingstone, New York: Dover, Four Volumes Bound as Two, 1963.

Park, Robert E. (1921), *Introduction to the Science of Sociology*, Chicago: University of Chicago Press.

Park, Robert E., and Ernest W. Burgess (1925), *The City*, Chicago: University of Chicago Press, 1967.

Parkin, Frank (1972), 'System Contradiction and Political Transformation', *European Journal of Sociology*, **13**.

Parsons, Talcott (1937), *The Structure of Social Action*, New York: McGraw-Hill.

Parsons, Talcott (1938), 'The Role of Theory in Social Research', *American Sociological Review*, **3**: 13–20.

Parsons, Talcott (1940), 'An Analytical Approach to the Theory of Social Stratification', in Parsons 1954.

Parsons, Talcott (1945), 'The Present Position and Prospects of Systematic Theory in Sociology', in Parsons 1954.

Parsons, Talcott (1947), 'Introduction', in *The Theory of Social and Economic Organisation [Max Weber]*, edited by T. Parsons and A. M. Henderson, New York: Free Press.

Parsons, Talcott (1951), *The Social System*, New York: The Free Press.

Parsons, Talcott (ed.) (1954), *Essays in Sociological Theory, Revised Edition*, New York: Free Press.

Parsons, Talcott (1960), 'Pattern Variables Revisted: A Response to Robert Dubin', *American Sociological Review*, **25**: 467–83.

Parsons, Talcott (1961), 'An Outline of the Social System', in Parsons *et al.* 1961.

Parsons, Talcott (1963a), 'On the Concept of Influence', in Parsons 1969.

Parsons, Talcott (1963b), 'On the Concept of Political Power', *Proceedings of the American Philosophical Society*, **107**: 232–62. Also in Parsons 1969.

Parsons, Talcott (1966a), 'Full Citizenship for the Negro American?' in Parsons 1969.

Parsons, Talcott (1966b),*Societies: Evolutionary and Comparative Perspectives*, Englewood Cliffs: Prentice-Hall.

Parsons, Talcott (1968), 'On the Concept of Value Commitments', in Parsons 1969.

Parsons, Talcott (1969), *Politics and Social Structure*, New York: Free Press.

Parsons, Talcott (1970), 'Equality and Inequality in Modern Society, or Social Stratification Revisited', *Sociological Inquiry*, **40**: 13–72.

Parsons, Talcott (1971), *The System of Modern Societies*, Englewood Cliffs: Prentice-Hall.

Parsons, Talcott (1978), *Action Theory and the Human Condition*, New York: Free Press.

Parsons, Talcott and Robert F. Bales (1956), *Family, Socialization and Interaction Process*, London: Routledge and Kegan Paul.

Parsons, Talcott and Edward Shils (eds) (1951), *Towards a General Theory of Action*, Cambridge, Mass.: Harvard University Press.

Parsons, Talcott and Neil J. Smelser (1956), *Economy and Society*, New York: The Free Press.

Parsons, Talcott, Robert F. Bales and Edward Shils (1953), *Working Papers in the Theory of Action*, New York: The Free Press.

Parsons, Talcott, Edward Shils, Kaspar D. Naegele and Jesse R. Pitts (eds) (1961), *Theories of Society, Volume 1*, New York: Free Press.

Peel, John D. Y. (1971), *Herbert Spencer: The Evolution of A Sociologist*, London: Heinemann.

Perrucci, Robert, and Harry R. Potter (eds) (1989), *Networks of Power: Organizational Actors at the National, Corporate, and Community Levels*, New York: Aldine De Gruyter.

Philp, Mark (1985), 'Michel Foucault', in *The Return of Grand Theory in the Human Sciences*, edited by Q. Skinner, Cambridge: Cambridge University Press.

Pickvance, Christopher G. (1973), 'Althusser's "Empiricist" Conception of Knowledge', *Economy and Society*, **2**.

Pickvance, Christopher G. (ed.) (1976), *Urban Sociology: Critical Essays*, London: Methuen.

Popper, Karl R. (1944), 'The Poverty of Historicism', *Economica*, **II**.

Poulantzas, Nicos (1968), *Political Power and Social Classes*, London: New Left Books, 1973.

Poulantzas, Nicos (1975), *Classes in Contemporary Capitalism*, London: New Left Books.

Pusey, Michael (1987), *Jürgen Habermas*, Chichester: Ellis Horwood.

Quinney, Richard (1970), *The Social Reality of Crime*, Boston: Little, Brown.

Radcliffe Brown, Arthur R. (1940), 'On Social Structure', *Journal of the Royal Anthropological Institute*, **70**.

Radcliffe Brown, Arthur R. (1952), *Structure and Function in Primitive Society*, London: Cohen and West.

Ratzenhofer, Gustav (1893), *Wesen und Zweck der Politik*, Leipzig: F. A. Brockhaus.

Ratzenhofer, Gustav (1898), *Die Soziologische Erkenntnis*, Leipzig: F. A. Brockhaus.

Ratzenhofer, Gustav (1907), *Soziologie: Positive Lehre von den Menschlichen Wechselbeziehungen*, Leipzig: F. A. Brockhaus.

Renner, Karl (1904), *The Institutions of Private Law and their Social Function*, London: Routledge and Kegan Paul, Revised Edition 1928.

Rex, John A. (1961), *Key Problems of Sociological Theory*, London: Routledge and Kegan Paul.

Rex, John A. (1970), *Race Relations in Sociological Theory*, London: Weidenfeld and Nicholson.

Rex, John A. (1974a), 'Capitalism, Elites and The Ruling Class', in Stanworth and Giddens (eds) 1974.

Rex, John A. (1974b), *Sociology and the Demystification of the Modern World*, London: Routledge and Kegan Paul.

Rex, John A. (1981), *Social Conflict*, Harlow: Longman.

Rex, John A. and Robert Moore (1969), *Race, Community and Conflict: A Study of Sparkbrook* [Corrected Edition], London: Oxford University Press.

Ricardo, David (1817), *Principles of Political Economy and Taxation*, London: J. M. Dent, 1911.

Riker, W. H. (1962), *The Theory of Political Coalitions*, New Haven: Yale University Press.

Ritzer, George (ed.) (1990), *Frontiers of Sociological Theory*, New York: Columbia University Press.

Robertson, Roland and Bryan S. Turner (eds) (1991), *Talcott Parsons: The Origins of Modernity*, London: Sage.

Rocher, Guy (1974), *Talcott Parsons and American Sociology*, London: Nelson.

Rock, Paul (1979), *The Making of Symbolic Interactionism*, London: Macmillan.

Roemer, John (1988), *Free To Lose*, London: Radius.

Rossi, Ino (1983), *From the Sociology of Symbols to the Sociology of Signs*, New York: Columbia University Press.

Rousseau, Jean-Jacques (1755), *A Discourse on Inequality*, Harmondsworth: Penguin, 1984.

Rousseau, Jean-Jacques (1762), *The Social Contract*, Harmondsworth: Penguin.

Runciman, W. Garrison (1989), *A Treatise on Social Theory, Volume 2*, Cambridge: Cambridge University Press.

Sacks, Harvey (1965–72), *Lectures on Conversation*, Oxford: Basil Blackwell, 1992.

Sacks, Harvey, Emanuel Schegloff, and Gail Atkinson (1974), 'A Simplest Systematics for The Organisation of Turn-Taking', *Language*, **50**: 696–735.

Santos, Theotonio dos (1970), 'The Concept of Social Classes', *Science and Society*, **34**.

Saussure, Ferdinand de (1916), *Course in General Linguistics*, New York: McGraw-Hill, 1966.

Savage, Stephen (1981), *The Theories of Talcott Parsons*, London: Macmillan.

Scheff, Thomas J. (1967), 'Toward a Sociological Model of Consensus', *American Sociological Review*, **32**: 32–46.

Scheff, Thomas J. (1990), *Microsociology: Discourse, Emotion and Social Structure*, Chicago: University of Chicago Press.

Scheler, Max (1923–24), *Schriften zür Soziologie und Weltanschauungssetzung*. Leipzig: Der Neuve Geist Verlag.

Schroyer, Trent (1975), 'The Repoliticization of the Relations of Production', *New German Critique*, **5**: 107–28.

Schutz, Alfred (1932), *The Phenomenology of The Social World*, London: Heinemann Educational Books, 1972.

Schutz, Alfred, and Thomas Luckmann (1973), *Structures of the Life-world*, Evanston: Northwestern University Press.

Scott, James Finlay (1963), 'The Changing Foundations of the Parsonian Action Scheme', *American Sociological Review*, **28**.

Scott, John (1978), 'Critical Social Theory: An Introduction and Critique', *British Journal of Sociology*, **29**.

Scott, John (1985), *Corporations, Classes and Capitalism, Second Edition*, London: Hutchinson, Second Edition, (originally 1979).

Scott, John (1990), 'Corporate Control and Corporate Rule: Britain in an International Perspective', *British Journal of Sociology*, **41**.

Scott, John (1991a), 'Networks of Corporate Power: A Comparative Assessment', *Annual Review of Sociology*, **17**: 181–203.

Scott, John (1991b), *Social Network Analysis*, London: Sage.

Scott, John (ed.) (1994a), *Power*, London: Routledge.

Scott, John (1994b), 'Class Analysis: Back to the Future', *Sociology*, **28**.

Sharrock, Wesley W. and Robert D. Anderson (1986), *The Ethnomethodologists*, London: Tavistock.

Shott, Susan (1979), 'Emotion and Social Life: A Symbolic Interactionist Analysis', *American Journal of Sociology*, **84**: 1317–34.

Simmel, Georg (1900), *The Philosophy of Money*, London: Routledge and Kegan Paul, 1978.

Simmel, Georg (1908), *Soziologie: Untersuchungen Über die Formen der Vergesselshaftung*, Berlin: Düncker und Humblot, 1968.

Simmel, Georg (1917), *Grundlegen der Soziologie*, Berlin: Walter de Gruyter.

Skinner, B. F. (1953), *Science and Human Behaviour*, New York: Free Press.

Skinner, B. F. (1957), *Verbal Behaviour*, New York: Appleton-Century-Crofts.

Small, Albion (1905), *General Sociology*, Chicago: University of Chicago Press.

Smith, Adam (1759), *The Theory of Moral Sentiments*, New York: Augustus Kelley, 1966.

Smith, Adam (1766), *The Wealth of Nations*, London: J. M. Dent, 1910.

Smith, Dennis (1988), *The Chicago School: A Liberal Critique of Capitalism*, London: Macmillan.

Stanworth, Philip and Anthony Giddens (eds) (1974), *Elites and Power in British Society*, Cambridge: Cambridge University Press.

Stein, Lorenz von (1831), *Der Begriff der Gesellschaft*.

Strauss, Anselm, Leonard Schatzman, D. Ehrlich, Rue Bucher and M. Sabshin (1963), 'The Hospital and Its Negotiated Order', in Friedson (ed.) 1963.

Sudnow, David (1967), *Passing On: The Sociology of Dying*, Englewood Cliffs: Prentice Hall.

Sudnow, David (ed.) (1972), *Studies in Social Interaction*, New York: Free Press.

Sumner, William Graham (1883), *What Social Classes Owe to Each Other*, New York: Harper and Brothers.

Sumner, William Graham (1906), *Folkways*, New York: Dover, 1959.

Therborn, Goran (1976), *Science, Class and Society*, London: New Left Books.

Thompson, John (1989), 'The Theory of Structuration', in Held and Thompson (eds) 1989.

Tilly, Charles (1978), *From Mobilization to Revolution*, Reading: Addison-Wesley.

Tönnies, Ferdinand (1889), *Community and Association*, London: Routledge and Kegan Paul, 1955 (based on the 1912 edition).

Tönnies, Ferdinand (1931), *Einführung in die Soziologie*, Stuttgart: Ferdinand Enke.

Touraine, Alain (1964), 'Towards a Sociology of Action', in *Positivism and Sociology*, edited by A. Giddens, London: Heinemann, 1974.

Touraine, Alain (1965), *Sociologie de l'action*, Paris: Editions du Seuil.

Touraine, Alain (1981), *The Voice and the Eye: An Analysis of Social Movements*, Cambridge: Cambridge University Press.

Turk, Austin T. (1969), *Criminality and the Legal Order*, Chicago: Rand McNally.

Turner, Jonathan (1988), *A Theory of Social Interaction*, Cambridge: Polity Press.

Turner, Ralph (1962), 'Role-Taking: Process Versus Conformity', in *Human Behaviour and Social Processes*, edited by A. Rose, London: Routledge and Kegan Paul, 1962.

Turner, Roy (ed.) (1974), *Ethnomethodology*, Harmondsworth: Penguin.

Urry, John (1973), *Reference Groups and the Theory of Revolutions*, London: Routledge and Kegan Paul.

Urry, John (1982), 'Duality of Structure: Some Critical Issues', *Theory, Culture and Society*, **1**: 100–106.

Van den Berghe, Pierre (1963), 'Dialectic and Functionalism: Toward a Theoretical Synthesis', *American Sociological Review*, **28**: 695–705.

Vico, G. (1725), *The New Science*, New York: Doubleday, 1961.

Vierkandt, Alfred (1923), *Gesellshaftslehre*, Liepzig and München: Düncker and Humblot.

Wallerstein, Immanuel (1974), *The Modern World System I: Capitalist Agriculture and the Origins of the European World-Economy in the Sixteenth Century*, New York: Academic Press.

Wallerstein, Immanuel (1980), *The Modern World System II: Mercantilism and the Consolidation of the European World-Economy, 1600–1750*, New York: Academic Press.

Wallerstein, Immanuel (1989), *The Modern World System III: The Second Era of Great Expansion of the Capitalist World-Economy, 1730–1840s*, New York: Academic Press.

Ward, Lester (1883), *Dynamic Sociology*, New York: D. Appleton, 1913.

Ward, Lester (1897), *Outlines of Sociology*, New York: Macmillan, 1913.

Ward, Lester (1903), *Pure Sociology*, New York: Macmillan, 1914.

Warner, W. Lloyd and P. S. Lunt (1941), *The Social Life of a Modern Community*, New Haven: Yale University Press.

Warner, W. Lloyd and P. S. Lunt (1942), *The Status System of a Modern Community*, New Haven: Yale University Press.

Wearne, Bruce C (1989), *The Theory and Scholarship of Talcott Parsons to 1951*, Cambridge: Cambridge University Press.

Weber, Alfred (1920–21), *Fundamentals of Culture-Sociology: Social Proc-*

ess, Civilization Process and Cultural Movement, New York: Columbia University Press, 1939.

Weber, Max (1904–5), *The Protestant Ethic and the Spirit of Capitalism*, London: George Allen and Unwin, 1930.

Weber, Max (1914), 'The Economy and the Arena of Normative and De Facto Powers', in *Economy and Society*, edited by G. Roth and C. Wittich, New York: Bedminster Press, 1968.

Weber, Max (1915), *The Religion of China*, New York: Macmillan, 1951.

Weber, Max (1916), *The Religion of India*, New York: Macmillan, 1958.

Weber, Max (1917), *Ancient Judaism*, New York: Macmillan, 1952.

Weber, Max (1920), 'Conceptual Exposition', in *Economy and Society*, edited by G. Roth and C. Wittich, New York: Bedminster Press, 1968.

Wellman, Barry and Steven Berkowitz (eds) (1988), *Social Structures*, New York: Cambridge University Press.

Whitehead, Alfred North (1926), *Science and the Modern World*, Harmondsworth: Penguin Books, 1938.

Whitehead, Alfred North (1927), *Symbolism: Its Meaning and Effect*, New York: Macmillan.

Whitehead, Alfred North (1929), *Process and Reality*, New York: Free Press.

Whitehead, Alfred N. and Bertrand Russell (1910), *Principia Mathematica*, Cambridge University Press, 1963.

Wieder, D. Lawrence (1974), 'Telling the Code', in Turner (ed.) 1974.

Wiese, Leopold von (1924-29), *Allgemeine Soziologie, Two Volumes*, Liepzig and München: Düncker and Humblot.

Williamson, Oliver E. (1975), *Markets and Hierarchies*, New York: Free Press.

Wilson, T. P. (1970), 'Normative and Interpretive Paradigms in Sociology', in Douglas (ed.) 1971b.

Winch, Peter (1958), *The Idea of a Social Science*, London: Routledge and Kegan Paul.

Wollstonecraft, Mary (1790), *A Vindication of the Rights of Men*, London: Joseph Johnson.

Wollstonecraft, Mary (1792), *A Vindication of the Rights of Woman*, Harmondsworth: Penguin, 1975.

Wright, Erik Olin (1978), *Class, Crisis and State*, London: New Left Books.

Wrong, Denis (1961), 'The Oversocialized Concept of Man in Modern Sociology', in Coser and Rosenberg (eds) 1971.

Young, Jock (1971), 'The Role of Police as Amplifiers of Deviancy, Negotiators of Reality and Translators of Fantasy', in Cohen (ed.) 1971.

Zald, Meyer and J. D. McCarthy (eds) (1979), *The Dynamics of Social Movements*, Cambridge, Mass.: Winthrop.

Zald, Meyer and J. D. McCarthy (eds) (1987), *Social Movements in an Organizational Society*, New Brunswick: Transaction.

Zimmerman, Don H. and D. L. Wieder (1970), 'Ethnomethodology and the Problem of Order: Comment on Denzin', in Douglas (ed.) 1971b.

Index